African
American

The Farrakhan Phenomenon

The Farrakhan Phenomenon
Race, Reaction, and the Paranoid Style in American Politics

ROBERT SINGH

GEORGETOWN UNIVERSITY PRESS / WASHINGTON, D.C.

Georgetown University Press, Washington, D.C.   20007
© 1997 by Georgetown University Press. All rights reserved.
Printed in the United States of America.
10 9 8 7 6 5 4 3 2 1   1997

Library of Congress Cataloging-in-Publication Data

Singh, Robert.
    The Farrakhan phenomenon :   race, reaction, and the paranoid style
in American politics / Robert Singh.
        p.   cm.
    Includes bibliographical references and index.
    1. Farrakhan, Louis.   2. United States—Race relations.   3. Afro-
Americans—Politics and government.   4. Hate—Political aspects—
United States.   5. United States—Politics and government—1989– .
I. Title.
E185.615S564   1997
305.8'009732—dc21
ISBN 0-87840-657-3 (cloth). —   ISBN 0-87840-658-1 (pbk.)
                                                97-6103

For my parents

Contents

Preface

In March 1990, upon being asked by the late Professor Aaron Wildavsky for my dominant impressions of America—on only my second visit to the country and my first to Washington, D.C.—I'd tentatively commented upon the feature that had struck me most forcefully: the overarching importance of race to the nation's political and social affairs. Fortunately, for a young British graduate student, the reply elicited the eminent professor's typically gruff approval: "That's right. When people ask me what they should understand about American politics, I tell them race, the first five times." Although I had no way of knowing, then or subsequently, whether Wildavsky actually did offer such repetitive advice to aspiring Americanists, neither academic study nor personal experience since that enjoyable encounter have altered my original view.

The decision to write this book about Louis Farrakhan in part reflected the strongly held conviction that examining the politics of race in America remains a necessary and central—though by no means sufficient—condition of a comprehensive and accurate understanding of politics in the United States today as much as, and probably more than, ever. For as the twentieth century draws to its close, it requires no special critical faculty nor an exceptional gift of intellect to see that the American dilemma of race is little closer to resolution now than at its outset. In over one hundred years, the great progress achieved by black Americans—though remarkable in many respects—has remained manifestly insufficient to bring them fully into the republic's economic and social mainstream. In consequence, of the many emotions invariably occasioned by both public and private discussions of race among American citizens today, that of pessimism is unmistakably widespread. That sentiment, moreover, constitutes an especially conspicuous and resilient exception to the generally optimistic cast of most Americans' speculations upon the future development of their nation.

Compounding that pessimism was most certainly not a motive for composing this treatise, but for some readers it may be an inadvertent and unfortunate result. The monograph originally began life as a much more modest academic paper, whose animating rationale was simply to examine the extent to which it was possible to locate Louis Farrakhan within what the distinguished American political historian, Richard Hofstadter, first identified as the "paranoid style" in American politics. During the course of composing that paper, however, it rapidly became clear not only that the leader of the Nation of Islam (NoI) could indeed be appropriately understood within a framework of authoritarian/paranoid politics in the United States, but also that Farrakhan's meteoric and controversial ascent to national leadership status among African-Americans merited an altogether lengthier, more considered and detailed analytic treatment.

Part of the reason for this extended examination is essentially internal to the Farrakhan phenomenon, residing in the very novelty of the NoI leader's views, leadership style, and ongoing political project. In this relatively narrow but popularly familiar sense, Farrakhan represents an appropriately menacing, divisive, and sharply polarizing political figure for the fin de siècle and, hence, an especially rich and compelling subject for study. Some of the most fascinating and crucial aspects of his recent rise are external to Farrakhan, however; they lie in the varied responses and reactions of other black and nonblack Americans to the NoI's charismatic leader. For few other political figures across American history of any race have elicited the extreme, contradictory, and often virulent reactions that Farrakhan unerringly provokes among a citizenry noted for their tenaciously favoring consensus and moderation over conflict and extremism. Love and hate are deeply emotive terms not readily or widely used in connection with American politics, save perhaps in the more salacious details concerning the ethical lapses of some members of the U.S. Congress. Yet these terms surface with an astonishing regularity in both popular and elite discussions of Farrakhan; the many passions that the Black Muslim arouses are almost palpable, even on paper.

Tempting though it may therefore be to treat Farrakhan in such terms of emotive hyperbole, this monograph eschews such a course. Rather, it is an attempt to consider the Farrakhan phenomenon in an engaged but dispassionate manner, from a physically distant but analytically clear vantage point. At the outset, it must readily be conceded that studying American politics from afar is an odd and sometimes difficult intellectual enterprise. As a long distance observer of African-American politics, in particular, one is constantly reminded of possessing an outsider status, as both a noncitizen and a professional political scientist. If, however, a factor can be said to mitigate the limitations that necessarily accompany this external locus, it is perhaps that the complex dynamics of racial politics in modern America are not inappropriately studied by individuals who have avoided the specifically American version of the scar of race, the universality of which, nonetheless, seems a tragic constant in our contemporary affairs.

The research for the book has drawn extensively upon both published and unpublished secondary data about and by Farrakhan (including his speeches, interviews, and written works), supplemented by a series of background interviews conducted with American politicians, academics, and journalists over the period 1993–96. Although approached several times (in Washington, D.C. and New York City), the NoI proved consistently unwilling to permit either interviews or archival research. The arguments contained herein are therefore made from limited, but sufficient, sources to admit of a comprehensive and accurate analysis of Farrakhan's political beliefs, ascendancy, and significance. The extensive use of secondary data that informs the text is designed both to substantiate my interpretation of the Farrakhan phenomenon (the NoI leader is frequently apt to accuse those whom he deems to be hostile critics of deliberate misinterpretation of his views), and to allow readers the opportunity to follow up those references that time and space have not permitted a full and thorough development of herein. As often as is appropriate, Farrakhan's own words are presented unadorned and unabridged.

Inevitably, substantial intellectual and personal debts are owed to the many individuals and institutions that have assisted in the genesis and evolution of this project, though they are all, of course, absolved of any responsibility for errors of fact or interpretation herein. Most important, the "Oxford Mafia" of Americanists have been tirelessly encouraging and supportive throughout. In particular, the evolution of my thoughts on Farrakhan owes much to Desmond King, a constant source of constructive and pertinent criticism, unceasing professional encouragement, and invaluable scholarly support. Further debts are also owed to my long-established and long-suffering mentors, Nigel Bowles and Byron Shafer, both of whom have maintained with customary equanimity, patience, and great good humor their constant support and outstanding critical skills. My accounts at their banks of expert advice and assistance are now embarrassingly overdrawn, an indebted state for which I continue to crave their forgiveness and ongoing indulgence.

In Ireland, the Department of Political Science at the University of Dublin, Trinity College, provided a very congenial and stimulating intellectual environment in which to work from 1994–96. The refinement and revision of my ideas and arguments benefited considerably from the opportunity to present a research paper on Farrakhan at a departmental seminar in November 1995, as well as from numerous informal discussions. Thanks are especially due to John Gary, Ron Hill, the trinity of Trinity Michaels (Messrs. Gallagher, Laver, and Marsh), John Lyons, and Ben Tonra. Miriam Nestor was also an incomparable source of friendship, encouragement, and administrative assistance. The research for the book was also vitally assisted by grants from the Arts and Social Sciences Benefactions Fund and the Provost's Academic Development Fund, for which I am most grateful.

Invaluable reviews, comments, and advice about particular chapters, specific arguments, and life in general were also generously forthcoming from Martin Conyon, Jon Exten-Wright, Anna-Marie Jatta, Neil Masuda, Louise Owens, Luisa Perrotti, and Lee Roberts. Their continued friendship and humor have afforded the ample sustenance essential to the project's completion. Thanks are also due to Adolph Reed, for initially sparking my critical interest in Farrakhan during my year as an exchange student at Yale University in 1990–91; to Juji Johnson, for introducing me to the practical politics of race in America and for her continued commitment and exceptional faith; and especially, to John Samples of Georgetown University Press, who was a particularly helpful, enthusiastic, and positive publisher. My great thanks go to him and his expert staff at Georgetown for all their professional efforts.

Finally, immense thanks are due to my parents, who have faced, fought, and overcome the ignorance, bigotry, and prejudice of weak and narrow minds in a locus some distance from the United States. It is in grateful recognition of their unceasing love, generosity, and patience that the book is dedicated to them both.

1

The Politics of Organized Hate

Disorganized love is not as effective as organized hate.

Louis Farrakhan, 1994[1]

Supporters and defenders of Minister Louis Farrakhan, leader of the Nation of Islam (NoI), are often apt to draw a simple analogy between the racial problems of the United States of America and a house that is on fire: when a building is burning, they sagely advise the unenlightened, its occupants need not enquire too deeply about the identities of the firemen who have arrived to battle the raging flames. The difficulty here, however, is that when one of those firemen invariably insists upon bringing voluminous quantities of oil instead of water to tackle the blaze, the prospects for its full extinction are decidedly more distant than close at hand. And in the generally smoldering edifice—and sometimes barely latent inferno—that is contemporary race relations in the United States, Louis Farrakhan contributes much gasoline and precious little water to still the ongoing heat.

Speaking a paranoid language of conspiracies, conversations with the dead, and visitations to spaceships that hover above the Earth waiting to rain down their awesome bombs, Farrakhan is easily the most controversial black American to have achieved a public position of national political influence in the United States since Malcolm X was assassinated a generation ago.[2] The leader of an obscure, unorthodox, and sectarian black separatist organization, Farrakhan has provoked the sharpest and most bitterly protracted exchanges between African-Americans and Jews in the United States in the twentieth century; has won the type of enthusiastic ovations from exceptionally large African-American audiences that elude all other contemporary black political leaders; has alternately embarrassed, antagonized, and condemned prominent national and local black politicians and civil rights activists; has assembled one of the most financially profligate and ethically disreputable black religious organizations in the United States; has elicited admiration and praise from white supremacists and black progressives alike; and has mobilized collective action by African-Americans in the 1990s on an unprecedentedly large scale. In his impressively unerring ability to prompt the most powerfully emotive responses from American citizens of all races, religions, and creeds—and thereby sharply polarize American political opinion—Louis Farrakhan has several demagogic rivals but no contemporary peer.

Farrakhan, political controversy, and mass black popularity have together formed a symbiotic trinity that has gradually but inexorably propelled the Black Muslim minister into the ranks of national African-American political leadership in the 1990s. Unlike most American political figures, Farrakhan's ascendancy has occurred not so much despite, but in large part as a direct result of, his successfully courting national and international controversy. Implicated in the assassination of Malcolm X in 1965, the minister was himself rumored to be the target of such a plot by one of Malcolm's daughters thirty years later. Having nonchalantly described Adolf Hitler as a "wickedly great man" in 1984, Farrakhan was subsequently characterized by the then mayor of New York City as a "Nazi in clerical garb" with "more followers than Hitler," who deserved to "burn in hell."[3] Banned by the British government from even entering the United Kingdom in 1986 on the grounds that his visit "would not be conducive to the public good,"[4] Farrakhan has been enthusiastically received by the brutal authoritarian despots of Iran, Iraq, and Nigeria, and offered a combination of arms, admiration, and generous financial assistance by the Libyan dictator and sponsor of international terrorism, Colonel Mu'ammar Gadhafi. Such deeply discordant national and international reactions together have shaped Farrakhan's steady emergence during the last thirteen years as, simultaneously, the personification of the aspirations and grievances of thousands of African-Americans and the apprehensions and fears of at least as many whites.

For the former, Farrakhan's elegantly clad figure, courageously unbowed demeanor, and fire and brimstone oratory represent a singularly powerful and impeccably heroic symbol of implacable racial defiance to a white America that is apparently distant and hostile—enduringly and increasingly so—to the political, economic, and social interests and aspirations of U.S. blacks. Such a view is itself parasitic upon the multiplicity of negative assessments of the NoI's leader made by many white Americans. For the latter, Farrakhan represents an inglorious blight upon an otherwise dazzling American mosaic. He constitutes a deeply troubling black political figure, whose rhetoric is replete with fear and loathing. Farrakhan's contemporary political locus is thus founded upon an apparently bifurcated emotive apparatus of a frequently professed and unqualified love for his own race, and a more-or-less coded, but equally undiscriminating, hatred of others. For Farrakhan, the content of an individual's character frequently seems effectively determined by the very color of that person's skin, a peculiar, perverse, and pernicious inversion of the Reverend Dr. Martin Luther King Jr.'s inspiring humanitarian dream of the potential racial future of the United States.

The Farrakhan phenomenon, however, is a far more complex political and social entity than either Farrakhan himself or the two explanations most frequently advanced to account for his gradual ascendancy—widespread anti-Semitism and increasing racial bitterness among African-Americans toward whites—in fact allow. Though assuredly apposite, these two factors alone are insufficient to account for Farrakhan's political longevity and recent rise. More than a decade has elapsed since Farrakhan first entered the American national political consciousness in 1984. Despite frequent attempts by many Americans of all races variously to counter his mass black appeal, urge his unequivocal political ostracization by African-American elites, and deny the brute fact of his broad social and political influence among black Americans at large, the NoI's leader has steadfastly refused to disappear from American national politics. Instead, the diffuse public and private efforts of Farrakhan's many critics and political opponents that have sought to achieve his full and enduring exclusion from the ranks of national black political leadership have in part facilitated his increasing inclusion therein.

The roots of the Farrakhan phenomenon are thus evidently deep and resilient. Although political scientists and other critics strongly disagree about both the nature and significance of Farrakhan's current political role, as well as the precise extent of his influence among African-Americans, the NoI's leader has undoubtedly emerged as a national black political figure provoking the starkest, deepest, and most conflicting reactions from American citizens of all races and creeds. For some (especially and overwhelmingly—though not exclusively—among the African-American community), Farrakhan and his besuited, bow-tied Fruit of Islam guards represent beguilingly reassuring and potent political symbols of dignity, responsibility, aspiration, pride, hope, courage, and autonomy. They embody in their outspoken words, fearless deeds, and defiantly independent demeanors the most positive and admirable traits that any human being might aspire toward or strive to emulate.

For others, though, among white Americans in general and Jews in particular, Farrakhan and his militaristic Black Muslim minions more recall brown-shirted fascistic militias, invariably being accorded the type of deep revulsion, fear, and (less commonly) intense ridicule normally reserved for the most outlandish, preposterous, and eccentric of cranks, bigots, and extremists. Far from being worthy of admiration and approbation, they represent much that is most ignoble, mendacious, and poisonous in modern American public life; that threatens ultimately to unravel the delicately sewn and still-frail fabric of American social relations that has for so long been richly embroidered with the painful struggle to achieve lasting racial comity; and that, therefore, merits the most fulsome contempt and unequivocally clear condemnation.

Most politically telling of all, however, few public or private responses to Farrakhan—from either black or white Americans—occupy a neutral, indifferent, or uncertain ground. That this should be the case powerfully reflects the continued centrality and the enduringly controversial character of race in American society and politics at the close of the twentieth century. Expressions of intense interracial conflict in the United States have assumed numerous forms through the republic's checkered history. Attempts to analyze the several painful horns of the "American dilemma" of race that Swedish social scientist Gunnar Myrdal first identified in 1944, however, show that Louis Farrakhan has clearly emerged as one of its sharpest and most vivid contemporary expressions.[5] Where white Americans typically find it at once inexplicable and outrageous that a public figure espousing Farrakhan's beliefs can be taken seriously at all, African-Americans see such incredulous attitudes as complacently ignoring the very real and desperate conditions of much of black America to which Farrakhan so regularly, directly, and forcefully speaks. Just as the racially bifurcated reactions to the O. J. Simpson trial and verdict in October 1995 so starkly revealed, once more, the profound racial gulf that exists at the very heart of modern American social life, so the pronounced dissonance that surrounds black/white evaluations of Farrakhan speaks volumes to the distinct lenses through which the races increasingly view American social, economic, and political affairs in general, and each other in particular.

This book charts such discordant reactions in the context of an exceptionally controversial and compelling case. Its purpose is to explain, as fully and accurately as possible, the nature, causes, and political significance of the Farrakhan phenomenon. Central to its analytic project is a simple, pressing, but as yet unanswered intellectual problem: how has an individual so reviled, repudiated, and reactionary—a man for whom racial hatred is in every sense an abiding article of faith—achieved a social and political impact of substantial consequence among African-Americans at large? In sum, this treatise seeks to analyze how and why such an unabashed leader of organized hate—one both espousing and attracting such intense emotion in kind—has achieved the leadership status he has among an American social group more enduringly the victims than the perpetrators of hatred, prejudice, and bigotry, a minority whose members have more often represented the courageous vanguard in realizing the noble vision of a color-blind society in the United States than bigots succumbing to being blinded by race.

FARRAKHAN AND THE PROMISE OF RACIAL DISHARMONY IN AMERICAN POLITICS

Although it is often said that the true theater of a demagogue is a democracy, organized hatred has only rarely been the province of American politics. Indeed, to outside observers of the United States especially, one of the most striking features of the American polity has invariably been its apparently stable, consensual, and harmonious character.[6] Compared to the European experience, in particular, American politics is frequently and widely viewed as having been mercifully free from the recurrent threats of tyranny, dictatorship, and totalitarian political regimes that have so often brutally quashed personal liberty and have—intentionally and otherwise—precipitated global wars over the course of the twentieth century. Commitment to the protection of the fundamental civil liberties and rights of individual citizens and minority groups, enshrined in the U.S. Constitution of 1787 and broadly and deeply rooted in American political culture, has survived and prospered for more than two centuries in the United States while struggling—even in the 1990s—to secure a firm and enduring grounding in many European, Asian, and African nations. Although government in general and the federal government in particular have admittedly been familiar targets of widespread and persistent popular political abuse in the United States, rarely has either (with few, though significant, exceptions) been a source of substantial or lasting political oppression to its own citizens—a remarkable political testament to the values and principles bequeathed successive generations of Americans by the founding fathers in the U.S. Constitution.[7]

Moreover, compared to countries in the rest of the world, the citizens of the United States have been remarkably and enduringly unreceptive to either appeals or demands for fundamental change in the nature of their established political, economic, and social arrangements. Although periods of deep social unrest and intense internal political conflict have occurred on many occasions throughout America's history, deriving in part from interpretative conflicts over the values of the American Creed and their distinctive applications to contemporary political problems and social maladies,[8] the liberal democratic consensus underpinning the U.S. polity has ultimately remained robust and fundamentally undisturbed. Thus when discussing revolution in America, we are well accustomed to using the prefix "the" rather than "which," in marked contrast to the revolutions of other regimes.

The primary causes of this systemic phenomenon of pronounced political stability have long been contested by intellectuals: the early achievement of the franchise by the mass of white American males; the geographic security afforded the United States by being bounded by two large oceans; the country's rich abundance of natural resources; the nation's unusual capacity for persistent economic growth; the absence of a feudal past and of fractious conflict over the institution of private property; the extremely limited extent of class consciousness; and the political genius of the design, and subsequent evolution, of the U.S. Constitution.[9] Whatever the various merits and flaws of the principal explanations for its occurrence, however, the empirical fact of the comparative stability of the American political system is clear and undeniable.

When American society is confronted by the abrasive incidence of extremist political figures or social movements, it is therefore not surprising that something appears to be deeply deficient, disturbing, and even malignant about the contemporary body politic. Expressions of political extremism strongly suggest an atypical malfunctioning in the basically centrist, consensual, and moderate nature of American political discourse. Although James Madison certainly envisaged the

United States as a new democratic republic in which conflict rather than consensus would undoubtedly predominate, the bounds of such domestic antagonisms—social, economic, and political alike—were conceived as limited and were constitutionally designed to ensure that they would indeed prove to be so.[10] Thus, the popularity of McCarthyism in the later 1940s and early 1950s; the intense social and political conflicts surrounding the postwar desegregation movement, in both the American South and the North; the prolonged and acute dissension, and sometimes violent domestic disturbances, over American military involvement in the Vietnam War; and the several bloody city riots that broke out from the urban crises of the 1960s, all manifested periods of pronounced and unusually protracted internal dissensus from the historically dominant pattern of domestic politics in the United States. Each has been widely viewed as an essentially aberrant expression of disharmony within the more general environment of a stable American polity whose political development has been fundamentally premised upon an inclusive and broad consensus, and that has been strongly sustained by the achievement of mostly incremental reforms and modest adaptations to changing eras and imperatives (whether domestic or international).

It is, nonetheless, within this context of periodic challenges to the dominant political milieu of American consensus and stability that the Farrakhan phenomenon is most appropriately and clearly located. For since 1984, the name of Louis Farrakhan has become popularly synonymous with notions of an extensive and deep interracial animus and with the existence of a fundamentally disharmonic American polity whose preeminent social division is that of race. To the extent that inscribed upon the names of certain individuals and locations over recent American political history is the controversial legacy of the deep fissures and cleavages in American society based centrally upon race, that of Farrakhan now assumes its full and appropriate historical place alongside those of Bernie Goetz, Howard Beach, Bensonhurst, Tawana Brawley, Crown Heights, Marion Barry, David Duke, Clarence Thomas, Rodney King, Mike Tyson, O. J. Simpson, and Mark Fuhrman as emblematic of the American dilemma, a dilemma no less central to American politics and entrenched in American society in the 1990s than it was during the 1890s.

For sadly, at the twilight of the twentieth century, as much as and, in many ways, more than at its outset, race continues to contribute consistently, powerfully, and divisively to the definition and the sharpening of virtually every social, economic, and political issue in the United States: from unemployment to welfare; from education to crime; and from the family to employment. Despite over thirty years of civil rights legislation and over twenty years of affirmative action policies in both public and private education and employment, black and white Americans in the last decade of the twentieth century remain to a conspicuously striking and alarming degree two separate and mutually suspicious societies, unequal, hostile, and apt to view the same facts and events through diametrically opposed interpretive lenses and emotive prisms. Race, more than any other social division, has been the most persistent and bitter apple of internal domestic discord in America for over 150 years; and it remains demonstrably and disconcertingly so today. [11]

Given the longevity of their deeply troublesome presence, it is hardly surprising that elite and mass responses among the American citizenry to the racial tensions and problems of the United States are far from uniform in character. Thus, for many Americans, both black and white, the reemergence in the 1990s of the starkest indices of racial separation, inequality, and mutual hostility is a tremendously sad, painful, and powerful indictment of what has emerged over recent decades as an unusually recurrent and critically important instance of chronic national failure; this in a nation especially rich in, and justifiably proud of, its long and enviable history of political achievement, social progress, and sustained economic success.

For Farrakhan, however, the obvious and increasing signs of American racial separatism are more a cause for celebration and hope than a depressing stimulus to despair and disillusion. The central problem in contemporary America for the leader of the NoI is not that black and white Americans inhabit two largely separate, suspicious, and increasingly distinct, unequal, and mutually hostile worlds within one nation. Rather, it is that the races in America are not yet set sufficiently apart. Where most American politicians continue to strive bravely for greater social proximity and increasing comity between the races, Farrakhan instead seeks to move them in precisely opposite physical, spiritual, and emotive directions. Where many Americans sincerely wish for the political, social, and economic distance between the races to be irrevocably reduced through increasing integration, Farrakhan desires its substantial and permanent extension through the complete separation of blacks and whites. Where the vast majority of Americans continue to vest enduringly strong faith in the oft-touted virtues of the "American Dream," its inspirational vision of universal and constant individual and collective potential, and the full realization of its inclusive societal appeal, Farrakhan instead emphasizes its multiple vices and failures and evokes the darkest visions of an imminent, violent, and all-encompassing American racial nightmare.

Thus, although Farrakhan bears—in common with all Americans—the "scar of race,"[12] he does so with a particular personal pride and political militancy that, rather than demanding its gradual, surgical removal through further public and private efforts at racial integration or assimilation, champions its rapid and irrevocable elimination through a radical, alternative route: the complete and enduring separation of black and white Americans in the United States.[13] The noble and compelling political and social ideal of a multiracial, pluralist American democracy, so beloved of King and the desegregation movement during the 1950s and 1960s—and still courageously strived for by Jesse Jackson, Colin Powell, John Lewis, and the overwhelming majority of national black political, civic, and religious leaders in the 1990s—is one that the leader of the NoI has manifestly never adhered to and does not currently share. Farrakhan's diagnosis of the American polity's cancerous racial ills is clear and straightforward. Racial integration represents at best a forlorn black American fool's political, economic, and social paradise, at worst a malign and repugnant recipe for a hellish national disaster. Farrakhan's emphatic response to Rodney King's plea after the Los Angeles riots of 1992 for black and white Americans to "get along" is therefore a consistent, vociferous, and unequivocal "no."

At the most fundamental level, then, Louis Farrakhan represents an especially intelligent, shrewd, and articulate African-American advocate of collective black consciousness, black political unity, and separate racial development in modern America. Black power in Minister Farrakhan's view is not a matter of power over white Americans, nor even parity with them; it is power set entirely apart from an oppressive and degenerate white society. Farrakhan's politics are thoroughly informed and infused not by integrative and inclusive racial impulses, but rather by an overwhelming imperative of complete black political, economic, and social disengagement from the majority-white American population. Black independence from white America, not integration with it, is the ultimate political goal for Farrakhan and the organization over which he presides, the tantalizing prize to which he must incessantly draw and keep focused the eyes and attentions of black Americans. Separation of the races is to be effusively celebrated rather than censured, representing a positive societal goal to be zealously encouraged, rather than inhibited, by public policy and private endeavor alike. However illuminating or impaired it may be to his fellow citizens, Farrakhan's vision is therefore one that is most definitely not "deeply rooted in the American Dream"; it stands squarely as an uncompromising and unrelenting challenge to that dream's most commendably uplifting humanitarian aspirations.

In this respect, one of the most acute ironies with which the Farrakhan phenomenon is notably replete resides in the timing of the political ascendancy of the NoI's leader. Manifesting a curious unorthodoxy—even a perversity—that characterizes much of his increasing appeal among African-Americans, Farrakhan's domestic social and political impact has grown in America at precisely the moment that the immense promise of multiracial harmony and interracial cooperation has won new and invigorating political hope abroad, with the dramatic but mostly peaceful revolution in South Africa. Just as the inspirational transformation of South Africa from an apartheid state predicated on keeping the races apart and unequal to a multiracial, pluralist, and liberal democratic regime was being forged, so Farrakhan's strident calls for the achievement of a complete separation of the races in the United States resonated strongly with increasing numbers of American blacks. As national and international political figures, Nelson Mandela and Louis Farrakhan have thus come during the 1990s to represent powerful symbols of national racial futures that point in entirely different directions for the black and nonblack populations of their respective countries: the former striving with immense courage and dignity to lead a long-divided nation decisively away from a deep swamp of historic racial hatred and a ruinously pernicious and discreditable public philosophy of group separatism; the latter enthusiastically encouraging its continued, fulsome, and destructive growth.[14]

As Americans watch Farrakhan prosper upon racial division, antagonism, and animosity, the poignancy of the contrast with South Africa in the 1990s is especially pronounced. W. E. B. Du Bois, the distinguished black American historian and social activist, famously declared in the early years of the 1900s that the main source of prospective national and international social and political conflict in the twentieth century would be centered upon the color line. In several respects, as African-Americans eventually achieved formal civil and political equality with the landmark passage of the Civil Rights Act of 1964 and the Voting Rights Act of 1965, respectively, and as black

African states contemporaneously secured independence from their former colonial rulers and gradually overcame segregation in Rhodesia (and ultimately South Africa), Du Bois's prediction appeared to be realized in the most complete, but at the same time the most positive and liberating, fashion. Progress for black Americans toward their final inclusion as full citizens in the American polity was strongly paralleled outside the United States by the liberation and maturation of Asian and African states attaining national independence.

As the century approaches its close, however, the fundamental features of racial conflict that Du Bois discerned remain substantially in place in the United States and, of course, in the much of the rest of the world. After struggling for such a prolonged period and at such pronounced and grievous cost in human life to achieve equality before the law, the failure of formal, procedural equality to bring about material social and economic improvements in the lives of millions of African-Americans is an extremely vivid and graphic one.[15] For many African-Americans, the bitter and brutal legacies of slavery, segregation, racism, and discrimination that have informed American history have barely been challenged by their collective experiences in the post–civil rights era, just as the legacy of colonial rule has not been erased by the checkered development of African states since independence that has offered so few reasons for enduring optimism about the long-term prospects of black Africa.

Farrakhan, in his unremittingly vehement rejections of integrative ideals and his shrill calls for racial separation, succinctly articulates the sentiments of an increasing number of black—and many nonblack—Americans, for whom the post–civil rights era of race relations in the United States has proven to be a very deep, painful, and persistent disappointment. The once-potent promise of equal treatment before the law has, for many black Americans, been bitterly exposed by the harsh—and in several instances horrific—socioeconomic realities of daily life in America's central cities and rural backwaters in the 1990s as a largely hollow political illusion. King's oft-cited dream of the achievement of a genuinely "beloved community" in the United States has, for many African-Americans, evolved since his tragic assassination as a siren call, an illusive and futile quest for social peace and fraternal cooperation between the races in the face of a growing material nightmare of inter- and intra-racial disharmony, and a rapidly deteriorating and debilitating quality of life for millions of black American citizens nationwide.[16]

Moreover, such disenchantment and disillusion has encompassed many more African-Americans than the disadvantaged and
impoverished inhabitants of blighted central cities alone. Even for the
rapidly expanded black American middle class, the brutally stark
facts of persistent racial prejudice, discrimination, and intermittent
conflict in the post–civil rights era remain tenaciously unavoidable.
Notwithstanding the day-to-day slights that many African-Americans
regularly suffer from authority figures and ordinary citizens alike, the
vicious beating of Rodney King by law enforcement officers in Los
Angeles in 1992 and the brutal revelations of detective Mark Fuhrman
during the O. J. Simpson trial about the prevalence of racial prejudice,
discrimination, and coercion in the Los Angeles Police Department in
1995 both issued especially clear and unequivocal national messages
to all black Americans: economic affluence and upward social mobility
provide substantial, but very much incomplete, protection against
still-prevalent patterns of racial prejudice, stereotyping, discrimination, and their many attendant effects.[17] In this sense, Farrakhan's
popular black appeal is understandable not only to the deprived and
disadvantaged urban African-Americans who form his most eagerly
receptive and enthusiastic core political constituency, but also to many
socially secure suburban and economically affluent blacks, even if that
appeal is encouraged and condoned by relatively few of the latter.

For the foundations of the Farrakhan phenomenon critically
encompass the reactions of elite, as well as mass, black Americans. In
particular, Farrakhan's current occupation of a wholly distinctive
niche in national black American politics reflects powerfully upon the
established black American political leadership cadre in the United
States more broadly, in terms of both its many achievements and its
several purported deficiencies. Farrakhan's rise is, in substantial measure, a direct function of the latter, especially. In the aftermath of the
Los Angeles riot of 1992, for example, the apparent lack of effective
black American political leadership was one crucial factor often cited
by American academics and media commentators to account for the
lawlessness of the black youths that took to the city streets soon after
the acquittal of the L.A.P.D. officers for beating Rodney King. According to Maulana Karenga, for example:

> Those black brothers out there in the street don't listen to the so-
> called black leaders because they know they aren't leading any-
> one but themselves. They're simply fed up with preachers and

politicians who seem to have no understanding of their situation and of the reasons for their rebellion.[18]

Whether or not one dignifies the riot with the term "rebellion," the horrific scenes of violent brutality transmitted across the nation, so powerfully reminiscent of the 1965 Watts riots in Los Angeles, suggested that little had altered in the intervening twenty-seven years, save perhaps for the rapidity and graphic detail with which sophisticated television outlets such as CNN were now able to reveal to a national and international audience the gravity and violence of an essentially local catastrophe. Both riots, though set almost thirty years apart, were characterized by murders, injuries, extensive damage to private property, and mass confusion adjoined to deep anger on the part of many Americans of all races, not to mention the perplexity of non-Americans that, in the putative land of the free and home of the brave, at a time of relative peace and prosperity, so many of its citizens once again appeared joyfully insistent upon abusing that precious liberty and denying it to their compatriots.

Moreover, as in 1965, the L.A. riots of 1992 offered a parallel in the apparent impotence and ineffectiveness of established local and national black American political leadership in the tumultuous face of mass urban disturbances. The African-Americans among the rioters appeared not only to be intent upon wreaking havoc—whether criminally opportunistic or in violent expression of pent-up frustrations borne of disillusionment with and alienation from the American political and the criminal justice systems—but also to be implacably resistant to the putative authority of community and national black civic and political leaders and their desperate appeals for public order and calm.

Framed by such an explosive context, Minister Louis Farrakhan was the one African-American leader who arose as qualified to address mass black American malcontents and the disaffected. Chicago Alderwoman Dorothy Tillman, for example, stated that:

> I can't think of any black leader other than Minister Farrakhan who could command the attention of our angry and frustrated black youth. Not only could Minister Farrakhan get young people's attention, but he also can transform them from a criminal preying on their own neighborhood to a hard-working asset to the neighborhood.[19]

Many other African-Americans concurred with the view that, despite his obviously advancing years, "Louis Farrakhan is probably the only national figure most youths pay any attention to."[20]

While such sentiments were broadly articulated among black commentators, however, they met with especially vehement criticisms from many members of established black American professional and intellectual elites of "the mindlessness of Louis Farrakhan and other spokespersons for what is marketed as 'black self-help'"[21] and the "blind alley" of black capitalism into which Farrakhan was seeking to lead his assembled African-American flock.[22] The veteran civil rights activist and NAACP board member, Julian Bond, scathingly described Farrakhan as "a black Pat Buchanan or David Duke . . . notoriously and unapologetically anti-Semitic, anti-Catholic, anti-white, misogynist, and anti-gay."[23] Rep. Major Owens (D-NY), a Brooklyn-based member of the Congressional Black Caucus, characterized Farrakhan's organization, the NoI, as a "hate-mongering fringe group" that persistently disseminated "dangerous poison."[24] For one leading black American intellectual, Harvard University's Cornel West, the increasing emergence of strong black nationalist sentiments among many African-Americans, younger blacks in particular, that formed the apparent foundation of Farrakhan's growing appeal essentially represented:

> . . . a revolt against this sense of having to "fit in." The variety of black-nationalist ideologies, from the moderate views of Supreme Court Justice Clarence Thomas in his youth to those of Louis Farrakhan today, rest upon a fundamental truth: white America has been historically weak-willed in ensuring racial justice and has continued to resist accepting fully the humanity of blacks.[25]

For the influential African American economist, Glenn Loury, however, Minister Farrakhan constituted simply "the leader of a black fascist sect . . . a hysterical preacher of hate"[26]; while the former Black Panther, Eldridge Cleaver, lambasted Farrakhan as an unadulterated opportunist, a "slimeball, scheming, renegade bandwagoner. . . ."[27]

That a single black American religious activist should elicit such stark, intense, and strongly conflicting reactions from within black communities in the 1990s—flatteringly heralded by some as a uniquely influential and important political authority figure, and harshly excoriated by others as a bigoted black extremist, a marginal social force, and a transparently opportunistic and fraudulent charlatan—is at once striking, unusual, and significant. Few, if any, other African-American public figures have attracted such extreme and contradictory responses since the 1960s. Of post–civil rights era black American public figures, only the nomination of Supreme Court Associate Justice Clarence Thomas provoked an intense political controversy and broad dissensus among African-Americans nationwide on a scale even remotely comparable to Farrakhan.[28] The black reactions to Thomas, however, were in part shaped by contingent factors of essentially transient popular salience. African-American responses to Farrakhan have been much more clearly located in political, economic, and social conditions of a far deeper and more enduring character, and have hence accorded the Farrakhan phenomenon a more pronounced and controversial public salience among black Americans.[29]

When the very forceful and invariably unfavorable responses that the NoI's leader evokes from many nonblack Americans are also considered, Louis Farrakhan assumes a singular political distinction and novelty. The former U.S. Senator and 1996 Republican presidential nominee, Bob Dole, for example, described the NoI minister unequivocally as "a racist and anti-Semite, unhinged by hate."[30] Rep. Peter King (R-NY), one of the NoI's most outspoken national critics, publicly decried Farrakhan during congressional hearings in 1995 as "a racist and a hate monger," and labeled his separatist organization an "empire of hate."[31] Nor was David Broder, the doyen of eminent national American columnists, in isolated critical company when he explicitly identified Farrakhan as "a racist demagogue."[32] Literally scores of white American mass media pundits and editors have repeatedly repudiated Farrakhan in the harshest terms as a "crackpot bigot"; have explicitly denounced his public message as being consistently and graphically "hateful"; have condemned his public discourse as comprising a clear, "unrelenting," and sickeningly offensive diet of rabidly vicious anti-Semitism; and have included Farrakhan among the self-deluded ranks of "America's most demented."[33] According to one representative and succinct summation of such unenamored journalistic views:

> Louis Farrakhan represents a variant of American fascism. His organization is authoritarian, his message dead-end demagoguery and his dope the bracing narcotic of hate.[34]

Few, if any, other contemporary political figures in America, of any race, religion, or creed, attract this type of hostile and unforgiving critical commentary on a scale and with a frequency and passionate intensity even remotely comparable to that of Louis Farrakhan. An exhaustive list of those many Americans who have vigorously repudiated, vilified, and condemned the NoI's leader would assume an almost encyclopedic dimension.

Notwithstanding the many deeply critical interpretations that have been regularly advanced by American media pundits and popular commentators since 1984, however, no systematic academic studies of Farrakhan currently exist. The few American scholars who have offered more or less considered critical interpretations of the Nation of Islam's leader (mostly in op-ed pieces and journal articles) have, moreover, reached strongly conflicting—indeed, contradictory—conclusions about the content of Farrakhan's ideological beliefs, the nature of his evolving political role, and the precise extent of his contemporary political influence among black Americans at large. Like shaking hands with a shadow, accurately identifying Farrakhan's appropriate political locus has thus far seemed an especially elusive and exasperating critical enterprise.

The scholarly dissensus over Farrakhan and his organization is unmistakably marked. In ideological terms, for example, Farrakhan has been identified variously by American social scientists as a "conservative black nationalist,"[35] a "left-wing black nationalist,"[36] and a "proto-fascist."[37] The black American separatist organization that Farrakhan leads has, on the one hand, been included in an international compendium of revolutionary social and political movements[38] while, on the other, a dictionary of radical right-wing organizations around the world also lists the Nation of Islam, but notes, somewhat ambiguously, that the Black Muslim group is "not avowedly right-wing."[39]

Farrakhan's evolving political role and influence among African-Americans at large have also animated competing commentaries and divergent critical assessments. Thus, John White's interpretation of the organization's leader sees Farrakhan as causing the NoI's "fragmentation and decline,"[40] and Nicholas Lemann views Farrakhan, somewhat dismissively, as far "more a popular orator than the leader of an organization."[41] Still others, however, argue convincingly that no analysis of contemporary national black American politics in the

United States can exclude a consideration of the NoI's mercurial leader. Thus, Claudette McFadden-Preston views Farrakhan as having "struck a chord" among many black Americans far more resonant, resilient, and deep than any black or white American religious and political figure since Malcolm X during the 1960s.[42] Clarence Lusane, concurring, argues that Farrakhan "exerts an inordinate amount of stature, visibility, and sway" in current African-American politics.[43] Even some of Farrakhan's strongest critics in the American Academy (such as Henry Louis Gates Jr. and Adolph Reed Jr.) and his most implacable political opponents alike have been noticeably unwilling to dismiss entirely the possibility of the minister's ultimately achieving a disturbingly influential position in national black politics.[44]

That no comprehensive scholarly analysis of the Farrakhan phenomenon yet exists despite the several popular commentaries on his political role, influence, and goals is reflective, in part, of the relatively recent and controversial entry of Farrakhan into the burgeoning ranks of the national black American leadership cadre. As long as Farrakhan remained a largely peripheral and quixotic figure in national African-American politics during the 1980s, his marginal leadership role seemed not to merit systematic and detailed treatment by social scientists. Lack of rigorous academic attention also reflects the very substantial difficulties facing any analyst in researching the head of the Nation of Islam, a highly secretive, exclusionary, and hierarchical race-based organization that remains deeply hostile to outsiders, whatever their national, racial, and ethnic origins. Furthermore, scholarly reluctance to tackle the Farrakhan phenomenon itself reveals the inordinately delicate sensibilities that surround—and, increasingly, help to suppress—informed public discussion of American race relations in general and the NoI's leader in particular. The mutual tolerance, laudable candor and painfully honest reflection that characterize many private discussions of the subject in the United States rarely dignify and enlighten American current public debates. As Nathan Glazer, reflecting succinctly upon the increasing hypersensitivity of the subject in America, once aptly put it, "how can you talk about race when you can't talk about race?"[45]

Thus, for some American critics, inattention to Farrakhan's alleged anti-Semitism, for example, immediately condemns any discussion of the NoI's leader as wholly misplaced, partial, and inadequate; for others, however, any reference to it whatsoever is itself entirely misleading, reductive, and inappropriate. For still others, a focus upon Farrakhan's paranoid style of politics inevitably diminishes the very real significance of the material deprivations of black American communities that exists and that the NoI's leader consistently seeks to address. Yet, for many, no amount of social deprivation, however pronounced and persistent, justifies the promulgation of wild conspiracy theories, defamatory insults, and bigoted and vicious demagoguery on Farrakhan's scale. As many have discovered previously, writing about Farrakhan therefore assumes an almost incendiary quality. It is somewhat akin to lighting a critical fuse to an explosively taboo racial bomb, the existence of which we are all too painfully aware but which most prefer—for the sake of temporary peace, tranquillity, and social comity—studiously to ignore. But such taboos, however powerful, frequently merit exposure, challenge, and, on occasion, explosion, no matter how tenaciously ostrichlike our critical aversion to candid discourse on sensitive matters may have become.

If the obstacles to rational and scholarly inquiry are clearly significant impediments to analysis, they nonetheless do not represent insuperable barriers to a reasonably clear and judicious understanding of Farrakhan's political goals, methods, achievements, and significance. Through careful and informed analysis and suitably balanced judgment, Farrakhan's role and significance not only can be evaluated, but also ought to be assessed at length. This book therefore represents a modest attempt to rectify in part the failure of social scientists to examine the Farrakhan phenomenon in depth, and thereby, it seeks to fill an important void in the scholarly literature of contemporary African-American politics in particular and the politics of race in the United States more broadly. The monograph makes pretensions neither to inside knowledge of the NoI nor to personal interest in advancing a given critical or political goal of either repudiating, endorsing, or defending Farrakhan. Rather, it stands or falls upon its scholarly argument alone, based upon the accumulated evidence as it currently exists. If emotive, rather than (or, in addition to) intellectual, provocation does result, it will be as by-product rather than an intended design, but the treatise was composed with the knowledge that emotive reaction typically accompanies, occasionally eclipses, and frequently transcends rational inquiry into the tragic terrain of race in contemporary America.

FARRAKHAN, RACE, AND REACTION IN AMERICAN POLITICS

The subject of this book is Louis Farrakhan as a political phenomenon. Conversely, it is neither about Farrakhan as a person—issues of his personal qualities, whether saintly, insane, inspired, or otherwise, are not examined herein—nor about the Black Muslim movement in general. In terms of the former, biographies of Farrakhan, of a generally hagiographic and extremely tendentious cast, are already publicly available.[46] Regarding the latter, several studies of a broadly sympathetic character also exist on the Black Muslims in America generally and the Nation of Islam in particular.[47] To the extent that the NoI is a powerfully leader-centric entity, this monograph addresses issues of the wider movement indirectly, insofar as an analysis of Farrakhan must, at least in part, encompass some consideration of his organization as well. It is not, however, upon the organization of the NoI that the main intellectual interest of this study is founded.

Rather, Farrakhan eminently qualifies as a contemporary American sensation by virtue of the peculiar evolution of his political, economic, and social influence among African-Americans in particular, and the treatment accorded him by other political and civic actors in the United States in general, since the early 1980s. Although extensive critical dissensus surrounds the nature of his political role and influence, and especially the sources and significance of the latter, few academics and popular commentators who have seriously observed his development as leader of the NoI contest that Farrakhan has achieved a social and political impact in black American politics of unusual note and undoubted importance. Whatever their distinct assessments of the normative merits and demerits of his recent national rise and the exact reach of his considerable political appeal among African-Americans at large, the brute fact of Farrakhan's current political influence incontestably stands as one of manifest consequence; and one, moreover, that most attentive observers of current American politics find increasingly difficult to deny with either confidence or equanimity.

Farrakhan thus assuredly merits extended critical analysis in terms of his representing a contemporary American political phenomenon of substantial note. The *Oxford English Dictionary* offers a threefold definition of a phenomenon:

> (1) a fact or occurrence that appears or is perceived, esp. one of which the cause is in question (2) a remarkable person or thing

(3) the object of a person's perception; what the senses or the mind notice. [48]

In this triadic definitional sense, the term is indeed strikingly apt in characterizing Louis Farrakhan.

First, Farrakhan's political occurrence or rise has undoubtedly been widely commented upon, such that his presence in current national American politics is difficult—indeed, quite impossible—to ignore. The substantive causes of his current political role and influence are, furthermore, shrouded in some critical confusion and have become the subject of notable academic disagreement.

Second, Farrakhan's personal status as a remarkable individual is self-evident from even the most cursory examination of his political career thus far. Both despised and admired, hated and loved, and repudiated and championed with exceptional intensity by his many opponents and supporters, respectively, Farrakhan constitutes a national African-American political leader who falls fully within Max Weber's traditional definition of "charismatic authority." [49] Even his many avowed critics and adversaries readily concede that Farrakhan is an altogether exceptional character in contemporary American politics.

Third, both scholarly and popular evaluations of Farrakhan frequently occur through observational and critical prisms of decidedly varied hue and distinctive (and sometimes imperfect) design. The elements of Farrakhan's public discourse that are emphasized by analysts and commentators, whether for approbation or censure, are often identified in an extremely selective and partial fashion and evaluated according to demonstrably subjective political tastes, judgments, and overarching goals. [50]

Nonetheless, the Farrakhan phenomenon constitutes significantly more than the mere sum of its component parts. Farrakhan's recent rise to an influential national leadership position in contemporary African-American politics merits rigorous analysis not only in itself, but also because Farrakhan serves as a particularly compelling and remarkably rich embodiment of—and hence an especially powerful and clear window upon—broader developments in recent American politics, and in the politics of race, especially. The analysis of the Farrakhan phenomenon that follows is, hence, neither exclusively nor most importantly about the Black Muslim minister and his ascent to national political leadership status among black Americans. Rather, in order clearly and comprehensively to understand the contemporary Farrakhan phenomenon, it is necessary to locate the NoI's leader within the broader strains of the political environment of post–civil rights era American politics.

This is not, it should be immediately stressed, to seek to diminish the political significance of the particular individual. Individual political actors and entrepreneurs matter a great deal in American politics, as elsewhere, whatever the particular configuration of the broader social forces and societal fissures that necessarily surround and shape their activity. Indeed, an important subtheme of the central argument of this monograph is that, while Farrakhan has undoubtedly capitalized upon—and consistently exploited to substantial effect—conditions that are deeply rooted in the post–1960s structure of black Americans' political, social, and economic development in the United States, it has been his own individual strategic contributions and his particular tactical choices as the leader of the NoI that have powerfully shaped both the direction and the fluctuating pace of his rise to national black American political leadership. Nonetheless, the main analytical significance of the Farrakhan phenomenon resides more in what it reveals about the contours and fissures of contemporary American politics in general than in what it demonstrates about the Nation of Islam or its particular leader per se.

Two broad themes are especially significant in this respect. First and most obvious, Farrakhan reveals and powerfully contributes to the contemporary fissures and divisions in the politics of race in America at the end of the twentieth century. Precisely by virtue of the juxtaposition of Farrakhan's manifest popular appeal among black Americans and the extreme (and predominantly critical and condemnatory) reactions that he invariably elicits from black and, especially, nonblack American elites, the NoI's leader stands squarely upon the racial fault lines of American politics. Farrakhan represents an intensely compelling political figure as the United States continues to grapple with the pressing problem of its inter- and intra-race relations and seeks to define and shape the political meaning and legacy of the 1960s. In this sense, and although their explanations of and solutions to the U.S.'s racial predicament differ markedly, Farrakhan articulates the sentiments shared more broadly among many black (and some nonblack) Americans, at both elite and mass levels: that the landmark achievement of formal black civil and political equality in the mid-1960s was a limited and shallow, if not entirely Pyrrhic, victory for many African-Americans.[51]

To this extent at least the NoI's leader, like his former friend and mentor, Malcolm X, represents a considerably more complex and immeasurably more fascinating political phenomenon than is frequently acknowledged by his many American critics and detractors. Farrakhan certainly does express unyielding hatred, explicitly, frequently, and without apparent regret, remorse, or sufficient reason to seek to atone for that unmistakably clear and consistent animus. Simply to reduce assessments of Farrakhan to being the contemporary arch African-American exemplar of "the hate that hate produced," however, is a grossly inaccurate and misleading oversimplification of both his political base and his substantive national role. Analysis of extremists in general, and of Farrakhan in particular, is assuredly not assisted by "interpretation through diabolism,"[52] eminently susceptible though the NoI's leader undoubtedly is to such a crudely demonic characterization. Precisely by virtue of his currently representing one of the sharpest and most striking horns of Myrdal's American dilemma, the scholarly imperative to grapple dispassionately with both the causes and the broader political significance of the Farrakhan phenomenon is especially great, pressing, and (potentially) intellectually rewarding.

In addition, though, in serving as an especially clear and powerful window upon that racial dilemma as it has manifested itself in America during the 1990s, Farrakhan does so from an unusual political location: as a black American radical right-wing leader. Studies of authoritarian politics in America have conventionally concentrated principally upon the distinctive and heterogeneous fanaticist forces of the extreme white American right-wing.[53] Most detailed examinations of extremism in contemporary racial politics in the United States focus upon the expressions, extent, and manner of the conservative exploitation of race-related concerns among white Americans by avowedly right-wing and populist politicians, political parties, and other organized groups. Thus it is that the Rockwells, Wallaces, Dukes, Helmses, and Buchanans occupy the vast bulk of scholarly attention to modern American right-wing political extremism and authoritarianism.

It is the markedly conservative and overwhelmingly illiberal traditionalist character of Farrakhan's ideological values and beliefs—an unabashed conservatism that is frequently obscured for many observers by his militant black nationalism, anti-Semitic pronouncements, and informal associations with African-American liberals and progressives, such as Jesse Jackson and the Congressional Black Caucus—that casts the Black Muslim leader in a very peculiar, curious, and distinctive contemporary political role. Although the ideological match is imperfect, the parallels between Farrakhan and the radical white right-wing in America, both in their analyses of the current political, economic, and social problems in the United States, and in their political goals and aspirations, are at once several and striking. Farrakhan is perhaps not viewed most appropriately as the bastard black political twin of Louisianan David Duke, the ex-Ku Klux Klan Grand Wizard and Republican party senatorial candidate, but they remain undeniably close relatives in the peculiar dysfunctional extended family of conservative American extremism and political paranoia.

Farrakhan's political rise is also intimately connected to his esoteric brand of theologically based black nationalist conservatism and to the political responses of other U.S. and foreign actors—black and nonblack, secular and religious, at elite and mass levels—to both his individual public pronouncements and his organization's direct action interventions to combat drug use and ameliorate gang violence in many of America's inner-city black communities. An accurate analysis of the Farrakhan phenomenon therefore demands that the Black Muslim leader be assessed in his appropriate political and social context: not as an isolated political figure waging an atomistic and unorthodox course of his own design, but as a religious activist whose political pronouncements, activities, and style are deliberately and precisely calculated to produce strongly outspoken reactions among others which, in turn, contribute further to the consolidation of his own burgeoning political role and influence. Ironically, the responses of some American political elites to the NoI's leader, designed precisely to confront, challenge, and ultimately undermine the Farrakhan phenomenon, frequently serve inadvertently to reinforce its very momentum. Some of Farrakhan's most ardent and implacable American critics thus often end up serving as unwitting accomplices in his unconventional and prophetic national racial project.

The Farrakhan phenomenon, then, is not exclusively about race in contemporary America. It also concerns political reaction in a twofold sense: first, in ideological terms, as the repressive features of Farrakhan's reactionary worldview are made manifest, despite their

being frequently obscured, disregarded, or ignored by both his supporters and critics; and, second, in practical and logistical terms, in
the dogged efforts of black and white American elites alike to
respond effectively—according to their frequently divergent defini-
tions of effective response—to the Black Muslim leader and his sectarian, separatist organization. It is in large part through the tactical and
strategic responses of other political and social elites—both black and
white—to Farrakhan that his novel locus and evolving role and influence in current American politics can most appropriately be delineated and profitably assessed.

Consonant with this two-dimensional focus, a dual narrative
therefore threads the examination of the Farrakhan phenomenon that
follows in this treatise. The peculiarly compelling story of Farrakhan's
rise to national political prominence and influence among African-
Americans is the first element. As a black political actor of evident—
though greatly contested—consequence, Farrakhan merits an extended and thorough examination. In addition, though, the scope and
character of the political responses to Farrakhan from other Americans form an integral part of the analysis. For it is in the political
responses to the Black Muslim leader—whether hesitant or forceful,
condemnatory or laudatory, fearful or encouraging—that many of the
deepest racial fault lines of recent American politics can be most
clearly identified and, thereby, fruitfully examined.

These twin themes of race and reaction form the underlying core
of the entire book. In chapter two, Farrakhan's recent rise to national
political leadership status among African-Americans is examined,
with particular reference to the two presidential nomination campaigns of the Reverend Jesse Jackson, during 1984 and 1988, and the
Million Man March on Washington of October 16, 1995. Farrakhan's
ideological and religious beliefs are then outlined and analyzed in
chapter three. Therein, the combination of a strident racial separatism
(based upon deeply unorthodox theological foundations) with a profoundly conservative economic and social agenda is examined. Prevailing popular notions of Farrakhan's leftist radicalism, and of his
status as an effective successor to Malcolm X for black Americans in
the 1990s, are also challenged as being at once profoundly misplaced
and as ignoring Farrakhan's fundamentally reactionary and repressive worldview.

Chapter four then locates Farrakhan within the broader American tradition of authoritarian political movements and paranoid activists, arguing that Farrakhan is not only a conventional conservative

authoritarian populist, but that he also represents the preeminent contemporary African-American exemplar of the paranoid style in American politics. The agents of the alleged conspiracy against black Americans that forms a central political leitmotif of Farrakhan's public discourse are explicitly identified (namely, Jews, the federal government, whites, and African-American accommodationists) and discussed in detail. Although deliberate and premeditated actions against black Americans have undoubtedly occurred over many decades, the impressive scope and passionate intensity of Farrakhan's style of paranoid politics are, at minimum, unusual. In implying an independence of thought and courage of action that his fellow black civic and political leaders do not possess, Farrakhan's brand of political paranoia also contributes strongly to the NoI leader's national self-projection as the autonomous personification of his race's "authentic" collective interests.

Having identified the appropriate political context in which Farrakhan's distinctive ideas and values should be located, the minister's recent popularity and his influence among black Americans at large are explored in chapter five, which draws upon both opinion surveys and secondary accounts to affirm the significant popular appeal of Farrakhan among African-Americans. Consonant with such an affirmation, the chapter also rejects the notion, prevalent among some critical analyses, that the Farrakhan phenomenon is either exclusively or primarily a media creation. Instead, it argues that print and televisual attention has been a necessary, but not sufficient, condition of Farrakhan's recent political ascendancy.

The substantive reasons for the popularity of Farrakhan's distinctive brand of black reactionary and paranoid politics are then examined at length in chapter six, which concentrates upon the Black Muslim minister's exploitation of post–civil rights era interracial differences and intrablack socioeconomic cleavages; the disjunctures between black American elite and mass political opinions; and Farrakhan's antielitist appeals and outsider, "spatial leadership" strategies. In the latter respect, Farrakhan essentially runs for national black American political leadership by running against, and running down, not only whites in the United States but also—both directly and indirectly—black political and civic leaders. Farrakhan's incessant appeals to intraracial unity are, ironically, based upon a political strategy and praxis that is premised fundamentally upon provoking sharp polarization, antagonism, and division among African-Americans themselves, as well as between blacks and whites, in the United States.

In chapter seven, Farrakhan's importance to current black national political leadership is discussed, and his broader significance in contemporary American politics is evaluated. Farrakhan's main political significance lies in the extent to which he vividly demonstrates how far advanced—though still incomplete—the recent incorporation of black American national political leadership into the pluralist American mainstream has become. In this sense, Farrakhan represents, paradoxically, a product and a confirmation of the overarching success, not failure, of traditional black American aspirations to inclusive political empowerment in the United States. In the absence of material improvements in the lives of most African-Americans, however, such inclusion will be insufficient either to remove the fertile ground upon which the Farrakhan phenomenon has thus far depended for its destructive growth or to disturb Farrakhan's hastening of an impending American apartheid.

For both better and worse, Louis Farrakhan is an influential and enthusiastic participant in national black American politics in the 1990s. For political scientists especially, but also for all those interested in the current character of politics in the United States and its evolving racial dimensions, examination of the Black Muslim leader is an integral though insufficient—and at times frustrating, perplexing, and even painful—necessity for a comprehensive and accurate understanding of its contemporary structure and dynamics. However unpalatable, offensive, and eccentric many Americans (and non-Americans) may rightly find Farrakhan's public discourse, lurid rhetoric, and policy prescriptions, simply to demonize and dismiss the NoI's leader as either an aberrant fanatic, an irrelevant lunatic, or an essentially ephemeral and marginal extremist figure is wholly to misinterpret his political salience and mass appeal and, thereby, to lend his own defense more cogency, vigor, and popularity than it otherwise merits. Equally, though, to exaggerate unduly Farrakhan's recent political influence is to ignore the extent to which the NoI's leader thus far remains a still-isolated force in the much broader national black American political leadership cohort and, moreover, confronts many intractable constraints to his achieving an enduring, mainstream national leadership role.

Farrakhan therefore merits careful but disinterested analysis, in the most accurate senses of those terms. Careful, because the nuances and subtleties of his role, influence, and beliefs are often too easily lost amidst the disproportionate attention that is devoted to his more provocative rhetoric and deliberately incendiary public comments; and disinterested, not in terms of diminishing or marginalizing his political and social importance, but in the sense of consistently and dispassionately inquiring as to the purpose and reasons for his actions, their wider public reception, and the political consequences thereof. Without doubt, the Farrakhan phenomenon is of manifest importance to the current and future shape of American race relations in the twentieth and twenty-first centuries, not so much for what Farrakhan himself either says or does, but for what his public discourse and behavior and the reactions to them suggest about the past, present, and future shape of racial politics in America.

NOTES TO CHAPTER 1

1. Quoted in William Gaines and David Jackson, "Profit and Promises," *Chicago Tribune*, 15 March 1995, sec. 1, p. 10.

2. I use the terms "black," "black American" and "African-American" interchangeably throughout the book to refer to people of African descent in the United States. The usage reflects the continued preference of a majority of the social group in question for the appellation "black" or "black American," despite the increasing use of the alternative term. For compelling, though contrasting, discussions of the changes in appellations, see: Ben L. Martin, "From Negro to Black to African American: The Power of Names and Naming," *Political Science Quarterly* 106, no. 1 (1991): 83–107; and Tom W. Smith, "Changing Racial Labels: From 'Colored' to 'Negro' to 'African American'," *Public Opinion Quarterly* 56, no. 4 (1992): 496–515.

3. The remarks were made by Mayor Ed Koch, a noted Jewish target for Farrakhan's public ridicule during the 1980s. See Christopher Thomas, "Black radical taunts US Jews with 'God's oven' gibe," *The (London) Times*, 10 October 1985, p. 7.

4. Farrakhan had been invited by the Hackney Local Council in London, under the control of the Labour Party, and was also due to address the Islamic Council of the United Kingdom. The decision to refuse him entry by then Home Secretary Douglas Hurd, M.P., was made in response to an appeal from Michael Latham, M.P., chairman of the British-Israel Parliamentary Group. See "Black activist barred from Britain," *The (London) Times*, 17 January 1986, p. 2.

5. See Gunnar Myrdal, *An American Dilemma: The Negro Problem and Modern Democracy*, vols. 1 and 2 (New York: Harper and Row, 1944, 1964).

6. Throughout its history, the stability of the regime in the face of pronounced ethnic, racial, religious, and regional heterogeneity has been strongly emphasized by most non-American writers. See, for example: Alexis De Tocqueville, *Democracy in America* (New York: Vintage Books, 1945); and James Bryce, *The American Commonwealth* (New York: Macmillan, 1888).

7. For an extensive and important recent treatment of the extent to which the federal government both legitimated and diffused segregated racial practices in the first half of the twentieth century in the United States, both within and outside the South, see Desmond S. King, *Separate and Unequal: Black Americans and the US Federal Government* (Oxford: Oxford University Press, 1995).

8. The most prominent exponent of this view is Samuel P. Huntington, *American Politics: The Promise of Disharmony* (Cambridge, Mass.: Belknap/ Harvard University Press, 1981). See also the concise discussion of the nexus of stability and conflict in Michael Foley, *American Political Ideas* (Manchester: Manchester University Press, 1991).

9. See the classic "consensus school" accounts: Richard Hofstadter, *The American Political Tradition* (New York: Knopf, 1948); and Louis Hartz, *The Liberal Tradition in America* (New York: Harcourt, Brace, and World, 1955).

10. See Alexander Hamilton, James Madison and John Jay, *The Federalist Papers*, with introduction by Isaac Kramnick (Harmondsworth: Penguin 1987), No. 10.

11. See Andrew Hacker, *Two Nations: Black and White, Separate, Hostile, Unequal* (New York: Ballantine Books, 1992).

12. Paul M. Sniderman and Thomas Piazza, *The Scar of Race* (Cambridge, Mass.: Harvard University Press, 1993). See also Paul M. Sniderman, Philip E. Tetlock, and Edward G. Carmines, eds., *Prejudice, Politics, and the American Dilemma* (Stanford: Stanford University Press, 1993).

13. As chapter three notes in greater detail, Farrakhan's racial separatism has never waned, but it has waxed and wavered over time between advocations of a largely cultural retrenchment by African-Americans (akin to many black nationalists' prescriptions; see William L. Van Deburg, *New Day in Babylon: The Black Power Movement and American Culture, 1965–1975* [Chicago: University of Chicago Press, 1992]) and endorsement of an actual physical separation of the races. On several occasions, the latter has entailed the exodus of black Americans from the United States, most typically with Africa as the proposed destination for their new homeland.

14. Farrakhan's meeting with Mandela in January 1996 attracted widespread international attention. President Mandela's lecturing Farrakhan upon the three foundations of the new South Africa—nonracialism, nonsexism, and freedom of religion—represented a powerful and telling rebuke to the NoI's leader and his prescriptions for America's blacks. See James Bone, "Prophet of Hate," *The London Times (Magazine)*, 3 February 1996, pp. 26–30; and Christopher Munnion, "Farrakhan Tells Whites to Atone for Apartheid," *The Daily London Telegraph*, 29 January 1996, p. 11.

15. On the general shape of post–civil rights black American politics, see: Steven F. Lawson, *In Pursuit of Power* (New York: Columbia University Press, 1985); Hanes Walton, *Invisible Politics: Black Political Behavior* (New York: State University of New York Press, 1985); and Huey L. Perry and Wayne Parent, *Blacks and the American Political System* (Gainesville: University Press of Florida, 1995). Manning Marable provides quasi-Marxist interpretations in *Race, Reform and Rebellion: The Second Reconstruction in Black America,*

1945–1982 (Jackson, Miss.: University of Mississippi Press, 1984) and *Black American Politics: From the Washington Marches to Jesse Jackson* (London: Verso, 1985).

16. See Derrick Bell, *And We Are Not Saved: The Elusive Quest for Racial Justice* (New York: Basic Books, 1979); and James H. Cone, *Martin and Malcolm and America* (London: HarperCollins, 1991).

17. See Robert Gooding-Williams, ed., *Reading Rodney King/Reading Urban Uprising* (New York: Routledge, 1993); and Rochelle Stanfield, "Black Frustration," *National Journal*, 16 May 1992, pp. 1162–66.

18. Cited in Salim Muwakkil, "Leaders Lacking in a Black and White World," in *Inside the L.A. Riots: What Really Happened and Why It Will Happen Again* (New York: Institute for Alternative Journalism, 1992), pp. 106–8, at 107.

19. Muwakkil, "Leaders Lacking," p. 107.

20. Cited in Gooding-Williams, *Reading Rodney King*, pp. 146–47.

21. Jerry G. Watts, "Reflections on the Rodney King Verdict and the Paradoxes of the Black Response," in Gooding-Williams, *Reading Rodney King*, pp. 236–48, at 246.

22. Manning Marable, "In the Business of Prophet Making," *New Statesman*, 13 December 1985, pp. 23–25, at 25.

23. The remarks were made in a memo circulated by Bond to other NAACP board members in the aftermath of the Million Man March. Quoted in Kevin Merida, "Four Months After March, Controversy Follows Farrakhan," *The Washington Post*, 25 February 1996, p. A6.

24. Cited in Michael Wines, "Farrakhan is Bitterly Denounced by House Black Caucus Member," *The New York Times*, 5 February 1994, pp. 1, 7.

25. Cornel West, "Learning to Talk of Race," in Gooding-Williams, *Reading Rodney King*, pp. 255–60, at 257. See also West's collection of essays, *Race Matters* (Boston: Beacon Press, 1993).

26. Quoted in Sylvester Monroe, "The Mirage of Farrakhan," *Time* 144, 30 October 1995, p. 52.

27. Quoted in Henry Louis Gates Jr., "A Reporter at Large: The Charmer," *The New Yorker*, 29 April-6 May 1996, pp. 116–31, at 121.

28. It is mildly ironic that, prior to his confirmation hearings for nomination to the Supreme Court in 1991, Thomas felt compelled to issue public statements repudiating his previous praise for the Nation of Islam's leader. In two speeches in 1983, Thomas praised Farrakhan as "a man I have admired for more than a decade." His statement of July 13, 1991, however, included comments of his unalterable opposition to "anti-Semitism and bigotry of any kind, including . . . Louis Farrakhan." See Robert Pear, "Despite Praising Farrakhan in 1983, Thomas Denies anti-Semitism," *The New York Times*, 13 July 1991, pp. 1, 7.

29. Most notable among the contingent factors conditioning the Thomas furor were his nomination by President George Bush to fill the vacancy created by Thurgood Marshall's retirement, the enthusiastic sponsorship of Senate Republicans, and the allegations of sexual harassment leveled against Thomas—and accorded prime-time network television coverage—by Anita Hill. Though the Thomas nomination animated deep dissensus among black

Americans and spoke directly to many themes of inter- and intra-racial division and tension, the mass salience of the controversy was neither as enduring nor as sharply defined as that surrounding Farrakhan and the NoI. On the Thomas nomination and its associated political controversies, see: Toni Morrisson, ed., *Race-ing Justice, En-Gendering Power: Essays on Anita Hill, Clarence Thomas, and the Construction of Social Reality* (London: Chatto and Windus, 1993); Timothy M. Phelps and Helen Winternitz, *Capitol Games: The Inside Story of Clarence Thomas, Anita Hill, and a Supreme Court Nomination* (New York: HarperPerennial, 1993); and Stephen L. Carter, *The Confirmation Mess: Cleaning Up the Federal Appointments Process* (New York: Basic Books, 1994).

30. Quoted in John Kifner, "With Farrakhan Speaking, a Chorus of G.O.P. Critics Join In," *The New York Times*, 17 October 1995, p. A18.

31. United States House of Representatives, 104th Congress, First Session, Hearing before the Subcommittee on General Oversight and Investigations of the Committee on Banking and Financial Services, March 2, 1995, *Security Contracts Between HUD or HUD Affiliated Entities and Companies Affiliated With the Nation of Islam* (Washington, D.C.: U.S. Government Printing Office, 1995), p. 3.

32. David Broder, "Farrakhan reminder that U.S. still has its own racial problems," *The Atlanta Journal*, 18 September 1985, p. A15.

33. See, respectively: "The Man and the March," editorial, *The New Republic* 208 (1995), p. 9; Andrew Sullivan, "Call to Harm: the Hateful Oratory of Minister Farrakhan," *The New Republic*, 203 (1990), pp. 13–15; Michael C. Kotzin, "Louis Farrakhan's anti-Semitism: A look at the record," *The Christian Century* 111 (1994), pp. 224–25; and Joe Queenan, "America's Most Demented: A Startling Scientific Analysis," *The Washington Post*, 30 May 1993, p. C1. Similar references to Farrakhan's politics of hate can be found in: Bob Herbert, "The Hate Game," *The New York Times*, 9 February 1994, p. A18; and Charles Krauthammer, "The 'Validation' of Louis Farrakhan," *The Washington Post*, 20 October 1995, p. A19.

34. Richard E. Cohen, "At Nuremberg-on-Potomac, A Chanting of Jews, Jews," *International Herald Tribune*, 3 March 1994, p. 7.

35. Manning Marable, *How Capitalism Underdeveloped Black America: Problems in Race, Political Economy and Society* (Boston: South End Press, 1983), p. 84. See also his several references to Farrakhan in the collection of essays, *Beyond Black and White: Transforming African-American Politics* (New York: Verso, 1995).

36. Nicholas Lemann, *The Promised Land: The Great Black Migration and How It Changed America* (London: Macmillan, 1991), p. 289.

37. See the series of articles and op-ed pieces by Adolph Reed Jr.: "The Rise of Louis Farrakhan," *The Nation* 252 (January 21, 1991), pp. 51–52, 54–56; "All for One and None for All," *The Nation* 252 (January 28, 1991), pp. 86–88, 90–92; "Behind the Farrakhan Show," *The Progressive* 58 (April 1994), pp. 16–17; and "Black Leadership in Crisis," *The Progressive* 58 (October 1994), p. 16.

38. See *Revolutionary and Dissident Movements: An International Guide*, 3rd ed. (Harlow: Longman, 1991).

39. C. O. Maolain, *The Radical Right: A World Dictionary* (Harlow, U.K.: Longman, 1987).

40. John White, *Black Leadership in America: From Booker T. Washington to Jesse Jackson*, 2nd ed. (London: Longman, 1990), p. 178.

41. Lemann, *The Promised Land*, p. 302.

42. Claudette McFadden-Preston, "The Rhetoric of Minister Louis Farrakhan: a pluralistic approach" (unpublished Ph.D. thesis, Ohio State University, 1986), p. 162.

43. Clarence Lusane, *African-American Politics at the Crossroads: The Restructuring of Black Leadership and the 1992 Elections* (Boston: South End Press, 1994), p. 29.

44. See, in particular, Reed, "All for One." Reed has been among the most consistent and courageous of Farrakhan's critics and has persistently sought to expose the reactionary features of the NoI leader's beliefs. If some of his interpretations of Farrakhan's political significance are not entirely compelling, much of his analysis of the Black Muslim's mass appeal nonetheless merits close scrutiny.

45. The question was the title of an American politics seminar paper delivered by Glazer at Nuffield College, Oxford, UK, in the summer of 1989. For a related discussion, see the polemic monograph by Arthur M. Schlesinger Jr., *The Disuniting of America: Reflections on a Multicultural Society* (New York: Norton, 1992).

46. See Jabril Muhammad, *Farrakhan, The Traveller* (Phoenix, Ariz.: PHNX SN and Co., 1985); C. Alan Marshall, *The Life and Times of Louis Farrakhan* (New York: Marshall Publications, 1992); and Arthur J. Magida, *Prophet of Rage: A Life of Louis Farrakhan and his Nation* (New York: HarperCollins, 1996).

47. The most useful analyses in an extensive literature on the Black Muslims are: Walter D. Abilla, *The Black Muslims in America: An Introduction to the Theory of Commitment* (Kampala: East African Literature Bureau, 1977); E. U. Essien-Udom, *Black Nationalism: A Search for an Identity in America* (Chicago: University of Chicago Press, 1971); Mattias Gardell, *Countdown to Armageddon: Louis Farrakhan and the Nation of Islam* (London: Hurst, 1996); Martha F. Lee, *The Nation of Islam: An American Millenarian Movement* (Lewiston, N.Y.: E. Mellen Press, 1988); C. Eric Lincoln, *The Black Muslims in America*, 3rd ed. (Grand Rapids, Mich.: Williams B. Eerdmans, 1994); Clifton E. Marsh, *From Black Muslims to Muslims: The Transition from Separatism to Islam, 1930–1980* (London: Scarecrow Press, 1984) and *From Black Muslims to Muslims: The Resurrection, Transformation, and Change of the Lost-found Nation of Islam in America, 1930–1995*, 2nd ed. (Lanham, Md.: Scarecrow Press, 1996); Morroe Berger, "The Black Muslims," *Horizon* 6, no. 1 (1964): 49–65; Leon Douglas Bibb, "A Note on the Black Muslims: They Preach Black to be the Ideal," *Negro History Bulletin* 28, no. 6 (1965): 132–33; H. M. Kaplan, "The Black Muslims and the Negro American's Quest for Communion: A Case Study in the Genesis of Negro Protest Movements," *British Journal of Sociology* 20, no. 2 (1969): 164–76; Joseph M. Kirman, "The Challenge of the Black Muslims," *Social Education* 27, no. 7 (1963): 365–68; James H. Laue, "A Contemporary Revitalization Movement in American Race Relations: The Black Muslims," *Social Forces* 42, no. 3 (1964): 315–23; and Vincent Monteil, "La Religion des Black Muslims," *Esprit* 32, no. 16 (1964): 601–29.

48. R. E. Allen, ed., *The Concise Oxford English Dictionary of Current English*, 8th ed. (Oxford: Clarendon Press, 1990), p. 893.

49. See the collected essays in the volume by Hans Gerth and C. Wright Mills, *From Max Weber: Essays in Sociology* (London: Routledge, 1991).

50. This is perhaps most obviously the case in the pamphlets published by the New York-based Anti-Defamation League of B'Nai B'rith, but it can also be said to characterize the writings of a broad range of academic and popular commentators, such as Richard Cohen, Adolph Reed, Carl Rowan, Cornel West, and Juan Williams. Their assessments of Farrakhan are typically as much polemics against him as examinations of his role, influence, and popular appeal.

51. One of the strongest, though largely unpersuasive, critiques of the integrationist public philosophy of the civil rights movement is Harold Cruse, *Plural But Equal: A Critical Study of Blacks and Minorities in America's Plural Society* (New York: Quill, 1987).

52. Seymour Martin Lipset and Earl Raab, *The Politics of Unreason: Right-Wing Extremism in America, 1790–1977* (Chicago: University of Chicago Press, 1978), p. 484.

53. None of the principal academic studies of right-wing extremism in the United States include discussions of the incidence of the phenomenon among African-Americans. See, for example, Lipset and Raab, *The Politics of Unreason*; Paul Hainsworth, ed., *The Extreme Right in Europe and the USA* (London: Pinter, 1992); Richard Hofstadter, *The Paranoid Style in American Politics* (Chicago: University of Chicago Press, 1979); and Lynne Tower Sargent, ed., *Extremism in America* (New York: New York University Press, 1995).

2

From the Margins to the Mainstream: The Rise of Louis Farrakhan

Louis Farrakhan is a problem.

William A. Henry III, 1994[1]

Although Lou Reed was typically idiosyncratic in including Louis Farrakhan in a rock song, ("Good Evening Mister Waldheim"),[2] the New Yorker was hardly alone in finding in the Nation of Islam (NoI) leader and his followers ample cause for unease, disquiet, and consternation. The Black Muslim minister's rise to a position of national leadership among African-Americans during the 1980s and 1990s has represented a political development that is not only deeply troubling, and even chilling to many white and black Americans, but also extremely difficult for most observers of contemporary American politics to comprehend fully and to explain adequately.

Had Farrakhan's ascendancy occurred as the obvious result of a new issue cleavage arising or a nascent political movement emerging among African-Americans, it would no doubt be more easily explicable. The Farrakhan phenomenon, however, has not arisen as a clear response to some sudden critical event or catastrophic new development among black Americans in which Farrakhan has assumed the leadership of a newly emergent political movement by capitalizing upon a rapidly transformed political situation or an unexpected socioeconomic crisis. The pattern of African-American political, economic, and social development in the post–civil rights era in the United States has been internally differentiated, to be sure, but its overall shape and direction—though profoundly bifurcated by social class and income—has been relatively stable and consistent nonetheless.

Notwithstanding the deep recession of 1982, no sudden lurch or dramatic downturn has occurred in black Americans' collective fortunes since the later 1960s; the pace of socioeconomic change has been steady and gradual rather than precipitous in its nature, scope, and consequences. No functional political equivalent therefore exists for Farrakhan in the 1980s and 1990s comparable to the Montgomery, Alabama, bus boycott for Martin Luther King Jr. and the fledgling civil rights movement in 1955–56.[3]

Furthermore, Farrakhan is neither a new nor an unfamiliar presence in black American communities, having first joined the NoI in 1955, eventually assuming its leadership in 1978. Nor does Farrakhan share the religious convictions of the overwhelming majority of black Americans. It is not simply that Farrakhan is a Muslim, but also that the version of the Islamic faith to which he (and the NoI under his leadership) subscribes is itself extremely unorthodox and adhered to by only a very small minority of the growing Muslim American population in the United States.[4] Although, then, Farrakhan has been very active in African-American public life for several decades, the unconventional "product" that he has offered his compatriots has traditionally attracted very few buyers among black Americans nationwide.

The causes and consequences of Farrakhan's increasing inclusion within the national black political leadership cadre in America have therefore prompted both popular disagreement and substantial academic and critical dissensus. Only in the principal events that have informed Farrakhan's curious but steady political ascendancy has broad critical agreement been reached. It is hence appropriate in this chapter to review the main features of Farrakhan's gradual but inexorable rise to a position of national political leadership among black Americans, before moving on to analyze both the causes and the broader political significance of the Farrakhan phenomenon in contemporary American politics.

Though not an exhaustive list, it is possible to identify four developments as especially influential political landmarks along the Black Muslim's checkered, bumpy, but very carefully calculated road to national leadership status among African-Americans at large: Jesse Jackson's presidential campaigns of 1984 and 1988; the conclusion of a "Sacred Covenant" between the Congressional Black Caucus and the NoI in 1993; the public reconciliation between Farrakhan and Betty Shabazz, the widow of Malcolm X, in January 1995; and the triumphal Million Man March in Washington, D.C., on October 16, 1995.

Together, these four developments have powerfully conditioned and propelled Farrakhan's quixotic political journey from the margins of African-American political respectability to a location, if not centrally within, at least proximate to, the national black political mainstream.

THE JACKSON FACTOR:
THE NATIONALIZATION OF LOUIS FARRAKHAN

If elections in liberal democracies have always been more emotional orgies than feasts of reason,[5] then it was perhaps especially appropriate that the quadrennial bout of sensory overload that an American presidential election typically occasions should form the catalytic engine of the entire Farrakhan phenomenon. For prior to 1984, Louis Farrakhan was a relatively marginal political figure for many black Americans and a wholly unknown one for the vast majority of non-blacks in both the United States and the rest of the world. Farrakhan's position as the leader of the recently revived NoI, an unorthodox and racially exclusive religious group that commanded few members—in either relative or absolute terms—among African-Americans and that preached a peculiar and uncompromising public gospel of racial separatism, made this fact (at best) unsurprising.

Within the space of a mere two years, however, between 1984 and 1986, Farrakhan found himself invited onto prime-time national television news and current affairs programs in the United States to give interviews about his religious beliefs and political aspirations; engaging in a remarkably well-attended and successful speaking tour of the fourteen most populous American cities in 1985; embarking in 1986 upon a series of international visits that took him around the world from Ghana and Pakistan to China and Japan (and that led to rumors of his facing possible prosecution by the U.S. Attorney General for violating federal prohibitions on travel to Colonel Gadhafi's Libya); and being subjected to vociferous, persistent, and near universal condemnation, by black and nonblack American political commentators alike, as a hysterical preacher of racial bigotry, sexism, and homophobic hatred—a veritable "black Hitler."

The rapid (and, for the minister, not unwelcome) transformation in Farrakhan's national public visibility was effected in two distinct, though related, stages during the period 1983–84. First, Farrakhan's initial entry into national black American politics occurred with his participation in the 1983 March on Washington. The march was a broadly based political gathering, organized both to commemorate the landmark civil rights mobilization of twenty years earlier and to bring substantial public pressure to bear upon the Reagan Administration and the U.S. Congress to halt, and subsequently reverse, the enactment of conservative economic and social policies that most black politicians deemed deeply inimical to mass African-American advancement.

The 1983 event represented an especially important attempt by the mainstream American civil rights establishment to reach out to a broader alliance of African-American and nonblack political forces that were all intent upon defending the hard-won liberal policy gains of the 1960s, an extremely heterogeneous political coalition that included democratic socialists, non-Marxist progressives, and black nationalists. Among the latter category, the NoI, as a result both of its historic longevity in the black community and its more recently revived urban activism, was undoubtedly the most significant nationalist group. Farrakhan, as its leader, was included as a principal speaker at the event, where he delivered an eloquent and well-received multiracial unity message to an ethnically diverse and racially mixed audience. For the Black Muslim minister, the content of his message was as uncharacteristic as the composition of his audience was unusual.

Both the message and the audience reflected the novelty of the event, which was particularly politically significant for Farrakhan's emergent national black leadership pretensions. Although he had previously attended black American political gatherings in the capacity of Elijah Muhammad's "national representative"—most notably, addressing the 1971 Black Solidarity Rally in Harlem and attending the 1972 National Black Convention in Gary, Indiana—the 1983 march represented Farrakhan's de facto national debut as the leader of the new NoI. For the first, but by no means the last, occasion in his intriguing career, Farrakhan achieved inclusion in a mainstream national political demonstration that drew extensive mass black American participation. Moreover, as Marable argued, the appearance of the NoI's leader on a national platform with figures such as Coretta Scott King was a powerful political symbol of elite, as well as popular, black legitimation, one that was not lost upon veterans of the civil rights movement.[6] That the putative heir to the black separatist tradition of Elijah Muhammad should now share a national platform with the widow of the most influential integrationist civil rights leader in American history was a cardinal political boost to Farrakhan's popular black standing and leadership credentials. In seeking both mass and elite black American legitimation, the march represented an initial, but vitally important, political victory for Farrakhan.

If the 1983 march signaled the tentative beginnings of Farrakhan's national political odyssey, however, the second and far more influential catalyst of his increasing national and international political prominence—indeed, the central, though inadvertent, launchpad for the entire Farrakhan phenomenon—occurred the following year, with the Reverend Jesse Jackson's insurgent campaign for the Democratic Party's presidential nomination.[7] The Jackson campaign of 1984 served, crucially, to nationalize Farrakhan's leadership status among African-Americans. Simultaneously, it cast the Black Muslim minister from a position of national obscurity (and almost total anonymity among white Americans) to one arousing widespread recognition, as well as a heady mixture of admiration and deep public animosity, across the entire United States.

The elevation reflected the landmark nature of the Jackson campaign. While it failed to secure him the party's nomination, the Jackson campaign nonetheless served as the principal political focus for a unity of purpose and an emotive and affective response among black Americans at the mass level that had rarely been in evidence since the high watermark of the civil rights movement, some twenty years previously.[8] Although its political significance remains widely and intensely disputed,[9] the evangelizing political crusade that Jackson tirelessly fought clearly succeeded in mobilizing large numbers of black Americans to register, vote, and take a new interest in political participation in general. Moreover, it established a wholly novel level of national media attention for Farrakhan in America and, in the intense furor over anti-Semitism that rapidly engulfed him, a deeply contentious issue that would subsequently become virtually inseparable from public discussions of the NoI's leader. In inadvertently ensuring him the vital American political oxygen of nationwide publicity and rapt media attention, the Jackson campaign thereby accorded Farrakhan the necessary ballast for his national African-American leadership aspirations.

Farrakhan's tentative entry into national U.S. politics was thus inextricably and very fortuitously bound to the four-yearly spectacle of the American presidential race and the intense concentration of media and public attention upon a set of tangible, concrete individual personalities that it invariably affords. Although it was not the first electoral campaign for the U.S. presidency mounted by an African-American, either within or outside the Democratic party, the Jackson bid did represent the first one to be accorded extensive news media coverage and to be treated by many political elites as serious in character, a requisite but insufficient condition of the aspirant's either winning the party nomination or exerting meaningful political influence subsequently upon the eventual nominee.[10]

Jackson's candidacy was the first by an African-American for the Democratic party's presidential nomination since Congresswoman Shirley Chisholm (D-NY) had made her disastrously unsuccessful and ineffectual bid in 1972. The twelve-year hiatus was itself of notable political significance. That a campaign by any African-American should have occurred in 1984 reflected three developments of increasing political import: the growing presence of black American activists and public officials within the ranks of local, state, and national Democratic party organizations; the contemporary imperative to challenge President Ronald Reagan's reelection effort; and the increasing desire of many African-American elected officials and voters loyal to the Democratic party to achieve a greater degree of responsiveness to their public policy concerns from its highest echelons than had hitherto been conceded by the party's elites, since 1980 at least.

In Jackson, however, that responsiveness was ironically sought through an insurgent African-American candidate who was expressly not an elected party official and who had never previously run for any elective public office in America: the quintessential "outsider" candidate. Despite the presence in the presidential race of white candidates whose commitment to civil rights and black American social and economic advancement was undeniably strong—most notably, former Vice President Walter Mondale and Senator Gary Hart (D-CO)—the entry into the Democratic party primaries of a fledgling black candidate who had never held a position of public authority represented an unusual and important political development, for both black (at both elite and mass levels) and white Americans.

Not the least of the politically significant aspects of the Jackson campaign was the manner in which it fully and dramatically encapsulated the acute dilemmas, for both aspirant and established national black American political leaders, that the polarizing figure of Louis Farrakhan would subsequently pose. It was also, moreover, replete with the many ironies that have surrounded Farrakhan's recent political rise and current national role. If, in effectively playing Hardy to Farrakhan's Laurel, Jackson found that the national political mess in which he was apt to be mired was worryingly deep and not prone to easy extraction, this was nonetheless a disconcerting discovery that other black American politicians would subsequently imitate, whether consciously or, more commonly, through strategic blunders and tactical miscalculations.

The genesis of the contemporary association was relatively recent. Jackson had asked Farrakhan in the winter of 1983 to participate actively in his prospective campaign for the Democratic party's presidential nomination. The links between the two black clergymen had been forged several years previously, however, in their common political and religious base of Chicago, Illinois. Both programmatic and strategic political factors had encouraged their informal political coalescence. The two ministers adhered to racially bounded capitalist economic tenets of self-help, individual entrepreneurship, and black private sector enterprise: Jackson through his modestly entitled organization, People United to Save Humanity (PUSH), founded in 1971; and Farrakhan, through the NoI's many and varied business enterprises and retail outlets. Jackson and Farrakhan also possessed very strong self-conceptions as the principal contemporary African-American heirs to the dominant black political figures of the 1960s and the political and racial traditions that they respectively embodied: the integrationism of Martin Luther King Jr., and the black nationalism of Malcolm X. Moreover, both ministers, albeit in dramatically different manners, were personally connected not only to their respective spiritual and political mentors, but also to their brutal assassinations.

Jackson's initial political socialization as a young assistant to King and an organizer in the civil rights movement was well-known to many black Americans. His presence at the Memphis, Tennessee, motel where King was shot on April 4, 1968, had accorded the young Baptist preacher a tragic but priceless personal legacy—and a controversial and contested one—that he readily and persistently attempted to exploit over subsequent years for political advantage. Implicitly and explicitly, Jackson sought as both a civil rights activist and an electoral candidate to enlist his links to the slain leader as one of the central foundations of his claims to be the rightful and appropriate successor to the reverend doctor's national political mantle among African-Americans for the 1970s and 1980s. In the latter decade, especially,

Jackson increasingly projected himself as the preeminent post–civil rights era legatee of King's fundamental goals of an integrated America, the achievement of a beloved interracial community, and the guarantee of economic security for minorities, the poor, and the disadvantaged of all races.

By contrast, Farrakhan's political inheritance was at once far more ambiguous, controversial, and unenthusiastically received by many black Americans at large. Befriended and tutored in the NoI by Malcolm X during the 1950s, Farrakhan's initially pronounced fraternal admiration for the charismatic black American political agitator had been rapidly transformed into an intense enmity and deep hostility by Malcolm's decisive break with the separatist organization in 1964–65.[11] Although regarded by some African-Americans (and nonblacks, too) as the effective successor to Malcolm's militant and uncompromising national black political mantle, the implication of Farrakhan in plots to assassinate the Black Muslim activist served as a political albatross for the NoI's leader among many American blacks. Until 1995, fully thirty years after Malcolm's assassination, rumors of the profound animosity harbored by the Shabazz family toward Farrakhan were accorded widespread credence in the black community in the United States.[12] By comparison even with Jackson, Farrakhan's reputation among African-Americans was, in consequence, far less than unimpeachable, and his legitimacy remained seriously tarnished and impaired.

Despite their divergent historical paths and distinct religious associations, however, Jackson and Farrakhan shared important political features that facilitated their coalescence. Most notably, both were ministers of faith, occupying positions with traditionally powerful historic roles in not only the spiritual, but also the secular and the political, lives of African-Americans generally.[13] Both were also accomplished, confident, and frequently compelling public orators whose mass black popularity and claims to political legitimacy rested to a substantial extent upon their self-evident possession of charismatic authority.[14] Unable to rely upon (or unwilling to attempt to achieve) the conventional forms of rational and legal authority that are typically conferred upon politicians by elective public office in liberal democratic polities, both Jackson and Farrakhan depended instead upon their personal qualities to win popularity and political support alike among black Americans.

Moreover, as "protest" leaders who possessed no formal public authority, both Jackson and Farrakhan stood demonstrably outside the increasingly dominant mode of political representation of black American interests in the post–civil rights era, that of black elected officialdom. Passage of the Voting Rights Act of 1965, enfranchising southern blacks, had powerfully assisted the growth of black American elected officials nationwide, from mayors and state legislators to members of Congress. Electoral channels represented the logical outgrowth of the pre-1965 protest and extrasystemic forms of black American political participation (such as sit-ins, boycotts, and marches) that had been advanced so effectively by the traditional civil rights movement. This new elective cadre of black politicians thus rapidly came to be viewed by many black Americans as not only the legitimate, but also as the principal, bearers of African-Americans' political, economic, and social interests.

Although few African-American civic leaders and elected officials believed that increased black political representation was itself sufficient to ameliorate black economic and social problems, putting black Americans into elective public offices nationwide nonetheless represented a necessary condition of collective black advancement. Moreover, the steady emergence of black elected officials as the de facto repositories of black Americans' public policy priorities and preferences was a development that was reasonably clearly delineated. Primary responsibility for the conversion of black Americans' social and economic interests into public policy agenda items and outputs increasingly resided with this new black political elite of elected officials, whose claims to democratic legitimacy could be tested transparently and whose institutional behavior in general (and voting records, in particular) could be made accountable to African-Americans by means of prescribed elections. Black political behavior in the post–civil rights era United States thus increasingly exhibited characteristics common to traditional modes of nonblack American politics.[15]

Two features of this "modernization" process among black American political elites were especially salient to the emergence of the Farrakhan phenomenon and to the evolving political fortunes of the NoI's leader subsequently. First, significant and persistent political tensions inevitably arose after 1965 between the growing set of African-American elected officials and the established constellation of protest-era black organizations, such as the National Association for the Advancement of Colored People, the Southern Christian Leadership

Conference, the Student Non-Violent Coordinating Committee, and the National Urban League. The claims of the latter organized black interest lobbies to fully representative status among African-Americans were now increasingly undermined—though not entirely endangered—by the democratically derived challenges posed by the new and expanding elected cadre of black American public officials.

Second, for black American elected (and appointed) officials themselves, loyalty to the Democratic party emerged as a fundamental article of political faith and typically a cardinal condition of personal career advancement (whether at the federal, state, or local level).[16] Efforts at independent African-American political campaigns or insurgent forms of activism were hence very powerfully constrained by the entrenched dominance of established party interests and the formidable boundaries to effective black political independence that these necessarily established.[17] A dual accountability structure within national black politics therefore emerged. On the one hand stood the increasing set of African-American elected officials, whose democratic political legitimacy was self-evident and transparent but whose jurisdictional bases were relatively narrow and whose political behavior was fundamentally conditioned by a near-universal one-party allegiance. On the other hand was the group of nonelected black American actors, whose racially organicist credentials (as representing all blacks) were still intact and were not subject to the demands of particular constituents, but whose effective and appropriate political roles in the post–civil rights era—which they had struggled so successfully to bring about—were far less certain and clear.

Most political and scholarly attention to this newly bifurcated structure of national black American politics was devoted to the new and increasing elite cadre of elected officials. Their growing numbers, novel political organizations, institutional behavior, and variegated policy influence encouraged extensive academic examination of the phenomenon of the so-called "new black politics."[18] (That the "old" black American politics persisted and remained influential was often complacently neglected or ignored.) Within this new structure of dual political authority, prior to 1984, both Jackson and Farrakhan occupied the more marginal and less academically noteworthy political positions in the protest category of nonelected, traditional black leadership. The entry of both into the conventional American electoral political arena—Jackson directly as electoral candidate, Farrakhan indirectly as his political confidant and zealous supporter—therefore represented a dramatic political development for African-Americans in general and national black political elites in particular. Jackson's candidacy attracted extensive media attention and comment in America and abroad. Not only did Jackson's entry into the Democratic party primaries in 1984 increase his personal name recognition and elevate the candidate's national political status among both black and white Americans, but national and international public awareness of Farrakhan was also wholly transformed as a result of the landmark Jackson presidential nomination campaign.

The two ministers certainly made for a peculiar political alliance: the Baptist progressive and King associate in search of an integrated, inclusive coalition of blacks, whites, labor, environmentalists, women, Latinos, Native Americans, Asians, and gays; and the fundamentalist Black Muslim separatist for whom the only color worth any apparent concern—to many of his critics at least—was black. The symbolic significance of their association was, by virtue of such manifest differences, both striking and substantial. The historic public and private divisions between the nonviolent, principally southern-based struggle for multiracial unity and integration personified by King, and Malcolm X's aggressive, and predominantly northern, urban militant black separatism were deep and, almost by definition, irreconcilable. For many black Americans, the *rapprochement* of Jackson and Farrakhan therefore represented an altogether new, regenerative, and welcome dimension of intraracial political unity, as an unprecedented coalition of traditionally distinct and antagonistic ideologies and religious tendencies around the common cause of black American political empowerment.

The political incentives structuring the association were distinct, but in essence complementary, for the two African-American preachers. For Jackson, Farrakhan's clear endorsement provided him with a particularly valuable political resource with which to appeal to the growing minority of American Muslims in the United States (although the NoI was unorthodox within this broader family, Farrakhan spoke Arabic sufficiently fluently to address Arab Americans on Jackson's behalf, for example). Also, and equally important, Farrakhan's imprimatur significantly enhanced Jackson's credentials among the more militant sections of the black nationalist movement in

America. Both groups represented constituencies traditionally uninvolved in, and generally very much opposed to, conventional forms of electoral and party politics in the United States.

Historically, the Nation of Islam had always rejected any participation in American politics in general, and electoral politics in particular. In a manner analogous to white Christian fundamentalist groups prior to their remarkable mobilization during the 1970s,[19] involvement in conventional, secular American political processes was seen as essentially sacrilegious by the Black Muslim movement. Moreover, the NoI viewed electoral participation as a strategy that was completely futile and ineffective for improving black Americans' social and economic conditions, the fundamental precondition of which remained (as chapter three explains in more detail) the complete and enduring separation of the races in the United States.

Nonetheless, despite facing significant internal NoI opposition, Farrakhan personally registered to vote at the Chicago Board of Elections on February 9, 1984.[20] The minister's expressed rationale for the novel departure from the NoI's traditional tenets of noninvolvement in American public life drew extensively upon claims that his spiritual father, Elijah Muhammad, had deemed electoral support for a black American candidate permissible in the event of that politician both emerging from within the black community in the United States and his additionally being fearless and unrelenting in pressing the cause of genuine African-American empowerment and liberation, conditions which Farrakhan made it abundantly clear during early 1984 that he held Jackson to have adequately and courageously fulfilled.[21]

For the leader of the NoI, the link with Jackson served two vital strategic functions in his personal political project. First, it accorded Farrakhan, an African-American figure even more obscure to most Americans than Jackson, national and international publicity; such attention represented an invaluable political asset for Farrakhan's burgeoning national black leadership ambitions. Second, the link encouraged Farrakhan's popular (albeit inaccurate and misleading) portrayal as a political radical, in the long historic tradition of black American progressives and liberals challenging established social, economic, and political structures. Although the sources and expressions of his purported radicalism were rarely accurately or fully disaggregated by most observers, either in the United States or abroad, Farrakhan's evident racial militancy accorded him significant political interest from leftist groups and African-American organizations alike. Jackson's political beliefs were, for most Americans, extremely liberal (and even unconventional) and a reasonable inference to make was that individuals especially close to his campaign broadly shared his political views. Given the persistently pronounced electoral support and political endorsements accorded ideologically liberal candidates by black Americans since 1965, Farrakhan's apparently radical, antiestablishment credentials thus served as a useful adjunct to his national black leadership claims and aspirations among African-Americans at large.

Although its early role was undeniably significant, the initial involvement of Farrakhan's NoI in the 1984 Jackson campaign nonetheless attracted relatively modest and circumspect media attention. The organization provided campaign workers for Jackson and, through its male and female Fruit of Islam guards, also provided personal security for the candidate, a function especially important in the initial stages of the campaign when the Reagan Administration denied Jackson the professional protection of trained Secret Service personnel. As the NoI's leader, Farrakhan personally and eagerly provided extensive political support to Jackson, through his weekly program on Chicago's WBEE radio station, in his public rallies and lectures (during which he regularly set aside time to encourage his black American audiences enthusiastically to register, turn out, and vote for Jackson), and by frequently serving as the warm-up speaker at campaign rallies immediately prior to Jackson's keynote addresses—sometimes even eclipsing the principal speaker in his oratorical zest and skill.

Anonymity and Farrakhan have been relatively rare bedfellows over recent years, however, and the initially limited media and popular attention was rapidly and definitively ended by the intense national political controversy that erupted in March 1984. The reaction of the NoI's leader to revelations in *The Washington Post* that Jackson had privately referred, in a conversation with one of the newspaper's black reporters, Milton Coleman, to American Jews as "Hymies" and to New York City as "Hymietown," strongly compounded Farrakhan's immoderate credentials. Jackson, in a remarkably inastute fashion, first denied making the statements, before stating that he had no memory of having made them, and then finally issuing a public apology for having made them. On February 25, 1984, in Chicago, Farrakhan came to the candidate's defense, standing beside Jackson and issuing an explicit warning to American Jews generally that, "If you harm this brother, it will be the last one you harm." Farrakhan also threatened all of Jackson's opponents with "retaliation if they harmed Jackson in any way." Though the exact form that such retaliation would assume remained unclear, the implicit threat of violence in Farrakhan's speech was not lost upon even the least attentive of listeners. It was, moreover, clarified further in Farrakhan's weekly radio broadcast on March 11, 1984, when he stated:

> But we're going to make an example of Mr. Coleman. I'm going to stay on his case until we make him a fit example for the rest of them. "What do you intend to do to Milton Coleman?" At this point, no physical harm. But at this point we're going to keep going until we make it so that he cannot enter in on any black people. One day soon we will punish you with death.[22]

American public outrage was nonetheless concentrated less upon the Coleman threat[23] and upon Farrakhan's declaration that, if Jackson's candidacy was not taken seriously by white political elites, he would "lead an army" to Washington, D.C., to "negotiate for a separate state or territory of our own,"[24] than upon the NoI leader's contemporaneous anti-Semitic comments. Most important, the national mass media focused persistently upon Farrakhan's by now notorious descriptions of Adolf Hitler as a "wickedly great man," and of Judaism as a "dirty" and "gutter" religion—deliberately incendiary rhetoric that one source persuasively held to have represented "the most serious injection of anti-Semitism into a national American political campaign in recent memory."[25] Despite his impeccably dapper personal appearance, such calculated and provocative declarations ensured that the NoI's leader provided a remarkably stark, controversial, and compelling contrast to the besuited and blow-dried politicians familiar to most Americans from the 1984 presidential campaign trail.

In its intensity and scope, the ensuing national controversy represented the first instance of a pattern of reactions to Farrakhan that was subsequently to become a familiar, repetitive, and (for him) generally beneficial feature of his gradual political ascendancy. The pattern comprised three interlinked stages: first, Farrakhan issues a deliberately provocative public statement, one that inevitably and deeply offends a sizeable section of the American populace; second, outraged elite commentators (primarily, but not exclusively, white) demand his immediate and unequivocal repudiation by prominent national black American figures for the offensive or defamatory remark; and third, those African-American figures variously comply, refuse, or equivocate in response, according to their personal circumstances, philosophies, and electoral imperatives. In this particular instance, Jackson disavowed Farrakhan's statements, but refused to repudiate the NoI leader's political endorsement, stating defiantly that "I am not going to negotiate away my integrity trying to impress somebody."[26]

That intrablack electoral imperatives powerfully informed and reinforced Jackson's personal integrity was readily apparent, but the candidate's refusal to denounce Farrakhan nonetheless prompted dozens of outraged editorial denunciations across America. The tactical exigencies and strategic imperatives of American party politics in 1984 sustained media and critical attention on Farrakhan and his immoderate political credentials still further. For the Democratic party, African-Americans constituted a core bloc of their general electoral coalition and their presidential base in particular, one that could be neither safely antagonized nor easily ignored. The New Deal policies of Franklin D. Roosevelt during the 1930s had initially begun an inexorable process of mass black electoral and political realignment away from the Republicans—the party of Lincoln, Emancipation, and Reconstruction.[27] Although that realignment was gradual, from the mid-1960s onward black electoral loyalty to the Democrats was comprehensive and near-complete.[28] Since 1948, and especially from 1968, a high black turnout in American elections emerged as crucial not only to the fortunes of the Democratic presidential nominee, but also to many of the party's incumbent and aspirant senators and representatives, especially in the South.[29] For many Democrats, therefore, inveighing too enthusiastically or strongly against Jackson was effectively to invite mass black disaffection and to court electoral suicide.

However, while Democratic party leaders risked seriously alienating black Americans if they denounced Jackson's informal associations with Farrakhan and his refusal fully to repudiate the NoI's leader, they also faced the deeply unattractive prospect of sacrificing significant Jewish American support—electoral, editorial, and financial—if they failed to do so. Although their relative proportions in the American population differed significantly, Jewish votes, money, and intellectual support for the Democrats were together vitally important to the party's leadership and to many of its elected officials nationwide. Democratic leaders were therefore mired in a catch-22 political predicament of epic proportions.

The tantalizing opportunity to accrue political profit from the Democrats' dilemma was, for the Republican party, too obvious to require either detailed elaboration or concerted pressure to exploit. Then Vice President George Bush predictably attacked Mondale, Hart, and Jackson collectively for their failure to denounce "the intrusion of anti-Semitism into the American political process," arguing that American society possessed "no room for hate and no place for haters."[30] President Reagan was also declared by White House spokesperson, Larry Speaks, to be "forthrightly" against Farrakhan.[31] For the GOP's campaign strategists, the incentive to denounce the NoI's leader was as powerfully compelling as the imperative to appeal to black American voters at large was demonstrably slight. Writing off black voters by vigorously attacking Farrakhan and Jackson was hardly a prohibitive political cost, since African-Americans barely figured in the Republican's electoral script in the first place. Highlighting the warring forces within the Democratic base, by contrast, offered a likely political reward from white voters well worth the minimal risk. If Farrakhan had not existed, the GOP's political operatives in 1984 would have been especially eager to have invented him.

Republican party officials' denunciations of Farrakhan, deliberately aimed simultaneously at increasing the Democrats' acute political discomfort, attracting Jewish American votes, and exploiting latent societal conflicts over race by exaggerating Jackson's political role and influence within the party, also strongly implied that Farrakhan was no ally of American conservatives. Ironically, the message was as formidably misleading as it was effective. Set against the deliberately bland—though electorally powerful—"Morning in America" theme of Reagan's 1984 reelection campaign, Farrakhan symbolically represented a hangover of a wake-up call to many white voters, as far as Republican strategists were concerned, much as the figure of Willie Horton would subsequently (though to far greater political effect) for the Bush presidential campaign in 1988.[32] In the context of the 1984 campaign, Farrakhan served as a near-functional totemic equivalent for animating white racial fears and arousing interracial animosities. Although the wedge of the NoI's leader prised few voters from the Democratic party, this was not for a want of effort on the Republicans' part.[33]

By the summer of 1984, Jackson's prospects of retaining any of the marginal credibility that he still possessed with Jewish voters was rendered determinate upon his expressly repudiating Farrakhan. Though Jackson had asked the Black Muslim privately to refrain from public works for his campaign in March, only in June was a clearly negative evaluation of Farrakhan forthcoming. Benjamin Hooks, Executive Director of the NAACP, acted as a catalyst, when he issued a statement on June 27, 1984, in which Farrakhan's "inflammatory" statements were deplored and "such forms of racism and anti-Semitism," as he termed them, were wholly rejected. Farrakhan's inclusion within the remit of prejudice and bigotry was implicit, but unmistakable and significant nonetheless.[34] The denouement came two days later when a similar declaration was finally made by Jackson, in which he labeled Farrakhan's comments "reprehensible and morally indefensible" and publicly disavowed them. Too late to salvage Jackson's campaign, which had faltered long prior to June, neither did the declaration defuse Farrakhan's newly acquired national mantle of black American militant number one.

Consonant with that status, controversy surrounding Farrakhan did not abate either during or after the 1984 campaign. Farrakhan's position as a political pariah and a substantial albatross upon Jackson's electoral aspirations continued into the black Baptist's second unsuccessful campaign for the Democratic party nomination in 1988. Moreover, whereas the 1984 campaign had served the crucial function of nationalizing Farrakhan's name recognition and controversial public profile, the 1988 campaign accorded him a further political totem of substantial utility in his national African-American leadership bid: the full and exclusive mantle of the national black prophet of racial authenticity. In attempting, however ineffectively, to build a broader multiethnic and cross-class "rainbow" coalition in 1988—a bold strategy that necessarily entailed deemphasizing the centrally racial dimensions of his candidacy that he had stressed four years earlier—Jackson left open a vacuum into which Farrakhan eagerly stepped to claim his position as the true repository of authentic, collective black American interests. The critical value of the 1988 presidential campaign for Farrakhan thus resided, ironically, in eclipsing rather than confirming the racial foundations of Jackson's preeminent leadership status among African-Americans at large. For Farrakhan, the second Jackson campaign offered renewed opportunities to assume a national mantle as the dominant spokesperson for black nationalism. The legacy of prior attacks by whites, Jews, and established African-American politicians had also left Farrakhan sufficiently shrouded in an aura of racial martyrdom to render that new position especially congenial to such efforts.

According to the candidate's press secretary during that campaign, Jackson's proximity to Farrakhan over the years had occurred for "politically symbiotic reasons."[35] By 1984, Jackson had perceived himself unable to sever his ties with Farrakhan, in large part because it would have been viewed by black Americans as giving in to the demands of whites. Although Jackson dissociated himself from Farrakhan in 1984 and once again in 1988, the issue of explicit and unequivocal denunciation represented a de facto litmus test of the veracity of Jackson's denials of anti-Semitism, not only for whites in general (and Jews in particular), but also for many African-Americans. One Jewish editor of the *New York Times* stressed in 1988 that, "Until Jackson publicly breaks with Farrakhan and finally resolves that issue, he'll never be accepted by the Jews."[36] Whether he would be fully accepted even if he did publicly denounce Farrakhan remained unclear, at best; but denunciation of the NoI's leader represented a minimal, though not necessarily sufficient, condition of his attracting even marginal levels of Jewish support.

The continued significance of the Farrakhan factor to Jackson was evidently, but uncomfortably, manifest to the candidate. An anonymously authored background paper on "Jackson and his relationship to the Jewish community," issued to the press by his campaign organization during the 1988 primary season, contained an entire section devoted specifically to the subject of the candidate's fluctuating relations with Farrakhan. This elaborated Jackson's "final" position on the matter: the NoI leader was not a part of the 1988 campaign and Jackson had four years previously dissociated himself from Farrakhan's "objectionable" public remarks. It nonetheless also stated, explicitly and emphatically, that Jackson would never "repudiate the personhood of Farrakhan":

> This he refused to do! Rev. Jackson is a minister who believes in separating the sin from the sinner. One should condemn the sin, not the sinner. Black civil rights activists like Rev. Jackson repudiated the rhetoric and behavior of Bull Connor, Orval Faubus and George Wallace in the 1960s but did not repudiate their personhood. When Rev. Jackson debated with KKK head David Duke on television, he repudiated Duke's statements, his philosophy and his behavior—but not his personhood. In the nonvio-

lent tradition, this is perceived as strength (not as a weakness) in the civil rights movement.[37]

The gross political ineptitude of the Jackson campaign in this regard was especially striking, though not exceptional in the broader context of his still neophytic style of national electioneering. By making explicit the analogy between Farrakhan and the racist demagogues of the white far-right, the paper served inadvertently to fuel rather than to quell continued political suspicion of Jackson among Jews and other white (and black) Americans, to compound their marked antipathy toward Farrakhan, and to confirm their increasing ambivalence about Jackson. To place the NoI's leader on an equivalent political level with the white southern segregationists of the past and the vicious racists of the present—though in accord with the prevalent views of Farrakhan among many black and white American observers—was an effective (and astonishingly politically naive) admission of the unusual severity of Jackson's political problem. It conceded, in effect, that Farrakhan self-evidently stood outside the broad range of acceptable views in mainstream American politics in the 1980s. Moreover, it inadvertently lent some credence to Mayor Ed Koch's deliberately provocative claim during the New York Democratic party primary, that Jewish New Yorkers would have to be "crazy" to cast a vote for Jackson.

According to Elizabeth Colton, Farrakhan was completely "anathema to Jews and to many other sensitive whites and even some blacks who recognized the dangers he posed." One white Jackson aide questioned why the candidate himself seemed curiously unable to comprehend that "Farrakhan could reappear any day and wreck his campaign? He should renounce him once and for all." The more important factor in Jackson's continued refusal to denounce Farrakhan than his long-held philosophy of nonviolence, however, was the Baptist's acute political fear that an unequivocal renunciation of Farrakhan would alienate a substantial number of otherwise supportive black American voters. The electorally beneficial consequences of maintaining the appearance of collective intraracial unity still assumed a far greater political importance for Jackson than did the socially divisive interracial results of failing to condemn individual black American bigots and racists.

In retrospect, the political damage that association with Farrakhan caused Jackson's hopes of securing either the presidential or vice-presidential nomination of the Democratic party, in both 1984 and 1988, was probably not especially great in purely electoral terms. That the Farrakhan nexus contributed to the marked antipathy of established Democratic party elites toward the Jackson campaign and compounded the serious doubts of many black and nonblack American politicians regarding the candidate's credentials for elective office in general, much less the presidency in particular, is clear enough. But Farrakhan hardly cost Jackson the party's presidential nomination. Influential white and black Democratic public officials had been highly skeptical of the Jackson insurgency from the outset[38]; established party constituencies—labor, feminists, environmentalists, educationalists, and gay and lesbian activists—possessed their own formal and informal links to several other well-established candidates; and important aspects of Jackson's distinctive and unconventional political resume, such as embracing Fidel Castro and Yasir Arafat (both literally and figuratively), made him deeply unattractive to many Democratic sympathizers seeking a credible aspirant for the White House who could appeal to as broad a range of American voters as possible. The Farrakhan imbroglio served to confirm the preexisting negative dimensions of many Democrats' assessments.

Though no empirical evidence exists by which to evaluate the overall effect that the Farrakhan factor had upon Jackson's primary campaigns, some observers have argued that Jackson's urban victories could probably not have been achieved without Farrakhan's active and aggressive support.[39] But such assessments tend to exaggerate the Black Muslim leader's importance at the time and his substantive political influence among African-Americans at large. To the extent that Jackson's 1984 and 1988 victories relied overwhelmingly upon the support of black Americans who were not members of the NoI, the galvanizing effect of his campaign was in itself a sufficient political incentive for many blacks to have turned out to vote, Farrakhan notwithstanding. The balance of evidence suggests that the compensating gains among black American voters that Jackson achieved through refusing to denounce Farrakhan were probably not much greater than the nonblack votes he thereby forfeited from otherwise sympathetic and potentially supportive constituencies within the Democratic party.

For the NoI's leader, however, the Jackson association had no adverse political consequences of note at all. Rather, the two Jackson campaigns served the vital political goal of raising Farrakhan's public profile among black and white Americans in general, a necessary but insufficient condition of his ultimate admission to the national black political leadership cadre in the United States. Moreover, the 1988 campaign also allowed Farrakhan to present himself publicly to white and African-American audiences alike as the preeminent national black political spokesperson for collective black American interests: the definitive and exclusive repository of a putatively essential, universal black identity. Unburdened by the demands of compromise and conciliation that the coalitional requirements of conventional American electoral and institutional politics typically impose upon elected officials of all races, Farrakhan moved to occupy the ground of racial essentialism that Jackson had initially assumed in 1984, but forfeited in 1988. The mantle of defining racial authenticity among black Americans nationally—of what it meant to be truly "black" in character, values, and beliefs as well as physical appearance—had passed to a new and more enthusiastic torchbearer with whom it thereafter remained as a core feature of Farrakhan's leadership pretensions and claims to national black political authority.

Precisely how future black American presidential aspirants might treat the leader of the NoI remained unclear in the aftermath of the Jackson campaigns. That they would have to develop a strategy to do so, however, represented an unequivocal testament to the assumption of a powerful national leadership role and distinctive political appeal among many black Americans that Farrakhan had long craved, and subtly but surely achieved after the 1984 controversy first arose.[40] Subsequently, over a relatively short period of time, the NoI's leader consolidated his political position and advanced his national black leadership claims, at once purposefully, aggressively, and effectively. Farrakhan's initial dramatic burst upon the national political consciousness of America was dominated by elite discussions of the complete unacceptability of his iconoclastic public discourse and by a near-universal emphasis in popular commentaries upon the pressing imperative of his total exclusion from the ranks of mainstream African-American political leadership. Nine years later, however, it was the topic of Farrakhan's effective inclusion within those ranks that occupied most critical commentary.

SACRED COVENANTS: THE INCLUSION OF THE UNEXCLUDABLE

Farrakhan and the Congressional Black Caucus

By the early 1990s, it was increasingly apparent from both his tactical political behavior and his evolving public discourse that Louis Farrakhan coveted a more enhanced leadership role among black Americans at the national level. Since 1988, a gradual but unmistakable thawing of his conventionally cool and distant relations with other black social and political elites and with institutions traditionally anathema to the separatist NoI had occurred. Most notably, Farrakhan traveled the country in support of African-American congressional and municipal candidates in 1990 and conducted several extended interviews with nonblack national media outlets. In the latter, the markedly temperate tone of his language and the largely unobjectionable content of much of the agenda that he advanced—emphasizing the beneficial role of the NoI among inner-city black American communities and stressing the values of individual responsibility that he sought to inculcate among African-Americans—together suggested a mature moderation, a newfound responsibility, and a sincere desire to achieve a genuine and lasting national political legitimacy on his part.[41]

Not only did the conservative tenor of his public pronouncements on matters of personal morality and family structure accord strongly with other contemporary traditionalistic strains in American public life in the early 1990s but, more important, the fact of the NoI's new activism in deeply inhospitable urban environments was indisputable (although its motives and material effects were less universally agreed upon).[42] In 1990, for example, Farrakhan launched a nationwide "Stop the Killing" speaking tour of African-American urban centers aimed at highlighting and countering the terrible problem of black-on-black homicide. Not since the peak of its popularity in the early 1960s had the NoI achieved comparably effusive and positive critical commentary even from white Americans and won such widespread respect among black Americans at both elite and mass levels for its courageous and dedicated efforts to reduce drug consumption and to combat gang violence among urban blacks. Thus, it was upon this combination of his organization's practical achievements and the newly temperate and apparently conciliatory character of his public behavior—which even included a public rendition of a Felix Mendelssohn violin concerto as a symbolic gesture of reconciliation with American Jews[43]—that Farrakhan sought to advance his growing case for full and unequivocal inclusion among national black American political elites.

The most important indication that Farrakhan's shrewd and determined political strategy was reaping substantial rewards occurred in 1993 at the "Race in America" panel of the annual legislative weekend of the Congressional Black Caucus (CBC), the organization of African-American members of the U.S. Congress.[44] The September gathering represented the Caucus's institutionalized national political forum. A long-established opportunity for black American social, political, and business elites to converge on Washington, D.C., it had evolved since the first dinner in 1971 as one of the most prestigious and high-profile events in the national black American calendar. Democratic presidential aspirants were regular attendees, incumbent Democratic occupants of the White House often made speeches there, and the national news media devoted substantial coverage to the glittering occasion.[45]

The 1993 CBC weekend assumed particular political significance for the supporters and admirers of the NoI's leader. Having been controversially excluded from the previous month's thirtieth anniversary of the 1963 March on Washington, Farrakhan was invited to attend the CBC forum. Farrakhan had not previously been extended such an invitation by the Caucus to share a national platform and the CBC, like the vast majority of national black American politicians and organizations, had generally maintained a respectful but clear political distance from him and the NoI. The focus of the CBC session was the grievous problem of intraracial crime, however, a subject that made Farrakhan—given the NoI's increasing interventions in inner-city black American neighborhoods—an especially appropriate and attractive candidate for inclusion on the Caucus panel.

The session received widespread media attention and was covered live by C-SPAN, and Farrakhan was well-received by the predominantly black American audience at the Convention Center in Washington, D.C. There, Ben Chavis, the then recently appointed Executive Director of the NAACP, issued an unequivocal public apology to the Black Muslim leader, describing his exclusion from the previous month's march as "a mistake," a stark contrast to the principled denunciation of Farrakhan nine years previously delivered by Chavis's predecessor, Benjamin Hooks. Although Farrakhan was criticized at times for attacking and belittling African-American politicians, the general tone of the panel was incontrovertibly conciliatory, inclusive, and forward looking. At the end of the session, to great applause, the Caucus's aggressively independent-minded chairman in the 103rd Congress, Kweisi Mfume (D-MD), solemnly pledged the CBC to enter a "Sacred Covenant" with a range of black organizations, including

Farrakhan's Nation of Islam. Declaring that "no longer will we allow people to divide us," Mfume stated that:

> We will support the efforts of anyone committed to the restoration of hope through self-help and self-empowerment, whilst at the same time reserving the right to disagree on other matters of principle.[46]

Given its prestigious source, the announcement represented an especially controversial legitimation of Farrakhan and his organization. The CBC represented the most important national black political organization in America. It entered the 103rd Congress with substantially increased numbers from the 1992 elections. With forty members (the largest congressional delegation of blacks in American history), it also faced a Democratic president in the White House, Bill Clinton, for the first time since 1981. Through the covenant, black federal legislators publicly accorded the NoI a consultative role in formulating legislative proposals to bring before the U.S. Congress. They thereby implied that the NoI occupied an equivalent political position to the NAACP, with whom the Caucus had recently concluded a similar agreement: a group widely regarded as comprising extremist, sectarian bigots wedded to a bizarre cosmology now occupied the same moral standing as the oldest and most influential civil rights organization for blacks in American history.

The covenant effectively conceded Farrakhan's occupation of a uniquely influential position within national black American politics; its implicit message was that the issues of anti-Semitism and black racism that continued to shroud Farrakhan and his organization in a negative veil of the vilest bigotry were essentially secondary to the formulation of a common national black American political agenda.[47] There could be few more telling testimonies to Farrakhan's emergence as an African-American leader of singular and distinctive political importance and to the social concerns upon which he evidently touched among many African-Americans. Though the original catalyst for Farrakhan's rise to national prominence and the central explanation for the unprecedented involvement of the NoI in national American politics had occurred some nine years earlier in the Jackson campaign, the genie of separatist black nationalism, once released from the bottle of national public obscurity, had exploited his opportunity to gain political capital to the fullest and most substantial effect. With gradual but increasing assurance, the leader of the NoI had steadily inveigled his way from the obscure outer fringes toward the central arenas of mainstream national black American political leadership.

That political transition nonetheless remained incomplete. Moreover, at precisely the moment that Farrakhan's new leadership centrality was being consolidated, it was also deeply compromised. The catalyst was a series of remarkable revelations concerning a speech made at Kean College, New Jersey, on November 29, 1993, by Khalid Abdul Muhammad, Farrakhan's national spokesperson (and de facto second-in-command). Though unpublicized until January 1994, when the Anti-Defamation League (ADL) of B'Nai B'rith reprinted the full text of the address in an advertisement in *The New York Times*, the speech represented a profoundly embarrassing rebuke to those forces seeking a *rapprochement* with the NoI. Viciously anti-Semitic, anti-Catholic, racist, and homophobic in content, both the text and the African-American college audience's favorable reaction to the speech were widely publicized and roundly repudiated by the ADL. Nationwide editorial condemnation of the speech, Farrakhan, and the CBC covenant with the NoI followed its publication.[48] For many critics, the Muhammad speech represented the most dramatic, damning, and convincing refutation of Farrakhan's apparently newfound moderate credentials and constituted the clearest confirmation that the NoI's traditional racism, pervasive prejudice, and uncompromisingly exclusionary politics all remained intact.

Such adverse impressions were publicly compounded by the prompt actions of the U.S. Congress. The Senate forthrightly condemned Muhammad's remarks in a resolution offered by John Danforth (R-MO) and Edward Kennedy (D-MA) as an amendment to an education bill (H.R. 1804), on February 2, 1994, by a 97:0 vote. The House of Representatives followed by denouncing the speech in a resolution (H.R. 343) on February 23, 1994, which passed by a margin of 361 to 34 (with 29 members voting "present"). The principal sponsor of the motion, Rep. Tom Lantos (D-CA), argued compellingly that "When free speech is abused in a vile and vicious way to promote hatred and to incite murder on a gigantic scale, it is the duty of responsible legislative bodies to condemn such speech in clear and certain terms."[49]

The clarity, speed, and assurance of Congress's repudiation of Muhammad contrasted sharply with the responses of Farrakhan himself. For although Farrakhan subsequently removed Muhammad from his national post—after some predictable prevarication—his public assessment of the controversy was designed to fuel rather than diminish its political salience. Condemning in "the strongest terms" the malicious and mean-spirited manner in which Muhammad had made his comments, Farrakhan stated that he nonetheless stood by the "truths" that his assistant had inelegantly articulated. These "truths" included references to Jewish Americans as "blood-suckers" of the black community who controlled the White House, owned the Federal Reserve, and managed national policy from "behind the scenes"; descriptions of the Pope as a "no-good cracker" ("Somebody need to raise that dress up and see what's really under there."); and calls to black South Africans to kill their white compatriots (a later Muhammad speech also included professions of love toward Colin Ferguson, the young black American male who had indiscriminately murdered white passengers aboard a Long Island commuter train in December 1993). For good measure, Farrakhan added further that no rebuke would have been issued at all by him had Muhammad made the remarks in private rather than in a public forum, a statement hardly designed to bolster the minister's alleged newfound political maturity, increasing moderation, and putative mainstream leadership impulses.[50]

The controversy over the sickeningly offensive Muhammad speech served rapidly to reestablish the political distance between the CBC and the NoI. According to one source, the universal disgust and contempt occasioned by the pernicious and foul remarks ensured that the Caucus had no further formal contact with Farrakhan after the Khalid controversy.[51] But informal contacts continued to occur with representatives of the NoI, nonetheless. Moreover, the initial NoI coalescence with the CBC—however uncertain and tentative some of the latter's members undoubtedly were about the dangerous liaison—had itself represented a sufficiently clear and unequivocal confirmation of the dramatically altered dynamics of the relationship between Farrakhan and national black American political elites that had developed since 1984. That many Caucus members and other black politicians harbored profound reservations about, and deep disdain for, Farrakhan's values, beliefs, and methods is clear enough. Both privately and, less commonly, in public, several CBC members made their intense disquiet—and even anger—manifest.[52] Mfume also publicly revoked the previous fall's covenant, reluctantly conceding that the Caucus's ability to work for change with the NoI was severely jeopardized "as long as there remains a question by some of our membership about the Nation of Islam's sensitivity to the right of all people and all religions to be free from attacks, vilification and defamation."[53]

The very fact of the NoI's leader having been accorded a public platform at the Caucus's leading annual national gathering, however, had represented a development of cardinal political significance. Mfume's subsequent denunciation of Muhammad's speech had asserted that "nowhere" in American life could sanctuary be given to such appalling "garbage."[54] Yet the former Baltimore congressman's own organization had extended such sanctuary—albeit temporarily—to its most persistent, vociferous, and unrepentant African-American purveyor in national public life in America in modern times. As one of the Caucus's own members candidly observed (though without apparent irony or discernible regret), "Farrakhan in 15 minutes can draw more people than 40 members of the black caucus."[55] Clearly, for many black politicians, Farrakhan had emerged by 1993 as a national African-American leader at once too influential to be ignored and too controversial to be embraced.

Rapprochement and Reconciliation: the NAACP and Betty Shabazz

Even prior to the Million Man March, then, the CBC–NoI *rapprochement* had signaled Farrakhan's increasingly successful bid for an inclusive role within the national African-American leadership cadre. Two further developments over 1994–95 compounded the new environment of leadership inclusion that Farrakhan had long cherished and now enjoyed. First, Farrakhan's political ascent was assisted by the protracted, deep, and tragicomic convulsions that accompanied Ben Chavis's tenure as head of the NAACP during 1993–94. Facing profound political and financial difficulties upon his securing its Executive Directorship in 1993 (over Jesse Jackson, to the somewhat misplaced joy of the Clinton White House), Chavis pioneered a twin-track strategy to reinvigorate the prestigious civil rights organization: first, to champion aggressively the ecumenical cause of intraracial leadership inclusion, and, second, to target younger, militant, and nationalist black Americans for membership recruitment to the NAACP.[56]

Consonant with such an ambitious project, Chavis sought to incorporate Farrakhan, the itinerant *enfant terrible* and errant cousin, fully within the national black leadership "family." The invitation that he issued to Farrakhan to attend a two-day national African-American leadership "summit" in June 1994 served not only as a practical attempt to realize the strained and intellectually challenged concept of "operational unity" that had been widely and enthusiastically articulated at the previous year's CBC weekend, but also to demonstrate publicly Chavis's apparently independent political credentials. In forging closer links with Farrakhan, the NAACP Director issued unmistakably clear signals of his unwillingness to be unduly influenced by either white American interest lobbies or adverse media commentary, as well as his marked attentiveness to the urban African-American constituency from which Farrakhan drew the bulk of his popular black support.

The strategy's effectiveness was nonetheless strangled almost at birth. Though it drew a chorus of criticism from white elites who had traditionally been sympathetic to the NAACP,[57] the more telling influence upon Chavis's failure was internal. Chavis was forced to resign his position after revelations that he had used over $300,000 of NAACP funds to pay the legal costs of an action brought against him by a former NAACP staffer, a black American woman, who had charged Chavis with sexual harassment. The ultimate derailing of the pronationalist strategy and the utter disgrace that enveloped Chavis provided a peculiarly resonant image, curiously appropriate to his fledgling political liaison with Farrakhan. Like Marion Barry previously, personal failure and political discredit served as particularly strong incentives for Chavis to seek redemption through enlisting Farrakhan's approbation and assistance. Chavis represented another example of the expanding ranks of what Reed termed the "rogues' gallery" of disgraced malcontents and extremist black American figures whose dubious and doubtful causes Farrakhan rapidly embraced and eagerly championed, and who thereby served as further proof for the African-American public of Farrakhan's obligingly unqualified and abundantly selfless "love" for his own race.

The second factor that embellished such a sensitive and nondiscriminating affective emotional apparatus for his race and that eased Farrakhan's hesitant entry into the portals of national black American political leadership still further derived from a particularly unexpected quarter: Malcolm X's widow, Betty Shabazz. The persistent controversy that had dogged Farrakhan since the assassination of Malcolm thirty years previously threatened to engulf him entirely in 1995 with the arrest of one of Malcolm's own daughters, Qubillah Shabazz, on charges of conspiracy to assassinate the NoI's leader. Rumors of the Shabazz family's deep antipathy toward Farrakhan had been widespread among African-Americans for many years after Malcolm's assassination. Betty Shabazz had persuasively labeled the NoI leader "an opportunist who creates public disarray" in 1985 and as late as 1994 described Farrakhan's incrimination in her husband's vicious murder as having represented "a badge of honor" for him in the NoI.[58] The possibility that one of Malcolm's daughters might enlist the assistance of a professional assassin to murder Farrakhan was therefore viewed as neither a preposterous nor an incomprehensible proposition.[59]

Ironically, however, the charges served as a particularly propitious political opportunity for Farrakhan to reestablish his national leadership credentials among skeptical African-Americans. Claims that the arrest was the result of a malicious plot by federal government authorities and white outsiders to divide the black American community were predictably but effectively invoked by Farrakhan to issue a national appeal for racial unity and political solidarity among African-Americans. At a New York City rally to raise funds for Qubillah Shabazz's legal defense costs in January 1995, the Farrakhan–Shabazz accommodation was tensely consummated.[60] Even Rep. Charles Rangel (D-NY), one of the most widely respected, influential, and electorally secure black members of Congress, felt it necessary to appear at the unity rally in Harlem in which Farrakhan was the principal speaker and main political attraction.[61] As ever, the NoI's leader once more sought successfully to make substantial political profit from apparently bankrupt leadership credentials.

The Farrakhan–Shabazz reconciliation not only constituted an apparent healing of a deep political wound between former black American allies, it also represented an invaluable symbolic seal of public legitimation that Farrakhan's inclusion within the ranks of national black American political leadership desperately required and that the Nation's leader deeply desired.[62] The emergence of Malcolm X as a popular contemporary black icon among African-Americans constituted a potentially more formidable barrier to Farrakhan's securing political support among many poorer, working class, and young black Americans than did the controversies over anti-Semitism by which so many white critics of the NoI's leader were persistently preoccupied. Farrakhan's historic role in Malcolm's murder, though decidedly unclear, had still cast an exceptional and substantial pall upon his leadership credentials among black Americans. In forging a new *entente* with Malcolm's widow and family—however much, even after the charges against Qubillah were dropped in May 1995, its genuinely cordial and sincere nature remained open to substantial doubt—Farrakhan thereby effectively neutralized an important political obstacle to his national leadership aspirations among many black Americans, aspirations that were ultimately realized in especially dramatic and decisive fashion on October 16, 1995.

THE MILLION MAN MARCH: FROM THE DREAM TO THE NIGHTMARE

The Million Man March represented the culmination of Farrakhan's bold attempts to achieve political legitimacy and full inclusion within the ranks of the national black American political leadership cadre.[63] To the deep chagrin of his many implacable opponents and ardent adversaries, it succeeded spectacularly. Farrakhan achieved a greater political legitimacy among African-Americans than ever before through the manifest success of the march's mass mobilization. Inspiring and organizing over 400,000 black American men to come to Washington, D.C., the march constituted one of the largest mass gatherings in the nation's capital in American history and represented an unprecedented affirmation of collective racial pride and self-love by African-American males.[64] By comparison even with the landmark 1963 March on Washington—whose striking numbers it more than doubled—the 1995 event was an undeniable and impressive political triumph for Farrakhan and the NoI in three important respects.

First, the 1963 march had occurred at the very height of the civil rights movement's protracted campaign to achieve effective southern desegregation. In converging upon Washington, the march had been founded upon a clear, noble, and broadly shared political objective: to bring irresistible public pressure to bear upon President John F. Kennedy and the Democratic Congress finally to enact a meaningful civil rights law that would give effective teeth to the Supreme Court's landmark desegregation ruling of 1954.[65] The practical goal of the march was integral to its purpose and assumed an importance that, in addition to being brilliantly encapsulated in King's soaring oratory, at least matched the great symbolic political significance of the mass gathering in the nation's capital.

By contrast, the 1995 event was far more symbolic than substantive in purpose. The declared public goals of the march were multiple and varied in emphasis both between its sponsors and over time: to counter the racist stereotype of all black American men as irresponsible, violent, and lazy; to serve as a reaffirmation of the commitment of African-American males to their families and local communities; and to register a clear and strong protest against the new Republican 104th Congress (1995–96). But beyond the notions of challenging prevailing stereotypes of African-American males and offering the latter an opportunity to atone for their errors (the October 16 date was symbolically selected by Farrakhan as the day of atonement from the Book of Leviticus), the march was entirely bereft of programmatic political, economic, and social content.[66] Lacking substantive programmatic purpose, with no intent to pressure either governing institutions, political parties, or corporate organizations, and pressing no concrete legislative agenda, policy program, or political strategy, the march represented a symbolic demonstration of collective racial pride and unity that advanced an unobjectionable and uncontentious vision, but one that simultaneously neglected to point the way forward to material socioeconomic or political achievements.[67]

The second factor that distinguished the march from its 1960s predecessor concerned its social composition. The 1963 march (and its successors in 1983, 1988, and 1993) had been an explicitly inclusive and ecumenical political initiative, an invitation to all Americans to consider the nature of U.S. citizenship, of what it meant fundamentally to be an American. Consonant with the integrationist objectives of its sponsors, the gathering was open to men and women of all races, religions, and creeds, a central explanatory factor in its effectiveness and eloquent affirmation of the irrelevance of arbitrary social and demographic distinctions to the possession of American citizenship. By contrast, the 1995 event was deliberately and consistently promoted as an event designed exclusively for black American males. Although some African-American women and nonblacks (including the author) attended the gathering, they had not been invited to do so. Powerfully reflecting the rotten core of Farrakhan's paranoid politics of hatred, polarization, and division, the march was infused by a dominant spirit of racial exclusion rather than inclusion—an emphasis on the myriad features that separated its attendees from other Americans rather than on what they shared in common.

The third factor differentiating the two marches was their wider public reception. The national civil rights leadership in 1963 had overwhelmingly—though by no means universally—agreed upon both the merits and objectives of the March on Washington. By contrast, national black American elected officials and civil rights leaders were deeply divided over both the virtues and the goals of the 1995 march.[68] Most significant, whereas the 1963 march had represented a collective interracial enterprise associated with a multiplicity of civic and political groups that were all dedicated to advancing the overarching goal of racial integration, the 1995 event was inextricably and principally linked to Farrakhan and the avowedly separatist NoI. The association of the gathering with such a divisive and polarizing public figure, and the potential prospect of Farrakhan's delivering an intemperate and bigoted tirade as the abusively offensive climax of the occasion, served greatly to quiet the enthusiasm of many black American elites for the march.

Thus, neither the NAACP nor the National Baptist Convention supported the march, while many prominent African-American politicians, such as Julian Bond and Douglas Wilder, refused to lend credence to its originator by attending. The several differences between the two occasions were most vividly personified by Rep. John Lewis (D-GA), the veteran civil rights activist whom *Time* magazine had once heralded as a "saint" for his incomparable courage and fortitude during the landmark Freedom Rides of 1963. Whereas, in that year, the then chairman of the SNCC had been pressured into rewriting and moderating the tone of his keynote speech and had, nonetheless, been the most progressive speaker on the platform, the increasingly influential black American congressman felt entirely unable to support its 1995 successor. The march's exclusionary nature, the central role of Farrakhan, and the occasion's strongly offending against the fundamental democratic values of "tolerance, inclusion and integration" were the proximate causes of Lewis's typically principled refusal.[69] For such a shining beacon of political and ethical integrity to dissociate himself from the 1995 march shed an abundant and humanitarian light upon its principal sponsor and ultimate political beneficiary.

For Farrakhan, however, the march represented a daring and eminently shrewd political gambit, the risk of which paid off very handsomely in the form of personal political and social profit. On the basis of a much smaller pool of potential participants, the 1995 event doubled the size of its predecessor of thirty-two years. It thus served simultaneously as the most foolproof manner for Farrakhan to once more gain unprecedented national and international attention and to mobilize collective action by African-Americans on a staggering scale, thereby confirming his national leadership credentials among both blacks and white Americans. The strategy that had informed the CBC–NoI coalescence in 1993 was revived and massively expanded in scope. By mounting an initiative whose ostensible political goals were fundamentally positive and universally unobjectionable to both black and nonblack Americans alike, Farrakhan posed established African-American political and civic leaders with an especially acute political dilemma: to oppose a novel and exciting initiative that sought to unite the black American community nationwide behind highly laudable civic and political objectives, or to support the march and thereby lend its leader and the bigoted creed that he consistently espoused an entirely new and potentially dangerous level of national political legitimacy. Eminently rational and reasonable impulses were thus cross-cut for many African-Americans, even as the principal object and political beneficiary of the march, Louis Farrakhan, became increasingly obvious to many of them.

Characteristically, then, the initiative was deliberately conceived by the NoI's leader to precipitate an extensive and intense nationwide political controversy, to advance a spurious unity through vigorously spreading the seeds of division. Within the African-American community, the principal focus of discontent centered upon the exclusion of black American women from attending the march, even as bystanders. The prohibition not only diminished the potential size of the crowd but also, more important, revived the accusations of rampant sexism that had previously been leveled at the NoI under both Farrakhan and, before him, Elijah Muhammad. The public rationale of Farrakhan and his spokespersons for the gender-based exclusion assumed two unconvincing forms: that the focus of the march—to challenge and alter perceptions of black American men—would be undermined if both sexes (and, of course, whites) participated, and that the march was, in itself, a manifest "tribute" to the dignity and burden of black American womanhood. Although neither explanation appeared persuasive to many female African-Americans, the exclusion nonetheless served its general political purpose of raising the public profile of the initiative among African-Americans at large.

The impact of the march was also greatly heightened by two entirely contingent political developments that dramatically accentuated its national and international public salience, again substantially to Farrakhan's benefit. Taking place less than two weeks after the former black football star O. J. Simpson was controversially acquitted of murdering his white wife and a male friend of hers, and in the midst of intense speculation about whether General Colin Powell would enter the 1996 presidential election, the march helped to concentrate national American public attention directly and explicitly upon matters of race (albeit for a short span) for the first time since the Los Angeles riot of 1992.

Simpson's trial and acquittal had occupied the national psyche and worldwide attention alike in a wholly unprecedented fashion. Replete with themes familiar to modern American life—the cult of celebrity, the taboo of interracial relationships, the frequently litigious destination of domestic strife, the sometimes dubious methods of police investigation, and the soap opera quality of national public affairs in the United States—the trial rapidly emerged as a peculiarly burlesque national spectacle unparalleled in its regular TV audience and curiously compulsive character. Yet, more than the verdict itself, America's deep racial fissures were starkly revealed in the contrasting reactions of the races to the jury's "not guilty" decision: on black Americans' part, jubilation and relief; on that of whites, disbelief, despondency, and anger. In a curious reversal of the more general historic pattern, the jury verdict suggested to many African-Americans that the criminal justice system for once worked and, to many more whites, that in this instance, it manifestly did not do so.

Most telling, the reactions themselves seemed to confirm to both groups the immeasurable distance that separated them from each other. For, unlike the King case, this was an instance in which both white and black Americans were overwhelmingly united as discrete national communities in desiring entirely different verdicts, and holding those, further, to be legally required; a satisfactory compromise was an impossibility. And the combination of the jury's composition and the actual verdict offered a disconcertingly clear lesson in modern racial politics: to blacks, that justice could be secured with a "fair" hearing only by a predominantly African-American jury; to whites, that black criminals would be acquitted by such a jury simply by virtue of their race. However mistaken those perceptions assuredly were, the evident separation, reciprocal incomprehension, and mutual hostility of black and white America were all glaringly on display in the trial's aftermath.

If the Simpson verdict confirmed both diffuse white suspicions of widespread African-American criminality and black American views of white indifference and hostility, Colin Powell—a figure who symbolically provided to whites proof positive of America's firm colorblind foundations and effective individualistic public philosophy—stood as a dramatic political counterpoint. Where Simpson had thrown aside a popular public mantle, Powell contemplated the most prestigious office that America could offer a citizen virtually being thrust upon him through the sheer brute force of a public clamorous for clear, decisive, and assured leadership. Where Simpson ostentatiously exhibited the many trappings of national celebrity, Powell consistently eschewed vulgar public displays. Where Simpson chose a white bride for his second wife, Powell's "blackness" remained a central—if complex—part of both his personal identity and his multiracial mass political appeal.[70] Where Simpson remained a fundamentally flawed and suspect figure to most white Americans even after the jury verdict was delivered, Powell's ethical credentials remained beyond reproach. Ironically, the only "blemish" upon them stemmed from Powell's responding to a Farrakhan phone call and contemplating attendance at the Million Man March, a lapse of political judgment uncharacteristic for the former general but a testament to the potent resonance of Farrakhan associations among white political elites.

Framed by these starkly polar symbolic visions of America's present and possible future racial relations, the march was critically important in confirming the disarray of national African-American leadership and black American elites' acute discomfiture in dealing with the growing political threat posed by Farrakhan. Once more, of all national black political, civic, and religious figures, it was Farrakhan—the most widely repudiated, divisive, and polarizing—who was determining the national African-American political agenda and conditioning the behavior of established national black American political elites, a plea for racial harmony articulated by the most deeply disharmonic of African-American voices. Although many of the speeches at the march, and much of the popular commentary upon it, focused upon the issue of black discontent with both the federal government and white American political leaders, the central political significance of the event was intraracial in character.

Thus, with black political representation at its highest-ever level in American history, the provocative revival of protest-era tactics by Farrakhan dramatically focused national American attention not only upon the failings of established African-American politicians, but also on the dynamism of the NoI's leader. The most common observation made by critics and supporters of the march alike (to which there were remarkably few dissenters) was that no one but Louis Farrakhan could have succeeded in mobilizing such an impressive demonstration of mass black American male unity; yet no black public figure was as divisive, despised, and polarizing a political actor in American racial politics. In a perverse inversion of Samuel Huntington's conceptual nexus of a disharmonic American polity in which conflict derived from universal consensus upon basic creedal values, here, instead, an event of broad intraracial consensus was the child that Farrakhan egregiously fathered from genes of pronounced interracial conflict.[71] Farrakhan's ascendancy to national black leadership was forged not so much despite, but precisely because of, what President Clinton persuasively termed his message of "malice and division."

Separating from the march that ignominious message and its ignoble messenger was a conceptual feat of which most of its participants and observers were eminently capable of achieving. Whether they actually should be so separated, however, represented a normative issue of more pressing political significance and extended elite–mass disagreement.[72] For no matter how subtle and carefully calibrated the distinctions they sought painstakingly to draw, the fundamental fact of the 1995 event was that a long succession of established and widely respected black American elected officials and civil rights activists eagerly assumed secondary positions behind the leader of the NoI. Jackson, Mfume, Rep. Donald Payne (D-NJ), Rangel, Rep. John Conyers (D-MI), Joseph Lowery of the SCLC, Betty Shabazz, Rosa Parks, and even Harvard's Cornel West—an erstwhile enlightened agitator for black-Jewish reconciliation—all gave their ringing personal endorsements to an occasion the principal organizing force and keynote speaker of which was one of the most controversial, heavily criticized, and polarizing figures in American public life; the platform of which was shared by the ranks of the politically disgraced and the disgraceful, a veritable who's who of zealots and demagogues, from Marion Barry through Gus Savage to Al Sharpton; and the spirit of which was infused by an uncompromising separatism and pleas for collective racial solitude as much as for black solidarity. For progressive critics who argue that the most important political dimension of Farrakhan's role is the threat that he poses to black Americans at large, rather than the racial animus that he promotes toward whites and Jews, the event was both a cause for sanguine reflection and a substantial confirmation of the deep dilemmas of contemporary national African-American leadership in general.[73]

For if, as Alonzo Hamby argues, the first essential of successful political leadership in America is "an ability to perceive the dominant needs of an era and to align oneself with them,"[74] Farrakhan achieved his epochal African-American leadership status by touching on some desperate and distressing racial imperatives. For many who watched the march, the peculiar spectacle of respected African-American politicians attending the court of an individual widely viewed as a combination of jester, bigot, and lunatic was as poignantly sad as it was politically significant and deeply discomforting.[75] The central irony of the peculiar plot of "Minister Farrakhan Goes to Washington" in 1995 was that many black American politicians were there many years before, and would remain long after, the NoI's leader opportunistically came and went; but that, thirty years after black Americans had achieved civil and political equality, many of their elected representatives who relied upon neither white votes nor white funds should line up behind an unelected, extremist, and bitterly divisive purveyor of political polarization and racial separatism represented a powerful indictment of the parlous and fissiparous state of contemporary racial relations in the United States. Where Malcolm X had once claimed that he would consider retiring if there were ten Adam Clayton Powells sitting in Congress,[76] now, with forty African-Americans there, it was the apparent redundancy of established black leaders that Farrakhan's day in the autumnal D.C. sun appeared to signal. Indeed, where Malcolm had once characterized the 1963 march as the "farce on Washington," now his verdict appeared to be premature by thirty-two years.

For Farrakhan's extraordinary political triumph was forged upon the fundamental failure—strategic, tactical, and otherwise—not only of U.S. public policy-makers in general, but also of black elected officials in particular, to address effectively the grievous socioeconomic problems of many African-American communities across the nation. Farrakhan enthusiastically exploited, and in exploiting knowingly aggravated, an edifice of racial antagonism that had been constructed upon the foundations of prejudice, discrimination, and despair. On a day publicly billed as one of mass black male atonement, the modern African-American leadership figure whose political career had been most strongly forged upon a path of unrelenting bigotry and prejudice offered no such personal precedents, only proverbial lessons in mass repentance to his assembled flock that once more demonstrated how glass houses remain vulnerable to their zealously stone-throwing occupants.[77] Although his political ascent had been gradual and occasionally halting, the Million Man March undeniably marked Farrakhan's firm incorporation within the national black American leadership cadre. From the grim ruins of King's noble dream had arisen the black phoenix of his ashen nightmare.

SUMMARY

Farrakhan's gradual but inexorable rise to a national political leadership position among American blacks in the 1990s was punctuated by several critical events, each of which contributed incrementally but positively to the increasing political legitimation of the NoI's leader among African-Americans at large. The Jackson association established Farrakhan's national political recognition by black and white Americans, at elite and mass levels, and eventually accorded the NoI's leader a unique and uncontested mantle of racial authenticity. The CBC's "Sacred Covenant" conceded Farrakhan's popular appeal among African-Americans and the NoI's effective activism in several urban black communities across America. The Shabazz controversy effectively neutralized the negative reactions among blacks to Farrakhan that derived from his implication in Malcolm X's assassination. The Million Man March provided a dramatic indication of Farrakhan's wholly exceptional capacity for national agenda-setting, mass mobilization, and widespread popular appeal among African-Americans. Though partial and unstable, rocked by tactical errors, and punctuated by impolitic pronouncements, the political legitimation that these developments afforded Farrakhan was nonetheless sufficiently deep and enduring to furnish him a clear mooring at the dock of national black American political leadership.

In seeking to explain Farrakhan's political rise and current influence, some critics draw parallels between Farrakhan and white right-wing extremists.[78] In issue concerns, organization, and rhetoric, comparisons with the white radical right are, to some extent, instructive in analyzing Farrakhan's role in contemporary American politics; but they are often invidious and tend to obscure as much as they reveal about the nature of the Farrakhan phenomenon. Admittedly, in several respects, Farrakhan and David Duke (the most common focus for comparative analysis) represent contemporaneous mirror images, adhering to parallel political analyses and policy prescriptions on the topic of America's racial ills, and having sought nationwide outlets for their unconventional views. In analyzing Duke's campaigns for the Senate and gubernatorial office in 1990 and 1991, respectively, Gary Esolen argues that the Louisianan's strategy resembled that of other latter-day "extremists-turned-moderates," among whom he included Farrakhan:

> The formula—develop a message acceptable in the mainstream, remake your image accordingly, keep at least one foot planted in your original constituency, and capitalize on personal notoriety and controversy—resembles the path taken by Louis Farrakhan, Yasir Arafat, and many others, with varying degrees of sincerity in their conversions. Some have succeeded in gaining a broader audience; many have failed.[79]

Both Duke and Farrakhan have certainly succeeded in winning a broader American—and even international—audience. But although Duke's efforts to improve his public image and enhance his electoral opportunities by moderating his rhetoric and approach were readily apparent (though assessments of his actual success vary), Farrakhan's conversion from extremist to moderate is difficult, by comparison, to discern as even remotely sincere. That Farrakhan has achieved a social impact which few would have anticipated upon his assumption of the NoI's leadership in 1978 is certainly manifest. That he has managed to do so by genuinely moderating his views is far less persuasive. Rather, it is the maintenance of an uncompromising conservative extremism and a comprehensive and distinctive political paranoia—one exclusive in its scope and intensity to Farrakhan among current national black leaders—that functions as the principal basis of the NoI leader's claims to political independence and, hence, political authority. Therein, moreover, resides the fundamental source of the threat that he poses to the established national black American political leadership cadre.

It may therefore reasonably seem to many that, like a bad bottle of wine, Farrakhan seems to immature with age, leaving the bitterest of tastes upon sensitive American palates. Upon being tentatively received anew, the grapes of black wrath and the old corrosive potion of racial animus and hostility invariably seep sourly through. At each point that Farrakhan has offered a fleeting and tantalizing glimpse of shedding a past of hatred, controversy, and demagogic confrontation, the minister has—unwittingly or intentionally—compromised a broader public acceptance through a return to his more intransigent and adversarial demeanor. The "World Friendship Tour" of 1995–96, which saw Farrakhan take his "message" to eighteen countries, including Iran, Iraq, and Libya, was only the latest and most spectacular instance of a well-established pattern of squandering newly acquired—if limited—legitimacy upon an altar of intense controversy.

However, the many controversies that have punctuated Farrakhan's political rise have served more to propel his elevation to the ranks of national African-American leadership than to limit the salience of his distinctive message among blacks at large, hence his apparent addiction to regularly stimulating such furors as a necessity for his leadership aims. Moderation, compromise, conciliation, pragmatism, and consensus are the dominant terms of conventional American politicians; they form the common currency of political exchange familiar to even the most cursory students of the dynamics of American politics. Farrakhan, however, bargains with a political capital culled unrepentantly from immoderation, nonnegotiable demands, dogmatism, intransigence, and incessant confrontation, in short, one that assumes an altogether different character to that of most American political actors and that ensures the NoI's leader of an exceptional niche within the ranks of black leadership.

Moreover, these controversies have also simultaneously rendered the substantive religious and ideological content of Farrakhan's distinctive message less clear than might otherwise have been the case, ironically, an important factor in explaining the mass black appeal that Farrakhan has achieved among both members and nonmembers of the NoI in the national African-American community. Precisely by virtue of the unconventional modes of political discourse and operation that have accorded him an ascendant position in national black politics, the content of his political and religious beliefs demands careful analysis. It is the peculiar nature of the belief system that Farrakhan propounds which we address next.

NOTES TO CHAPTER 2

1. William A. Henry, "Pride and Prejudice," *Time* 26 February 1994, pp. 21–27, at p. 21.

2. The song, from Reed's "New York" album (Sire Records, 1989), was an inventive attack upon anti-Semitic sentiments and prejudice that linked together Jesse Jackson; former Nazi, UN Secretary General, and

Austrian president Kurt Waldheim; and Pope John Paul II. Farrakhan is also mentioned by name in the late Frank Zappa's sharply satirical tribute to Jackson, "Rhymin' Man," from "Broadway the Hardway" (Zappa Records, 1989).

Farrakhan has also featured heavily in rap and hip-hop music, winning extensive support from black artists such as Ice Cube, Public Enemy, and Afrika Bambaataa. As Matthias Gardell observes, while some rap artists belong to the radical left, the majority of the more popular American rappers adhere to the broad black nationalist Islamic tradition. (See the discussion in Gardell, *Countdown to Armageddon*, pp. 293–301.) Ice Cube, in particular, has been one of the most consistent supporters of Farrakhan. Sleeve notes and photographs in his albums have variously encouraged membership in the NoI, praised Farrakhan, and depicted Cube reading the Nation's newspaper, *The Final Call*, backed by suitably stern-looking bow-tied Black Muslims.

3. This is not to suggest that the civil rights movement turned upon the Montgomery protest, but that King's particular role in the movement owed a substantial debt to his activism in the critical Alabama dispute. On the civil rights movement in general, and Montgomery in particular, see: Taylor Branch, *Parting the Waters: America in the King Years, 1954–1963* (New York: Simon and Schuster, 1988); the excellent rational choice treatment of the movement by Dennis Chong, *Collective Action and the Civil Rights Movement* (Chicago: University of Chicago Press, 1991); David J. Garrow, *Bearing the Cross: Martin Luther King, Jr. and the Southern Christian Leadership Conference* (London: Jonathan Cape, 1988); Doug McAdam, *Political Process and the Development of Black Insurgency, 1930–1970* (Chicago: University of Chicago Press, 1982); Aldon D. Morris, *The Origins of the Civil Rights Movement: Black Communities Organizing for Change* (New York: The Free Press, 1984); and Juan Williams, *Eyes on the Prize: America's Civil Rights Years, 1954–1965* (New York: Viking-Penguin, 1987).

4. On the tensions within American Islam, see: Amir M. Ali, *Islam or Farrakhanism?* (Chicago: Institute of Islamic Information and Education, 1991); and Marsh, *From Black Muslims to Muslims*, 1st edition.

5. The author first encountered the application of these terms to election campaigns in the conclusion to the volume by David Butler and Austin Ranney, eds., *Electioneering: A Comparative Study of Continuity and Change* (Oxford: Clarendon Press, 1992).

6. Marable, *Black American Politics*, p. 120.

7. The value of counterfactual speculation is inherently limited, of course. Nonetheless, it is difficult to conceive of Farrakhan achieving the leadership position that he has over the last two decades without the extensive publicity and acute controversy that attended his often stormy association with Jackson.

8. 1964 saw the passage of the most significant civil rights legislation in American history. For a detailed account, see Charles Whalen and Barbara Whalen, *The Longest Debate: A Legislative History of the 1964 Civil Rights Act* (New York: New American Library, 1985).

9. The most skeptical interpretation of Jackson's political role and substantive significance was first advanced by Adolph Reed in *The Jesse Jackson*

Phenomenon: The Crisis of Purpose in Afro-American Politics (New Haven: Yale University Press, 1986). For alternative, more sympathetic, but less persuasive, analyses, see: Lucius J. Barker and Ronald W. Walters, eds., *Jesse Jackson's 1984 Presidential Campaign: Challenge and Change in American Politics* (Chicago: University of Illinois Press, 1989); and Charles P. Henry, *Culture and African American Politics* (Bloomington: Indiana University Press, 1990).

10. On the role of the black vote and African American candidates in presidential elections, see: Ronald W. Walters, *Black Presidential Politics in America: A Strategic Approach* (New York: State University of New York Press, 1988); and Katherine Tate, *From Protest to Politics: The New Black Voters in American Elections* (Cambridge, Mass.: Harvard University Press, 1993).

11. Contrasting accounts of Malcolm X's evolving belief system and relations with the NoI can be found in: Steven Barboza, *American Jihad: Islam after Malcolm X* (New York: Doubleday, 1994); George Breitman, ed., *Malcolm X Speaks: Selected Speeches and Statements* (New York: Grove Press, 1965); George Breitman, ed., *By Any Means Necessary: Speeches, Interviews and a Letter by Malcolm X* (New York: Pathfinder Press, 1970); Louis DeCaro, *On the Side of My People: A Religious Life of Malcolm X* (New York: New York University Press, 1996); David Gallen, ed., *The Malcolm X Reader* (New York: Carroll and Graf, 1994); Benjamin Karim, *Remembering Malcolm* (New York: Carroll and Graf, 1992); Bruce Perry, *Malcolm: The Life of a Man Who Changed Black America* (Barrytown, NY: Station Hill, 1991); and Oba T'Shaka, *The Political Legacy of Malcolm X* (Chicago: Third World Press, 1983).

12. On the assassination of Malcolm X, see: George Breitman, Herman Porter, and Baxter Smith, *The Assassination of Malcolm X* (New York: Pathfinder Press, 1976); Michael Friendly, *Malcolm X: The Assassination* (New York: Carroll and Graf, 1992); Peter Goldman, *The Death and Life of Malcolm X*, 2nd ed. (Urbana: University of Illinois Press, 1979); and the brief discussion in David E. Scheim, *The Mafia Killed President Kennedy* (London: W. H. Allen, 1988), pp. 278–82.

13. The most accessible and influential works on the black religious experience and its influence in American politics are: Charles V. Hamilton, *The Black Preacher in America* (New York: William Morrow and Co., 1972); and C. Eric Lincoln, *The Black Church in the African American Experience* (Durham, N.C.: Duke University Press, 1990).

14. See Hans Gerth and C. Wright Mills, eds., *From Max Weber.*

15. For a concise summation of the changing environment of national black American politics after the civil rights movement, see Robert Smith, "Black Power and the Transformation From Protest to Politics," *Political Science Quarterly* 96, no. 3 (1981): 431–43.

16. On the consistent lock of the Democrats upon black Americans' voting loyalties, see Louis Bolce, Gerald De Maio, and Douglas Muzzio, "The 1992 Republican 'Tent': No Blacks Walked In," *Political Science Quarterly* 108, no. 2 (1993): 255–70.

17. The dominance of party interest derived from both electoral and institutional sources. Electorally, the vast majority of black Americans since 1964 have remained consistently, and disproportionately, loyal to Democratic party candidates. At an institutional level, in addition, the Democratic party enjoyed a comprehensive lock upon the House of Representatives and (with the exception of 1981–87) the U.S. Senate in the years 1955–95. As the majority party in Congress (and in many state legislatures), black elected officials therefore had powerful institutional incentives to remain within the Democratic party fold.

18. See: Michael B. Preston, Lenneal S. Henderson, and Paul Puryear, eds., *The New Black Politics*, 2nd ed. (New York: Longman, 1987); and Clarence Lusane, "Black Political Power in the 1990s," *The Black Scholar*, January/February 1989, pp. 38–42.

19. Steve Bruce, *The Rise and Fall of the New Christian Right, 1978–1988* (Oxford: Clarendon Press, 1988).

20. See E. R. Shipp, "Candidacy of Jackson Highlights Split Among Black Muslims," *New York Times*, 27 February 1984, p. 10.

21. The reasons underlying Farrakhan's endorsement of Jackson are explained at length by the Nation of Islam leader in his article, "Farrakhan on Jesse Jackson: A Warning to Black Leaders, A Warning to Black People," in the black American female-oriented publication, *Essence*, February 1984, pp. 30–34. Therein, Farrakhan characterizes Jackson's candidacy as "one of the most far-reaching and significant events of this century" and argues that Jackson represented "an instrument that Allah is using for a much larger purpose than perhaps he [Jackson] himself realizes."

22. Farrakhan, "Register and Vote" radio address, 11 March 1984. Also quoted in McFadden-Preston, "The Rhetoric of Minister Louis Farrakhan," pp. 176–77.

23. The Reagan Administration's Justice Department did investigate the possibility of prosecuting Farrakhan for the threat, but rejected the notion on the grounds of insufficient evidential proof being available.

24. See *The New York Times*, 23 April 1984, p. 1.

25. Jerome H. Bakst, ed., "Louis Farrakhan: An Update," *Anti-Defamation League Facts* 30, Spring 1985 (New York: Anti-Defamation League, 1985), p. 1.

26. Faye S. Joyce, "Farrakhan Warns Press on Jackson," *New York Times*, 10 April 1984, p. 1.

27. See: Nancy Weiss, *Farewell to the Party of Lincoln: Black Politics in the Age of FDR* (Princeton: Princeton University Press, 1983); and Anthony Badger, *The New Deal: the Depression Years, 1933–1940* (New York: Hill and Wang, 1989).

28. On the pattern of black partisan allegiances, see: Louis Bolce, Gerald D. De Maio, and Douglas Muzzio, "Blacks and the Republican Party: The 20 Percent Solution," *Political Science Quarterly* 107, no. 1 (1992): 63–79.

29. See: Earl Black and Merle Black, *Politics and Society in the South* (Cambridge, Mass.: Harvard University Press, 1987) and *The Vital South: How Presidents are Elected* (Cambridge, Mass.: Harvard University Press, 1992); Alexander P. Lamis, *The Two-Party South* 2nd ed. (New York: Oxford University Press, 1990); and Nicol C. Rae, *Southern Democrats* (New York: Oxford University Press, 1994).

30. Joyce, "Farrakhan Warns Press on Jackson," p. 1.

31. "President Opposes Farrakhan," *The New York Times*, 28 June 1984, p. 22.

32. See Thomas Byrne Edsall and Mary D. Edsall, *Chain Reaction: The Impact of Race, Rights, and Taxes on American Politics* (New York: W. W. Norton, 1991).

33. Three out of every four Jewish Americans voted for the Democratic candidate, Walter Mondale, in 1984, a marginal increase from 1980 when a substantial minority of Jews voted for the independent candidate, John Anderson. See Paul R. Abramson, John H. Aldrich, and David W. Rohde, *Change and Continuity in the 1988 Elections* (Washington, D.C.: Congressional Quarterly Press, 1990), pp. 130–31.

34. *The New York Times*, 29 June 1984, p. 10.

35. Elizabeth O. Colton, *The Jackson Phenomenon: The Man, the Power, the Message* (New York: Doubleday, 1989).

36. Colton, *The Jackson Phenomenon*, p. 205–6.

37. Cited in Colton, *The Jackson Phenomenon*, p. 207–8.

38. On their skepticism in 1984, see: Lorenzo Morris, ed., *The Social and Political Implications of the 1984 Jesse Jackson Presidential Campaign* (New York: Praeger, 1990); Reed, *The Jesse Jackson Phenomenon*; and Maulana Karenga, "Jesse Jackson and the Presidential Campaign: The Invitation and the Oppositions of History," *Black Scholar* 15, no. 5 (September-October 1984). On the 1988 context, see: Paulette Pierce, "The Roots of the Rainbow Coalition," *Black Scholar* 20, no. 2 (March/April 1988), pp. 2–16; and Ronald W. Walters, "The American Crisis of Credibility and the 1988 Jesse Jackson Campaign," *Black Scholar* 20, no. 2 (March/April 1988), pp. 31–44.

39. See, for example, James Melvin Washington, "Jesse Jackson and the Symbolic Politics of Black Christendom," in *Annals of the American Academy of Political and Social Science* 480 (July 1985): 89–105, at 102.

40. Even an unannounced candidate, Colin Powell, encountered (in the context of otherwise near-universal praise) remarkably adverse critical comments for his speaking to Farrakhan on the phone about, and contemplating participation in, the Million Man March over the weekend of October 14–15, 1995. Though publicly rejecting the invitation as a result of book promotion duties in New York, the very fact that Farrakhan's contact cast a doubt upon his fitness for highest office says much about the litmus test that the NoI's leader has come to represent for many Americans.

41. See Bill Turque, Vern E. Smith, and John McCormick, "Playing a Different Tune: Louis Farrakhan Is Trying to Reach Out to the White Mainstream," *Newsweek* 121, 28 June 1993, p. 30.

42. See: Kenneth T. Walsh, "The New Drug Vigilantes," *U.S. & World News Report*, 9 May 1988, p. 20; and Lorraine Adams, "Nation of Islam: A Dream Past Due," *The Washington Post*, 2 September 1996, pp. A1, A8. Adams documents at length how the NoI and its related security offshoots became embroiled in severe debts by the mid-1990s and attracted strong criticism from housing tenants for their ineffectiveness and proselytizing on behalf of

Farrakhan, being "more concerned about converting people than security" (p. A8).

43. Farrakhan's rendition occurred as part of a three-day symposium, "Gateways: Classical Music and the Black Musician," at the Reynolds Auditorium in Winston-Salem, North Carolina, on 18 April 1993. He prefaced the recital by declaring that he would "try to do with music what cannot be done with words and try to undo with music what words have done." See Bernard Holland, "Sending a Message, Louis Farrakhan Plays Mendelssohn," *The New York Times*, 19 April 1993, p. C11. It is perhaps not inappropriate to treat the material political significance of the recital with a healthy degree of skepticism. One wonders, for example, whether black Americans would be persuaded of David Duke's sincerity in recanting his previous pronouncements upon race in the event of the Louisianan's publicly performing a Marvin Gaye tribute or Muddy Waters medley as a conciliatory message to African-Americans.

44. See Robert S. Singh, "The Congressional Black Caucus in the United States Congress, 1971–1990," *Parliaments, Estates and Representation* 14, no. 1 (1994): 65–91.

45. See William L. Clay, *Just Permanent Interests: Black Americans in Congress, 1870–1991* (New York: Amistad, 1992).

46. Quoted in Richard E. Cohen, "Hatred Covenant," *The Washington Post*, 15 October 1993, p. 25.

47. See: Cohen, "Hatred Covenant"; Lynne Duke, "Congressional Black Caucus and Nation of Islam Agree on Alliance," *The Washington Post*, 17 September 1993, p. A3; and Cameron Humphries, "The Sacred Covenant," *Diversity and Division* 3, no. 3 (Spring-Summer 1994).

48. See, for example: William A. Henry, "Pride and Prejudice," *Time* 143, 28 February 1994, pp. 21–27; Joe Klein, "The Threat of Tribalism," *Newsweek* 123, 14 March 1994, p. 28; Sylvester Monroe, "Khalid Abdul Muhammad: Is the Fiery Speaker Undermining the Nation of Islam?," *Emerge* 5, September 1994, p. 42; and Nat Hentoff, "Black Bigotry and Free Speech," *The Progressive*, May 1994, p. 20.

49. Cited in Janet Hook, "House Denounces Remarks as 'Racist' Speech," *Congressional Quarterly Weekly Report*, 26 February 1994, p. 458.

50. See Ian Brodie, "Muslim Racism Sparks Uproar," *The London Times*, 4 February 1994, p. 12.

51. David Bositis, *The Congressional Black Caucus in the 103rd Congress* (Washington, D.C.: Joint Center for Political and Economic Studies, 1994), p. 19.

52. See, for example, Juan Williams, "Hiding from this Rage Is Harmful," *International Herald Tribune*, 18 February 1994, p. 7.

53. Quoted in Janet Hook, "Mfume Cuts Renewed Ties to Nation of Islam," *Congressional Quarterly Weekly Report*, 5 February 1994, p. 219. See also Kevin Merida, "Black Caucus Says It Has No Official Ties with Nation of Islam," *The Washington Post*, 3 February 1994, p. A16.

54. Quoted in Brodie, "Muslim Racism."

55. Rep. Cynthia McKinney (D-GA), cited in Kevin Merida, "Lawmakers Uneasy Over Farrakhan: Black Officials Split on Summit Invitations," *The Washington Post*, 17 June 1994, p. A3.

56. See: Alex Kotlowitz, "A Bridge Too Far?," *The New York Times Magazine*, 12 June 1994, pp. 41–43; and George Curry, "Unity in the Community: Can Ben Chavis Pull It Off?," *Emerge* 5 (September 1994), p. 28.

57. See: Sylvester Monroe, "The Risky Association," *Time*, 27 June 1994, p. 39; Dorothy J. Gaiter, "Civil Unrest," *The Wall Street Journal*, 10 June 1994, p. A1; Denton L. Watson, "Chavis's NAACP: Embracing Farrakhan," *The Washington Post*, 29 June 1994, p. A23; and Nat Hentoff, "A Black Response to Black Bigotry," *The Washington Post*, 23 July 1994, p. A21.

58. See: *The Atlanta Journal*, 4 November 1985, p. A5.

59. See Tom Morganthau, "Back in the Line of Fire," *Newsweek*, 23 January 1995, p. 20.

60. Shabazz, eschewing any explicit talk of reconciliation, merely encouraged Farrakhan to continue broadening his "conceptual framework." See Malcolm Gladwell, "Farrakhan Seeks End of Rift with Shabazz; Apologizes for Hurt but Denies Involvement in Malcolm X Death," *The Washington Post*, 8 May 1995, p. A1.

61. Part of Rangel's calculations also involved the need to retain black support for his primary election constituency. Though he had triumphed easily over Adam Clayton Powell, the son of the (in)famous black congressman, in his October 1994 primary, the imperative to attend to the type of constituency to which Farrakhan targeted his general message clearly influenced the New York incumbent. Indeed, the following year, despite reports before the event that he would not attend at all, Rangel was also a featured platform speaker at the Million Man March in 1995.

62. See: Don Terry, "Shabazz Case: A Gain for Farrakhan," *The New York Times*, 3 May 1995, p. A15, B8; Charisse Jones, "Farrakhan-Shabazz Meeting Kindles Hope," *The New York Times*, 6 May 1995, p. 16, 23; and Joyce Purnick, "An Unlikely Matchmaker," *The New York Times*, 8 May 1995, p. B1, B12.

63. Given its notably more modest numbers and entirely stationary quality, the term is something of a misnomer, of course.

64. Farrakhan claimed 1.5 million African-American men had attended the march, and threatened to sue the National Park Service for its "racist" estimate of 400,000. It seemed to this author, both on the day and subsequently, that a figure somewhere between 400,000 and 600,000 was plausible—but no more than that.

65. *Brown v. Board of Education*, 347 U.S. 483 (1954).

66. The efforts to conduct a voter registration drive among black Americans that occurred on the day of the march and subsequently were not part of the original public literature promoting the event. Most of the emphasis upon African-American leadership inclusion and electoral influence that Farrakhan made occurred after, rather than prior to, the march itself. See, for example, Michael A. Fletcher and Hamil R. Harris, "Farrakhan Announces Voter Drive," *The Washington Post*, 19 October 1995, p. A3.

67. An implicit political goal of the march may, nonetheless, have been to demonstrate to black Americans both the possibility and the desirability of racial separatism. Many of the marchers commented upon the novelty of seeing so many black men gathered together, some recording that it felt as if they were in Africa. Given Farrakhan's separatist objectives, it seems plausible that the march was partly designed by him to encourage such sentiments and to reinforce the theoretical appeal of separatism by a practical demonstration of its putative viability.

68. For comparison with previous marches, see Marable, *Black American Politics*, chapter 2. One of the most lucid synopses of the arguments for and against participation in the 1995 march is made by A. Leon Higginbotham Jr., "Why I Didn't March," *The Washington Post*, 17 October 1995, p. A17.

69. Quoted in Martin Fletcher and Tom Rhodes, "Washington Mass Rally Rekindles Black Pride," *The London Times*, 17 October 1995, p. 11. It should be noted, though, that Lewis also relied upon, and enjoyed excellent relations with, white and Jewish supporters in his Atlanta district for his reelection to the House.

70. See Juan Williams, "President Colin Powell?," *Reconstruction* 2, no. 3 (1994): 67–78.

71. See Huntington, *American Politics*.

72. See: Richard E. Cohen, "Marching behind Farrakhan," *The Washington Post*, 19 September 1995, p. A18; E. J. Dionne, "So Many Could Have Been There," *The Washington Post*, 17 October 1995, p. A17; Matt Labash, "Inside the March: Farrakhan Is King," *The Weekly Standard*, 23 October 1995, pp. 26–29; and Glenn C. Loury, "One Man's March," *The New Republic*, 6 November 1995, pp. 18–22.

73. See the discussions in: Darryl Pinckney, "Slouching Towards Washington," *The New York Review of Books*, 21 December 1995, pp. 73–82; and Sean Wilentz, "Backward March," *The New Republic*, 6 November 1995, pp. 16–18. Many of Pinckney's points, especially on the respective racial dangers that Farrakhan poses, were also previously anticipated in Reed, "Behind the Farrakhan Show."

74. Alonzo L. Hamby, *Liberalism and Its Challengers: F.D.R. to Reagan* (New York: Oxford University Press, 1985), p. 9.

75. The international reception accorded the march provides interesting indications of the extent to which Farrakhan's rise has occasioned incredulity as well as curiosity outside America. Farrakhan was not only widely portrayed in the mass media in the United Kingdom, for example, as a racial extremist but was also ridiculed as a lunatic. See, for example, the references to the NoI as the "Nutters of Islam" in the satirical British fortnightly magazine, *Private Eye*, 3 November 1995, p. 15, and the question raised by the journalist Francis Wheen, as to whether Farrakhan was "loony as a coot?" in "Voice of Islam," *The Guardian*, 8 November 1995, sec. 2, p. 7. For black Americans who argued that distinctions needed to be made between the message and messenger, the international treatment of the march should serve as a

salutary reminder of the powerful symbolism that characterizes such events. Moreover, to the extent that advocates of the march sought to challenge the inaccurate and sometimes racist international perceptions of black American men that are represented in rap music and popular films, the external dimension of the coverage of the march assumed a particular importance. With Farrakhan as its principal sponsor, however, such stereotypes were apt to be less successfully countered than might otherwise have been the case. See also Martin Fletcher, "Prophet of Hatred Becomes Voice of Black America," *The London Times*, 18 October 1995, p. 11.

76. Malcolm X (with Alex Haley), *The Autobiography of Malcolm X* (New York: Penguin Books, 1968), p. 28.

77. Despite widespread anticipation that Farrakhan would use his keynote speech as an opportunity to offer public apologies for his own anti-Semitic and bigoted comments over the years (an anticipation admittedly tempered by Farrakhan's familiar reference to Jews as "bloodsuckers" in an interview the week before the march), the NoI leader scrupulously refused to apologize for his dubious record during his rambling monologue of over two hours duration. Though Farrakhan invited "dialogue" with Jewish leaders and others in the speech, his personal history provided few causes for optimism that such dialogues would either occur or produce tangible results in improved race relations.

78. See the lucid discussion in Dennis King, "The Farrakhan Phenomenon: Ideology, Support, Potential," *Patterns of Prejudice* 20, no. 1 (1986): 11–22.

79. Gary Esolen, "More Than a Pretty Face: David Duke's Use of Television as a Political Tool," *The Emergence of David Duke and the Politics of Race*, ed. Douglas Rose (Chapel Hill: University of North Carolina Press, 1992), pp. 136–55, at 140.

3

The Prophet Motive: The Theology and Ideology of Black Radical Reaction

Even Malcolm X . . . retreated from the impossible position of separatism.

Harold Cruse[1]

I really don't care if you think I'm a nut.

Louis Farrakhan[2]

Farrakhan's political ascendancy has been widely viewed as surprising by virtue of the anti-Semitism and racial militancy that pervade his national public profile in the United States. Perhaps the most common reaction among Americans to Farrakhan's public discourse, however, is not so much one of revulsion, outrage, or fear as sheer incredulity. Many can scarcely believe that a public figure articulating the beliefs that Farrakhan propounds can even take himself seriously, much less be taken so by others. The potent and eclectic amalgam of numerology, pseudo-history, theology, and prophecy that punctuates the Nation of Islam (NoI) leader's public pronouncements requires on the part of most listeners a willing suspension of disbelief to entertain even minimally. The veritable Stephen King of black nationalists, Farrakhan's fantastic world is inhabited by sinister Jews and malevolent Masons, spaceships waiting to drop bombs upon the Earth on an imminent judgment day, and African-American spirits miraculously returned from the dead. It is almost as if America patiently waits for Farrakhan eventually to smile, wink knowingly, and candidly concede that his political opportunism and vivid imagination are far more deeply entrenched and enduring than is the elaborate fictional landscape that he publicly relates.

Such reactions are certainly understandable. For though Farrakhan's rise to a position of national black American political leadership has afforded a reasonably large stock of public information and commentary about the Black Muslim leader, much of this remains essentially impressionistic, lacking comprehensive detail and accuracy. For most Americans, Farrakhan therefore continues to represent a largely foreboding and mysterious black American figure of malice, spite, and hatred. Relatively little is known at large of either his personal or political background beyond a national reputation rich in racial militancy, vitriolically aggressive speeches, and barely coded anti-Semitic public utterances. In short, many elite evaluations of, and popular political responses to, Farrakhan occur against a background of very partial and limited knowledge of the minister's substantive political values, beliefs, and attitudes.

Farrakhan has, nonetheless, been active in the NoI for over forty years. Having delivered literally thousands of speeches and sermons across America, the Black Muslim has created a voluminous record of his values and beliefs.[3] What that record clearly reveals is a minister whose political project of racial regeneration is thoroughly infused by a set of keenly held theological doctrines of a deeply unorthodox and extremely tendentious hue, whose connection with orthodox Islam—much less reality—is far more tenuous than certain. Although Farrakhan is a quintessential American political entrepreneur, highly attentive to opportunities to increase his personal role and influence among African-Americans, his pragmatism is powerfully constrained by the very distinctive religious and ideological beliefs that are entirely inseparable from the minister's locus within the NoI. In this regard, Farrakhan's extensive and varied experiences in the black separatist organization have altered few (if any) of the fundamental religious and ideological beliefs that first drew him to joining the NoI in 1955. What has changed significantly over subsequent decades, however, has been the lessons that Farrakhan has absorbed, adapted, and reapplied about internal organization, self-publicity, and political leadership.

As a political operator in recent American politics, Farrakhan's sophistication is more pronounced than many of his critics are either able to recognize or willing to concede. Moreover, the theological convictions that inform his political beliefs also render his public discourse somewhat more nuanced than is frequently admitted. Neither the sensitivity of Farrakhan's political judgment nor the coherence of his belief system should be obscured by the apparent crudity of his public persona and by his regular public denials that he either is, or harbors aspirations to become, a national politician in America. For if Mahatma Gandhi can be said to have first invented the politician as saint, Farrakhan has equally vigorously promoted the self-proclaimed prophetic savior as politician.[4]

That this should be so reflects Farrakhan's distinctive organizational base. The NoI represents an esoteric and eccentric mix of cosmological, religious, and ideological tendencies that powerfully distinguish it from all other national political, religious, and civic organizations seeking black Americans' socioeconomic and political empowerment in the United States. Farrakhan's zealous adherence to the religious teachings of its founders, W. D. Fard and Elijah Muhammad, leads to his self-conception and national projection as a prophetic figure and race savior. That figure, however, is one who advances a public philosophy far closer to that of Jesse Helms than Jesse Jackson, a soothsayer whose offers of cathartic comfort to African-Americans conceal a deeply conservative and reactionary set of convictions and, moreover, a material practice that clearly contradicts those avowed political principles. The adverse and incredulous reactions that Farrakhan frequently elicits from his American compatriots are in this respect not merely eminently understandable, but are also in large part fully merited.

THE CHARMING DEMAGOGUE

Farrakhan's early personal background provided several useful preparatory experiences and skills for his eventual role as leader of the NoI. The minister's political socialization was founded upon formative experiences that subsequently enabled him to forge a public persona as readily able variously to identify with many African-Americans' concerns and aspirations from personal experience; to work with and across social classes among African-Americans; to be tutored in different styles of political and organizational leadership; to be afforded an early exposure to public performance, spectacle, and the critical importance of the mass media in personal political promotion; and to invoke Christian theological tenets and parables as a means of tempering and reinforcing his unorthodox Islamic message to black

Americans at large. The demagogic aspects of Farrakhan's political career and public persona have thus drawn deeply upon many important facets of his early life.

Minister Louis Haleem Abdul Farrakhan was born on May 11, 1933, in the Bronx, New York City. His mother, Mae Manning, had migrated to New York from the British colony of Saint Kitts, in the West Indies. She married a Jamaican, Percival Clark, who soon disappeared, before falling in love with another West Indian, Louis Walcott. Walcott fathered Farrakhan's older brother, Alvan, before Clark returned briefly and made Manning pregnant with a second child, prior to disappearing once more. Manning attempted to abort the baby three times with a coat hanger before eventually changing her mind and giving birth once again, at the age of 15. The child was given the name of Louis Eugene Walcott, after a man who was not his natural father and whom he would never know.

Three years after Louis's birth, Manning left for Boston, Massachusetts, where she raised the young child alone. Despite his lacking a father at home, Walcott's upbringing in the thriving West Indian neighborhood of Roxbury was conventionally middle-class in character. Walcott took up the violin from the age of five, for example, and received private music tuition. He also grew up as a devout Episcopalian, winning a place at the Boston Latin School (one of America's then best, and overwhelmingly white, state schools). After high school, Walcott gained a modest athletics scholarship to the Winston-Salem Teachers' College in North Carolina, a black academy where he majored in English. Returning to Boston with few serious prospects after college, Walcott married his high-school sweetheart, Betsy (later known as Khadijah). Walcott eventually fathered nine children by her, and has at least twenty grandchildren, some of whom have become active and influential members of the NoI and its several institutional enterprises and offshoots.

One of the first black Americans ever to appear on national television in the United States, Walcott achieved his initial exposure to a national American audience when he appeared on *Ted Mack's Amateur Hour*, playing the violin, in 1946. Soon taking up the guitar and the ukulele, he quickly assumed a journeyman role as a Calypso singer and dancer, rapidly gaining the affectionate sobriquets, "The Charmer" and "Calypso Gene." There, but for the grace of Harry Belafonte, Walcott might have remained.

Instead, Walcott's initiation into the NoI occurred in 1955, when (on a tour of Chicago nightclubs) he attended a lecture by Elijah

Muhammad, at the end of which he promptly joined the organization. Upon joining, however, he was instructed (whether by Elijah or by other members of the group is unclear) that life as a performer was incompatible with NoI membership. Now termed Louis X (the name "Farrakhan" does not appear to have been embraced by him until 1975), he thereupon gave up his fledgling performing career to participate fully in the NoI through its Boston mosque. Nonetheless, his artistic bent still found typically didactic expression in several plays that he wrote—and, presaging his later political ambitions, starred in—that documented the nature and scale of black oppression in the United States at the hands of white Americans.[5] As Louis X, Farrakhan also went on eventually to release a calypso record redolent of his developing political and religious beliefs, "The White Man's Heaven Is the Black Man's Hell" (which won anthemic status within the NoI but achieved neither popular nor critical acclaim, although it was, admittedly, better received than his disc commemorating America's first sex-change operation).[6]

In the Boston temple, Louis X was rapidly appointed to the rank of "Captain," in charge of training and instructing the male members of the NoI in the mosque. Outside the temple, he worked successively as a storm door and window salesman at a wage of $35 per week, as a dishwasher, and then in Boston's Garment District at $45 per week. Success as a Captain resulted in further rapid promotion to the prestigious position of Minister of the Boston mosque, Temple No. 11, which subsequently emerged under his ministership as one of the fastest growing of the NoI's temples in the entire United States.

When Louis's early friend and mentor, Malcolm X, was brutally assassinated on February 21, 1965, the NoI was plunged into internal turmoil and the mosque in New York over which the latter had presided was left in deep disarray. Louis was transferred by Elijah from Boston to act as minister of the prestigious Mosque No. 7 in Harlem, and shortly thereafter was selected to be Elijah's national spokesperson for the NoI, in addition to his responsibilities in New York City. In the NoI's history up to that point, only Malcolm and Louis had been selected to serve as national spokespersons for the organization; both were personally chosen by Elijah for the role. The choice clearly reflected Farrakhan's diverse and compelling personal qualities: a man, according to C. Eric Lincoln, "of extraordinary charisma and charm, but, armed, with a rapier-like wit, he is well practised in polemical skills."[7] Such skills would be tested before a nationwide audience by the 1980s when Farrakhan's early reputation as the Charmer became largely and justifiably eclipsed by that of the Demagogue.[8]

THE NATION OF ISLAM: ELIJAH, MALCOLM, AND LOUIS

Farrakhan's early immersion in a religious environment was hardly unusual for an African-American of his generation, but his particular choice of organization was decidedly atypical for members of his race. For although religion and the institution of the Church have historically performed many vitally important social, economic, and political functions in the lives of most black Americans, the overwhelming focus of African-American religious allegiance in the United States has been Christianity.[9] The Islamic faith has never been adhered to by more than an extremely small proportion of Americans, either black or white, the vast majority of whom have remained firmly wedded to various denominations of the Christian faith. Thus, although in 1995 African-Americans made up 42 percent of the approximately five million Muslims in the United States, approximately 92 percent of all black Americans were Christians.[10]

In the African-American case, although Syrian Muslim immigrants and black returnees to Islam established local religious organizations as early as 1912 and 1913, respectively, it was not until the 1950s that a significant organization by orthodox Muslims on a national level was formed in America: the Federation of Islamic Associations (FIA). Established in June 1952, the Federation sought to promote the growth of Islam and to facilitate its greater understanding by the non-Muslim American majority.[11] The theological orthodoxy of the FIA, however, stood in sharp contrast to the Nation of Islam and the Bilalian faith to which its members subscribed.

Regarded by most Muslims as deeply unorthodox, Bilalian Islam arose from a belief system propounded and popularized by Robert J. Poole, a former automobile factory worker, before whom Allah—or God—allegedly appeared in the person of Master W. D. Fard Muhammad, in Detroit, Michigan, on July 4, 1930 (Poole later changed his name to "Elijah Muhammad," adopted as a symbolic rejection of all associations with white American society, its slave history and tainted legacy). Although few existing studies of the Black Muslim movement have commented upon it, the date of Fard's appearance was evidently of substantial political significance for African-Americans: American Independence Day. The arrival of Fard in the United States was intended to represent the day of future black American independence from the land of their enslavement and subjugation.

Bilalianism comprises six key beliefs: first, there is one God called Allah, who is identified as being black; second, Elijah Muhammad was his last messenger on Earth; third, heaven and hell are states that are deemed actually to exist on Earth and, therefore, there is no life after death; fourth, it is necessary to pray seven times daily and to fast each December; fifth, Elijah assumes the place of the Prophet (the justification for this is that Elijah knew Allah personally in the form of Fard Muhammad, which represents a double heresy in the orthodox Islamic faith, by making God both visible and personified in human form); and, sixth, Bilalians adhere to the notion of black supremacy, an inverted type of racism that characterizes Caucasians as intrinsically evil. Together, these six fundamental beliefs powerfully distinguish the Bilalian faith from orthodox Islam.

The Nation of Islam represents the institutional expression of Bilalianism in America. Established by Fard in July 1930—after the NAACP (1909) and the National Urban League (1910), but before the Congress of Racial Equality (1942), the SCLC (1957), and Jesse Jackson's Operation PUSH (1971)—the NoI's political locus was firmly within the relatively new ideological tradition of black nationalism in America. Though derided by early scholastic observers as a "voodoo cult"[12] and a "Muslim goon squad,"[13] the NoI has achieved an impressive institutional longevity that has eluded many other African-American organizations in the twentieth century. Much of the explanation resides in its consistently combining a distinctive theological belief system with a set of political goals, public rhetoric, and practical urban activism that have together singled out the organization as enduringly different from all other groups concerned with advancing African-American welfare in the United States.

Black Nationalism and the Early Nation of Islam

Nationalism is conventionally defined by political scientists as the belief of a group that shares (or alternatively, as a normative aspirational goal, ought to share) a common heritage of language, culture, and religion. Moreover, that heritage, way of life, and ethnic identity are conceived as being manifestly distinct from—though not necessarily superior to—those of other groups. Nationalists believe that members of a particular group ought to rule themselves and should enjoy full autonomy in determining their own destinies. They should therefore be demonstrably in control of their own social, economic, and political institutions, to shape entirely as they so desire.[14] The existence of such beliefs among African-Americans is conventionally termed "black nationalism" and, although its particular political expressions have differed both over time and among black nationalist groups, it is within this basic conceptual notion that the NoI is most clearly and appropriately located.[15]

Although its antecedents date at least as far back as Frederick Douglas during the second half of the nineteenth century, black nationalism first emerged as an influential political form and assumed an identifiable organizational expression in the United States in the years following the end of World War I. The contemporary political environment was especially conducive to the development of a racially bounded nationalism in postwar America. Having risked their lives in defense of American democracy abroad during the "Great War," black servicemen returned from Europe to the United States to face extensive racial discrimination and expressions of the deepest prejudice at home. Black veterans confronted intense competition for employment and housing opportunities, and many were subject to grotesque forms of coercion and physical violence, including numerous lynchings. Moreover, far from actually challenging segregation, the federal government itself perpetuated and spread segregated practices—both in and outside the South—through its own departments and programs.[16] Many African-Americans therefore became especially receptive to the political appeals of two nationalist movements then emerging among U.S. blacks: the United Negro Improvement Association (UNIA) of Marcus Garvey and the Moorish Science Temple of Noble Drew Ali. The NoI's early development drew substantially—though not exclusively—upon both the urban black constituencies and the separatist beliefs of these two movements.

The NoI shared many ideological tenets with Marcus Garvey and the UNIA, in particular.[17] Garvey had arrived in New York from the Caribbean in 1916 and the following year established a Harlem branch of the UNIA, which he had originally founded in Jamaica. The U.S. organization rapidly acquired a membership estimated to exceed one million black Americans by 1922. Vehemently rejecting the racial integrationism of the fledgling NAACP, Garvey was the most influential early African-American exponent of a distinctive version of black separatism: Pan-African nationalism. Garvey held that, ultimately, the only workable solution to black Americans' multiple problems in the United States was physically to leave America and to "return," albeit selectively, to Africa. Although the precise form of the African state that he hoped to establish has been the subject of academic dissensus, its initial intended foundation is generally agreed to have been the (now independent) state of Liberia, to which Garvey had sent several exploratory missions before Britain and France terminated the association.[18]

That Garvey's unequivocal racial separatism was wholly anathema to the integrationist ideals of many members of the black American middle class and intelligentsia was immaterial to the Jamaican agitator. Like Farrakhan subsequently, Garvey's principal target constituency was working class and deprived African-Americans. Seeking to increase their racial consciousness, Garvey vigorously exhorted the mass of African-Americans to revel and glory in their blackness, and argued—again anticipating Farrakhan by over half a century—that the white version of Christianity with which they had been indoctrinated since slavery was designed to achieve their collective racial subservience, not their true and lasting liberation. In its pernicious place, Garvey offered instead an explicitly black form of the Christian faith, complete with black icons, black parables, and a black Christ. Stressing the common origins and shared interests of black peoples throughout the world, Garvey advocated the selective emigration of black Americans to Africa in order to achieve their true freedom and independence.

The parallels with Farrakhan's NoI are at once several, striking, and significant. Drawing recruits largely from impoverished and disadvantaged black Americans in central cities in the Northeast and Midwest, Garvey's message was one of unabashed racial militancy, but one that neither offered nor demanded fundamental political or economic change in established American structures. In offering black Americans a new version of their collective history and in raising their racial pride, Garvey's movement was undeniably of dual political significance to African-Americans. Garvey, however, was fundamentally conservative in terms of his economic philosophy. He strongly urged his black supporters to emulate the white man's dedication to hard work, thrift, and individual responsibility, and called upon black Americans to establish separate industrial, commercial, and financial structures from whites, in order to counter white economic power in America. Enthusiastically championing black free market capitalism, the Jamaican fiercely attacked trade unions, socialists, and Marxists, all of whom he deemed to be implacable foes of black Americans. In the 1924 presidential election, Garvey even urged his (enfranchised) black followers to cast their votes for the Republican nominee, Calvin Coolidge, one of the most racially conservative candidates for the American presidency in the entire twentieth century. The jarring combination of racial militancy and deep conservatism of the Garvey movement thus powerfully presaged that of Farrakhan in these important respects. (Garvey was convicted of mail fraud after a campaign by integrationist activists, committed to prison in 1925, and deported in 1927, eventually to die in London in 1940. Deprived of its leader's crucial guidance, the UNIA rapidly experienced major internal divisions and soon atrophied.[19])

In contrast to Garveyite tenets, members of the Drewish cult essentially sought psychic rather than physical escape from white American oppression. Although both movements shared an abiding and fundamental belief in racial separatism as the only viable solution to black Americans' grievous problems in the United States, that of Noble Drew Ali (Timothy Drew) was essentially religious rather than political in character.[20] Black Americans were instructed by Ali that the white man's destruction both in and outside America was imminent, and that it would be signified by the appearance in the sky of a star with a crescent moon, the traditional symbol of Islam. Although most estimates of its membership put it at a maximum of 30,000, the eschatological beliefs of the Drewish cult accorded its members a collective racial self-confidence and an abiding contempt for white Americans that emboldened them greatly. The movement rapidly splintered, however, when Drew Ali attempted to prevent some of the cult's less spiritually inclined members from exploiting their cofollowers through selling goods and artifacts for profit. Ali was rapidly removed and eventually murdered, and the cult subsequently fragmented and ceased to be even a minimally influential force among urban black Americans by the later 1920s.

By 1930, the vacuum of racial militancy among black Americans caused by the decline of the Garvey and Ali movements was increasingly filled principally, though not exclusively, by Fard's fledgling Nation of Islam. Located within the same black nationalist and separatist traditions, the NoI vigorously espoused the merits of black capitalism and attempted strongly to recruit and win support from deprived urban blacks in central cities across America. Ironically, while its racial nationalism was pronounced, the Black Muslims (like the Garveyites previously) also celebrated and cherished many of the basic values and aspirations of the white petit-bourgeois American society that they superficially appeared to loathe and despise. Indeed, for all their virulent and contemptuous denunciations of the evil white man and congenitally oppressive "blue-eyed devils," the Black Muslims assiduously modeled themselves after certain familiar and conventionally "white" middle-class American ideals: personal clean-liness, fastidious care of the home, thrift, sobriety, diligent and honest hard work (even for a white employer), and obedience to civil authorities—except on grounds of religious obligation—all became moral duties incumbent upon NoI members. Although, therefore, the Black Muslims vehemently rejected the evil white man, they zealously embraced his Protestant ethic, nonetheless. [21]

Having rapidly acquired sufficient African-American support-ers and finance to procure a temple for the NoI, Fard was thus able during 1930–33 to attract many of the former followers of Drew Ali and members of the much larger UNIA to join his fledgling black nationalist organization. Like the previous movements, the NoI's history was to prove extremely turbulent. Unlike its immediate spiritual predecessors, however, the NoI was destined to enjoy an institutional longevity and a political future of substantial consequence.

From Fard to Farrakhan: The Nation of Islam in Transition

Farrakhan's political and religious socialization within the NoI has evolved with each of the three distinct stages of political development that the organization has undergone since its initial establishment by Fard in 1930: fundamentalist separatism, liberalization and reform, and revived fundamentalism. Each period was associated with a par-ticular leader of the organization, one who powerfully shaped its doc-trinal beliefs and activities according to his personal tenets and particular perceptions of both the demands and opportunities of con-temporary circumstances. The two earliest stages also contributed very powerfully to Farrakhan's theological and political education, providing him with the peculiar intellectual legacy and spiritual bal-last that have robustly supported his gradual but inexorable ascent to the ranks of national African-American political leadership in the 1990s.

The first phase of the NoI's development, *fundamentalist separatism*, occurred between 1930 and 1964. It was during this period that the Bilalian faith to which Farrakhan so assiduously subscribes assumed its first coherent, if curious, shape. Fard, a traveling salesman, proclaimed in his teachings to black Americans in Detroit that he was a direct descendant of the Prophet Muhammad, his spiritual mission on Earth being to retrieve "The Dead Nation in the West." This nation comprised all American blacks, who had collectively lost their original Islamic faith and, with it, their true self-knowledge as Allah's chosen people, as a result of the peculiar institution of slavery and egregiously harmful white Christian indoctrination. Arrested in May 1933 in connection with a human sacrifice (described in police reports of the time as a "voodoo murder"), Fard was never charged, but was nonetheless ordered by concerned local authorities to leave Detroit.

Assuming the name Elijah Muhammad, Robert Poole rapidly took over the NoI's leadership from Fard. Widely held responsible for Fard's apparently mysterious and untimely disappearance, Muhammad fled several death threats from disgruntled NoI members and rapidly reestablished the organization in Chicago, Illinois, where he first enunciated two of the most important Bilalian doctrines: that Fard had in fact been Allah in human form, and that he, Elijah, was in turn the holy Messenger of Allah. (If necessity is indeed the mother of invention, this new doctrinal departure was certainly very convenient and effective for Elijah in explaining Fard's disappearance to his discontented followers.) Eventually arrested and incarcerated in 1942 for avoiding the U.S. military draft and allegedly being sympathetic to the Japanese cause during World War II, Elijah nonetheless continued to direct his movement from prison, with the outside assistance of his wife. Upon his final release in 1946, Elijah returned to his proselytizing religious work in full.

Under Elijah, Black Islam rapidly became synonymous not only with the Bilalian theology but also with the doctrine of black separatism, by now a well-established and increasingly important strand of American black nationalism. Elijah's NoI advocated separate black development in all spheres, and promoted both collective and individual racial self-reliance and self-assertion as the only legitimate and effective black responses to racial segregation in the United States (both de jure in the American South and de facto in the North). These injunctions essentially entailed the creation of an entirely separate black economy within the United States and the fostering of an identifiable and clear black American national consciousness. The black separatist creed was also a shrewd political recruitment strategy explicitly targeted at disadvantaged, poorer black Americans in the country's major urban centers. Combined with a rigorously conservative code of personal morality, the NoI promoted thrift and sobriety, and strongly disapproved of all displays of hedonism or frivolity, among both members and nonmembers, in African-American communities. Drinking, drug-taking, smoking, fornication, adultery, sexual promiscuity, gambling, lying, stealing, and all forms of idleness among black Americans were entirely prohibited by Elijah and were made punishable by suspension and, ultimately, expulsion from the organization.

The NoI's second stage, *reform and liberalization* (1965–78) was associated with the dramatic internal crisis of 1964–65, and the subsequent rebuilding process. The organization's activism and national public profile among both black and white Americans had received a particular boost during the late 1950s and early 1960s from the activism of the charismatic African-American figure, Malcolm X.[22] Although Malcolm's effective political career was relatively short—lasting from 1952 to 1965—and while several assessments persuasively concur that his political and social influence was much greater in death than during his life,[23] most of it was spent as a loyally devoted follower of, and an extremely dynamic and compelling spokesman for, Elijah Muhammad. Like many of the organization's recruits both before and after, the former drug pusher and pimp had first been converted to the Islamic faith and the NoI while in prison, and he subsequently rose rapidly within the organization to become one of Elijah's most effective, trusted, and dedicated lieutenants in the Black Muslim movement.

A combination, however, of Malcolm's formidable personal power base within the Nation of Islam, his growing popular support among black Americans at large, his increasingly critical attitude to traditional Bilalian doctrines, and his vocal criticisms of Elijah's personal conduct (after revelations concerning the latter's fathering several children through illicit relationships with female NoI members) caused pronounced tensions within the black organization. Malcolm's inopportune description of President John F. Kennedy's assassination, in November 1963, as a case of "chickens coming home to roost" provided Elijah Muhammad with an appropriately convenient pretext upon which to discipline and suspend his preeminent but increasingly errant disciple from the role of national representative, in late 1963 and early 1964.

These increasingly disturbing tensions were rapidly transformed into a formal and irrevocable split between Malcolm and the NoI after his return from a holy pilgrimage to Mecca in 1964, during which Malcolm had experienced a profound feeling of genuine brothership with Muslims of all races. The Mecca *hajj* encouraged Malcolm to convert to the orthodox Sunni Muslim faith and to found two new rival religious and political organizations to Elijah's NoI in the United States: the Muslim Mosque, Inc. and the Organization for Afro-American Unity, respectively. Although both organizations remained closed to white Americans, Malcolm now rejected the core Bilalian belief that whites were intrinsically evil and accepted the legitimate possibility of engaging in selective cooperation with politically sympathetic white Americans in pursuit of racial equality, comity, and economic justice in the United States.[24]

Such clearly heretical views inevitably earned widespread denunciation and fierce criticism from within the increasingly discordant ranks of the Nation of Islam, though not, publicly at least, from Elijah Muhammad personally. Farrakhan, despite (or, perhaps, partially because of) his previous closeness to Malcolm, notoriously denounced him as a "dog" in the NoI's house newspaper, *Muhammad Speaks*, declaring prophetically that:

> Only those who wish to be led to hell or to their doom will follow Malcolm. The die is set, and Malcolm shall not escape . . . Such a man as Malcolm is worthy of death.[25]

After receiving several death threats and surviving a bomb attack upon his family home, Malcolm X was eventually gunned down in controversial circumstances in Harlem's Audubon Ballroom, on February 21, 1965.[26] Although Farrakhan subsequently was widely incriminated in the plot to murder Malcolm, the minister reiterated in a speech in March 1994 that he had had "nothing to do with Malcolm's death." Farrakhan nonetheless conceded that he was among those influential contemporary black American figures who had "created an atmosphere that allowed Malcolm to be assassinated." Betty Shabazz, Malcolm's widow, was long convinced that

Farrakhan was indeed complicit in the murder, arguing that "everybody talked about it" and that its role for Farrakhan functioned as an invaluable, unmistakable, and morbidly distinctive "badge of honor" within the NoI thereafter.[27]

The NoI nonetheless gradually recovered from the consuming crisis precipitated by Malcolm's untimely demise. By the 1970s, the organization began to make an increasingly concerted political appeal to the growing black American middle class and to temper the more virulently offensive expressions of its traditional antiwhite racism. The NoI acquired a multimillion dollar corporate empire, including a bank, publishing facilities, an airplane, an import business, orchards, dairies, small businesses, 4200 acres of farmland, apartment complexes, a nationwide chain of supermarkets, barber shops, restaurants and clothing stores, over one hundred temples across the country, and a "palace" in Arizona. Its total assets were estimated by Lincoln to be worth between 80 and 100 million dollars.[28] Although several political, civil, and religious groups possessed significantly larger memberships and greater national political legitimacy among African-Americans, few could claim comparably extensive financial support.

Following Elijah's death in 1975, his son, Wallace Deen Muhammad, acceded to the NoI's leadership, as Farrakhan feared and many NoI insiders had both hoped and confidently predicted. As Marsh observed, upon assuming his father's leadership mantle, the strategic political choice confronting Wallace during the mid-1970s was between three stark alternatives: to continue to seek to change the nature of American society by acquiring a separate state, either therein or in Africa, exclusively for black Americans; to advocate the complete cultural separation of the races in America; or to alter substantially the organization's religious and political doctrines to become more fully compatible with the pluralist nature of the United States' social and political structures. Wallace chose the latter course and, for the subsequent three years, advanced an extensive, unprecedented, and extremely controversial reform process in the NoI.

The reforms ranged in both scope and importance. Most contentiously, the core doctrine of the intrinsic evil of whites was revised and modified to describe instead a more diffuse "devil mentality," which motivated some individual whites to commit evil deeds. Consonant with such reformist notions, whites were even invited by Wallace to join the organization. Demands for a separate American state for blacks were also abandoned, and members of the NoI were encouraged both to honor the American flag and to vote in elections to public office. The theological doctrines of the NoI were altered to conform more closely to orthodox Sunni Islam beliefs. Significantly, the interior decor of the NoI's mosques saw Arabic motifs replace the anti-American and anti-Christian symbols and slogans that had previously adorned the walls. The strict dress and grooming code of Elijah's organization was abandoned in favor of individual preferences, subject to the basic requirement that clothes remained neat, clean, and nondegrading to Islam. Presiding over such a radical relaxation of the NoI's strict codes of discipline, dress, and rules of personal morality, and dismantling the Fruit of Islam, the militia-style force of young men trained in martial arts (and sometimes firearms) who dealt with all aspects of the group's internal discipline and security, Wallace's leadership constituted the most profound and serious challenge to traditionalist conceptions of the Nation as an unorthodox black separatist, racist, and repressive cult.

Inevitably, such far-reaching reforms encountered strong internal opposition, sufficient ultimately to usher in the third and current stage of the NoI's development, *revived fundamentalism* (1978 to the present). The emergence of the third phase followed an irretrievably deep split between Wallace and Farrakhan, with the former becoming head of the larger and less sectarian World Community of Islam (WCI, within the United States, the American Muslim Mission [AMM]), while the latter assumed the NoI's leadership in 1978, announcing its eventual "rebirth" in January 1981. The WCI (disbanded in 1985) represented a nonexclusive entity that comprised Muslims who believe in Islam; rather than conceiving of themselves as Black Muslims, they were simply Muslims.[29] Farrakhan's group, by contrast, remained inextricably wedded to the unorthodox fundamentalism of Elijah's NoI.

The split—tellingly referred to in NoI circles subsequently as "The Fall of the Nation of Islam"—was occasioned by the increasingly stark and ultimately irreconcilable differences in opinion between Wallace and Farrakhan over the organization's racial vocation and religious philosophy after Elijah's death. Farrakhan had occupied a position as the international spokesman of the NoI under the Wallace interregnum but soon announced his departure in December 1977. He believed adamantly that the move to Orthodox Islam that Wallace had pioneered had caused a substantial decrease in the organization's financial assets and had also contributed powerfully to an increasing lack of discipline among its members, both individually and collectively. Farrakhan, as subsequent developments under his leadership would clearly demonstrate, maintained an uncompromising belief in the fundamentalist doctrines that had been enunciated and propagated by Wallace's father and by Fard Muhammad before him. As a matter of both theological faith and political strategy, Farrakhan held that the NoI's original doctrinal tenets were still central to its continued organizational vitality, its future prospects for recruiting new black members, and the likelihood of increasing its political influence among black Americans in general.

The internal power play also reflected the increasing marginalization of Farrakhan that Wallace Muhammad's acceding to the NoI's leadership appeared, at least to the former, clearly to presage. For Farrakhan, Wallace's assumption of the NoI's premier role entailed deep personal distress, as much for the manifest threat that it posed his demagogic national career prospects as for the material theological and organizational reforms that Wallace sincerely favored. Wallace Muhammad, for his part, perceived Farrakhan's new organization as markedly more political than religious in character. Elijah's son argued that it represented Farrakhan's attempt to stay abreast of the black political freedom movement.[30] The implicit critique was that Farrakhan's opportunism and desire for personal publicity as a serious player in national African-American politics weighed far more heavily upon his personal ambitions than did the Islamic faith to which he regularly paid the most lavish public tribute. Even the most charitable interpretations of Farrakhan's subsequent leadership of the NoI could not easily reject the accuracy of the Wallace interpretation.

For prior to Farrakhan's coup, most scholarly assessments of the NoI held the organization to have been of extremely limited political importance and effect in the United States. Prevailing views saw the black nationalist group as one that primarily promoted agitation and violence[31] and whose prison inmates could not safely be treated like followers of other religions[32]; as an unashamedly racist sect and a personality cult centered principally upon a visceral, collective black hatred of whites[33]; and as the religious dimension of racial strife in America and a genuine danger to American society.[34] In all these interpretations, however, the religious bounds to the NoI's activism were universally viewed as central. Resolutely eschewing participation in the growing civil rights movement, in which thousands of

African-Americans risked their very lives to achieve desegregation in the South, the NoI historically stood expressly outside that conflictual southern theater and, hence, occupied a place on the margins of black American society.

Critics such as Norton have therefore held the NoI's role among African-Americans to have been very limited. That the organization contributed to elevating black Americans' perceptions of their self-worth is conceded by him as an achievement of note. Even in increasing the level of collective race consciousness among northern urban black Americans, however, the NoI encouraged African-Americans to look beyond the NoI for effective political activism, thus compounding the group's political impotence and rendering it fundamentally unable to advance in either membership terms or national black prestige from 1965 onward. Marx, too, attributed the Black Muslims' fundamental lack of political success to the religiously derived separatist dimensions of the organization and to the related fact that black Americans "want in, not out" of mainstream America.[35]

The resurgence of the NoI under Farrakhan, however, has profoundly challenged such complacent assessments. Although Farrakhan's project has been unerringly attentive to opportunities for personal self-aggrandizement, the organization's revival and revitalization—and, not least, its securing new popularity, respect, and prestige—has also been integral to the minister's political advance. The third stage of the NoI's development reflects the dual forces of continuity and change upon which Farrakhan's strategic leadership calculus was originally founded: the former, in the decision explicitly to return the NoI to its traditional theological precepts and organizational disciplines; the latter, in the innovative and unprecedented participation of the NoI in American politics. Above all, though, the NoI's resurgent popularity and the success of the Farrakhan phenomenon have represented functions of the broader changes of post–civil rights era America, which have caused many black Americans to doubt both the possibility and the desirability of ever breaking "in" to the American political, social, and economic mainstream. In response, many have found in the NoI and its charismatic leader new and attractive sources of collective support, solidarity, and even potential salvation.

FARRAKHAN AS LEADER: THE POLITICS OF RADICAL REACTION

Although the political dimension of the NoI's activities under Farrakhan represented a substantial and dramatic departure from its traditional organizational role and doctrinal precepts, the group none-theless displayed substantial continuity with its first incarnation, under Fard and Elijah Muhammad. Upon assuming the leadership of the NoI in 1978, Farrakhan charted an explicit course of rebuilding and revitalizing the organization by reviving its original fundamental-ist theological values and beliefs, and by reintroducing the doctrinaire internal organizational codes and rigid practices that had existed under Elijah's lengthy period as leader. Farrakhan's leadership thus represented the most unequivocal rejection and comprehensive repu-diation of the liberalizing course upon which Wallace Muhammad had embarked in 1975.

Evaluations of the overall organizational success of Farrakhan's leadership strategy are heavily complicated by the unavailability of accurate statistics on the NoI's membership base. Speculative assess-ments by social scientists and media commentators have varied dramatically, even wildly. Dennis King, for example, estimated a membership of around 5,000–10,000 in 1985,[36] whereas Farzana Shaikh argued in favor of a figure of "less than 50,000" in 1990 (this compared with figures for the less sectarian AMM of between 150,000 and almost 1,000,000).[37] C. Eric Lincoln, however, contends that a black membership of between 70,000 and 100,000 in 1993 is "consis-tent with what is known about other aspects of the community."[38] Most critical estimates nonetheless tend to converge around an approximation of only 10,000–20,000 formal NoI members.

Evaluating Farrakhan's political achievement in recruitment terms alone, however, is a very misleading indicator of the effective-ness of his leadership of the NoI since 1978. The NoI's members and publications alike consistently and strongly emphasize that the orga-nization's influence within the national black American community and beyond should not be judged, either exclusively or principally, by the number of its formal, registered members, an argument that is largely persuasive in the light of its evolution during the last two decades. Members of the NoI adhere tenaciously to the (conveniently enigmatic) public maxim that "those who say they know don't know and those who know won't say." More important, however, Farra-khan's political ambitions upon assuming the organization's leader-ship were neither exclusively nor primarily concerned with recruiting new, bona fide members of the NoI. Rather, as Reed argued, the objec-tive that Farrakhan sought in terms of his popular appeal among African-Americans occupied an "intermediate zone" of mass black endorsement, lying somewhere between actual membership of the NoI and a more pro forma popular black American legitimation.[39]

That Farrakhan has largely achieved this core objective is especially notable when the actual content of the NoI's belief system is examined. For the NoI under Farrakhan comprises, at best, a very distinctive—even uniquely eccentric and bizarre—amalgam of cosmological, religious, and ideological currents. Together, these tendencies render the NoI entirely exceptional within the universe of national organizations in the United States dedicated to the improvement of black Americans' political, economic, and social fortunes in the post–civil rights era. Indeed, it is, ironically, in this very distinctiveness, in standing so vividly apart from other black organizations, that much of both the NoI's popular appeal and the most formidable limits to its potential social impact reside among the national African-American community.

Cosmology

The NoI's status as a cosmocentric community accords an exceptionally strong priority to two overarching organizational precepts: first, the need for complete conformity and obedience by its members to authority figures and established doctrines, and second, the preeminent and infallible role of the organization's leader. Membership in the NoI powerfully resembles that of a sectarian political movement, requiring energetic and complete devotion to the cause, enthusiastic imbibing of its canonical sources of collective wisdom, and regular recitation of the required mantras of faith.[40] To be a member in the NoI demands belonging fully to the group, in "body, mind, and spirit," in return for which the NoI belongs to its constituency, corporately and individually. The organization's achievements and mystique are thus replicated in each true believer. The group's primary unifying bond derives from direct, personal allegiance to its leader's exceptional vision, wisdom, will, program, and putative indestructibility. Salvation for individual members consists essentially in the recognition by, and approbation of, the leader, and hence is attainable in this life. In such an avowedly cosmocentric society, as Lincoln argues, "there can be but one loyalty, and it must be to one leader."[41]

The emphasis traditionally accorded the leadership role in the NoI has been of particular political importance for Farrakhan. It is the preeminence accorded the central role of unquestioned fidelity to the leader that Farrakhan has invoked not only to bolster his own position of political authority internally within the NoI, but also as an explanation—to both NoI members and outsiders—for his actions and pronouncements against Malcolm X in 1964–65. Thus, in explicit reference to the NoI's internal mores and codes of practice, in a speech in 1993, Farrakhan said of Malcolm's murder that, "if we dealt with him like a nation deals with a traitor, what the hell business is it of yours?"[42] According to Farrakhan, only the personal instructions of Elijah Muhammad not to harm Malcolm prevented him (and others in the Black Muslim movement) from engaging in more concerted and vigorous attempts to undermine Malcolm in order to assuage the compromised honor of the then leader of the NoI. The doctrine of leadership infallibility has thus served as an extremely useful and powerful legitimating device for Farrakhan, not only in defending his past actions as a loyal and dedicated follower, but also in compelling continual support among the NoI's members currently for his innovative strategic and tactical political decisions, and doctrinal interpretations, as the group's leader since 1978.

Theology and Ideology

Conjoined to its unusual cosmological currents is a distinctive ideological set of beliefs, one that is informed and driven by a theological foundation that is as logically coherent (accept its initial premise, and the rest follows logically) as it is intellectually vapid and morally bankrupt. At its most fundamental, the Nation's ideology combines a stridently aggressive black nationalism with a series of profoundly conservative economic tenets and social convictions. The peculiar combination of biblical allusion, racial militancy, and reactionary public philosophy is one that renders the NoI distinctive and unusual in comparative terms. It also serves to lend the organization and its leader a degree of public ambiguity, in terms of their appropriate ideological locus, that has strongly assisted the broad and amorphous appeal of Farrakhan and the NoI to African-Americans at large.

The NoI's separatist version of black nationalism is most obviously manifest in the organization's core political aims, which comprise: separate black economic and social development; employment and educational equality; freedom for black prisoners; rejection of all attempts at integration with whites; and the achievement of a separate, mineral-rich state (or states) for black Americans as minimum compensation for slavery.[43] Such goals represent relatively familiar core features of the ideological content of the programs of many black nationalist groups since (and, in some instances, prior to) the civil rights movement's landmark political successes during the 1960s.[44] Indeed, the symbolic continuity with the era of "black power" is made explicitly manifest through Farrakhan's personal links with prominent African-American agitators of the time, such as Kwame Toure (formerly Stokely Carmichael), probably the most influential popularizer of that famous slogan. Toure is one of a select group of favored black American political activists—past and present—regularly invited to address larger NoI gatherings, immediately prior to Farrakhan's keynote speeches. The racially separatist political goals of the NoI are not, then, particularly novel in comparison with other black American nationalist groups.

The separatist black nationalism of the NoI under Farrakhan, however, is infused by an explicitly religious dimension that is at once central, esoteric, and frequently overlooked or ignored in both elite and popular evaluations of the organization and its leader. The key feature of Farrakhan's public discourse is not so much its black nationalist or separatist character, which is shared in more or less muted forms by many historic and contemporary black political actors and organizations alike, but rather its particular and peculiar theocratic content, which is shared by none at all. For Farrakhan, neither he, the NoI, nor its members are primarily political actors, in the conventional sense of that term. Rather, they are religious disciples, spiritual warriors engaged upon a divine mission of racial revival and national salvation that is ultimately of nothing less than global importance. The political dimensions of the NoI's activities are principally a function (or, more accurately, an indirect consequence) of its central and dominant religious vocation. Although the theological and spiritual dimensions of Farrakhan's NoI are often neglected or minimized in popular accounts that tend to stress instead its racial militancy and uncompromisingly separatist creedo, the "Islam" component of the organization's title is in fact at least as significant as that of the "Nation." Moreover, the theological origins of Farrakhan's belief system have important political consequences in both ideological and strategic terms for Farrakhan's ongoing public praxis in and outside America.

Theology

Central to both Farrakhan's determined rise within the pre-1975 organization and his subsequent public activities and pronouncements as its leader since 1978 are the two key figures of W. D. Fard and Elijah Muhammad. Together, their theological teachings form the foundation stone upon which the entire edifice of Farrakhan's religious and political faith, and in turn public behavior, is shakily and unattractively constructed. As Elijah's former national representative to America and the world, and subsequently as leader of the NoI, Farrakhan's conception of his national role has been inextricably tied to these two men and their combined social and spiritual legacy: to representing his God (Fard) and spiritual father (Elijah) while the latter was alive and, subsequently, to resurrecting their divinely enlightened teachings after Elijah's death.

According to Bilalian tenets, Elijah was God's solitary student for three years and four to five months (that is, until Fard's untimely disappearance). Farrakhan was thus guided and taught by God, through his final messenger on Earth, Elijah. Thus, Farrakhan and members of the NoI are completely convinced in the fundamental rightness—indeed, the complete infallibility—of the values, analyses, and prescriptions to which they zealously adhere, since these are all divinely derived and therefore possess a uniquely righteous, and hence unchallengeable, authority. As Farrakhan's opening remarks to the National Press Club on July 30, 1984, proclaimed:

> I represent the Honorable Elijah Muhammad, a Messenger and Warner from Allah to Black people, and the world. I do not speak to you from mere personal desire, I speak in the Name of the God who raised up the Honorable Elijah Muhammad and I am backed by them both.[45]

Like Malcolm before him, Farrakhan frequently prefaces his public remarks by stating, "The Honorable Elijah Muhammad teaches that..." Farrakhan's "voice" is therefore most assuredly not one of complete autonomy and independence, but rather that of the most loyal and assiduous student, articulating a litany of divinely revealed truths and prophecies, conveyed directly and personally by the holiest and most infallible of enlightened spiritual teachers.

Farrakhan's frequent self-reference as simply a dedicated student of Elijah serves three important political functions for the NoI's leader. First, it enables him to draw upon an historic lineage that is unavailable to many other contemporary national black American political leaders. Farrakhan's political entrepreneurship is not a matter of personal career aggrandizement or advancement, in this interpretation, but is instead located within deep historic roots and in direct encounters with (and instructions from) God's final messenger on Earth. Second, and connected to such a powerful historic lineage, the self-reference provides a useful pretext of personal modesty and deep humility to a political role that is, in every other respect, based upon the most persistent self-promotion and the steady but unrelenting accumulation of nationwide political attention centered unremittingly upon the individual leader. Third, the avowed student status underlies Farrakhan's recurrent public claims that both he and the organization that he leads are frequently misrepresented in and by the American mass media. Farrakhan's erroneous ascriptive designation as "leader" of the NoI by print and television commentators—when he is a mere representative and a follower of its genuine spiritual leader—is portrayed by him as an example of the deliberate failure (or the clear inability) of outsiders accurately and fully to understand the Black Muslim movement, its structure, and its most cherished beliefs.

As his Million Man March speech demonstrated to a national American audience, Farrakhan draws liberally upon both the Koran and the Bible to support his many claims. An accomplished and keen student of scripture, Farrakhan invokes apposite parables and verses at ease. The shrewd strategy reflects both his own early Christian upbringing and the tactical necessity of appealing to the mass of African-Americans by invoking their own religious beliefs. In doctrinal terms, however, the two most important sources of instruction for Farrakhan's theological claims and political arguments—as for Malcolm X before him—are Elijah Muhammad's treatises, *Message to the Black Man in America* and *The Fall of America*.[46] Together, these turgid tomes serve as the twin functional theological equivalents for Farrakhan that Karl Marx's secular *Communist Manifesto* and *Capital* once represented for Lenin and Trotsky. Farrakhan's contemporary public discourse and rhetoric flow directly from what Elijah taught him between 1934 and 1975 and from the divine pearls of collected wisdom contained in the two texts. If Farrakhan departs from Elijah's voice at all as the NoI's contemporary leader, it is merely to accord his mentor's beliefs greater conceptual clarity, and to lend them a more modern application, where such is either necessary or desirable (such as in endorsing Jesse Jackson's 1984 presidential bid as divinely sanctioned and blessed, for example).

Four distinct, though related, features of the religious dimension that is contained in Elijah's writings are especially prominent, important, and, to many Americans, utterly preposterous features of Farrakhan's public discourse: first, the biblical ancestry of African-Americans; second, the inevitable and violent fall of America in a global apocalypse; third, the overarching need for separation of the races in the United States prior to God's final judgment and the resulting Armageddon; and, fourth, Farrakhan's personal status as a messianic figure and prophetic race savior. Collectively, these beliefs serve powerfully to distinguish the NoI not only from other Islamic groups, but also from every other organization seeking currently to improve black Americans' political, economic, and social welfare in the United States. Together, the beliefs mark Farrakhan vividly apart from all other African-American leaders. Although muted or accorded varying degrees of emphasis according to the particular venue, occasion, and (actual or intended) audience, these four convictions are, nonetheless, absolutely fundamental to Farrakhan's worldview.

Central to the black nationalism of the NoI under Farrakhan is a core theological belief in the privileged biblical ancestry of black Americans collectively. In an ironic mirror of Judaistic belief in the Jews' role as the Almighty's "chosen" people, the 30 million-plus black Americans in the United States currently represent, for Farrakhan, "God's elect." According to Farrakhan, the "peculiar institution" of black slavery in America was an historic inevitability, since it was actually preordained and divinely sanctioned by Allah (God). The presence of blacks in America therefore assumes a major religious significance, their current condition being fundamentally prophetic in nature. The shameful and tragic character of blacks' history in America marks them out for their divine status. The Bible prophesied a people living at the temporal end of the world to whom a "warner" would be sent and, among the four "races" of the world (according to Farrakhan, Jews, whites, Muslims, and blacks), only blacks had not yet received such an enlightened visitor by 1930.

The basis for Farrakhan's idiosyncratic view, and the foundation upon which the NoI's predictive assertions of imminent black American deliverance rest, is typically identified as being the Book of Genesis, chapter 15, verses 13–14:

And he God said unto Abraham, know of a surety that thy seed shall be a stranger in a land that is not theirs, and shall serve them, and they shall afflict them four hundred years; And also that nation whom they shall serve, will I judge; and afterward shall they come out with great substance.

Black Americans are argued by Farrakhan to be the direct descendants of the family of the biblical Abraham, the "lost-found nation of the tribe of Shabazz" and the seed of God. Forcibly removed from the continent of Africa in the 1500s, the descendants of the tribe were brutally imported, as private property, to the land that subsequently became known as America. The present black American population is thus the direct progeny of the original Shabazz tribe.

The peculiar institution of slavery in the United States was therefore unavoidable, since it formed part of a broader plan designed by God some 6000 years previously. However, after a period of 430 years of painful oppression, the Book of Exodus notes that the children of Israel eventually left their land of bondage to achieve their true liberation. The date of black Americans' freedom was thus set, according to Farrakhan, for midnight, December 31, 1985, some 430 years after their initial bondage in America. Fard's arrival in 1930 was designed to alert African-Americans to the circumstances of their plight and the methods by which freedom could be secured by that date, fifty-five years hence. Had Elijah not recognized his divine credentials, however, Fard would have left America earlier than 1934, and the fate of African-Americans would have thereby been irretrievably sealed in doom-laden perpetuity.[47]

This belief distinguishes Farrakhan sharply from the vast majority of contemporary national black American political and civic leaders in two key respects. First, while most black religious, civic, and political leaders would undoubtedly concur that black American history—and the turbulent shape of America's social and political development in general—has been profoundly influenced by African-Americans' forced importation to America as private property, few (if any) would accord the peculiar institution the pervasively malign influence that Farrakhan discerns. For Farrakhan, however, the present condition of blacks in America is by definition inseparable from, and is adequately explained by, the slave period. The origins of black Americans have ensured that they remain a totally "invented" people, without a homeland either in America or Africa, materially impoverished, emotionally crippled, and psychologically destitute. The Thirteenth Amendment admitted into American society as full participants a social group whose members were wholly unprepared and unsuited for their new status. Slavery was deliberately intended, originally, to bring about the creation of a new type of earthly being, neither necessarily nor fully human in character. According to Farrakhan, even the term "Negro" originated not from the Spanish word for "black," but rather from the Greek term "necropolis," meaning "cemetery" or "place of the dead." Black Americans are thus conceived by Farrakhan to be psychologically, spiritually, and emotionally dead and, hence, in need of the most complete and enlightened reeducation, a function that he and the NoI under him exist exclusively and selflessly to provide in the most generous of fashions.

The second consequential facet of black Americans' privileged ancestry concerns the date of their divinely prescribed release from collective racial bondage in the United States. The notion of black freedom being set for the beginning of 1986 onward has afforded a clear religious rationale—even a spiritual imperative—for Farrakhan's concerted efforts exponentially to increase the secular activism of the NoI in conventional American politics. Although occurring prior to the date of African-American freedom, the courageous activism of black American civil and political leaders such as Garvey, Du Bois, King, and Malcolm X was not entirely futile, in Farrakhan's view; it served as a necessary foundation for the current black political struggle. Nonetheless, black Americans at large only possessed sufficient potential to achieve their full mental and spiritual independence from 1986 onward. The imperative to reeducate them in order to ensure that they fully realized that potential has therefore served as the central basis for Farrakhan's leading the NoI into hitherto uncharted territories of mass mobilization and "mainstream" political activity, such as voter registration drives and election campaigning. Collective deliverance of African-Americans requires divinely influenced guidance; Farrakhan generously offers such enlightened and spiritually informed leadership at the appropriate historic moment for American blacks.

Linked to black Americans' uniquely privileged biblical ancestry and the momentous historic opportunities of the present is the second crucial constant in Farrakhan's theological black nationalism: belief in the inevitability of the decline, and ultimate fall, of the United States, in what the NoI's leader refers to variously as "the War" and the "Battle of Armageddon." Four centuries of brutal enslavement in America have left black Americans as the "lost sheep," "the dry bones in the valley," and the "despised and rejected." America represents the biblical Babylon; its president is the effective evil King of the corrupt, degenerate, and doomed land; and the cities of Los Angeles and San Francisco serve as its modern Sodom and Gomorrah.[48] Armageddon—the ultimate and decisive conflict between good and evil—will bring about the end of the present, evil, white-dominated world and the illustrious beginning of a newly righteous kingdom of God on Earth, one in which black Americans are finally spiritually, emotionally, and mentally reborn. Although the ensuing apocalypse will be global in scale, the war will commence in America, precisely because of its history of African enslavement and its subsequent mistreatment of American blacks. African-Americans will, nonetheless, emerge as the brave vanguard of human liberation in the war and as its clear eventual victors. Finally achieving true and complete emancipation, their role thereafter in the new righteous world will be to serve as its humanitarian leaders and hortatory teachers, offering appropriately enlightened spiritual instruction both to America and the rest of the world.

The inevitable global conflagration that awaits humanity gives logical rise to the third critical feature of Farrakhan's iconoclastic theological system, namely, the need for the full separation of the races in America prior to the imminent Armageddon. Racial separation is a necessary prerequisite and prelude to the collective judgment that is prophesied in Genesis as being inevitable for both Abraham's offspring and the corrupt Babylonian land that they currently inhabit. God did not desire his chosen people to be linked to their tyrannical master at the time of the latter's punishment, and he therefore encouraged the Israelites to leave the land of Pharaoh to establish their own independent nation. As Farrakhan observes:

> God raises up Moses not to tell Pharaoh "let's get chummy," not to tell Pharaoh "let's integrate," but God came to Pharaoh through Moses to warn Moses that . . . the time of Israel's deliverance had come.[49]

In this interpretation, the bondage of Jews by the Egyptians was not historical fact but rather prophetic allegory—the Jews of the Bible are the black Americans of today, not the Jews of ancient times.

The need for racial separation in America further reflects the inherent evil of the white race. Whites, along with all nonblack races, were originally conceived in a failed medical experiment on the island of Patmos by a mad black scientist named Dr. Yakub, a troublesome malcontent who was exiled from an original black Eden centered in Mecca, many thousands of years ago.[50] The most degenerate of all the half-breed races, whites were accorded the role of persecuting blacks, until the appearance of an enlightened Messenger (Fard). The Messenger would alert blacks to their true state, the real nature of their white oppressors, and the means by which genuine and lasting freedom could best be attained. Farrakhan's version of history also bears out the original doctrinal teachings of Fard, according to which whites have indeed been responsible for most of the evil that has occurred in the world. People of color, in particular, have consistently been the subject of white abuse and assault through colonialism, imperialism, and segregation, and so, for Farrakhan, the imperative for black Americans to distance themselves absolutely from such manifestly evil forces is self-evidently great.

The precise form that the necessary and complete separation of the races must assume has varied in character and over time, from an ambitious Garveyesque goal of physical and territorial separation to a somewhat more modest objective of mental and cultural retrenchment. Initially, the NoI sought the achievement of independent black territory or a block of mineral-rich American states to be set aside as a black homeland, owned, maintained, and developed exclusively for and by African-Americans. This remains the goal of the demands printed each week in *The Final Call*. Over recent years, however, the emphasis in Farrakhan's lectures and sermons has increasingly altered toward stressing a mental and cultural separation from white America.[51] Black Americans must, by this interpretation, studiously refrain from adopting "white" American norms, values, ideologies, mores, folkways, and lifestyles. Only through a true and complete knowledge of both Allah and self can black Americans achieve their full and authentic independence of thought and action as human beings. Whether physical or mental, though, the attempts that have been made in the postwar era in general, and the post–civil rights era in particular, to integrate the races in America have vividly demonstrated to Farrakhan the total futility of hope for peaceful coexistence between the races and the centrality of misguided integrative efforts to the United States' current (and, should such foolish efforts persist, future) racial problems.

The NoI's emphasis under Farrakhan on racial separation echoes the arguments of the Kerner Report on Civil Disorder in 1968, albeit with an implicit enthusiasm rather than explicit regret. Indeed, Farrakhan even cited Otto Kerner's famous conclusions in his speech at the Million Man March. Established by President Lyndon B. Johnson to investigate the sources of and potential solutions to America's urban crises of the mid to late 1960s, the Commission report represented a damning indictment of the contemporary condition of relations between black and white citizens in America. Prescriptively, Kerner argued that, in the absence of meaningful and effective public and private action to reduce the socioeconomic differences between the races, within twenty years the distance between black and white Americans would have become so wide as to be unbridgeable. Unity and comity would become impossible. Black and white Americans would physically inhabit the same nation but they would do so as two effectively separate, unequal, and hostile communities.

For Farrakhan, by the mid-1980s, American politics and society were indeed replete with multifarious indications of black and white relations in the United States having finally, completely, and irrevocably exhausted themselves. Among white Americans, the resurgence of the Ku Klux Klan, Aryan Nation, and other white supremacist groups; the several antiaffirmative action decisions of the U.S. Supreme Court under Chief Justices Warren Burger and William Rehnquist; the conservative policies of successive Republican administrations; and the incidence of sporadic, violent attacks upon black Americans and black institutions by whites all represented powerful symptoms of a white America that was attempting, increasingly and aggressively, to free itself from the troublesome aftermath of slavery and its unwanted black legacy. Among African-Americans too, growing disorder, rebelliousness, and disrespect for what were widely perceived as white-controlled institutions, laws, and practices suggested to Farrakhan that the great U.S. racial divide was widening even further in an inexorable fashion. Subconsciously, at least, black Americans were gradually responding to a majority-white nation that neither needed its black members any longer, nor cared for them, nor even knew precisely what to do with them. Otto Kerner's fears were thus being fully realized in the most dramatic and unequivocal of fashions.

Such clear signs of increasingly imminent racial crisis of course offered rewarding opportunities to advance the fourth feature of Farrakhan's theological worldview: his own, personal role as the prophetic race savior. The German philosopher Hegel once defined the "great man" as being the one "who actualizes his age." And in his words and deeds since assuming the NoI's leadership, Farrakhan manifestly conceives himself to be a great man—a messianic and prophetic figure of destiny whose historic hour had finally arrived. The biblical analogy is clear, after all. Black Americans resemble the people to whom Jesus arose, a people possessing eyes but not sight, ears but not hearing, tongues but not speech. Farrakhan views his national task as being to activate the dormant senses and the stunted critical faculties of black Americans at large. For Farrakhan, "Jesus" is a job description rather than the name of a particular historic figure—a revolutionary opponent of inequality, injustice, and prejudice whose passivity, patience, and tolerance in the face of oppression is a gross misrepresentation of the truth, originally perpetrated upon gullible black Americans by a manipulative and mendacious white slaveowner class, intent upon exercising complete social control and diffusing all forms of African-American protest. If the truth be told, there are in fact five entities known as Jesus, of which he, Farrakhan, (alongside the original Jesus, Fard, Elijah, and NoI members collectively) is one. The language in which Farrakhan's prophetic mission of racial salvation is described hence draws heavily upon resonant biblical images that project him as a beneficent savior of his long-oppressed people:

> I want to provide some comfort for the sheep of Almighty God who have not been led to green pastures, whose soul has not been restored, who have not been led in the path of righteousness for God's namesake. I want to be a good shepherd in the midst of a people who have had thieves and robbers in front of them as leaders. [52]

If the four claims that form the nucleus of Farrakhan's theology evince an undeniably coherent logic (bizarre and incredible, admittedly, but by no means incoherent), they nonetheless raise many more questions than they purport to answer. As a purely theological matter, for example, it is notably unclear how Farrakhan's claim that black slavery in America was preordained by God can be either fully or adequately reconciled with his argument that the United States is ultimately to be judged, and held to final account, by God because of its enslavement of blacks. It would appear, at best, perverse that God should hold to account a nation or people for a course that he had predetermined and for which they could hence exercise no free or conscious choice. The important argument for Farrakhan, though, is that Armageddon, the impending end of the existing (that is, white-dominated) pattern of race relations, and the full emancipation of black Americans is an historical inevitability, according to divine prescription. The apocalyptic conflagration of the races around the world is as inevitable as the sun's rising in the morning.

Of course, Farrakhan's manifest confidence in the inevitability of Armageddon also confronts certain evidential problems in terms of the accuracy of his prophetic analysis. For example, during the early 1980s, Farrakhan predicted—much as he has continued to do so subsequently—that the inevitable racial apocalypse was imminent. President Ronald Reagan then represented a "blessing in disguise" to black Americans, a deliverance from God. Reagan professed a strong personal belief in good and evil; included among his Cabinet and White House staff evangelical Christians who themselves adhered to explicitly fundamentalist conceptions of the ultimate conflict between good and evil; presided over America at the date of blacks' release from the slave mentality (thus making the president the most important white man ever to have lived); and possessed a name (Ronald Wilson Reagan) whose letters, when added sequentially, totaled 666, the notorious biblical number of the Beast.[53] Although God knew that black Americans wanted former Vice-President Walter Mondale to win the 1984 presidential election, he apparently returned Reagan to the White House, in a landslide popular and electoral college victory, to give blacks not what they wanted, but what they instead needed to free themselves, according to Farrakhan. (No doubt the families and accountants of many professional political consultants and media advisors were especially appreciative of GOP operatives' ignorance about the presence of such decisively divine electioneering interventions in 1984.)

Reagan's momentous temporal presence, and the imminent global war that it presaged, thus strongly encouraged Farrakhan's energetic bouts of national activism. In typically individualistic and distinctive fashion, Farrakhan was one of the handful of outspoken national black American leaders during the 1980s to defend the conservative Republican president's personal integrity:

It is not that Mr. Reagan is insensitive. The man is looking at the economy of the country. You do not understand that the economy of the country is so weak today that Mr. Reagan must make cuts in order to save what he can. You know, if you're in an airplane and you lose an engine, they must look around for expendable baggage. "What can we jettison, what can we throw off to make it lighter?" I know you feel bad being in that position, as expendable baggage. Well, that's not Mr. Reagan's fault. That's our fault.[54]

Faced with such a grievously bleak picture, Farrakhan predicted that Reagan would soon proceed to undertake direct negotiations with the NoI's leader, personally, in order to save white America and that, unless this occurred, black Americans would either be "free or dead" by 1990. Americans probably needn't rush en masse to consult the history books at length to discover that these particular predictions were not, in fact, realized. Rather, they attested to a visionary quality on Farrakhan's part that remains more pathetically deficient than divinely prophetic in nature.

Perhaps, in this light, Farrakhan's many luridly colorful convictions should be dismissed as entirely irrelevant to his political importance. Whether on the grounds of the very tenuous and uncertain connection with reality that they manifest, or on the basis that they matter little to the true foundations of his popular appeal among African-Americans, such a view could certainly be plausibly advanced. While the religious beliefs that Farrakhan evinces are, however, at best distinctive and unusual in character, they nonetheless remain central to his view of the destiny of black Americans, as well as the ultimate fate of the United States and the entire world. Although his public discourse since the late 1980s has increasingly avoided a full enunciation of his theological beliefs (especially when white audiences are observing his pronouncements closely, as at the Million Man March), Farrakhan's values, attitudes, and prescriptions for black Americans' collective advancement are all inextricably bound to the revived fundamentalist theological foundation of the NoI. That the vast majority of African-Americans neither know of nor share his exotic theological views has not substantially inhibited his national political ascendancy thus far. Ironically, popular ignorance of Farrakhan's belief system represents a positive element in (and perhaps even a necessary condition of) his achieving mass African-American support. Nevertheless, the tangential relevance of Farrakhan's iconoclastic theology to his

popular black appeal hardly diminishes the profound significance—
and the peculiarity—of such an idiosyncratic public figure winning
broad African-American approval.

Ideology

The impressively eclectic theological dimensions of the Black
Muslim leader's worldview are important not only in themselves, but
also because they powerfully inform and shape the NoI's values, beliefs, and organizational practices more broadly. In particular, by
virtue of its connection to Farrakhan's avowedly theocratic, quasi-
Islamic, and separatist variant of black nationalism, the social, cultural,
and economic conservatism of the NoI is especially pronounced. On
matters of diet, gender, sexual and interracial relations, as well as
economic philosophy, Farrakhan's NoI endorses a markedly conservative—indeed, a quintessentially reactionary—agenda for African-
Americans and nonblacks alike. Like many conservatives, Farrakhan
zealously champions and celebrates what one critic has labeled the
"vigorous virtues" (most notably, independence, personal responsibility, and individual initiative).[55] Farrakhan's ideal American world,
however, is one in which professional women, unmarried mothers,
homosexuals, mixed-race couples, and free-thinkers are all decidedly
unwelcome. At once profoundly inegalitarian, strongly conformist,
deeply illiberal, and blessed by an expressly divine and infallible
imprimatur, Farrakhan's desperately bleak and dispiriting vision is a
reactionary's delight and an Epicurean's nightmare.

The critical religious and racial imperatives to reject dominant
American values, mores, and lifestyles that form such a prominent element of Farrakhan's worldview inevitably compel a profound alteration in the general behavioral patterns of the NoI's members.
Following Elijah's instructions and adhering to a strictly orthodox
interpretation of the Koran, strong emphasis therefore is attached
within the NoI to a very strict dietary code and to the tenets of personal discipline, respectable appearance and dress, individual responsibility, and an unremitting loyalty to the organization's leadership.

In achieving an effective mental and cultural separation from
whites, diet represents an especially important component of black
independence in modern America. Both Elijah and Farrakhan consistently stress the overarching imperative to end completely African-
American consumption of the "slave master's diet," and Elijah's

strictures and injunctions on the subject are regularly reprinted in weekly copies of *The Final Call*. For example, Elijah attributed the high incidence among black Americans of serious health problems, such as diabetes, heart disease, hypertension, and cancer, to an excessive intake by African-Americans of carbohydrates, sugars, and pork products, against which "divine" prohibitions were issued.[56] Fasting was also emphasized by Elijah as an especially desirable goal to which NoI members should dedicate themselves to achieving.

Farrakhan, too, has attributed the primary cause of many contemporary black health problems to African-Americans having never been properly taught how or what to eat, and hence having developed an unhealthy reliance principally upon food items produced by others, and in particular, by whites. To combat such deficiencies, dietary regulations of the NoI include eating only one meal in every twenty-four-hour period, and participating in a three-day fast at the end of each month. The general underlying goal is for blacks to strive to consume food in longer and longer intervals. The establishment of the NoI's Salaam restaurant on Chicago's south side, in 1995, represented a material realization of these convictions about the need for black autonomy in matters of diet (although, in common with the many inconsistencies that are a notable hallmark of the NoI under Farrakhan, its appetizing menus hardly represent great culinary frugality[57]).

Farrakhan's dietary prescriptions do not differentiate sharply between male and female NoI members, but the NoI leader's views on gender relations exhibit markedly traditionalist tendencies and deeply inegalitarian currents that draw very clear and rigid distinctions between the sexes. As can be inferred from the title of his mentor's main instructive treatise, the NoI's principal focus for attention has consistently been the black man in the United States. Nonetheless, Elijah Muhammad's message to the black American male also comprised an implicit, but equally fundamental, one to the black American woman: subordination. Thus, consonant with Bilalian biblical teachings, the role of women within the Black Muslim movement is carefully and deliberately prescribed, their being assigned to a fundamentally subordinate role within a patriarchal family, in which the functions of childbearing and childrearing assume their principal preoccupation and primary social importance. Farrakhan's (no doubt benevolent) paternalism is pronounced:

What black man can be a real man when he is unable to offer security to his wife and security to his children? Paul in the New Testament said, "As Christ is the head of the man, man is the head of the woman." But how can a man be a head of his woman, even be the head of his household, without knowledge, without wisdom, without economic wherewithal?[58]

For Farrakhan, the role of gender is fundamental not only in religious but also in historical terms for black Americans. As a result of white America's consistent and consciously destructive efforts, the black male in the United States has essentially been emasculated, and the black woman, in consequence, has been forced to bear a tremendous and excessive social burden. If the distant genesis of an emergent feminist discourse perhaps exists herein, however, it is nonetheless overwhelmed by Farrakhan's avowed view of the African-American woman's role. Following Malcolm X's epigrammatic advice that "to educate a woman is to liberate a nation," the unresolved issue in the modern NoI remains, educate to do what, precisely? Thus, Farrakhan's analysis typically conflates an apparently generous and lavish praise of black American women's ascribed personal qualities with interconnected explanations for the perceived failings and deficiencies of African-American males:

> . . . as Black men we've been castrated. We feel so threatened by the high degree of intelligence, aggressiveness, and forthrightness of our women. It only shows that we have not been afforded the opportunity under this social, economic, and political system to grow to our full potential as men. Our women have had a little more freedom to grow.[59]

That disproportionate African-American female liberty does not extend, however, to issues of reproductive rights, as far as Farrakhan is concerned. Abortion, for example, is opposed by the NoI's leader on the grounds that "when the black woman kills her unborn child, she is murdering the advancement of her nation."[60] Black Americans in general need to be taught techniques of "self-control" rather than birth control, according to the NoI's traditionalist social tenets.

While African-American women are admitted to the Black Muslim movement and have served selectively as both ministers[61] and security guards,[62] the NoI's prescribed views on gender roles are nonetheless stringently traditionalist and essentialist. Although Farrakhan appointed a female member of the NoI to the Mosque Maryam ministry in Chicago and has also made many public statements that apparently affirm the great importance of black women in the group, the internal organization of the NoI seems clearly to contradict such views. According to one female former NoI member, for example, upon joining the organization, black American women receive instruction in seven "basic" units: cooking; sewing; raising children; taking care of her husband; proper behavior inside the home; care of the home; and proper behavior outside the home.[63] Lest they be deluded into notions that such patronizing instruction might possibly hamper their full development as fundamentally equal human beings, NoI women are assured that they may pursue any area of interest and realize their many talents to the full—subject to the crucial condition that such ambitious endeavors do not compromise their "true nature." African-American women in Farrakhan's NoI are evidently intended to occupy a bleak state of "modified domestic purdah,"[64] such that even Murphy Brown might yearn for Dan Quayle's progressive and compassionate feminism by comparison.

The prohibition upon black American women participating in the October 1995 March on Washington was perhaps the most explicit and well-known example of the essentially patriarchal nature of the NoI's structure and public prescriptions. While black women were asked to assist in the national organization of the march, they were also requested not to participate or attend the event. The obvious tension was consonant with the subtly drawn distinction that Farrakhan offered in explanation, observing that "we are not saying that a woman's place is in the home; we are saying that a woman's base is in the home."[65] Although many black women attended despite the prohibition, the event was clearly intended by its organizers to be wholly exclusive in its gender, as well as in its racial, composition. While some critics attribute the patriarchal character of the organization to second-tier male administrators rather than to Farrakhan personally (despite his adamant rejection of female attendance at the march),[66] the hierarchical, leader-centric nature of the NoI strongly suggests that sexist stereotyping and paternalistic practices could effectively be eliminated if the NoI's leader so desired. That this has not occurred is a far more powerful indicator of the character of the NoI's gender politics

and its leader's convictions about the sexes than are Farrakhan's intermittent public commendations of the African-American woman's crucial social role and many admirable achievements.[67]

Almost inevitably, given his preoccupation with race as the sole
analytic category of social and political importance, issues of gender
relations are also crosscut by Farrakhan's unequivocal advocacy of
racial separatism in all social and cultural matters. Thus, paralleling
the prejudiced prescriptions of bigots, racialists, and white American
supremacist groups through the ages—and echoing the teachings of
Elijah and Malcolm X before him—Farrakhan opposes interracial relationships in the United States (in typically lurid and vitriolic terminology). The white American man having "pumped his blood" into
black females during slavery, African-Americans were as a result rendered persistently "weak and susceptible" to whites' "evil, filthy, and
indecent way of life." The prevalence among blacks of drug-taking,
alcohol consumption, prostitution, gambling, and other "sinful" activities can thus be directly traced to the forcible injection of impure and
degenerate "white" ideas into previously untainted and uncontami-
nated black American communities, through such brutally coercive
and vicious interracial liaisons. Black Americans must therefore steadfastly avoid further contamination by whites as a fundamental prerequisite of their collective purification and full redemption. Farrakhan's
antimiscegenistic message is, typically, directed at the African-American male:

> Take this beautiful Black woman—she's your Queen! She's your
> jewel! Don't let a white man get near this Black woman . . . And
> last but not least, Black Man, don't let that white man at anytime
> in your life give you his white woman! We don't want her! We
> don't want her![68]

Such puerile and base sentiments are, as far as groups such as the
Aryan Nation are concerned, evidently mutual. Moreover, given such
shared convictions, it is at best unclear as to whether Farrakhan
would agree—on either legal or normative grounds—with the
Supreme Court's landmark decision in 1967 that state prohibitions
upon interracial marriage violated the U.S. Constitution.[69] Farrakhan's organic conceptions of race are instead powerfully suggestive
of a wholesale rejection of the right of individuals to choose their

particular partners regardless of racial background; an anti-individualistic and morally contemptible position powerfully at odds with American creedal values, though not the nation's historic practice.

Farrakhan's views on sexual politics also encompass a miscellany of markedly illiberal and traditionalist views. The NoI's de facto constitution, "What the Muslims Want, What the Muslims Believe" (published in *The Final Call*), for example, calls for members found guilty of fornication or adultery to be suspended from the organization for certain prescribed periods of time (a suspension to which Elijah was, of course, notoriously and consistently exempt). Besides such immoral activity, though, Farrakhan also harbors a profound antipathy toward homosexuality, which he views as "submission to circumstances rather than anything genetic or innate." Derogatory references by Farrakhan to former New York City Mayor Ed Koch's alleged homosexuality and the vicious Kean College speech of his national spokesperson, Khalid Muhammad, attracted widespread accusations of virulent homophobia from gay rights groups. Viewing AIDS as an explicit and incontrovertible manifestation that "there is a problem somewhere in this kind of social behavior," Farrakhan advocates repressive measures to deal with both the disease and its carriers:

> . . . if AIDS is a communicable disease it has to be quarantined until we can correct it. If I were walking the streets with tuberculosis in the days when they didn't have the kind of cures for tuberculosis that they have today, it was almost mandatory that they take me off the streets. That's not a crime against my humanity; it is protection for my humanity and the humanity of others by taking me and putting me in a sanitarium until I can be relieved of that which I am suffering. Then I can enter back into society.[70]

Whether this entails the incarceration of all homosexuals as well as those diagnosed as HIV carriers is—no doubt deliberately—difficult to discern from Farrakhan's public comments. What is more certain, however, is that, as he argued in *A Torchlight for America*, homosexual behavior offends the proper standards of moral behavior established by God, and the "circumstances" that bring it about must be eliminated. Indeed, in encouraging less promiscuous sexual behavior, among both homosexuals and heterosexuals, Farrakhan even holds that ultimately AIDS "will turn out to be something good."[71] For

Farrakhan, fatal viruses evidently serve as timely and effective "cures" for sexually heretical behavior and inappropriate lifestyles.

Thus, in the conflict over issues of cultural values and "lifestyle" choice that has become such a prominent and divisive feature of recent national American politics, Farrakhan clearly occupies a strongly traditionalist rather than a progressive social stance.[72] The degenerative societal problem lies in the deficient behavior of particular individuals and social groups, not in the prejudiced attitudes of others toward certain modes of behavior. Were it not for the antiwhite bigotry in which they are frequently clouded, most of Farrakhan's traditionalist cultural values and moral convictions would be shared and heavily endorsed by Christian evangelicals such as Pat Robertson and Jerry Falwell, white conservative figures whose enthusiasm and activism on behalf of black American advancement have never assumed particularly prominent places on their political and religious resumes. Like them, too, Farrakhan's convictions on matters of morality and ethics tend to be strongly infused by the scapegoating discourse of censure and condemnation, to be dominated more by a lengthy litany of the many evils and vices that he is adamantly "against" than of the virtues that he is "for"—an exemplar of an antipolitics of familiar, though undistinguished, historical pedigree in the United States.

Farrakhan's cultural conservatism also encompasses his analysis of black Americans' current social and economic problems more generally, though. Paralleling his traditionalist views on matters of morality, Farrakhan's analysis of the so-called "Negro problem" is focused more on individual failings than on the historic, structural inequalities of American society, an analysis that—much as it targets homosexuals rather than homophobia for disapprobation and censure—frequently comes perilously close to blaming black people for not being economically successful. Farrakhan views the central societal problems confronting disadvantaged African-Americans in the contemporary United States through an ideological prism analogous to that of David Duke and the radical white American right, albeit one shaped by a peculiar theological derivation.[73] Given their shared belief in the notion of racial essences and purity, this interpretative commonality between Farrakhan and white racialists is hardly surprising. Nonetheless, it serves as yet another example of the very substantial distance that exists between Farrakhan and the vast majority of national African-American political actors.

Thus, in Farrakhan's view, the grievous maladies confronting many black American communities are neither exclusively nor primarily economic in character (poverty, unemployment, and dispossession) but are rather behavioral, attitudinal, and pathological in nature (drugs, crime, and general social dislocation). Separation of the races is hence, according to the Farrakhan analysis, fundamentally beneficial for African-Americans. Free from a malign white influence, black behavioral dysfunction can be diagnosed, challenged, and ultimately corrected under the beneficent auspices of the NoI. Consistent with such a notion, Farrakhan also holds that, historically, black-owned businesses were more numerous and successful under the legally sanctioned segregation of the Jim Crow era and, further, that the civil rights legislation that brought that era to an end has in fact caused black Americans general harm. Moreover, Farrakhan adamantly rejects the notion of governmental responsibility for citizen welfare in the United States and is, at best, ambivalent with regard to the secular character of the American state.

It is thus acutely ironic—and misleading—that many popular accounts often portray Farrakhan as the modern African-American national leadership successor to Malcolm X, as a comparable black nationalist icon for the 1990s. Certainly, Farrakhan and Malcolm share many beliefs regarding the cultural values that black Americans ought to adopt and profess. Malcolm X's ideological beliefs, however, evinced an enduring and marked hostility toward capitalism that contrasts sharply with Farrakhan's enthusiastic embrace of the free market. While some scholarly interpretations minimize the significance of Malcolm's prosocialist comments, arguing that these were made to marginal political groups and lacked either intellectual coherence, complexity, or sophistication,[74] such views are not especially compelling. Admittedly, Malcolm's beliefs were not definitively settled even at the time of his death. Nonetheless, the lack of faith in American capitalism that Malcolm displayed in the final eighteen months of his life was clearly substantial and evidently sincere. Certainly, Malcolm's anticapitalist convictions led progressive and socialist groups within and outside the United States, both at the time and subsequently, to claim his political legacy as their own, while characterizing its putative appropriation by Farrakhan as "distorted, caricatured, and sanitised."[75] Unsurprisingly, Farrakhan has consistently refused to compromise the notable popularity, among both African-Americans at large and leftists generally, that invariably attends such comparisons by conceding the profound ideological distance that has actually separated the two black American leaders—in death as well as in life.

Allied to its eschatological beliefs, leadership mystique, and black separatism, then, the NoI's pronounced cultural conservatism powerfully distinguishes Farrakhan's group from other African-American organizations—both integrative and separatist—concerned with improving black Americans' political, economic, and social welfare. Groups such as the NAACP or Urban League represent secular organizations that rarely issue recommendations of a cultural character (in relation either to their own members or nonmembers), concentrating their energies instead principally upon issues of economic and political empowerment. By comparison, Farrakhan's NoI adopts a very distinctive and unusual approach, even in its symbols. Following its conviction that blacks in America represent an oppressed nation within a nation, for instance, the organization developed its own flag to proclaim African-Americans' putative independence. Its symbols of the sun (representing freedom), moon (equality), and star (justice) are held by NoI members to render its flag superior to all others (including the Stars and Stripes) since none of these entities can be taken down by either government edict or military force. Again, the distinctive character of the NoI constitutes an important resource for Farrakhan's aspirations to national black political leadership, in affording him a status that is sharply differentiated from established African-American civic and political leaders.

Admittedly, on occasion, Farrakhan has issued public pronouncements that undermine the consistently conservative tenor of his worldview. The ideological identity of the NoI's leader has been complicated by Farrakhan's appeals to the progressive and liberal groups with whom a tactical alliance has frequently appeared both necessary and politically profitable. Neither the tactical appeals of the black nationalist nor the tentative embrace by political progressives is novel in historical terms, with white socialists and communists expressing interest in, and seeking to forge alliances with, black nationalist groups since the early part of the twentieth century.[76] As with black nationalists' efforts during earlier eras, the central features of Farrakhan's more recent attempts to create broader political links revolve around his rhetorical appeals for racial equality, the internationalist dimensions of his public discourse, and his calls for economic justice.

That Farrakhan strongly opposes black oppression by whites and sincerely seeks the improvement of African-Americans' economic and social welfare is clear from his many speeches and writings. The NoI's leader, however, has also made explicit attempts to appeal to nonblack racial and ethnic groups in America, in particular Native Americans and Latinos, to join black Americans in a broad-based anti-racist and antiestablishment coalition. Farrakhan issued such a call at the 1983 March on Washington, for example, and has often included Native and Latino Americans within the privileged ambit of his "black brothers." The actual strength of Farrakhan's commitment to multiracial and multiethnic unity both within and outside the United States, however, is implausibly great. It is at best difficult to reconcile such claims of inclusive humanitarian commitment with descriptions not only of Jews, but also of Arabs, Koreans, and other ethnic American groups as "bloodsuckers," for example. If it exists at all, Farrakhan's sincere desire to transcend racial and ethnic differences assumes such a minor role in his dominant political and religious agenda as to be effectively discounted.

In his apparent quest for an ecumenical racial unity, though, the NoI's leader has also sought to promote himself as an anti-imperialist, recalling the mantle of prior black leaders within the United States who had fought against American (and non-American) military involvement in foreign lands, such as Garvey, Du Bois, King, and Malcolm. Farrakhan's scathing criticisms of American foreign policy for being too favorable to the interests of Israel; his unrelenting defense of Palestinian rights; his personal ties to Arab regimes in general, and that of Gadhafi in Libya in particular; his close associations with African governments, such as that of Jerry Rawlings in Ghana; and his opposition to American sanctions against Cuba, Iran, Iraq, and other despotic regimes have provided overlapping areas of agreement for the NoI's leader with elements of the progressive Left in America.[77] In consistently opposing U.S. involvement in Central America and the Arabian Gulf, and in arguing that black Americans should never participate in any military action by the United States against black Africans, Farrakhan has evidently sought to echo the anticolonialist and anti-imperialist tenets of Malcolm X after his departure from the NoI. The relevance of such foreign policy positions to the advancement of African-American welfare in the United States is, nonetheless, at best marginal and indirect.[78]

An even more prominent theme in Farrakhan's speeches than foreign policy, however, is a recurrent call for economic equity between the races in America. Farrakhan has sought explicitly to deny the extent of his capitalist convictions by emphasizing his unyielding opposition to "exploitative" economic relations:

> I am not a capitalist, I don't believe in the exploitation of the wealth of the masses for the benefit of a few greedy people. I believe that since we are living in a capitalist society we should use the instruments of capitalism, but the ownership of everything must be the common ownership by the masses of the people. I don't believe the wealth of any nation should be in the hands of the few.[79]

The democratic-socialist and collectivist cast of Farrakhan's commitment to common ownership can nonetheless be heavily doubted. In 1985, for example, Farrakhan announced the establishment of a new and important NoI program, "People Organized and Working for Economic Rebirth" (POWER), which comprehensively embodied his black nationalist-capitalist tenets. The objective of POWER was to become a multiple-level business enterprise, marketing products produced and distributed exclusively by black Americans, for sale within and outside America. Farrakhan's goals were to tap into the estimated $200 billion purchasing power of African-Americans and to encourage a wholesale change in the prevailing patterns of their spending and saving habits. Black-owned firms would sell to black American consumers, with the resulting capital from sales being used to start small, all-black manufacturing companies. Based initially upon a black toiletries firm, Farrakhan's program for racial self-reliance invoked the inspirational argument that, if African-Americans continued to depend upon the white man for such intimate personal hygiene products, there would eventually be "a brown day in Detroit." Black Americans had, he eloquently averred, to attend assiduously to their own "wiping needs," free from the insidious and degenerative influence of the white man's toilet paper;[80] a noble, enlightened and compelling vision, indeed.

The program, which initially attracted significant support from black American businesspersons, reflected two of Farrakhan's core convictions: that African-Americans, with a "new" status as a freed people from 1986 onward, and a novel opportunity to be responsive to appropriately enlightened instruction, needed to be taught by example how to behave, and that economics represented the key mechanism by which collective black American advancement would most effectively be achieved. Prophesy and profit thus represented mutually reinforcing routes to collective black American emancipation, in Farrakhan's view. Subsequently, Farrakhan's entrepreneurial activities have increased in scope and diversity, though not at all clearly in terms of their commercial success.[81]

Farrakhan's core economic position is essentially a powerful echo of that of populists throughout American history, in its opposition to concentrations of economic power in the hands of wealthy conglomerates and in its antipathy toward multinational corporations. In favoring the "little man" against "big business," however, the racial twist to Farrakhan's American populism is manifest in economic tenets that are more deeply concerned with the racial control and size of the business than with challenging its capitalist mode of production. Although the little man may be an African-American, and the agents of big business white, the goals of Farrakhan's economic movement remain firmly located within the capitalist and free market tradition of American political economy. As Marable has argued, Farrakhan's economic philosophy essentially amounts to an ambitious black attempt to defeat the white American corporate elite by playing the free market game within its own rules of private enterprise.[82] Exploitation is directed by the NoI at the nonblack, rather than the African-American, poor in this guise. Farrakhan's strategy is therefore informed less by fighting social inequities and economic injustice per se than by simply inverting the identities of its victors and victims, according to race.

That Farrakhan's pronounced economic conservatism enjoys a deep historical lineage among African-Americans is clear enough, but this assumes a less significant role in terms of the minister's political ascendancy than does its current exceptionalism among national black American political elites. Certainly, the NoI's emphasis on self-help and economic individualism among African-Americans has a long historical pedigree. At the turn of the twentieth century, Booker T. Washington tirelessly advocated black capitalism and established the National Negro Business League to assist black entrepreneurship. A coalition of black businesspersons, the League promoted the development of all-black insurance firms, funeral homes, groceries, and retail establishments. In the 1920s, Garvey, too, endorsed similar race-bound economic tenets through his Black Star steamship line, which aspired to market black-produced goods to Africa and the Caribbean, and the Negro Factories Corporation, a group of black entrepreneurs that attempted unsuccessfully to dominate the black American consumer market.

However, the overwhelming majority of national black American politicians in the post–civil rights era have endorsed markedly liberal economic programs, social welfare assistance, and governmental regulation of economic affairs in a fashion wholly anathema to Farrakhan's laissez-faire precepts. As Charles Hamilton observed:

> Black Americans have always had to look to the national government for a more responsive hearing of their grievances . . . States' rights became synonymous with black oppression . . . (which) caused black political thought to be influenced very heavily by reliance on the federal government and to be very pessimistic about the ultimate willingness or ability of local governments to deal with black problems. [83]

By stark contrast, Farrakhan's combination of economic and cultural currents unmistakably mark him out as a conservative American populist. His avowed preference is consistently and overwhelmingly for order over freedom in social and cultural matters, yet simultaneously for liberty over regulation in economic ones. Equality does not figure prominently in his public philosophy beyond seeking an improvement of black welfare comparable to that of whites; redistributing resources within America on a more equitable basis is not the issue. On this point Farrakhan has substantially more in common with conservative white Republicans, such as Phil Gramm and Jesse Helms, than he does with liberal black Democrats, such as Jesse Jackson and John Lewis. Small wonder, then, that some critical observers were apt to doubt whether an imagined debate between Farrakhan and David Duke—an intriguing if deeply unedifying prospect—would witness any material disagreements arising between the two populist extremists, upon either the causes of America's racial problems or their most appropriate solutions.

That Farrakhan's conservatism has been largely ignored during his rise to national political attention is largely a consequence of the proximate causes of his increasing public notoriety. Although the ambiguous signals that his public pronouncements issued partly accounted for his ideological misplacement, the more influential sources of confusion surrounded his involvement in the Jackson campaign of 1984. A combination of the association with Jackson, the political capital that the Republican party sought to gain from the episode, and the intense and protracted political furor over his anti-Semitic remarks from 1984 onward, together conveyed a dominant media and public impression of Farrakhan as constituting simply a more extreme and crudely vitriolic version of the black American presidential aspirant himself. Since vigorously fighting against racial discrimination and prejudice necessarily entailed strong resistance to the status quo, and since Farrakhan appeared so obviously committed to challenging established structures in the most militant, aggressive, and uncompromising of fashions, the leader of the NoI was not easily cast as a conventional conservative.

More important, very few American political actors—black or white, progressive or conservative, supporters or opponents—have faced a sufficiently pressing political imperative or a compelling incentive actually to cast Farrakhan in such a light. Embracing Farrakhan's variant of right-wing conservatism was attractive to neither Republicans nor liberal Democrats. Although, for example, Charles Henry argues that Jackson's ultimate severance of his electoral ties with Farrakhan owed "more to the strategic needs and experience of each leader than . . . to ideological incompatibility,"[84] the latter was untested. Had it been, the substantial distance separating them would undoubtedly have become clear since, as Reed has compellingly and consistently argued, Farrakhan:

> weds a radical, oppositional style to a program that proposes private and individual responses to social problems; he endorses moral repressiveness; he asserts racial essentialism; he affirms male authority; and he lauds bootstrap capitalism.[85]

The Jackson-Farrakhan links were demonstrably less religious, philosophical, or ideological than politically pragmatic in their origins—a source of both their strength and frailty.

Abetted—inadvertently or intentionally—by his many erstwhile opponents, Farrakhan was therefore able to disguise a profoundly conservative political, economic, and social agenda behind his aggressively populist black nationalist public discourse, anti-Semitism, and his organization's direct action interventions in inner-city African-American communities to reduce black drug consumption and to combat black-on-black crime. The correct ideological locus of Farrakhan as an impassioned black conservative—indeed, as an African-

American exemplar of what might be most appropriately termed "radical reaction"—was thus left obscure for many Americans of all races.

A POLITICS OF CONTRADICTIONS: PROPHESY AND PROFITS

The most cursory examination of Farrakhan's prolific writings and speeches reveals that the minister eminently merits designation as a radical activist. In etymological terms, Farrakhan fully qualifies as an individual who vehemently believes in the overarching and immediate need to transform American society from its very roots, rather than through incremental changes, minor adaptations, and gradual reforms. Critical conceptions of both Farrakhan's personal politics and that of his organization are, nonetheless, frequently apt to diverge markedly between reformist and revolutionary interpretations.[86] Moreover, the notion of an uncompromising racial militant espousing deeply conservative, and even reactionary, positions and prescriptions renders the appropriate designation of Farrakhan particularly problematic.

Reformist social movements or political parties tend to be concerned with the achievement of incremental changes in existing patterns of political, economic, and social relations in a given polity. Their focus is upon the need to alter or repair laws, institutions, customs, or practices rather than to overhaul the prevailing system in its entirety. Revolutionary movements, by contrast, invariably emphasize the need for a complete regeneration of societal values and established institutional structures. They stress the desirability of either totally rebuking the old polity or bringing about an entirely new pattern of relationships between the individual and the state, between classes or ethnic and racial groups, and between individual citizens.

In this respect, Farrakhan occupies a political terrain decisively more reformist than revolutionary in nature. Admittedly, revolutionary themes and impulses infuse his public discourse. Farrakhan's NoI also advances a call for complete change in the values and priorities not just of American blacks, but also of the United States (and the West) as a whole. Farrakhan envisions an entirely new type of society, and a pattern of economic and political relations between the races, wholly novel and unprecedented in American experience. The NoI's theological precepts necessarily compel not a gradual and marginal set of alterations in existing structures and patterns of social and economic life in America, but their rapid, wholesale, and lasting transformation. Reformists, on the whole, tend not to endorse global Armageddon and all-consuming apocalyptic conflagrations as the most propitious incremental means by which existing political, economic, and social arrangements can best be improved to universal benefit.

Nonetheless, in demanding the full redress of black American grievances, Farrakhan advances no concrete plan or program of action, much less full-blown revolution. Although he explicitly and frequently directs American attentions to the socioeconomic gaps between blacks and whites in the United States, and demands their rapid and complete removal, there is surprisingly little in Farrakhan's public discourse that can be construed as even remotely encouraging the overthrow of the American state. The NoI's effective constitution, "What the Muslims Want, What the Muslims Believe," even includes a demand directed to the U.S. government to bring about "freedom, justice, and equality" for African-Americans, an explicit appeal to working within the existing state framework rather than threatening the polity's imminent demise. The organization has never engaged in extensive political activity to achieve a wholesale transformation of the state and of the established politicoeconomic system. Nor has the NoI resorted to coercive, violent, or terrorist acts to achieve its separatist goals. Farrakhan, it seems, desires power for himself and the organization that he leads. He wants to colonize governmental and civic institutions with his own loyal black forces, to bring about the multitude of comprehensive changes that he professes to desire. Were Farrakhan offered the U.S. presidency, he would most likely accept it as the most propitious national bully pulpit from which to press his radical transformation of American society.

The radical features of the NoI are a function of the centrality of race to Farrakhan's religious and ideological beliefs. Farrakhan's analysis of African-Americans' current woes consistently focuses on the racial rather than the class or economic causes of blacks' contemporary plight. Although the need for African-Americans generally to become economically self-sufficient is a prominent and critical theme in his speeches, that imperative is a product of the fact that black Americans have been mistreated and miseducated in the United States by virtue of their race, not their class positions. It is, therefore, in achieving a transformative racial unity that such deprivation must find its necessary, sufficient, and ultimate solution.

Thus, although Farrakhan's specific policy prescriptions on cultural and economic matters share substantially more in common with black American conservatives, such as Thomas Sowell or Clarence Thomas,[87] than progressives, the analyses of the NoI overlap with those of many avowedly liberal African-American politicians in their common emphasis on race. Unlike orthodox conservatives, both Farrakhan and progressive groups such as the CBC share a public dialogue whose preeminent analytic category—the cornerstone by which they assess policies, politicians, and institutions—is that of race. It is above all the racial variable that conditions the divergent collective fates of African-Americans and other social groups in the United States. Although their prescriptions for resolving the problems plaguing many African-American communities differ substantially, the source of those communities' difficulties is identified in remarkably similar fashion. For all their significant differences, the shared stress that is placed upon the achievement of racial unity by both Farrakhan and politicians such as Jesse Jackson reveals a basic commonality of vision and an adherence to a common notion of racial authenticity.

Consider, for example, Lani Guinier's definition of "authentic" black American leadership, regarding elected black officials: "Black Representatives are authentic because they are elected by blacks *and* because they are descriptively similar to their constituents. In other words, they are politically, psychologically, and culturally black."[88] Although Guinier and Farrakhan would disagree profoundly on what public policies black politicians should strive to enact in order to best benefit their African-American constituents, they share this fundamental notion that an authentic black persona can be identified, achieved, and (by definition) forfeited.

Moreover, in invoking race as the key prism through which prevailing public policies are evaluated, Farrakhan's prescriptions are precisely at odds with the calls from several influential African-American academics, such as the sociologist William Julius Wilson, for the development of a comprehensive and deracialized public policy program, capable of legislative passage and enactment, that can effectively address black Americans' social problems and economic grievances.[89] For Wilson and other neo-liberals, the grievous problems afflicting African-American communities require programs that do not make race their explicit basis or express goal in order to be effective. The deracialization of political discourse and the evolution of race-neutral public policy programs is a pressing necessity for the forging of multiracial, majority coalitions and a central precondition of the regeneration of many deprived and disadvantaged black communities across America. For Farrakhan, by manifest contrast, the extreme polarization of political forces and the explicit racialization of public policy is a requisite, though not sufficient, condition of meaningful black American empowerment.

Although, therefore, an explicit, pervasive, and important conflict exists between Farrakhan's militant racial posture, on the one hand, and his deeply conservative economic and social program, on the other, this does not represent a complete contradiction. Farrakhan's militancy is not only rhetorical but is also wholly compatible with the particular ideological nature of his demands. Much as Patrick J. Buchanan's increasingly aggressive promotion of a protectionist, nativist, and recidivist "America First" program since 1991 has hardly proven violative of an extremist and radical posture, so Farrakhan's "Black America First" discourse enthusiastically embraces rather than rejects deeply conservative and traditionalist tenets. Farrakhan represents a prophet of radical black reaction, propounding a populist right-wing message that, in order to achieve full emancipation, black Americans must adopt the avowedly conservative value system and the traditionalist behavioral modes that he vigorously espouses. Were his public philosophy to be articulated in similarly direct, vivid, and lurid terms by a white American politician, the latter would inevitably invite mass opprobrium and the ideas would probably compel censure rather than celebration or encouragement.[90]

Reed is thus absolutely correct to draw critical attention to the avowedly conservative nature of Farrakhan's agenda for black Americans.[91] One hundred years on, the NoI's leader essentially repeats Booker T. Washington's comprehensive indictment of black America during the 1890s for its collective failure to undertake proactive, private initiatives, to reject dependency upon government largesse, and to inculcate among black Americans responsible, bourgeois, and traditionalist cultural values in order to rejuvenate black communities. Like Washington previously, Farrakhan has come to national prominence in America at a moment of profound racial crisis, apparent impotence on the part of national black political and civic leadership, and increasing federal government retreat on matters of civil rights, welfare provision, and economic redistribution for African-Americans. Much as Washington's activism was centrally shaped by the collapse of the first Reconstruction, so Farrakhan's efforts have been directed at forging an influential popular base in the midst of the fragmentary remnants of the second. [92]

Admittedly, Washington was, unlike Farrakhan, ultimately an integrationist, and one whose genuine faith in the notion that separate could be equal remains in academic dispute. Nonetheless, his programs of self-help and moral regeneration bear substantial resemblance to the public prescriptions of Farrakhan's NoI currently. Espousing public policy positions that the Republican party in the House of Representatives under Newt Gingrich would mostly endorse with alacrity, it represents a signal achievement by Farrakhan that the full, repressive extent of his conservative agenda has not been effectively "smoked out" to the mass of black Americans. The threat that Farrakhan poses to his compatriots is far more potent in regard to black Americans than whites in its multifarious reactionary, authoritarian, and retrograde dimensions, a fact that many analyses of the Farrakhan phenomenon are apt to disregard or ignore.

The irony of Farrakhan's contemporary role, however, is not only a matter of his often mistaken and ambiguous ideological identity. It is also a function of the blatant contradictions between the conservative practices and autonomous modes of economic and social activity that the NoI publicly supports and the dependent state of its own private activities. Most notably, the free-market philosophy and self-sufficiency tenets that Farrakhan relentlessly advances in public forums across America is wholly belied by the extent to which his own organization's activities have depended on sources of substantial financial support that are external not only to the NoI, but also to the black American community in general. Thus, the POWER program, for example, was largely financed by an interest-free loan of $5 million from Libyan dictator Muammar Gadhafi (the second of three occasions, over twenty-three years, in which the dictatorial Libyan autocracy has financially assisted the NoI). Similarly, in 1993, a chain of health clinics run by a top NoI official willingly accepted federal monies to market a dubious "cure" for the AIDS virus, while at the same time the organization attributed the spread of that very virus among black Americans to a combination of deliberate federal governmental action and promiscuous homosexual activity among African-Americans. [93]

The NoI's efforts at reducing gang conflict and the drug trade in inner-cities through the Fruit of Islam and its several corporate relations have also relied critically, and controversially, upon the patronage of federal government funds. The NoI initially commenced voluntarily patrolling two housing projects in Washington, D.C., in April 1988. Subsequently, private security agencies affiliated with the NoI and the boards of which comprised NoI members—but which constituted legally separate and self-constituted corporations—secured in excess of $20 million of funds from local housing authorities for their activities in a total of nine American cities, in 1990–1995: D.C., Baltimore, Chicago, Dayton, Brooklyn, Buffalo, Philadelphia, Pittsburgh, and Los Angeles. The contracts were financed in part by funds that local authorities receive from the federal government, rendering the security firms subcontractors of the U.S. government.

Most accounts concur that the NoI security firms have been reasonably effective in tackling drugs and crime in the overwhelmingly black projects. The firms, however, hired almost exclusively black workers (in contravention of federal affirmative action guidelines on achieving racial and ethnic diversity in the workforce); invariably preferred NoI members over other African-Americans; numbered among their NoI employees many recently convicted black felons; and owed several thousands of dollars in back taxes. Moreover, the "firewalls" that existed between the NoI and the legally independent security agencies (the NOI Security Agency in Baltimore, the New Life Self Development Agency in Chicago, the X-Men Security Agency in New York, for example) were hardly thick,[94] while the evidence of proselytization by the latter on Farrakhan's behalf (from advertising his lectures to selling the NoI's newspaper and trademark bean pies in the blocks they patrolled) was considerable—all, indirectly, at American taxpayers' unwitting expense.

Nor was the suspicion that the federal government actively, though inadvertently and indirectly, subsidized the NoI laid to rest by congressional hearings on the matter in 1995. Replete with mutual recriminations and predictably hyperbolic accusations of "witch-hunts" being leveled at NoI investigators, the hearings revealed only that the security agencies' work won widespread plaudits from African-Americans in the projects and that their activities received federal support of a highly questionable (and likely illegal) nature.[95] The response of Henry Cisneros, then Secretary of Housing and Urban Development in the Clinton Administration, was to transfer the matter to the Equal Employment Opportunity Commission. Given the latter's two-year, 100,000 case backlog, the unrefuted charges against the NoI firms were thereby effectively buried (although eight security contracts at public or federally assisted housing projects in six cities either expired without being renewed or were terminated during 1995–96).[96]

For the frequency and ferocity with which Farrakhan preaches the merits of economic self-sufficiency and individualistic self-help, his organization practices a set of activities that is powerfully reliant upon sources of financial subsidy that are external to black Americans. No matter how effective they may have been in local black city communities, Farrakhan's organization and its affiliated security groups are markedly less self-sufficient than substantially subsidized (and, in spite of those subsidies, plagued by dire financial difficulties[97]). Much as Farrakhan's personally residing in a large mansion in a racially integrated neighborhood on Chicago's south side wholly contradicts his preaching in favor of separation of the races, so his practical business ventures are also directly violative of the self-help economic principles that he publicly promotes. But then, the NoI's leader would no doubt argue that the motives and methods of prophets throughout human history have frequently been misunderstood by the massed ranks of the infidels and the unenlightened.

SUMMARY

History may judge Farrakhan as neither an exotic political opportunist nor a certifiable madman. The esoteric religious dimensions of Farrakhan's message are nonetheless as central to his belief system and political behavior as his practice is violative of them. The Black Muslim leader's bizarre and byzantine theological analysis powerfully informs his explanations of black Americans' history, current position, and future social and economic prospects in the United States. Although distinctive to the point of being extraordinarily eccentric, risible, and repugnant, Farrakhan's political role and influence simply cannot be understood either fully or accurately apart from an appreciation of his prophetic self-conception and his profound, unshakeable conviction that he, personally, is imbued with divine influence and is set upon an irrevocable course of collective racial salvation. Farrakhan's theological beliefs remain fundamental to his leadership of the NoI—they form the fountain from which all his many other prescriptions and public behavior flow.

Farrakhan assuredly possesses the courage of his many colorful convictions. Those convictions, however, are deeply and overwhelmingly conservative in character. Indeed, if the project of many white

American conservatives over recent years has been to "take back" the United States by somehow transporting the country to an earlier period of its history (most typically, by reviving and recreating an idealized version of the 1950s), so Farrakhan's ultimate goal is to return black Americans to an earlier set of economic and social structures that shaped their development—albeit without the manifold black inequalities, indignities, and injuries so integral to the segregated system of Jim Crow. In advocating many of the reactionary positions he does, Farrakhan essentially calls for a return to the past in America: separate racial facilities and collective development; unequivocal and strong division of gender roles along traditionalist lines; an end to government programs to black American citizens; and a revival of traditional moral codes of behavior, subject to the strictest of sanctions for their violation. Louis Farrakhan's America is a nation in which all those many heretics who heinously breach his ascribed notions of racial authenticity and sexual and moral purity—fornicators, homosexuals, miscegenators, adulterers, drinkers, gamblers, and professional women—are effectively excluded; an imagined American community far less benignly beloved than brutally regimented, repressive, and deeply repugnant to civilized sensibilities.

Farrakhan therefore represents a substantially more reactionary than a progressive American political figure. Far less than three strikes would invite an "out" verdict under a Farrakhan regime, while the minister's great admiration of Saudi Arabian law and order methods suggests strongly that the conceptual (and constitutional) limits to "cruel and unusual punishment" in America would be tested to the full. Moreover, to the extent that his organizational practices are themselves clearly and deeply violative of his avowed public philosophy, Farrakhan also represents a fundamentally false prophet whose putative hopes for African-Americans are honed upon a hypocritical public praxis. Preaching a future panacea of racial separatism to deprived and impoverished blacks, Farrakhan resides in an integrated, affluent Chicago neighborhood; humbly affirming his essentially frugal and modest desires, he lives in resplendent luxury; persistently advocating black private enterprise and self-sufficiency, his organization depends crucially upon public subsidies and loans from foreign despots and international terrorist sponsors for its continued viability; and proclaiming deadly sexual viruses as of ultimately beneficial and cathartic social effect, the NoI markets dubious and doubtful cures for them. Professing a prophetic status, Farrakhan's plethora of promises and predictions emerges not only as bizarrely eccentric but also as a hollow and farcical fanaticist's facade. The conservatism and opportunism of Farrakhan's material practice dramatically contradict the supposed militancy and the elaborately principled character of his public preaching. The latter also marks him out, however, if not as insanely brilliant (or vice versa), at least as a modern exemplar of a distinctively black brand of American political paranoia.

NOTES TO CHAPTER 3

1. Cruse, *Plural But Equal*, p. 252.

2. Quoted in Martin Fletcher, "Anti-Semitic Gibes Mar Million Man March," *The London Times*, 16 October 1995, p. 10.

3. Most of Farrakhan's speeches are recorded, and many are sold by the NoI as cassette tapes. Some are also available as videos. In addition, collections of his speeches are contained in the following books: *Seven Speeches by Minister Louis Farrakhan* (New York: Ministry Class, Muhammad's Temple No. 7, 1974); and *A Torchlight for America* (Chicago: FCN Publishing, 1993). In addition to standard newspaper reports and interviews, a lengthy interview was also been published: *The Honorable Louis Farrakhan: a minister for progress; the complete historic interview with Michael Hardy and William Pleasant from The National Alliance* (New York: Practice Press, 1985). This pamphlet was reproduced in *Independent Black Leadership in America: Minister Louis Farrakhan, Dr. Leonari Fulani, Reverend Al Sharpton* (New York: Castillo International, 1990). See also "Excerpts of Interview," *The Washington Post*, 1 March 1990, pp. A16–17. I have drawn upon all of the available published sources, as well as audio-cassette recordings of Farrakhan's speeches, to attempt to distill his biographical details and the nature of his belief system with a reasonable degree of conciseness.

4. The notion is that of the eminent Marxist historian, Eric Hobsbawm. See *The Age of Extremes: The Short Twentieth Century* (London; Abacus Books, 1995), p. 208.

5. Excerpts from one of Farrakhan's plays were featured in the 1959 documentary by Lomax on the Black Muslims, "The Hate That Hate Produced." Another, entitled *Orgena* ("A negro" spelled backward) satirized so-called "Americanized" blacks, from well-dressed businessmen to alcoholics. As well as writing, Farrakhan starred in the productions.

6. Although he does not refer to Farrakhan by name, the record is noted by James Baldwin as accurately expressing the sentiments of many black Americans outside as well as within the Nation of Islam (see Baldwin, *The Fire Next Time* [New York: Dell, 1963], p. 64). A less well-known Farrakhan disc from the 1950s was released, according to one account, to celebrate America's first sex-change operation. Both the general subject and the specific lyrics of the song (which include the memorable lines: "People came out of curiosity/To see this amazing freak of the century/With this modern surgery/

They change him from he to she/But behind that lipstick, rouge, and paint/I gotta know—is she is, or is she ain't?") rest somewhat incongruously with Farrakhan's subsequent public views on gender and sexual relations. See Francis Wheen, "Voice of Islam."

7. Lincoln, *The Black Muslims*, p. 268.

8. A detailed discussion of Farrakhan's demagogic status can be found in Julia E. Gaber, "Lamb of God or Demagogue? A Burkean Cluster Analysis of the Selected Speeches of Minister Louis Farrakhan" (unpublished Ph.D. thesis, Bowling Green State University, 1986). Gaber affirms the appropriateness of the designation to Farrakhan.

9. See: Hamilton, *The Black Preacher in America*; and Lincoln, *The Black Church in the African American Experience*.

10. The remainder were made up mainly by immigrants (and their descendants) from Saudi Arabia, Iran, Egypt, Pakistan, and Morocco. Personal communication, American Muslim Council, Washington, D.C., 19 October 1995.

11. Farzana Shaikh, ed., *Islam and Islamic Groups: A World Wide Reference Guide* (Harlow, UK: Longman, 1992).

12. Erdmann D. Beynon, "The Voodoo Cult Among Negro Migrants in Detroit," *American Journal of Sociology* 43 (July 1937—May 1938): 894–907.

13. Arna Bontemps and Jack Conroy, *Anyplace But Here* (New York: Hill and Wang, 1966), p. 230.

14. See: J. Herman Blake, "Black Nationalism," in *Annals of the American Academy of Political and Social Science*, 382 (1969): 15–25; and Essien-Udom, *Black Nationalism*, pp. 6–7.

15. See August Meier, Elliott Rudwick, and Francis L. Broderick, eds., *Black Protest Thought in the Twentieth Century* 2nd ed. (New York: Macmillan, 1971).

16. See King, *Separate and Unequal*.

17. My use of the term "ideology" reflects the basic definition offered by David Kettler: "a pattern of symbolically-charged beliefs and expressions that present, interpret and evaluate the world in a way designed to shape, mobilize, direct, organize and justify certain modes or courses of action and to anathematize others." See his discussion in *The Blackwell Encyclopaedia of Political Thought*, ed. David Miller (Oxford: Basil Blackwell, 1991), pp. 235–38.

18. On Garvey's pre-1925 beliefs, speeches, and writings, see Amy-Jacques Garvey, ed., *Philosophy and Opinions of Marcus Garvey* (New York: Universal Publishing House, 1923).

19. The two most impressive biographies of Garvey are: Edmund David Cronon, *Black Moses: The Story of Marcus Garvey and the Universal Negro Improvement Association* (Madison: University of Wisconsin Press, 1962); and Theodore G. Vincent, *Black Power and the Garvey Movement* (San Francisco: University of California Press, 1972).

20. See Arna Bontemps and Jack Conroy, *They Seek a City* (Garden City, N.Y.: Doubleday, 1945).

21. See Lawrence L. Tyler, "The Protestant Ethic Among the Black Muslims," *Phylon* 27, no. 1 (1966): 5–14.

22. Among the voluminous literature on Malcolm X, see, in particular: Cone, *Martin and Malcolm and America*; Perry, *Malcolm X*; and Eugene Victor Wolfenstein, *The Victims of Democracy: Malcolm X and the Black Revolution* (London: Free Association Books, 1989).

23. See, for example: David Mervin, "Malcolm X and the Moderation of Black Militancy," *PAIS Papers*, Department of Politics and International Studies, University of Warwick, Coventry, UK, Working Paper no. 107 (April 1992); and Frederick Harper, "The Influence of Malcolm X on Black Militancy," *Journal of Black Studies* 1, no. 4 (1971): 387–402.

24. See George Breitman, ed., *The Last Year of Malcolm X* (New York: Pathfinder Press, 1967).

25. Louis Farrakhan, "Boston Minister Tells of Malcolm—Muhammad's Biggest Hypocrite," *Muhammad Speaks*, 4 December 1964, pp. 11–15.

26. See Breitman et al., *The Assassination of Malcolm X*.

27. Quoted in M. A. Farber, "In the Name of the Father," *Vanity Fair* 58 (1995), pp. 52–60.

28. Lincoln, *The Black Muslims*, p. 264.

29. On the split, see Lawrence H. Mamiya and C. Eric Lincoln, "Minister Louis Farrakhan and the Final Call: Schism in the Muslim Movement," in *The Muslim Community in North America*, eds. Earle Waugh, Baha Abu-Laban, and Regular Querishi (Edmonton: University of Alberta Press, 1983), pp. 234–51. The AMM was eventually dissolved in 1985. Subsequently, other Black Muslim groups have sought to establish mass memberships among African Americans by adhering to orthodox Islamic doctrines and stressing their opposition to the sectarianism and racial separatism of Farrakhan's Nation of Islam—though without conspicuous success.

30. Cited in Marsh, *From Black Muslims to Muslims*, p. 97.

31. Wallace E. Caldwell, "Black Muslims Behind Bars," *Religious Studies* 34, no. 4 (1966): 185–204.

32. Wallace E. Caldwell, "A Survey of Attitudes Towards Black Muslims in Prison," *Journal of Human Relations* 16, no. 2 (1968): 220–38.

33. Scott Grant McNall, "The Sect Movement," *Pacific Sociology Review* 6, no. 2 (1963): 60–64.

34. Ernst Benz, "Der Schwarze Islam," *Zeitschrift fur Religion und Geistesgeschichte* 19, no. 2 (1967): 97–113.

35. Philip Norton, "Black Nationalism in America: the Significance of the Black Muslim Movement," *Hull Papers in Politics*, University of Hull, no. 31, 1983.

36. King, "The Farrakhan Phenomenon." See also Marable, *Black American Politics*, p. 287; and Christopher Thomas, "The Man Who Haunts Jesse Jackson," *The London Times*, 8 August 1984, p. 6.

37. Shaikh, *Islam and Islamic Movements*, pp. 268–72.

38. Lincoln, *The Black Muslims*, p. 266.

39. Reed, "All for One," p. 86.

40. It is striking how closely life in the NoI compares to that of splinter political parties and extremist organizations in terms of fulfilling the necessary requirements for membership, expending substantial personal resources

(both in terms of time and finance) on the group, and in general ensuring that the organization assumes the preeminent focus of social life. For a non-U.S. secular comparison, see the study of Trotskyist "entryist" politics within the British Labour Party by Michael Crick, *Militant* (London: Faber and Faber, 1984).

41. Lincoln, *The Black Muslims*, p. 268.

42. The speech was made in Chicago and included in a 1995 documentary on Farrakhan's role in Malcolm's demise, *Brother Minister: The Assassination of Malcolm X*. The comments are also cited in *The London Times*, 13 January 1995, p. 13.

43. Shaikh, *Islam and Islamic Movements*, pp. 268–72.

44. See the examples in Meier et al., *Black Protest Thought in the Twentieth Century*.

45. Transcript of Farrakhan speech, 30 July 1984, National Press Club, Washington, D.C.

46. Elijah Muhammad, *Message to the Black Man in America* (Chicago: Muhammad's Temple No. 2, 1965); and *The Fall of America* (Chicago: Muhammad's Temple of Islam No. 2, 1973). See also Elijah's summation of the NoI's most important tenets in, "The Demands and Beliefs of the Black Muslims in America," *Islamic Review* 52, no. 10 (1964), pp. 25–27. Summations are also contained in Bernard Cushmeer, *This Is the One: Messenger Elijah Muhammad—You Need Not Look for Another* (Phoenix, Ariz.: Truth Publications, 1970).

47. Farrakhan's speeches attest to a view of history that is apparently determined in advance of itself by a council of Gods, in 25,000-year cycles. Fard, one of these Gods, dissented from their collective conviction that black Americans were beyond saving and came to America to warn them of their impending fate.

48. Among several other occurrences, Farrakhan predicted that the ensuing apocalypse would witness the destruction of the American 7th Fleet and the entire state of California collapsing into the Pacific Ocean, not as a result of the state lying on a fault line, but because of the corruptive and degenerate influence of the cities of Los Angeles and San Francisco.

49. Farrakhan speech, Cobal Hall, Detroit, 8 February 1985. Quoted in Gaber, "Lamb of God or Demagogue?," chapter 4, pp. 103–104.

50. Farrakhan confirmed in 1996 that he viewed the story of Yakub as fact rather than a metaphorical device, seeing the doctor as a "very real scientist." See his interview with Gates, "The Charmer," p. 124.

51. Although in an interview in 1990, Farrakhan restates his vision of a racial nightmare for America and the desirability of black Americans moving en masse to Africa. See Barbara Kleban Mills, "Predicting Disaster for a Racist America, Louis Farrakhan Envisions an African Homeland for U.S. Blacks," *People* 34, no. 11 (17 September 1990).

52. Quoted in Gaber, "Lamb of God or Demagogue?," p. 111.

53. Although an ingenious numerological device for identifying potentially satanic entities, it should perhaps be noted that, on this basis of inference, the number of Devils in the world is probably extremely large.

54. Quoted in Gaber, "Lamb of God or Demagogue?," p. 123.

55. Shirley R. Letwin, *The Anatomy of Thatcherism* (London: Fontana, 1992), p. 33–36.

56. Elijah Muhammad, *How to Eat to Live* (Chicago: Muhammad's Temple No. 2, 1968). *The Final Call* reprints Elijah's injunctions on health and diet in each issue, along with selective contemporary health briefs. One such example provided the striking warning (especially useful to academics) that "Students cannot pay attention and perform simple tasks after at least 22 days a month of marijuana smoking." See "Marijuana Use Impairs Performance," *The Final Call*, 3 April 1996, p. 28.

57. The restaurant was eventually completed and opened by Farrakhan in 1995. Its three separate areas included an array of dishes from curries to Creole cuisine and even permitted the sale of alcoholic beverages; food seems to be one of the few areas in which diversity evidently merits celebration and encouragement by Farrakhan and his organization.

58. Quoted in Gaber, "Lamb of God or Demagogue?," pp. 106–107.

59. Louis Farrakhan, *Independent Black Leadership in America: Minister Louis Farrakhan, Dr. Leonari Fulani, Reverend Al Sharpton* (New York: Castillo International, 1990), p. 47.

60. Cited in Robert Weisbord, *Genocide? Birth Control and the Black American* (Westport: Greenwood Press, 1975), pp. 96–104.

61. Farrakhan appointed a female African-American, Ava Muhammad, to the Ministry at the Nation's Chicago mosque (see R. X. White, "Minister Ava Muhammad: An Inspiration for Black Women," *The Final Call*, 27 January 1992, p. 17). The number of female ministers, however, still appears to be extremely limited and certainly not even in double figures as of September 1996.

62. Farrakhan's speech at Madison Square Garden on 7 October 1985 was the first and most notable occasion in which his normal guard of Fruit of Islam men was largely abandoned in favor of a phalanx of Black Muslim women. The decision evidently reflection a tactical ploy to counter accusations of sexism leveled at the NoI and to broaden Farrakhan's appeal among African-Americans of both sexes. A representative example of his views can also be garnered from his article, "Nation of Islam Offers True Liberation for Muslim Women," *The Final Call*, 24 August 1992, p. 28.

63. McFadden-Preston, "The Rhetoric of Minister Louis Farrakhan," p. 213, note 60.

64. Reed, "All for One," p. 87.

65. Quoted in Hamil R. Harris, "March of Black Men Is Planned in District; Farrakhan Seeks a Turnout of 1 Million," *The Washington Post*, 19 July 1995, p. B1.

66. See McFadden-Preston, "The Rhetoric of Minister Louis Farrakhan," chapter 6.

67. The suspicion that Farrakhan's personal values also encompass sexist notions is partially fuelled by some of his less sensitive public comments. One example was the interpretation that Farrakhan placed upon the conviction of the black boxer, Mike Tyson, for raping the African-American former beauty queen contestant, Desiree Washington: "You bring a hawk in at the

chicken yard and wonder why the chicken got eaten up." Quoted in Richard E. Cohen, "Marching behind Farrakhan."

68. Farrakhan speech, "Black Solidarity Day Address," 2 November 1970. Reprinted in Farrakhan, *Seven Speeches by Minister Louis Farrakhan*.

69. See the aptly titled case, *Loving v. Virginia*, 388 U.S. 1 (1967). Virginia was one of sixteen American states in 1967 that still retained antimiscegenation laws that both prohibited and punished racial intermarriage. (Fifteen others had repealed such laws over the previous fifteen years.) In the Court's 9–0 decision to invalidate the Virginia statute as an invidious racial classification prohibited by the Equal Protection Clause of the Fourteenth Amendment, Chief Justice Warren held that, "Under our Constitution, the freedom to marry, or not to marry, a person of another race resides with the individual and cannot be infringed by the State" (p. 12).

70. Farrakhan, *Independent Black Leadership*, p. 46. The analysis is analogous to Farrakhan's argument that black Americans need to be taken "out" of American society and "cured" (clearly by the Nation of Islam, under his tutelage) before being allowed to return to play a full role therein. It also jibes with the views of "moral" crusaders such as Jerry Falwell, who have also advocated the quarantining of homosexuals as a proper and proportionate response to AIDS. See Dennis Altman, *AIDS and the New Puritanism* (London: Pluto Press, 1986).

71. Such pronouncements rest curiously with the Nation of Islam's attempts to market among African-Americans what most respected medical practitioners view as an entirely fraudulent cure for AIDS. See Gaines and Jackson, "Profit and Promises."

72. Isaac Julien has also drawn attention to the very narrow view of the African-American male that informs Farrakhan's racial essentialism. As Julien argues: "Black romanticism is high on the political agenda of people like Louis Farrakhan and the Nation of Islam and various rap groups prioritizing their very narrow versions of black masculinity. It mythologizes the past as it erases memory." See Julien, "Black Is, Black Ain't: Notes on De-Essentializing Black Identities," in *Black Popular Culture*, ed. Gina Dent (Seattle: Bay Press, 1992), pp. 255–63, at 257.

73. See Douglas Rose, ed., *The Emergence of David Duke and the Politics of Race* (Chapel Hill: University of North Carolina Press, 1992); and Sargent, *Extremism in America*.

74. See Mervin, "Malcolm X."

75. Keith Ovenden, *Malcolm X: Socialism and Black Nationalism* (London: Bookmarks, 1992), p. 9.

76. For example, see: George Breitman, ed., *Leon Trotsky on Black Nationalism and Self-Determination* (New York: Pathfinder Press, 1978); and Cedric J. Robinson, *Black Marxism: The Making of the Black Radical Tradition* (London: Zed Press, 1983).

77. See Marable, "In the Business of Prophet Making."

78. It may reasonably be argued that some of Farrakhan's international ties could yield benefits for American blacks. The refusal of the Treasury Department's Office of Foreign Assets Control to allow Farrakhan an exemption from U.S. sanctions on Libya, in September 1996, is one possible instance of this. Farrakhan had sought the exemption so that Colonel Gadhafi's pledge of $1 billion to assist American blacks economically and politically could be delivered. Even if the monies were indeed forthcoming, however (which may legitimately be doubted), the precise form of their proposed expenditure by Farrakhan and the NoI remained—much like the resources raised at the Million Man March—unclear.

79. Farrakhan, *Independent Black Leadership in America*, p. 42.

80. Quoted in Gaber, "Lamb of God or Demagogue?," p. 131.

81. See: Michael Sanson, "Farrakhan Means Business," *Restaurant Hospitality*, April 1995, p. 22; and Ron Stodghill, "Farrakhan's Three-Year Plan," *Business Week*,13 March 1995, p. 40.

82. Marable, "In the Business of Prophet Making," p. 24.

83. Charles V. Hamilton, *The Black Experience in American Politics* (New York: Putnam, 1973), pp. 245–6.

84. Henry, *Culture and African American Politics*, p. 86.

85. Reed, "All for One," p. 87.

86. See Shaikh, *Islam and Islamic Groups*; and O'Maolain, *The Radical Right*.

87. See, for example: Thomas Sowell, *The Economics and Politics of Race* (New York: Morrow, 1983) and *Civil Rights: Rhetoric or Reality?* (New York: Quill, 1984); and Walter Williams, *The State Against Blacks* (New York: McGraw-Hill, 1982).

88. Lani Guinier, *The Tyranny of the Majority: Fundamental Fairness in Representative Democracy* (New York: The Free Press, 1994), p. 56.

89. William Julius Wilson, *The Truly Disadvantaged: The Inner City, the Underclass, and Public Policy* (Chicago: University of Chicago Press, 1987); and "The Underclass: Issues, Perspectives, and Public Policy," in "The Ghetto Underclass: Social Science Perspectives," *Annals of the American Academy of Political and Social Science* 501 (January 1989).

90. Consider, for example, the censorious reaction among African-American and progressive political elites to the book by Charles Murray, *Losing Ground: American Social Policy, 1950–1980* (New York: Basic Books, 1984). Murray's prescriptions for ending welfare were in many respects merely a more rigorously detailed and coherent elaboration of Farrakhan's basic beliefs on the sources and consequences of African-American welfare dependency.

91. Reed, "All for One."

92. The most comprehensive scholarly account of Washington is the two-volume biography by Louis R. Harlan, *Booker T. Washington: The Making of a Black Leader, 1865–1901* (New York: Oxford University Press, 1972); and *Booker T. Washington: The Wizard of Tuskegee, 1901–1915* (New York: Oxford University Press, 1983).

93. NoI minister and head of the Washington, D.C. Abundant Life Clinic, Dr. Abdul Alim Muhammad, told a 1992 NoI convention in Atlanta that President Bush had played a "leading role" in the development of "a policy of genocide against non-white people," a direct consequence of which was the spread of the AIDS virus. In April 1993, the Abundant Life Foundation

won a federal grant of $213,000 to fund a one-year contract to treat AIDS patients in D.C., and a total of $571,521 of federal monies were received by the clinic 1993–95. See Gaines and Jackson, "Profit and Promises."

94. The Chicago company's chief executive, for example, was Leonard Farrakhan Muhammad, the NoI's "chief of staff" and Farrakhan's son-in-law.

95. The cry of "witch-hunt" was raised by Rep. Maxine Waters (D-CA), whose political career has been forged upon a well-earned reputation for racial militancy in her south-central Los Angeles district. See U.S. House of Representatives, *Security Contracts Between HUD or HUD Affiliated Entities and Companies Affiliated With the Nation of Islam*. As well as the hearings and documentary evidence in the report, see the account by Marshall J. Breger, "Discriminating in Favor of Farrakhan," *The Wall Street Journal*, 24 July 1994, p. A12.

96. According to Lorraine Adams, a contract with a federally subsidized housing project in Brooklyn and three publicly assisted but privately owned projects in Washington, D.C., remained in effect as of September 1996. See Adams, "Nation of Islam."

97. Adams's detailed investigation claimed that, in a "pattern of nonpayment," the cumulative outstanding debts owed by the NoI in 1996 totaled $1.9 million (for which seventy-four lawsuits had been filed against NoI corporations and some of its key officials over 1986–96), in addition to which the organization owed $1.5 million in outstanding court judgments, unpaid liens, and secured claims. See Lorraine Adams, "Nation of Islam." Her findings corroborated entirely the previous research of David Gaines and William Jackson (dismissed by Farrakhan as a conspiracy) for *The Chicago Tribune*, in 1995.

4

The Paranoid Style in Black American Politics

We have a Congress, a Senate and a president working for the destruction of black people.

Louis Farrakhan, 1995[1]

The black community, as a product of their own experience, don't think that a conspiracy is such a bizarre phenomenon.

John Mack, Head of the Los Angeles Urban League, 1995[2]

To the extent that Americans have historically exhibited a marked proclivity toward embracing bizarre and ephemeral social and political phenomena, the political ascendancy of Louis Farrakhan is perhaps neither surprising nor entirely exceptional. What is truly unusual about the Farrakhan phenomenon, however, is not simply the confusion and ideological ambiguity that have enveloped the minister's controversial public persona in the United States, but more the unique brand of black separatist conservative populism that he so vigorously and consistently espouses. For Farrakhan represents far more than merely a conventional conservative authoritarian political actor or a right-wing black American populist. Rather, the NoI's leader constitutes the most powerful and comprehensive expression of political paranoia to be found in contemporary—as well as premodern—black American politics in the United States.

Although their religious and racial sources differ dramatically, Farrakhan's version of paranoid politics powerfully resembles that of many white American far-right extremist groups in its pronounced intensity, broad scope, and multiplicity of targets. Central to the worldviews of both the NoI's leader and the cadres of the white far-right is the concept of overarching conspiracy. Farrakhan consistently promotes the notion that a widespread and deeply rooted conspiratorial plot exists against African-Americans in the United States, and furthermore, the NoI leader publicly identifies the several agents of that sinister and far-reaching antiblack conspiracy. This dual project serves explicitly to draw popular African-American attentions to Farrakhan's own purported political autonomy and also to the relative moderation of the established national black American civil and political leadership elites in the United States. The political reactions that the minister thereby provokes from black and nonblack actors alike are invoked by Farrakhan to reaffirm and reinforce both the alleged veracity of his conspiratorial claims and his personal political authority as an independent, free-thinking, and courageous national black leadership aspirant. It is in his distinctive and fulsome embodiment of the paranoid style in contemporary black American politics that Farrakhan bases a substantial part of his national political leadership appeals as, simultaneously, a dedicated architect of African-American hopes and a forceful repository for white fears.

Farrakhan's novel locus in the paranoid hall of American political infamy is, moreover, doubly distinctive. First, expressions of paranoia in black American politics are relatively unusual (although certainly not unprecedented). At the very least, the legitimate concerns that many African-American politicians have often articulated over FBI surveillance and coercion, for example, are relatively few in comparison with the expansive scope and virulent nature of the many paranoid claims advanced by Farrakhan. Second, paranoid politics in the United States typically comprises, as a crucial feature, the notion of "un-American" activities and the identification of "un-American" conspirators. For Farrakhan, however, the claims of conspiracy that he persistently promotes are difficult to reconcile within the conceptual ambit of such notions. African-Americans have, after all, only been included in the United States as full citizens relatively recently. The ambivalence that many harbor toward their national identity— and both the historic and the contemporary inclusion of blacks within the broad "un-American" compass of many white paranoid groups— thus renders the relative absence of such claims from Farrakhan's brand of political paranoia rational and, at the same time, distinctive in comparative terms. While Farrakhan's paranoid convictions may therefore be incidental rather than central to his mass black support, they remain integral to his successfully stoking political controversy,

and hence achieving national notoriety, which together have powerfully assisted his black leadership ambitions.

AUTHORITARIANISM, POPULISM, AND THE
PARANOID STYLE IN AMERICAN POLITICS

In the years following World War II, in-depth examination of the
social foundations of political authoritarianism (and, in particular, of
anti-Semitic and fascist beliefs) became an important and understandable scholarly preoccupation for academics in general, and for European social scientists, in particular. The prewar rise of Nazism in
Germany had powerfully spurred academic interest in authoritarianism as a culturally fostered personality trait during the 1930s. The
banning and exile of leading members of the Frankfurt Institute during that decade led subsequently to their reconstituting at Berkeley,
California, where they conducted the seminal sociological study of
authoritarianism, *The Authoritarian Personality*. Drawing together the
themes of anti-Semitism, discrimination, and political ideology, the
text became a classic work of social science, "the most thoroughgoing
attempt yet seen to . . . search for the roots of social action in personal
motives displaced on public objects."[3]

Despite the book's controversial contemporary reception in the
Academy and the widespread criticisms that were subsequently leveled at the very concept of an authoritarian personality, the notion has
continued to retain a marked analytic resonance for social scientists.
In 1984, for example, a special conference was convened on the topic
of authoritarianism in Potsdam, New York. Several panels of the International Society of Political Psychology in 1990 were also devoted to
reviewing four decades of research into the subject and, in April 1995,
a workshop of the European Consortium on Political Research at
Bordeaux, France, was convened upon the subject of racist political
parties as a new authoritarian party "family."[4] The persistence of
intolerance, prejudice, and discrimination against racial and ethnic
minorities and the notable electoral successes of extremist right-wing
political parties in several West European states during the late 1980s
and early 1990s strongly encouraged renewed scholarly study of the
social bases of their support.[5]

By comparison with Europe, however, the attention accorded
American authoritarianism by political scientists has consistently
been much more limited. The analytic imperative has traditionally

been considerably weaker, given the very low incidence of mass-based, influential authoritarian American political movements. Such movements have confronted powerful and enduring societal and institutional obstacles to political success in the United States: a liberal political culture based upon a codified constitution and the protection of the fundamental civil liberties and rights of the individual citizen; the relative weakness and permeability of the American state; the complex division and pronounced fragmentation of governmental authority in America along both vertical and horizontal dimensions; extensive racial, ethnic, religious, and regional heterogeneity; and a dominant two-party system at once organizationally weak and ideologically inclusive. In consequence, authoritarian movements in America have been both more episodic and much less influential than their European counterparts.

Lack of political success has not deterred extremist American groups from persistent activism, though. Indeed, the significant popular attention devoted to white right-wing citizen militias and other extremist political activists during the mid-1990s has lent substantial credence to the conclusion of the most notable scholarly study of the authoritarian political fringe in the United States, published two decades earlier, that "the American population is still highly vulnerable to political extremism."[6] While the extent of that vulnerability may have been exaggerated in some of the more sensationalist of recent popular accounts, the novelty of extremist groups gaining growing public attention has itself been a noteworthy development in national American politics in the 1990s. It has also been one, moreover, that has offered a fittingly malevolent and macabre backdrop to the peculiar political ascendancy of Minister Farrakhan.[7]

An unusual constellation of factors encouraged the revival of both popular and populist coverage of extremist tendencies in American political life, and accounts for the renewed academic attention that the incidence and expressions of paranoid politics in the United States in general—and white right-wing authoritarianism, in particular—has increasingly received over the 1990s. The changing issue agenda of American politics, the perceived threats to domestic order from without and within the United States, and the dramatic and decisive victory of an increasingly conservative Republican party in the 1994 mid-term congressional elections together prompted editors and academics alike to analyze what some perceived as a sudden and alarming lurch to the right in American politics. Furthermore, over a relatively short period of time, the siege of David Koresh's sect of Branch Davidians at his ranch in Waco, Texas, in 1993; the fatal shooting of white extremist Randy Weaver's wife by agents of the Federal Bureau of Alcohol, Tobacco and Firearms in Rubyridge, Idaho in 1994; the bombing of a federal building in Oklahoma City (and arrest of suspect white supremacist Timothy McVeigh), in April 1995; the arrest of the Unabomber in March 1996; and the crude pipebomb attack on the Atlanta Olympics in July 1996 together concentrated national American attentions upon the activities of extremist right-wing individuals and organized groups (as well as the many allegations of conspiracy that they leveled at the federal government).[8]

The coincidence of these developments also focused attention upon deeper currents and fissures within the contemporary American polity. Perhaps most important, in the aftermath of the revolutions in Eastern Europe and the collapse of the Soviet Union in 1989 and 1990–91, respectively, the absence of an equivalent external threat to the national security of the United States cast open the opportunity for new and more concentrated attempts to identify possible internal sources of the various maladies and malaises afflicting American communities in the post–Cold War era: spiraling budget deficits, limited economic growth, diffuse perceptions of job insecurity in an era of rapid technological change, fear of violent crime, and widespread marital breakdown. In such a context, the politics of scapegoating—to which such a heterogeneous and diverse society has long been susceptible and has, on occasion, temporarily succumbed—enjoyed a new and unfortunate resurgence.

The political salience of attempts to identify internal sources of disorder also achieved an especially extensive reach in the context of the more conventional strains of American politics in the 1990s. Thus, some of the most dominant, recurrent themes of contemporary national political debate—crime, immigration, trade, and issues involving conflicts of cultural values (most notably, abortion, sexual orientation, and gun control)—were especially conducive to the eliciting of paranoid appeals. In particular, so-called lifestyle issues, which encompassed antagonism over moral and ethical values, were apt to animate the most fundamental and visceral bases of many Americans' outlooks upon both their individual lives and their nation as a whole. As Michael Barone and others have persuasively argued, the most acute, prolonged, and painful conflicts in American politics have derived as much, if not more than, from dissension over issues of culture, morality, and ethics than over ones involving economics.[9] Social issues, such as abortion rights and gun control, invariably force American citizens to address some of their most deeply held cultural beliefs and personal values.[10] For many Americans such issues have been prone to animate greater political interest and to encourage more extensive political mobilization than complex and abstruse public policy questions such as the federal budget deficit or social security reform. Although the Federal Reserve may be a target of their righteous animus, for example, few militias have actually formed around the cause of reforming national monetary policy.

Moreover, by virtue of their widespread salience to ordinary American voters and citizens, established politicians and aspirants to governmental office alike frequently felt compelled to make public pronouncements upon such issues themselves. Consequently, both the issue agenda of American politics and the substantive positions held by many national politicians were framed by, and often occupied ground that either overlapped with (or was not notably dissimilar to), the dominant concerns of the cults and extremist groups associated with the Texas, Idaho, and Oklahoma disasters. The political context of national U.S. politics was, after all, one in which a prime-time speech at the 1992 Republican convention included explicit references to the "cultural and religious war" allegedly being waged in America and in which the candidate making that acerbic speech, Pat Buchanan (who had not previously been elected to any public post), was subsequently treated by many media commentators and GOP operatives alike as an important force in the 1996 Republican presidential nomination battle, representing a sizeable—albeit somewhat disparate and inchoate—popular constituency.

The GOP's victory in the 1994 mid-term congressional elections also compounded popular perceptions of a dramatic and historic shift having occurred in the traditional social bases and issue concerns of American politics. In securing control of both houses of the U.S. Congress, the Republicans dramatically ended the brief return to unified party control of national government that Bill Clinton's election had heralded in 1992. Forty years of entrenched Democratic dominance of the House of Representatives was dramatically and surprisingly brought to an end. The Republicans triumphed, moreover, on the unusual basis of a program of government, the "Contract with America," which represented a decidedly conservative set of policy proposals. The new Speaker of the House even spoke publicly in terms of "renewing American civilization," bombastic language calculated intentionally to cast opponents of the Gingrich project on the side of the forces of barbarism. The marked enthusiasm of populist right-wing radio talk-show hosts, such as Rush Limbaugh, Oliver North, and G. Gordon Liddy, for the new GOP majority, and its electoral support by a majority of white southerners for the first time in the region's history, suggested that a politics of extremism that had traditionally been confined to the outer fringes of national American political life was increasingly entering the corridors of the Congress itself, a view that the politics of the 104th Congress did relatively little to disturb.[11]

The combination of these influences contributed powerfully to a revival of critical interest in extremist politics in America, but the overwhelming focus of such concern remained the extreme white right-wing. In this respect, the marginal attention that had always been accorded the incidence of authoritarian and conservative impulses among African-Americans was once more compounded. Traditionally, two factors have occasioned limited intellectual attention to be devoted to the phenomenon of black political extremism in the United States. First, and most notable, the combination of the absence of a substantial historic conflict over the institution of private property and the demagoguery of McCarthyism during the 1940s and early 1950s have together encouraged most postwar studies of American authoritarianism to examine white extremist groups, generally of the far-right.[12] Second, since black Americans have historically been among the most common targets of such white authoritarians, and since African-American extremism has traditionally been associated with leftist ideological tendencies, few political scientists have analyzed the black right-wing in general, or the Nation of Islam (NoI) in particular.[13] In addition, of course, as a secretive, racially exclusive organization, the NoI has not been readily amenable to conventional methods of scholarly investigation. Nonetheless, Farrakhan's NoI represents as powerful an exemplar of American conservative authoritarianism in its paranoid form as white far-right groups in the United States; albeit with its own particular, distinctive sets of racial, religious, and political identities and sources of popular black American support.

FARRAKHAN, POPULISM, AND PARANOIA

Despite the factors that have reliably informed the reluctance of scholars of American politics to apply extremist analyses to black leaders and African-American organizations in the United States, such a lack of attention is at once intellectually surprising and mildly disappointing: surprising, because extremist and unconventional politicians have certainly been present and active in black American politics during the twentieth century; and disappointing, because the absence of academic attention leaves something of an intellectual vacuum in the literature on modern black politics in the United States. Precisely because black American history has been so dominated by the long and inordinately costly struggle against their political, economic, and social deprivation, both the general absence and the occasional incidence of successful extremist political movements and currents among African-Americans in the United States merit the considered attention of researchers.[14]

The roots of political extremism in America are conventionally traced by political historians to early anti-immigrant or "nativist" social movements, which were invariably dominated by white Americans. "Aliens," whether foreign or indigenous, typically occupied the animus of such groups. Although some of the social and political movements, as well as the ideologies of both the left and right in America, admittedly manifest external origins and foreign influences of varying consequence (most typically, forms of Marxism for the left, and National Socialism and fascism on the right), many extremist groups in the United States have drawn heavily upon a distinctively homegrown American brand of populism.

Originating during the later nineteenth century, populism was a quintessentially American political movement, centered upon the rural and small-town Midwest and South. Two features were traditionally central to populist appeals: first, a demand for government intervention (whether state or federal) to aid particular groups that had fallen into social or economic distress, such as farmers; and, second, an appeal for effective political reforms to give the average American citizen more power in relation to public officials and large corporations. Neither component in themselves suggested, of necessity, especially adverse political results for African-Americans. If anything, in fact, the populists' demands for enlightened state intervention and assistance to the ordinary American citizen invariably promised beneficial consequences for often-deprived minority communities.

In addition, however, the role of race has been fundamental to American populism through the ages; so fundamental, in fact, as to encourage a near-exclusive concentration on white populist agitators in the United States by social scientists. Nineteenth century populists were frequently—and their twentieth century successors remain similarly—divided over the social cleavage of race. In the American South and southern parts of the Midwest, in particular, populists were generally extremely conservative on issues encompassing race and, in many cases (such as that of Alabama Governor and 1968 American Independence Party presidential candidate, George Wallace) made brutally racist political appeals. Even today, while the extreme left in the United States tends strongly to favor attempts to integrate the races and heartily supports racial and ethnic assimilation as a positive social ideal, the extreme right generally favors racial separation, either explicitly or implicitly. A substantial part of the extreme right (though not all) identifies America as a quintessentially "white" nation whose social, political, and cultural roots reside in northern Europe. Many such groups also incorporate into this essentialist vision of the United States additional notions of America as a fundamentally Anglo-Saxon and Christian democratic republic.[15] The formal, definitional neutrality of populist origins in theory has thus been frequently belied, and often very brutally and inhumanely so, by its historic practice in the United States.

The marked prevalence in the social science literature of studies of right-wing white American authoritarians is therefore eminently understandable in historical terms. Nonetheless, in generally eschewing consideration of nonwhite extremists, such studies provide a decidedly partial focus upon American extremist tendencies in general. This is particularly the case with regard to the NoI, in both its traditional and, especially, its modern guise under Farrakhan. For Farrakhan is most appropriately viewed not only as a conservative African-American populist, but also as an excellent contemporary example of the "paranoid style" in American politics.

Richard Hofstadter and the Paranoid Style in American Politics

Paranoia is conventionally defined as comprising, first, some form of mental disorder (typically characterized by persistent delusions of persecution and self-importance) and, second, an abnormal tendency to suspect and mistrust others.[16] Its most familiar and influential public exponent and arch-exemplar in modern American history, Senator Joseph Raymond McCarthy (R-WI), stimulated extensive academic inquiry into the origins, role, and consequences of paranoia within

U.S. social and political life.[17] Most notable, in order to locate McCarthy within his appropriate national historical setting, the late political historian Richard Hofstadter drew upon the standard definition of paranoia in order to develop the more specific notion of the American political paranoid. In so doing, Hofstadter's sweeping survey of American history since the republic's founding isolated the paranoid as an identifiable, distinctive, and peculiarly recurrent style in American politics through the ages.[18]

The paranoid politician represents an especially curious and compelling, though deeply unattractive, American public figure. In marked contrast to most politicians active in American national life, the political paranoid constitutes a distinctive activist. Most obvious, the stuff of "normal" politics—moderation and courtesy, comity and mutual cordiality, civility of manners and discourse, a consistent striving for conciliation and compromise—is not for the paranoid actor, for whom blandness and uniformity are traits to be zealously avoided at almost all costs. Indeed, it is partly by virtue of his vivid differentiation from conventional American politicians that the paranoid bases and sustains his public appeals and aspirations to mass popularity. Although it is unclear whether his typology is fully exhaustive, the paranoid exhibits six distinctive characteristics, according to Hofstadter. Possession of any one would classify the individual as an unusual political actor, but collectively they render the paranoid a distinctive and especially troubling political figure.

First, the perceived existence of an all-encompassing conspiracy is fundamental to the paranoid *Weltanschauung*, or worldview. The core feature that distinguishes paranoids from authoritarians—and that can be said, in an historic European context, to have separated Hitler from Mussolini during the 1930s, for example—is the former's vision of a vast and unrelenting conspiracy as the dominant force in human history. The central case advanced by the paranoid is that of "a gigantic yet subtle machinery of influence set in motion to undermine and destroy a way of life."[19] The paranoid is confronted by opponents whose goal is not merely the enactment and implementation of particular public policies but also, thereby, the effective eradication of an entire cultural or political tradition and, in the most extreme instances, the elimination of a whole people. Moreover, the latter is absolutely integral, not incidental, to the conspiratorial project. The paranoid thus constantly lives at an historic turning point, with time rapidly ebbing away and demanding a suitably forceful and prompt response from those under threat, should they wish to survive. The unavoidable choice that confronts the threatened group is between immediate, organized action to resist the conspiracy or its collective subjection to potentially apocalyptic consequences.

Second, the paranoid differs from most conventional American politicians in the fundamental nature of his political demands. The paranoid is a demonstrably militant leader, for whom the necessities and niceties of conventional politics are essentially tantamount to acquiescence in defeat. Compromise, concessions, consensus, and conciliation are the bankrupt political currency of appeasement. The paranoid's demands are, by contrast, wholly unavailable for bargaining and exist to be met in full rather than being mediated or compromised. Such militancy is a vital feature of the paranoid's public praxis. The strength, sophistication, and persistence of the conspiratorial forces ranged against the paranoid requires his opposition—and that of the vulnerable group whose cause he selflessly champions—to be full, unequivocal, and uncompromising.

Third, the paranoid explicitly identifies and demonizes political opponents—both domestic and foreign—as enemies. As Sargent argues, the identification of a conspiracy permits one to know who the enemy is, and the existence of enemies represents a constant and central feature of the American paranoid's peculiarly distorted political vision.[20] Those who participate in the conspiracy against a particular group or established way of life (whether directly or indirectly) represent far more than mere political opponents. So great are the stakes involved, and so fundamental and intense are the differences in respective worldviews, that the relationship between the paranoid and his political protagonists merits characterization in terms analogous to war. Moreover, the enemy is both readily identifiable in the paranoid mind-set and bears direct responsibility for many current maladies and for the threat of future disasters to come. (Ironically, however, precisely by virtue of his impressive political skills and potentially overwhelming power, the enemy also elicits from the paranoid a grudging admiration and even imitation.[21])

Fourth, in the intense and unrelenting struggle between virtue and vice, good and evil, the possibility of redemption as well as treason is an important paranoiac belief. Although the symbolic attractions and material blandishments of the conspirators' cause may frequently be great, the possibility exists that even members of the enemy's malign coalition may later be persuaded to reform their misplaced and dangerous views. Thus, the convert occupies an especially prestigious status in the paranoid world, serving as "living proof that all the conversions are not made by the wrong side."[22] The confessions of subversives in the federal government during the McCarthy era, for example, provided to many American observers clear and irrefutable confirmation of the truth of the Senator's claims of internal conspiracy and, thereby, further fuel for his anticommunist political project and zealous self-promotion.

Fifth, the paranoid possesses an abiding ambivalence—tending to outright hostility—toward abstract thought in general, and toward its practitioners in the academy and the mass media in particular. Frequently aiding and abetting his enemies directly, the intellectual represents a particularly grave political threat, given the authoritative professional status of the critic and the associated ability of such a thinker to undermine the veracity of the paranoid's case solely through rational argument. Nonetheless, the intellectual can also, by virtue of the very same mental resources and prestigious social status, confer a desirable degree of outside credibility upon the paranoid's claims, as both a source of independent and "objective" advice and as a counter to the enemies' arsenal of intellectuals.[23]

Sixth, the diverse movements manifesting the paranoid style tend to be episodic rather than enduring in character. The essentially temporary and transient nature of paranoid political forces suggested strongly to Hofstadter that the:

> . . . paranoid disposition is mobilized into action chiefly by social conflicts that involve ultimate schemes of values and that bring fundamental fears and hatreds, rather than negotiable interests, into political action.[24]

Thus, conflicts over complex but essentially incremental questions of fiscal or monetary policy, for example, are not the paranoid's preoccupation. Rather, catastrophe, tragedy, and disaster (or the fear and threat thereof) are most conducive to eliciting paranoid appeals. The paranoid tendency is aroused by a conflict of interests that the protagonists in the struggle perceive (rightly or wrongly) to be wholly and enduringly irreconcilable and that, therefore, are also entirely unamenable to resolution by conventional political processes and established procedures; an environment exacerbated further when the representatives of a particular social group or collective interest perceive themselves to be unable materially to influence either the political system or the governmental process to discernible effect. Ethnic, religious, and class conflicts have hence tended to constitute the major foci for paranoid politics in America, forming the main stages of the democratic theater upon which the various demagogues have strutted and starred.

Farrakhan and the Paranoid Style: A Suitable Case for Treatment?

Although Hofstadter referred in passing to the Black Muslims—observing that paranoid tendencies existed on both sides of the racial divide in the segregated America of the 1950s—the principal focus of his seminal treatise on paranoid politics was the American white far-right, and its specific expressions in McCarthyism and the John Birch Society, in particular. Farrakhan's distinctive brand of conservative black nationalism nonetheless merits analysis according to the basic framework of paranoid politics that Hofstadter outlined. For, although some popular commentaries have drawn attention to the paranoiac character of Farrakhan's public discourse,[25] the extent to which the categories identified by Hofstadter clearly and fully encompass Farrakhan is both striking and politically significant. Of course, many of Farrakhan's more remarkable paranoid claims derive—either directly or indirectly—from his eccentric theological beliefs, discussed in the previous chapter. Others, however, remain entirely separate and distinct from Farrakhan's unusual religious convictions. Whatever their source, though, they suggest that the Black Muslim minister meets Hofstadter's six paranoid criteria in full: belief in conspiracy; militancy; identification of enemies; faith in redemption; ambivalence toward intellectuals; and an essentially episodic character. Let us deal with each in turn.

An explicit and central feature of Farrakhan's worldview is his resolute conviction that a deep, far-reaching, and formidably powerful conspiracy—comprising both general and particular dimensions—currently exists against black Americans in the United States. Just as previously, for McCarthy, communist subversion within the U.S. federal government constituted the only persuasive explanation for postwar Soviet expansionism and the "loss" of China, so, for Farrakhan, the existence of a diffuse antiblack conspiracy represents the sole compelling rationale for the grievous socioeconomic plight of many African-

Americans in the post–civil rights era and the devastated character of many black communities across America currently. Only the fact of secret plots, premeditated machinations, and malign plans that are all deliberately designed to ruin African-Americans can adequately account for the atrophy, despair, and seemingly unremitting downward spiral of so many black lives.

Admittedly, a substantial component of Farrakhan's outspoken public lexicon emphasizes both the individual and the collective responsibilities of African-Americans themselves for their fate. Following his religious precepts, Farrakhan consistently and vigorously encourages black Americans to assume the responsibility for their own welfare, reject government programs as appropriate palliatives or effective solutions to current black problems, and adopt private, proactive initiatives to regenerate and revitalize African-American communities across the United States. Engendering such tenets of individual and collective responsibility among blacks, however, essentially represents a necessary response to conditions that have been externally created, imposed, and perpetuated by whites. In this context, African-Americans in the United States are:

> . . . of no further use to the children of our former slavemasters and when a thing loses its use or utility, it loses its value. If your shoes wear out, you don't keep them around. Once it loses its utility, you move to get rid of it . . . We cannot accept the fact that they think black people have become a permanent underclass . . . If we have become useless in a racist society, then you must know that, not public policy, but a covert policy is being formulated to get rid of that which is useless since the economy is going down, and the world is going down. [26]

Black citizens in America must recognize, according to Farrakhan, that they continue to suffer terribly from a dependent, welfare mentality and that, even in the 1990s (as a result principally of the peculiar institution of slavery), "we as a people are sick." Nonetheless, black Americans collectively are essentially absolved by Farrakhan from the full responsibility for their ignoble and parlous contemporary state; the overwhelming—though not the exclusive—locus for their tragic and disheartening modern condition remains essentially external. Thus, for example, the type of devastating fratricidal conflict in which almost 96 percent of the crime and violence in the African-American community is perpetrated by blacks upon other blacks, represents ". . . a field in which the wicked manipulate our ignorance to create genocide, but using our own hands as the destructive force."[27] African-Americans are essentially unwitting pawns, black dupes in a concerted and comprehensive (although heavily disguised) national project of racial genocide, one that is fundamentally determined, devised, and dominated by whites.[28]

The particularistic dimension of the antiblack conspiracy concerns the incessant harassment of national black U.S. politicians and the existence of recurrent, premeditated attempts at the complete destruction of "authentic" black American political and civic leaders. Militant black public figures who either achieve mass followings among African-Americans or who attain influential political roles are invariably made the subject of persistent and vicious attacks by a fearful, cowardly, and intimidated white establishment. For Farrakhan, such black leaders encompass a range of historic and contemporary African-American figures, from the controversial and flamboyant black congressman Adam Clayton Powell ("lynched because he got too close to the juice box"[29]) and Jesse Jackson, to former Chicago congressman Gus Savage, and Washington, D.C., mayor Marion Barry. Although the specific authors of such dastardly attacks and their exact methods are rarely identified by Farrakhan, their political goals nonetheless remain self-evident: the destabilization and eventual destruction of African-American political leaders who fearlessly represent and accurately articulate the true interests of black Americans. The long and distinguished list of black politicians in the United States who have been subject to external surveillance and various forms of political, economic, and social intimidation is ample proof of the many malign forces ranged against courageous African-American leaders.[30]

In this specific generic context, Farrakhan also perceives the existence of sinister and malevolent forces that are dedicated to achieving his own elimination. That this should be the case is not particularly surprising. Since the NoI's leader clearly views himself as the most honest, dedicated, and complete personification of authentic collective black interests in America, it is only to be expected that the many dangerous forces ranged against those interests in general should isolate Farrakhan in particular for especially concerted, aggressive, and persistent attack. Indeed, in this respect, the sheer number and diversity of these hostile anti-Farrakhan forces is impressive. Thus, for example, Farrakhan held (in 1990) that President George Bush wanted to have him murdered,[31] while the implication of Farrakhan in Malcolm X's assassination was, furthermore, inextricably linked to the deliberate, discrete attempt to discredit his increasingly influential political role as an African-American leader that has occurred since 1984. The revival of popular and elite black interest in Malcolm during the 1990s resulted from a long-term conspiracy to undermine the minister's increasing popularity among black Americans at large:

> . . . it is because I am popular today, and there's only one Black man in the Black community who has popularity dead to match my popularity living and that's Malcolm X and/or Martin Luther King [sic]! So if you can tie me to the murder of Malcolm X you can put a cloud over Louis Farrakhan and diminish him in importance to this community—and perhaps you can incite someone to murder him. That's the plot. That's the plan.[32]

The arrest of Malcolm's daughter, Qubillah Shabazz, in 1995, on a nine-count federal indictment that charged her with complicity in an assassination attempt on Farrakhan—and that ultimately resulted in the trial's abandonment—was yet another powerful example of the lengths to which antiblack conspirators would go in order to undermine the Black Muslim's increasing leadership credentials among the minority American community. It showed clearly that the "ultimate aim of this government is to destroy Louis Farrakhan by planting the seeds of public contempt and hatred" through a compliant news media, thus "setting the stage for my incarceration or assassination."[33] That homicidal stage was also powerfully aided by Farrakhan's 1996 World Friendship Tour "interfering with America's foreign policy objective in Africa and in the Middle East," interference that the minister held had prompted intense discussions in both the White House and the Congress as to how best to silence him.[34]

The unremitting and increasingly desperate attempts to isolate and discredit Farrakhan also include deliberate, concerted efforts to attack and undermine his popular political base, as well as his prestigious personal reputation. Thus, even the spread of crack cocaine and other "hard," addictive drugs in America's inner cities—the NoI's principal recruiting sites and mass constituency—since the early 1980s is explicable in terms of anti-Farrakhan conspiracies:

> I have noticed that since my coming to tremendous popularity, crack has come to prominence in the various metropolitan centers of this nation. I don't think this is accidental. I do believe with all my heart that there is a purposeful destruction of the black community.[35]

Indeed, according to Farrakhan, a revelatory series of investigative articles in the *Chicago Tribune* in March 1995, which persuasively argued that the NoI was an organization pervaded by debt, dominated by nepotism, and rife with corruption, was itself part of an ongoing conspiracy between American journalists and "international bankers" to destroy the NoI's leader.[36] Only the fortuitous combination of Farrakhan's immense vigilance, infallible judgment, and acutely sensitive political antennae have thus far foiled these accumulated foul and fiendish plots. A representative example of his unintimidated third-person response to his many unidentified and absent enemies occurred in 1991:

> Everything you try to do to destroy Farrakhan, it backfires on you and now you're just about at your wit's end! You really want Farrakhan? Well, here I am! I ain't going nowhere![37]

Unbowed, unbossed, and undefeated, Farrakhan clearly views himself as the most vilified black American man in the history of the United States; vilification that serves as yet further proof, were any either warranted or required, of the fact of his articulating eternal truths in the most brave and fearless of fashions. Farrakhan's opening remarks to a speech to the National Press Club in August 1984, for example, included a reference to his having "the distinction of being the most openly censured and repudiated black man in the history of this country,"[38] a spectacularly impressive political performance for a figure unknown to the vast majority of Americans a mere six months previously. Nevertheless, according to the NoI's leader, of all contemporary and prior black American political figures, only Malcolm X even approximates the disgraceful level of national (and international) vilification and censure directed at Farrakhan over recent years.

That unrelenting vilification also serves to embellish Farrakhan's claims of prophetic stature since, like the Messiah, he must of necessity suffer widespread insult, injury, and indignity before rising to appropriate public recognition and full and unchallenged leadership status among his people. Moreover, Farrakhan is evidently convinced that, like Jesus previously, his personal destruction is not merely political or social in character but necessarily encompasses his actual physical assassination. Public espousals of a belief in an all-encompassing conspiracy—the leitmotif of paranoids and demagogues around the world and through the ages—is thus a conspicuously prominent feature of Farrakhan's distinctive worldview.

That Farrakhan also merits appropriate designation as a militant is no doubt clear and compelling by now. Farrakhan's political, economic, and social demands are nonnegotiable in character. For Farrakhan, the constant and fundamental imperative to challenge the blindness, deafness, and muted character of his African-American audiences necessarily entails that his public rhetoric be consistently as clear, strident, and provocative as possible. To awaken a sleeping race (Farrakhan once even entitled a suitably modest and circumspect monograph, "I Am an Alarm Clock"), his message must be propounded in an uncompromisingly aggressive, articulate, and vocal fashion. Thus, the minister's sermons and speeches are incontestably infused by political extremism, and Farrakhan consistently and publicly condemns "crossover" black politicians who sell out by egregiously compromising with "the system." The establishment of a separate black American homeland; the quarantining of AIDS carriers (and, implicitly, homosexuals in general); the essentially domestic, secondary, and family-centered role of African-American women; the implacable opposition to abortion rights all clearly testify to a political figure whose values and policy prescriptions do not admit of compromise and are unavailable for negotiation. "Coalition-builder" is more a term of abuse than one deserving approbation in Farrakhan's militant political lexicon.

Indeed, even Farrakhan's lectures and rallies are frequently not public in the proper sense of the term; both African-American women and whites have frequently been excluded from attending. Admittedly, many private organizations scrutinize the credentials of those attending their meetings before allowing them admission. They tend, however, neither to exclude individuals merely on the basis of their race or gender, nor to deny entry to those citizens wishing to attend from genuine interest rather than a desire to cause disruption. Of course, in more general terms, given the context of America's inevitable fall and the imminent global apocalypse, compromise and conciliation would be manifestly self-defeating for Farrakhan and the NoI, black Americans collectively, and (indirectly, at least) the human race in general. Hardly surprising, then, that Farrakhan has frequently subscribed—both explicitly and implicitly—to the clear, simple, and uncompromisingly militant dictum that, "if you are not for us, you are against us."[39] Farrakhan's black and white view of the world is as wide-ranging in its inclusive compass as it is certain of its infallible veracity.

An additional, and very important, dimension to Farrakhan's militancy clearly fulfills the third of Hofstadter's paranoid criteria: the NoI leader frequently and relentlessly demonizes his many political opponents as either malign, misguided, or foolish enemies. Such demonization is in part a function of the pressing need to awaken black Americans from their slave-induced mental and spiritual slumber in order to reeducate them to their true worth, path to salvation, and proper national (and ultimately global) vocation. It also represents, however, a genuine reflection of Farrakhan's theological beliefs concerning the imminent worldwide conflict between the races and the Armageddon that this conflict will occasion. Given the immense magnitude of the stakes involved—apocalypse, global war, and the final emergence of God's righteous kingdom on Earth—demonization of opponents is less a risky gamble than a necessary condition of Farrakhan's preparatory teachings of black Americans prior to their full and enduring emancipation. It is in this aspect of the paranoid demeanor, in particular, that Farrakhan's prominent role as an assiduous architect of fear in contemporary America is most centrally to be found and that has occupied the dominant focus of national and international media coverage of the NoI's leader.

Although—like McCarthy previously—he rarely mentions specific individuals by name, preferring instead the characteristically comfortable demagogic luxury of anonymity and sweeping generalization, Farrakhan frequently invokes indirect assistance (generally of a divine nature) in explaining the existence of antiblack conspiracies and in ascertaining the identities of the various antiblack conspirators. He has referred most notoriously (in a richly exotic plot worthy of George Lucas or Isaac Asimov), for example, to a vision of being transported in 1985 to a spaceship hovering forty miles above the Earth, where Elijah Muhammad issued him instructions and prophesied the 1986 U.S. bombing raid on Tripoli, Libya.[40] Access to such privileged cosmic assistance has enabled Farrakhan to divine, and explicitly to identify for a mass black public, the several conspiratorial forces that are responsible for African-American disadvantage and degradation, both historically and in the modern era in the United States. Four of these malevolent agents of destruction are especially noteworthy and feature prominently in Farrakhan's regular public indictments of the enemies of black America: Jews, the U.S. federal government, white Americans, and black accommodationists.

Unlike both Elijah Muhammad and the pre-1964 Malcolm X—for whom white Americans in general were intrinsically evil devils and among whom neither made substantial distinctions—Farrakhan has increasingly isolated Jews (both within and outside America) as a particularly influential source of mass black oppression in the United States. Most notable, Farrakhan vigorously defended Jesse Jackson's "Hymietown" reference in 1984 and held Jewish groups responsible for anonymous death threats that were issued against Jackson during that year's presidential campaign. Almost a decade later, in January 1994, Farrakhan informed an African-American audience at the New York City Regiment Armory that "Jews are the most organized, rich and powerful people, not only in America, but in the world. They're plotting against us even as we speak." Farrakhan has also argued that Jews dominated the slave trade and has speculated that Jewish doctors deliberately inject the HIV virus into black American patients in order to advance black genocide, endorsing a Black Muslim aide's statement to this effect as "the truth."[41]

The themes of hatred, physical violence, and death represent regular components of Farrakhan's public references to or about Jews. Such ominous references are, of course, neither coincidental nor unintentional. As a rhetorical device, however unsophisticated, the premeditated and deliberate emphasis upon violence is one that is not only calculated to create the maximum possible amount of rapt audience reaction and media attention but also—given the systematic murder of millions of Jews in death camps under Nazi Germany (and the brutal incarceration and grotesque mistreatment of many others)—one that is especially powerful, deeply distasteful, and grievously offensive to many individuals, Jewish and non-Jewish alike. Farrakhan's most notorious comments, made during a radio address in Chicago in March 1984 are a good example of his more general rhetorical approach to black-Jewish relations in America:

> The Jews don't like Farrakhan, so they call me Hitler. Well, that's a good name. Hitler was a very great man. He wasn't great for me as a black person, but he was a great German . . . He rose Germany up from nothing. Well, in a sense you could say there's similarity in that we are rising our people up from nothing. What is it about Hitler that you love to call every black man who rises up with strength a Hitler? What have I done? Who have I killed? I warn you, be careful, be careful. You're putting yourself in dangerous, dangerous shoes. You have been the killer of all the prophets. Now, if you seek my life, you only show that you are no better than your fathers.[42]

Despite his apparently sincere expressions of personal admiration for many individual American Jews, and for the Jewish people as a whole, few of Farrakhan's public discussions of Jews omit a fulsomely lurid lexicon of murder, destruction, and retaliation. For example, the minister claimed, in a speech at the University of the District of Columbia in March 1988 that, "You (Jews) want my people to kill me."[43] The NoI even attributed the revival in 1994 of allegations concerning Farrakhan's complicity in Malcolm X's assassination to a Jewish plot, led by the New York-based Anti-Defamation League, to "incite the murder" of its leader. Farrakhan's many enemies having "already determined that I must die," Jewish-controlled media had shrewdly sought to enhance Malcolm's image in order "to use a dead man against the only living black American . . . who can't be bought."[44] In the same year, the universally negative and hostile nationwide media response to Farrakhan's "rebuke" of Khalid Muhammad's New Jersey speech also affirmed, for the NoI's leader, the stark reality of the continued Jewish conspiratorial project: "I see a conspiracy. I don't know what others see, but the conspiracy is to destroy Louis Farrakhan and the Nation of Islam."[45] As for those who hold Farrakhan's vision to be less than 20–20 and more than a little impaired, his morbid preoccupation with death and destruction reflects the obvious fact that, according to the NoI's leader:

The germ of murder is already sewed into the hearts of Jews in this country . . . The Jews talk about "Never again." Well, I am your last chance, too, Jews. Listen, Jews, this little Black boy is your last chance because the Scriptures charge (you) with killing the prophets of God. But if you rise up to try to kill me, then Allah promises you that he will bring on this generation the blood of the righteous. All of you will be killed outright . . . You cannot say "Never again" to God, because when He puts you in the oven, "Never again" don't mean a thing.[46]

Imitating the viciously unrelenting and unapologetic anti-Semitism of the Irish-American priest, Father Charles Coughlin, during the New Deal, Jews occupy a central role for Farrakhan. Instead of the three interlocking conspiracies of the 1930s that Coughlin identified (the New Deal, communism, and international banking), however, it is the Jews' alleged historic role in slave-ownership and their putative dominance of the American mass media and entertainment industries that occupy the focus of Farrakhan's virulent anti-Semitism. Thus, according to the Black Muslim, the United States is "being made ripe for a take-over from without" through a Jewish plot to use Hollywood and the music industry to corrupt Americans through the "sexual drive." That many Jewish writers, directors, and producers of films have sympathetically addressed the subject of black disadvantage in America (such as Steven Spielberg's adaptation of *The Color Purple*, a novel by the black American feminist Alice Walker), and that much of the most lurid, savage, and rabidly misogynistic sexual imagery in contemporary popular music is to be found among the recorded work of black American artists (including some of Farrakhan's most enthusiastic and outspoken public supporters, such as the rapper Ice Cube[47]), are facts that rarely seem to disturb the NoI leader's simple analysis of the key sources of "corrupting" influences in contemporary American society.[48]

For many Americans, Farrakhan's unrelenting public hostility toward Jews is more than a matter of its intensity and depth. Farrakhan's thuggish animus is also seen by several commentators as being sinister and politically dangerous, in comparison with both Coughlin previously and other anti-Semites currently.[49] This view is to a large extent attributable to the post–civil rights era political context of black-Jewish relations having been altered in ways that have increased the potential for economic competition, and for social and political polarization, between the two minority American communities.

First, the shared moral commitment that strongly informed black–Jewish cooperation in the civil rights movement during the 1950s and 1960s subsequently foundered on class and ethnic conflicts over affirmative action, education, urban violence, the Middle-East, and Africa.[50] Second, whereas shared working class origins and the political institutions of organized labor and the Democratic party mediated conflict between Jews and both Irish and African-Americans (and thereby limited Coughlin's appeal) in the 1930s, the contemporary political environment is characterized by largely dissimilar class interests and electoral affiliations between blacks and Jewish Americans. Although a decisive majority of Jewish Americans remain supportive of the Democratic party, their identification with, and loyalty to, the party's candidates is neither as overwhelming nor as reliable as that of African-Americans.

Third, Farrakhan's anti-Semitism encompasses an important foreign policy dimension that was wholly unavailable to Father Coughlin during the 1930s: opposition to the state of Israel and its international allies. Antipathy toward Israel among Americans is hardly confined to the NoI, of course; many others share Farrakhan's view of U.S. foreign policy toward Israel as being unduly favorable and as deriving principally from the "abnormal . . . power of the Jewish leadership."[51] Typically, though, few express it in the virulently aggressive and disparaging terminology of Farrakhan, for whom those nations that assisted in the original establishment of the state of Israel (an "outlaw act") and who currently lend it financial assistance, military aid, and diplomatic support constitute nothing less than "criminals in the sight of Almighty God."[52]

Farrakhan has nonetheless insisted that such adamant opposition to Israel is entirely unrelated to issues of anti-Semitic belief on his part, explaining that:

> When I made the statement that Israel had not had any peace in forty years and will never have any peace because there can be no peace structured on injustice, lying, thieving, and deceit, using God's name to shield your dirty religion or practices

under His holy and righteous name, this was termed to be an attempt on my part to discredit Judaism as a religion.[53]

Farrakhan's appeals frequently seek to invoke such allegedly neutral, nonreligious, anti-Israeli sentiments in order to reach across racial and ethnic lines to "patriotic" Americans generally:

> I am very concerned, not just for Black people, but for America. I see America like ancient Egypt, Babylon, and Rome, going down the tubes—not from external aggression, but from internal corruption. When a strong Jewish lobby can control the United States Senate, where anything Israel wants, she can get. This kind of lobby robs the American people of their vote when they have voted for representation in the Congress and that Congress is manipulated by a Jewish lobby and other lobbies, then this strangles the democratic process and, in my judgement, is the great danger to America's future.[54]

That Farrakhan's concern for the American nation as a whole rests curiously and uneasily with his stinging rebukes of black American parents for bringing up their children to "salute the conqueror's flag"[55] (i.e., the Stars and Stripes) is suggestive of either a somewhat confused intellectual apparatus or more than a mild deficiency in the minister's political sincerity. The NoI's own flag, after all, represents the Black Muslims' core belief in the status of black Americans as a nation within a nation, and Farrakhan has stated explicitly that, "As a Muslim, I cannot pledge allegiance to the flag; my allegiance is to God."[56] Much as Farrakhan condemned the U.S. Constitution as "racist" in the 1980s only to praise its First Amendment guarantee of freedom of speech in his Million Man March speech of 1995, so Farrakhan's economy with the truth about America's plight (not to mention his personal love of an America whose incipient destruction at Muslim hands he eagerly related to an Iranian audience as an impending and welcome "privilege") is such as to assure him of every award in the patriotic parsimony stakes.[57]

Nonetheless, such allegedly sincere patriotic appeals win Farrakhan political admirers and potential allies in what might otherwise be viewed as an unexpected quarter: far-right white American supremacist groups, such as the Ku Klux Klan and Aryan Nation. It is in their shared—and deeply rooted—perception of both Jews and the U.S. federal government as the true enemies of the American people that Farrakhan secures enthusiastic political support from white supremacists who zealously adhere to notions of the intrinsic inferiority of his own race. Roy Frankhouser, a former KKK Grand Dragon, for example, expressed the consensus of a meeting in October 1985, in Michigan, of over 200 neo-Nazis and Klansman nationwide that, "Louis Farrakhan is a man who understands the problems of this country the same as we do, and patriots shouldn't shy away from someone who speaks the truth, no matter what color he is."[58] Tom Metzger, whose KKK career was superseded by his heading the equally racist Aryan Nation, also attended Farrakhan's 1985 rally in Los Angeles, donating $100 to the NoI. Informal contacts between the NoI and far-right groups were established around this time, though the substantive results of their bigoted liaison remain unknown.

Although it remains one of the exceptional examples of Farrakhan actually serving as an agent for encouraging a curious form of black–white "understanding," the racist rapprochement was in some respects unsurprising. For while white hate groups retain their fundamental belief in the inherent racial inferiority of African-Americans, it is the Jewish community and the federal governmental institutions of Washington, D.C., that are increasingly viewed as the genuine political threats and the real controlling forces that are responsible for America's recent relative economic decline and current societal woes. As one Klansman argued:

> The Klan in the 20s made a mistake thinking that evil resided in men who came home drunk or in Negroes who walked on the wrong side of the street. Today we see the evil is coming out of the government. To go out and shoot a Negro is foolish. It's not the Negro in the alley who's responsible for what's wrong with this country. It's the traitors in Washington.[59]

It is difficult to identify anything in the above statement with which Farrakhan—for whom Washington, D.C., also represents the avowed "capital of oppression"—would disagree. In judging one's political allies according to the inverted logic of the traditional, strategic tenet of possessing shared enemies, the Jewish community within and outside the United States represents a central fulcrum of political friendship for black and white extremists in America.[60] By the very same logic, of course, the fact that Farrakhan's more enthusiastic admirers include such racist and terrorist groups is itself eloquent testimony to many black Americans as to the dubious—even disreputable—ethical and political credentials of the NoI's leader.

Though of course striking, neither the acute irony nor the historic precedents of these unholy extremist overtures are lost on many observers.[61] After all, such unlikely associations represent nothing new or original in the politics of race in the United States in the postwar era. American Nazi party leader George Rockwell, for example, attended a Black Muslims Washington, D.C., rally in 1961, observing that he and Malcolm X were in complete agreement about the causes of and solutions to the problems of race relations in America, and donating twenty dollars to the NoI.[62] (Subsequently, he was a featured speaker at the NoI's Savior's Day convention in Chicago in 1962, declaring to warm African-American applause his strong belief that Elijah Muhammad was "the Adolf Hitler of the black man.") Moreover, in 1964, Malcolm X argued in favor of conservative Republican presidential candidate Barry Goldwater's dictum that "extremism in the defence of liberty is no vice, moderation in the pursuit of justice is no virtue."[63] Without engaging in speculations upon the geometric configuration of the shape of ideological fissures in American public opinion in the 1990s, the consonance in the positions of extremists of the left and right across several issue dimensions is commonplace in current U.S. politics, but in particular with regard to issues involving race. Admittedly, Farrakhan and David Duke represent imperfect political parallels; nonetheless, the distortion of their ugly mirror image is more one of degree than of nature.

The biracial animus directed at Jews by the white far right and the NoI is also invoked by Farrakhan as a central explanation of his isolation by Jewish groups for particularly vehement and unrelenting public attack. Farrakhan holds that the vigor with which he has been condemned by Jewish groups is in fact entirely unrelated to his alleged anti-Semitism. Rather, he attributes such attacks to growing Jewish fears that non-Jewish white Americans will be alerted by Farrakhan's vocal, persistent, and increasingly effective activism to the disproportionate political, financial, and cultural influence that Jews, a mere 6 percent of the American population, wield in the United States. In this respect, much as Farrakhan seeks to teach his race the "truth" about America, so white supremacist groups are intellectually in advance of their racial compatriots in persistently and vigorously emphasizing both the scope and depth of Jewish domination of America. Hence, Farrakhan has even lavished fulsome praise upon *None Dare Call It Conspiracy*, an unrelentingly anti-Semitic tract penned by the self-confessed white supremacist, Gary Allen. The vociferousness with which Farrakhan refers to Jews is not aimed exclusively at black Americans, but also targets white Americans in need of patriotic "education" to the insidious clout of Jewish America.

Nonetheless, Farrakhan vigorously denies the charge of anti-Semitism, a denial that assumes two main forms. The first rebuttal charges that accusations of anti-Semitism are the invidious product of the misrepresentation of his views by the American mass media. In this respect, it is certainly true that Farrakhan's articulation of sentiments that express deep animus toward Jews and Judaism have been a relatively recent part of his public discourse in America. Prior to 1984, such references were relatively rare in his speeches. Moreover, it clearly has also been the case that media representations of some of his public speeches have—whether deliberately or unintentionally—omitted particular nuances that enter his public discourse, such as leaving out the qualification of "wickedly" from press and TV reports of Farrakhan's descriptions of Hitler as "great." Notwithstanding this, however, the argument that selective quotations taken out of their full context are responsible for erroneous notions that Farrakhan is an anti-Semite is extremely difficult—indeed impossible—to sustain. Even as late as 1995, for example, Farrakhan continued to inform worshippers in Chicago that Hitler's genocidal project had actually been bankrolled by Jewish financiers:

> Little Jews died while big Jews made money. Little Jews being turned into soap while big Jews washed themselves with it. Jews playing violin, Jews playing music, while other Jews (were) marching into the gas chambers.[64]

Most observers might be forgiven for wondering, if Farrakhan's many well-documented public comments do not qualify as anti-Semitic, how lurid, derogatory, and vicious must a defamatory public statement about an entire social group be to permit the designation as an accurate rather than an invidious one.

Second, Farrakhan invokes the claim that it is simply impossible for African-Americans to be racist. In an argument that has gained significant support among African-Americans at both elite and mass levels, Farrakhan contends that "For a black man to become a racist he must first have power."[65] Racism as a generic term, however, comprises three distinct meanings: a belief in the superiority of a particular race and prejudice based upon this belief; antagonism toward other races based upon this belief; and the theory that human abilities are essentially determined by race. Wielding power is not, and never has been, a necessary condition of professing racist views.

Of course, the adverse consequences for others of a belief among African-Americans of their own superiority or of racially predetermined differences in human abilities are limited, given the disproportionate exclusion from economic and political resources of African-Americans. Their situation hardly parallels the old white minority in apartheid South Africa or Hitler's Nazis after 1933. While they could only implement their genocidal policies once acceding to state power, however, the Nazis—themselves well-versed in the populist rhetoric of exclusion, disadvantage, vicitimization, and conspiracy—were no less racist in their beliefs prior to Hitler's becoming German Chancellor than subsequently. Power facilitated their carrying out their racist convictions as public policy, but the convictions preexisted.

Moreover, the possibility that prejudiced beliefs exist among African-Americans is a very real one, and indeed the notion of an inherent black racial superiority has traditionally been one of the doctrinal mainstays of the NoI. Even Farrakhan himself, both in his rebuke of Khalid Muhammad and in his unconvincing claims that the NoI has abandoned the notion of whites being congenitally evil devils, at least implicitly concedes that prejudice and bigotry can be harbored by members of any—and potentially all—social, racial, and ethnic groups. The notion that Farrakhan's contention that blacks cannot be racist actually exculpates ·him from the legitimate charge of anti-Semitism is a spurious and unconvincing one.

Still, Jewish conspirators constitute only one—albeit an especially influential—component of the multiplicity of nemeses and nefarious forces arrayed against African-Americans. Although Farrakhan holds Jews responsible for many of the most serious problems facing black (and white) Americans, the scale of organization necessary to import the quantity of hard drugs and to spread HIV sufficiently to wreak social and economic devastation among urban black American communities requires assistance by the one U.S. institution capable of concerted national and international action: the federal government. The federal role in the oppression of black Americans is substantial, and assumes a twofold dimension in Farrakhan's paranoid analysis.

First, through the combination of its inaction against black-on-black crime, its refusal to undermine indigenous and foreign drug barons and cartels, insufficient funding of AIDS research, and progressive regulations regarding homosexual relations, the federal government has effectively abetted black American genocide. Indeed, the secretive and sinister plots of the U.S. national authorities against African-Americans seem to know few apparent bounds. According to Farrakhan, the primary reason that the government has done nothing meaningful to stem intrablack crime, for example, is the increasingly desperate need among white Americans for organ donors.[66] As if this were not sufficiently obvious and compelling evidence of the government's anti-black malevolence, Farrakhan also argues that:

> . . . the government has done nothing to stem the tide of alcohol, which is the number one destroyer of the people, and tobacco, which is of course killing our people; the chemicals that they are putting in the foods are killing the people.[67]

That tobacco and alcohol companies represented some of the largest corporate donors to the CBC annual legislative weekend—presumably unprompted by the federal government—which Farrakhan enthusiastically attended in 1993, evidently escaped his otherwise wide-ranging attention, not to mention his righteous censure.[68]

The all-encompassing dimensions of the governmental conspiracy (like the multiplicity of anti-Farrakhan forces in existence) are indeed almost staggering to the uninformed and unenlightened mind. Thus, Farrakhan argues:

> Don't you know the wicked ones today don't need ovens like they did in Germany for the Jews? Chemical death can do the job just as easily. A little dab of this in the water, you don't know what it is, you don't know what effect it has on your reproductive organs. You're drinking water that is death. You're breathing air that is death. You're eating food that is death because you're too lazy to get up and do for yourself.[69]

The racially discriminatory properties of water and air may no doubt represent as yet undiscovered facts for most Americans, not to mention natural science in general. (Although, in this context, Farrakhan's otherwise surprising defense of the "crossover" black popular music icon, recluse, and androgynous oxygen tent–enthusiast, Michael Jackson, perhaps becomes a little more understandable.[70])

Farrakhan has also occasionally argued that the federal government positively assists in the importation of drugs and dissemination of HIV among African-Americans. In 1990, for example, the minister argued that "there is a war being planned against black youth by the government of the United States under the guise of a war against drugs and gangs and violence."[71] Myriad as the problems that face the U.S. government and successive administrations typically are, both a compelling imperative and sufficient resources evidently exist for federal authorities to devote to devising and implementing the destruction of over a tenth of the nation's population.

The second manner in which the national government acts against black Americans at elite and mass levels is through the Federal Bureau of Investigation. The FBI's historic record of black harassment extends from Martin Luther King through the Black Panthers to members of Farrakhan's NoI. Marion Barry's arrest in 1990 on felony charges and the 1995 trial of Qubillah Shabazz, over an alleged FBI-orchestrated plot to hire a professional assassin to kill Farrakhan, represent two of the more recent examples of the Bureau's deep complicity in the premeditated and deliberate destruction of national black American political leadership. The latter, in particular, was attributed by Farrakhan to an attempt by the FBI (in alliance with the Justice Department of the Clinton Administration) to create "conflict and hostility" between the NoI and the family of Malcolm X.[72] At base, the FBI functions essentially as a coercive force against those blacks who reject the compromises and coalitional requirements of conventional American politics.[73]

If the FBI's role in seeking to undermine black leaders historically has been well-documented, the contemporary scope of such efforts has been less clearly proven to be either as broad or anywhere near as sinister in nature as Farrakhan holds. Barry, for instance, was certainly the subject of a well-planned and orchestrated sting operation; but not so much on the basis of his race or the novelty of drug use as for egregiously abusing his public office as mayor of the nation's capital. Antipathy toward the Bureau ironically is another area in which the parallels between Farrakhan and white extremist groups is especially marked. For the latter, the coercive tactics and surveillance techniques of the FBI are deployed not against genuine subversives but rather against patriotic and loyal Americans, such as Randy Weaver, who are simply gun owners and enthusiasts seeking to protect "their" nation. Although the motives and sources of the FBI's actions in such cases demonstrably differ, the persecution to which black leaders and white patriots alike are subjected is evidently common in the paranoid lens.

The racial identities of other American conspiratorial forces are less clearly or fully shared between Farrakhan and his many white supremacist admirers and putative allies, however. Just as white supremacist groups remain wedded to notions of the inherent racial inferiority of blacks, so Farrakhan's organization is still committed to a belief in the fundamental racial superiority of African-Americans. Although he claims to have "long ago left the language of White devils behind,"[74] Farrakhan views white Americans as being fundamentally antiblack in their values, attitudes, and behavior. Whether through direct participation or acquiescence in black American oppression, whites are universally guilty. Farrakhan has referred to whites, for example, as "the enemy" that trains black American babies subversively in order to undermine collective black solidarity. Whites have been "chemical engineers of death" and have "practised a form of genocide" toward dark-skinned peoples in America and toward people of color all over the world.[75] As the minister told a black City College audience in New York:

> The white man is our mortal enemy, and we cannot accept him. I will fight to see that vicious beast go down into the lake of fire prepared for him from the beginning, that he never rise again to give any innocent black man, woman or child the hell that he has delighted in pouring on us for 400 years.[76]

White Americans' fundamental antagonism toward blacks is also manifest in racial disjunctures in partisan preferences in recent elections in the United States. Democratic presidential candidates have never secured a majority of the white vote since African-Americans achieved civil and political equality in 1964 and 1965, respectively, whereas blacks have overwhelmingly supported the Democratic party at all levels.[77] Even within the Democratic party, the Jackson campaigns demonstrated the pronounced reluctance of white Americans actively to support a black American candidate for public office; a reluctance manifest also in the narrowly successful campaigns of Harold Washington, David Dinkins, and Doug Wilder in the traditionally Democratic bastions of Chicago, New York City, and Virginia, respectively.[78]

For Farrakhan, the disastrous defects of white America are many, deep, and distressing to behold. Addressing a rally at the Washington Convention Center in July 1985, Farrakhan explained that, "It's because you (whites) are wicked and you fear in the sickness of your mind that you must control everybody . . . I say you're sick and you need a doctor or you need to be buried." The minister holds that it represents "an act of mercy to white people that we end your world" and a pressing imperative for black Americans to do so, since "Your world is killing you and all of humanity. We must end your world and bring in a new world."[79] At the NoI's annual Savior's Day Convention, in February 1994, Farrakhan also stated that whites' "history is written in the blood of the human family . . . Murder and lying comes easy for white people. . . . Your history is shedding the blood of all human beings." Such remarks powerfully negate the less-than-subtle analytic distinction that the NoI leader sought suddenly to draw in his Million Man March speech, between individual evil whites and the "mind-set" of white supremacy. That Farrakhan's rebuilding of the NoI since 1978 has entailed the explicit and complete reiteration of its founders' original teachings about the nature of Allah, the prospective racial Armageddon, and the character of whites "without change"[80] powerfully suggests that its traditional racism endures, robust and irrevocably central to Farrakhan's worldview.

The racial antagonists and enemies of African-Americans, however, are not exclusively white in identity. Abetting white American conspirators—whether intentionally or unconsciously—are black American allies of white political and economic power structures. For Farrakhan, such black Americans represent the functional political equivalents of citizens in an occupied nation who traitorously collaborate with their invaders and oppressors. In the contemporary United States, the main group of such treacherous accommodationists comprises so-called crossover black politicians who seek to build biracial coalitions and to practice the logrolling and exchange of favors that are central to conventional American politics. Farrakhan has thus strongly criticized black elected officials such as William Gray, Dinkins, and Wilder for their consensual and pragmatic approach to public office:

America is willing to use safe black men, non-threatening black men who will not rock the white boat by crying out for justice for black people.[81]

In Farrakhan's turbulent world, disturbing the white boat represents a de facto litmus test of racial purity for African-American elected officials and blacks in general; antagonism toward whites constitutes the anchor of black authenticity. Thus, Farrakhan's threat to the black *Washington Post* reporter who initially broke Jackson's "Hymietown" remark that, "One day we will punish you with death. . . . we're going to make an example of Milton Coleman," was also intended to be a dire warning to other black American members of the press corps who failed the demanding tests of racial essentialism and black authenticity established by the NoI's leader. Such threats of fatal retaliation remarkably extend as far as to encompass potential future race traitors who depart from Farrakhan's many prescriptions for collective black regeneration. Discussing the rebirth of black America after Armageddon under his divinely beneficent tutelage, for example, Farrakhan projects an American future abundant with employment opportunities for blacks. For African-American hustlers and drug dealers, however, "if you don't take that job and continue to deal death to our people, then we will deal death to you, make no mistake about it,"[82] an assuredly novel form of work incentives in a full employment economy.

Farrakhan has even held "moderate" black American politicians partly responsible for the fall of "authentic" black leaders:

May I remind you that whenever a strong black leader made a revolutionary stand, the moderate black leaders condemned that revolutionary leader, giving the signal that it was alright to move against him. That is how we have lost most of our brilliant leaders.[83]

To be more specific:

The moderate black leaders opposed Malcolm X and the Honorable Elijah Muhammad, and that gave the government the signals that it could destroy those leaders and their organizations. When Martin Luther King, Jr. spoke out against the war in Vietnam, moderate black leadership stood against Dr. King, and the signal was clear to the forces that wanted to destroy him that this was the right moment to do so.[84]

The parallels with Farrakhan's own controversial position in modern black politics are often drawn explicitly by the NoI leader and are sometimes left implicit for his audience to infer autonomously.

Notwithstanding the flawed history and conspiratorial cast, the organicist and racially essentialist worldview that such statements reveal serves not only as a useful strategic mechanism by which Farrakhan seeks to rally the black American masses to his eclectic, idiosyncratic, and bigoted banner—and to intimidate his more conventional elite black opponents and detractors. Such allegations also serve to reinforce prevailing perceptions among many white Americans of the fundamental homogeneity of black American culture and values, and the continued need for an identifiable, preeminent black political leader (titular or otherwise), exempted from the accepted tenets of democratic accountability and legitimacy that characterizes white, mainstream American politics.[85] (It is in this respect that, by adopting secondary roles in the Million Man March, other black leaders reinforced many white Americans' inferences of the failure of black leadership as being primarily a function of the absence of a single, dominant black leader.) Although many distinguished, responsible, and courageous African-American politicians refused to participate in the Million Man March, these "inauthentic" blacks are—along with Jews, whites, and the federal government—among black America's central and most consistently disturbing enemies.

While the notion of having enemies rather than mere opponents is one wholly alien to most American politicians and decidedly unusual in the general tenor of public discourse in the United States, it nonetheless serves as still further evidence to Farrakhan (in the very unlikely event that any were needed) of the fundamentally correct character of his analysis. Having been strongly criticized by the black activist, Paul Robeson, for having made enemies among the wrong people, for example, the Black Muslim leader's response was to seek to diminish the force of the criticism by invoking claims of his significant popular black American support. In an argument somewhat strained in coherence and clarity, Farrakhan responded that:

Well, I'm not the first to make enemies among the wrong people. The question is, are the wrong people the oppressors of the right people? No, I have impressed the *right* people—the masses.[86]

In sum, then, the existence of enemies of black America is a central and vital component of Farrakhan's public discourse.

Nonetheless, for Farrakhan, the possibility of black American redemption also represents a necessary and important feature of his religious and political worldview. Providing that they listen carefully to his enlightened warnings and vigorously adhere to his divine prescriptions, black Americans can successfully cast off their slave mentality and experience a complete spiritual, psychological, and mental regeneration, attaining a resplendent revival through embracing reaction, in effect.

Moreover, the possibility of mass black redemption is regularly reaffirmed by the addition to the NoI of new African-American members and by its popularity among disadvantaged urban blacks, black college students, and black celebrities. That Farrakhan commands speaking fees for college lectures far in excess of other national black politicians provides one indication of his exceptional leadership position among African-Americans. Furthermore, the embrace of Islam by disgraced black Americans in politics and entertainment/sport, such as former convicts Barry and boxer Mike Tyson, respectively (as well as black entertainers such as the rap and film star, Ice Cube), all provide additional—and very visible—examples of successful conversion. In Barry's case, the mayor's apparent spiritual and political rejuvenation was an especially piquant redemptive victory for Farrakhan, who had denounced him in 1990 as an immoral drug fiend, prior to Barry's subsequently embracing the NoI.[87] The public notoriety of figures such as Johnnie Cochran, the leading O. J. Simpson defense attorney, being escorted to court by Fruit of Islam guards also undoubtedly lends the NoI a particular social cache among many black Americans. The example of individual black Americans, apparently at the very depths of social life in America, being "raised" and rejuvenated by the NoI is a powerful religious metaphor and also a political symbol of manifest significance.

A distinct, though complementary, feature of Farrakhan's paranoid politics is his anti-intellectualism, which is in turn linked to a broader antielitism that frequently animates the NoI's leader and informs his public discourse. Given the divine source of his belief system, the hostility evinced by Farrakhan toward intellectuals is hardly surprising. Since the values, beliefs, attitudes, and prescriptions that the NoI's leader advances are by definition correct and wholly irrefutable, given their directly divine derivation, the position of most intellectuals is necessarily marginal and fundamentally redundant. In terms of recruitment to full membership in the NoI—as Malcolm X eventually found to fatal cost—independent thinkers need not apply. Critical faculties must essentially be sacrificed upon the altars of leadership loyalty and conformity to the prescribed NoI faith.

Nonetheless, a degree of ambivalence characterizes Farrakhan's antipathy toward the thinking and writing classes in America. Most notable, Farrakhan simultaneously denounces intellectuals who challenge the NoI's mass black credibility and eagerly cites those who either directly or indirectly affirm his own eclectic positions and esoteric arguments. Enlisting unspecified authorities or experts in the Farrakhan cause is a common rhetorical tactic:

> According to demographers, if the plummeting birth rate of white people in America continues, in a few years, it will reach zero population growth. As for blacks, Hispanics, and Native Americans, if their present birth rate continues, by the year 2080, demographers say, blacks, Hispanics and native Americans will conceivably be 50 percent or more of the United States population . . . If things continue just birthwise, we could control the Congress, we could control the Supreme Court, we could control state legislatures and then "Run, Jesse, run" or "Run, Jesse Junior, run," or "Run, Jesse the Third, run."[88]

The NoI's February 1985 Savior's Day convention also featured a major speech by Dr. Arthur Butz, a leading Holocaust "revisionist" historian and a prominent associate of white American neo-Nazi groups. The imprimatur of intellectual credibility is one eagerly sought by Farrakhan from either anonymous or unusual (and flawed), critical sources.

Farrakhan also frequently cites *The Secret Relationship Between Blacks and Jews*, a NoI text controversially adopted by Tony Martin, a black American professor in Wellesley College's African Studies Department, as authoritative confirmation of the Jewish role in black enslavement. Persuasively labeled the "bible of black anti-Semitism" by Henry Louis Gates, the book provides a fascinating window on the black paranoid disposition in general in the United States and toward intellectuals in particular. Vigorously promoted by Farrakhan and his followers, the book serves as the functional contemporary equivalent for the NoI that the *Protocols of the Elders of Zion* has done previously for many anti-Semitic groups. Most of its central arguments have been strongly countered and convincingly disproved. Contrary to its central argument, for instance, the existence of slavery in Africa was a Muslim invention long before the white man colonized the continent. Moreover, nothing in the orthodox Muslim writings of the Prophet forbids the institution of slavery, which is one of the central reasons for its development into an extremely profitable business dominated by Arabs. For Farrakhan and the NoI, *The Secret Relationship* (compiled by the NoI's "historical research department") represented a useful pseudo-intellectual attempt to neutralize such inconvenient facts.[89]

Although its distortive allegations were both condemned by the Council of the American Historical Association (in January 1995) and emphatically refuted in an extremely detailed, point-by-point analysis by the distinguished historian, Harold Brackman[90] (invoking in their full and accurate context many of the sources misused and misquoted in Farrakhan's version), the NoI book rapidly became a best-seller among black Americans. As the cultural critic Robert Hughes has persuasively argued, in spite of Brackman's extensive research, the author's clear exposure of the NoI text's pseudo-history:

> . . . could not penetrate the black community as *The Secret Relationship* has done, since it is in the nature of paranoid texts to inoculate naive readers against their rebuttal; any reply becomes part of the huge global conspiracy itself.[91]

Indeed, the particular instance of *The Secret Relationship* manifested a more broad and serious dilemma for Farrakhan's opponents generally. As the NoI's leader is evidently well aware—and as some of his strongest and most courageous critics, such as the *Washington Post* journalist Juan Williams, regularly point out—the challenge to or condemnation of Farrakhan's paranoid claims has a tendency to rebound and reinforce the claims' political salience and popular black appeal in inverse proportion to the ferocity of the attacks. For Farrakhan's political opponents, the strategic dilemma is one that is not only acute but also essentially intractable: on the one hand, to seek to refute Farrakhan's claims, and thereby to lend him an importance through dignifying his outrageous charges that he might otherwise forfeit; or, alternatively, to ignore the claims, and (as was previously the case for McCarthy's anticommunist allegations) thereby to provide an implicit and tacit acceptance of their veracity from the very groups whom Farrakhan accuses of continually conspiring against African-Americans.

Much as Hofstadter observed that, for American paranoids generally, the greatest evidence for the existence of an all-consuming conspiracy is the complete absence of such evidence, so, in Farrakhan's particular case, the greater the frequency and the more intense the vigor with which Jewish groups and others seek to refute his conspiratorial claims and "historical" arguments, the more those claims thereby acquire the status of potentially accurate and legitimate political views and perspicacious historical interpretations among many black Americans. Certainly, Farrakhan takes great nourishment in such attacks, which seem only to confirm the accuracy of his allegations about his enemies' diabolical motives and their unremitting personal animus. After all, a basic logic suggests that, if the claims that Farrakhan advances were so manifestly wrong or obviously preposterous, why bother to seek to repudiate them with such vigor and passion at all?

Although the bulk of Farrakhan's anti-intellectual critique is aimed at nonblack Americans, it also comprises a racial dimension that is addressed specifically and exclusively to black American professionals. Criticisms of African-American intellectuals and professionals are a regular feature of Farrakhan's speeches. For the NoI's leader, such African-Americans neglect their solidaristic duties to their race by working for white-dominated corporations, such as IBM and Microsoft, and by pursuing their individual careers at the expense of the collective social group. The mental resources and physical effort that they devote to furthering the corporate interests of such white businesses ought to be more effectively and responsibly employed in intrablack social and economic affairs. Along with white American critics in general, African-American intellectuals in particular therefore represent important objects of Farrakhan's fiery disapprobation.

That Farrakhan meets the first five of the six criteria of paranoia identified by Hofstadter appears incontrovertibly to be the case.

What, though, of the traditionally temporary and transient nature of the paranoid disposition and its multiple organizational expressions? Paranoid movements such as McCarthyism, and extremist forces in American politics in general, are largely ephemeral phenomena, the product of very specific, unusual, and transitory conditions, according to most analyses.[92] For Hofstadter, in particular, this observation was at once a cause for both optimism and caution: the former, in pointing to the fundamental resilience of the political moderation, liberal tolerance, and inclusive pluralism of American culture; and the latter, in the tenacious tendency of paranoid movements to reconstitute and reappear over time in a variety of distinct forms.

In this respect, Farrakhan and his organization could be argued to be manifestly ineligible for the paranoid designation. In particular, after sixty-seven years, the NoI represents a more enduring than ephemeral component of American authoritarianism in general, and black American social and civic life in particular. To this extent, both the specific organization, and the longevity of black American separatist political thought generally, might together be held to disqualify Farrakhan from the paranoid category of American authoritarians and extremists. Not only is his organization effectively institutionalized in the United States (despite its intermittent internal feuds and alleged factions), but Farrakhan fits into a political and ideological locus in American politics more permanent than transient during the twentieth century as a whole.

While the NoI does constitute an enduring component of the universe of American authoritarian movements this century, however, Farrakhan clearly represents an entirely novel leader of the organization in terms of his political strategy, tactics, and, most important, his broad social impact. The NoI's political activism, in particular, is unprecedented, and unquestionably represents Farrakhan's most important and innovative strategic contribution since he assumed its leadership in 1978: in 1984, Farrakhan registered to vote, a first for any member of the sect, and cast his vote for Jesse Jackson in the Illinois Democratic Party primary election of that year; the Fruit of Islam provided security for Jackson's 1984 campaign, and Farrakhan took a keen and supportive interest in the candidate's affairs; in 1986, Farrakhan's fund-raising world tour included visits to China, Ghana, Iran, Japan, Libya, Pakistan, and Saudi Arabia; Farrakhan has frequently addressed the national and international media and appeared on national television, in a fashion that both Elijah Muhammad and

Malcolm X largely eschewed; three NoI members unsuccessfully sought elective office in Washington, D.C., in 1990; during 1992–96, relatively successful overtures were made by Farrakhan toward mainstream black organizations and elected officials; October 16, 1995, saw Farrakhan organize and lead an unprecedentedly large national gathering of African-Americans in the Million Man March on Washington, D.C.; the beginning of 1996 saw Farrakhan once more travel across Africa and the Middle East, often to be treated by his hosts in the manner normally accorded a head of state; and Farrakhan mounted a campaign to register black, Arab, and Muslim voters in 1996, ostensibly in order to forge "a third force" that would be effective in the United States in defending their interests and ensuring their rights.[93] None of these initiatives had previously been advanced in theory or executed in practice by either Elijah Muhammad or Malcolm X.

The NoI's permanence should not, therefore, obscure the essentially episodic character of the Farrakhan phenomenon, insofar as it represents neither an extension of Elijah's leadership nor a guarantor of substantial political continuity under Farrakhan's potential successors.[94] Farrakhan's personal contribution as leader of the NoI has been critically influential in his achievement of national leadership status among African-Americans in the 1990s. In his strategic and tactical choices, his adaptation and contemporary reapplication of Elijah's original teachings, and his evolving relations with other African-American religious and political leaders, Farrakhan has displayed a wholly distinctive, entrepreneurial, and individualistic approach, neither imitative of, nor emulated successfully by, other black American actors. To this extent, Farrakhan evidently meets the sixth of Hofstadter's criteria of American political paranoia.

In sum, then, Farrakhan powerfully exemplifies an exceptional, black variant of the dominant tradition or "style" of political paranoia in American politics. The NoI's leader is, of course, only one (albeit particularly visible and controversial) exponent of paranoid politics in the contemporary United States. Both other black American activists, such as Sharpton and Leonara Fulani, and nonblack politicians, from Duke and Buchanan on the conservative far-right to former California governor Jerry Brown on the progressive left, manifest varying degrees of paranoia in their political critiques and policy prescriptions. Their fears, frustrations, and resentments are also unquestionably shared by substantial numbers of ordinary American citizens. Most notable, deep antipathy to government in general, and the federal government in particular, is a long-established but still extremely potent target for the expression of popular anger and mass disenchantment in the America of the 1990s.

The articulation of citizen grievances that such figures address has constituted a central feature of populist politics in general over the course of American history. In constructing a political battle centered upon a bitter struggle between "us" and "them," based on an apparently irreconcilable conflict of fundamental values that admits of no obvious compromise, populists seek to exploit genuine fears and resentments among sections of the citizenry by expressing such sentiments and allocating blame upon particular groups or institutions. Partly by virtue of the nation's long and rich history of representing a welcoming home to immigrants from all corners of the world, the populist strain in politics in the United States—one that stresses the precedence of values of social order and equality over freedom—is essentially as American as apple pie (if not always as palatable). Indeed, it is mildly ironic that aliens of some or another type have been—and remain—so evidently integral to America's social, political, and economic development and yet have so frequently formed the target for concerted and vitriolic attack. The politics of scapegoating that is rarely far from the surface of such populist appeals is a sadly familiar, recurrent, and unattractive feature of the American political landscape.

Political paranoia, by contrast, is not so clearly an integral feature of the American polity, however much it is a transparently recurrent one. The articulation of conspiracy theories is not a necessary feature of populist rhetoric. It is absolutely central, however, to the paranoiac's political praxis. Moreover, not only is it the case that few contemporary political figures fulfill the analytic criteria of American paranoid politics identified by Hofstadter as does Farrakhan; but, in addition, still fewer have achieved the notable social and political impact of the NoI's leader over recent years. As the head of a national organization of long historical standing, Farrakhan possesses an organizational base and an established mechanism of institutional support denied more marginal and sensationalist local political figures, such as Sharpton. Perhaps most significant, Farrakhan's political locus in the NoI accords him an historic and ideological legacy upon which to draw that few other contemporary African-American politicians can rely on in comparable fashion.

In addition, of course, the impact that Farrakhan has achieved has occurred as a member of a minority racial group that has been subject to grievous harms and deliberate mistreatment over the course of American history. The potency of Farrakhan's political paranoia consequently has assumed threatening dimensions to many non-black observers of his political rise. With the notable and mercifully brief exception of McCarthyism, the incidence of paranoid appeals among white Americans has conventionally been greeted by a curiosity and bewilderment that has been tempered by the confident expectation of its effective containment by the majority-white population. Its occurrence among a racial minority still suffering from disproportionate social and economic grievances during the 1990s is less deserving of a sanguine response, for many white and black Americans alike; not least when whites in general, and Jews in particular, are isolated as being particularly culpable for the distressing plight of the black disadvantaged in the modern United States.

It is in this respect that Farrakhan occupies an especially important and exceptional status among contemporary African-American political, civic, and religious leaders. The incidence of paranoid appeals among African-Americans is of vital importance in understanding Farrakhan's political rise and national role. As Andrew Hacker has compellingly argued, the fear that black Americans achieving political power will exact retributive justice upon whites for white Americans having previously treated blacks unfavorably is a powerful and widespread dread that continues to animate the white psyche and to condition relations between the races in contemporary America. Typically, though, few national political figures of either race have publicly interpreted the latent sensibilities of whites as succinctly and brutally as Farrakhan did when he stated that, "You fear we'll do to you what you did to us."[95] It is upon such deeply held (though rarely articulated) fears and resentments, among both blacks and nonblacks, that much of Farrakhan's public discourse is forged and that his viscerally reactionary and paranoid political appeal among many African-Americans is in part based. The scar of race is an ugly abrasion that Farrakhan invokes as a political scare tactic, simultaneously to provoke and embolden African Americans and to shock and intimidate white Americans—to significant political and social effect.

The fractious "threat" that Farrakhan personifies to many whites is therefore perceived by some critics to be especially great, by virtue not only of the glaring and incontrovertible historic fact of black mistreatment, subjugation, and murder in the United States at white American hands, but also as a result of the obvious deterioration in the quality of life and the socioeconomic infrastructure of many black communities since achievement of formal civil and political equality, in 1964 and 1965, respectively. For many people, Farrakhan represents the formidable symbolic and (rhetorically) violent African-American political repository of a powerful, constant, and barely suppressed black rage, a rage directed not only toward their historic mistreatment but also to their contemporary deprivation. More than "the hate that hate produced," the Farrakhan phenomenon constitutes the hate that equality before the law, growing black political representation, and the formal prohibition of public discrimination by race in America have together failed to quell in the post–civil rights era. The anger and disappointment that fuel Farrakhan's racial animus are of extensive and deep historical lineage.

Thus, in invoking the claims that Farrakhan does, the Black Muslim leader uses political paranoia for a dual political purpose. First, the extreme nature of his claims and the uncompromisingly aggressive rhetoric in which they are couched draw popular attention to the relative moderation of both the content and the style of established national black politicians' public discourse. In presentational and discursive forms, the NoI's leader vividly recalls earlier periods of American history in which apparently isolated African-American political, civic, and religious leaders waged entrenched battles against many powerful opponents and seemingly insurmountable odds. Eschewing appeals to the forging of broad-based coalitions, consensus, and interracial harmony, Farrakhan instead enthusiastically embraces a strident, radical rhetoric that most—though not all—black elected officials long ago discarded as outdated, inappropriate, and fundamentally self-defeating, both for them individually and for African-Americans collectively. Farrakhan, like his one-time friend and mentor, and subsequent enemy, Malcolm X, stands in sharp and vivid contrast to the bulk of contemporary black civic, religious, and political leaders. Like Malcolm before him, Farrakhan wins many thousands of adherents and plaudits among African-Americans—as well as many critics and opponents—for the caustic candor by which he "tells it like it is"; even, and especially, when he tells it like it is not.

Second, in making the exotic claims he does, Farrakhan invokes paranoia as supportive evidence of his extraordinary and exceptional political independence, and hence unique political authority, among national black political leaders. Uncompromised by the political demands of consensus-building and conciliation that typically confront elected or appointed black American public officials in the

United States, Farrakhan seeks to reinforce his "outsider" political credentials as an incorruptible and immutable voice on behalf of African-Americans' true, enduring, and shared collective racial interests. It is by a very deliberate and carefully constructed contrast with the established cohort of elected black officialdom—and the pluralist traits that it increasingly manifests—that Farrakhan seeks to embellish his putative essentialist credentials as the preeminent repository, indeed the personification, of his race's authentic values and aspirations. Thus, according to Farrakhan's own characteristically humble and unassuming assessment:

> . . . my experience today, standing up against the manipulation of Black politicians and Black organizations by elements of the white community, particularly Jewish persons, has created a crisis in Black leadership. You see, there was no crisis so long as nobody could present some alternative to what they are offering. It only became a crisis when another voice stood up that was not controlled by those same persons that they are responsible to. The pressure is put on them to repudiate this voice. So, then there is a big crisis.[96]

Unflinchingly independent, fearless, unbowed, and eloquent, Farrakhan stands fast as a uniquely outspoken and independent black leader who insouciantly treats sacred cows as mere ordinary heifers. Political disagreement with, or opposition to, Farrakhan among African-Americans is (according to the notions of collective group purity that informs his particular diagnosis of American racial dynamics) effectively suggestive of either control by nonblack forces or amounts to a form of racial "false consciousness" among black Americans. The political strategy represents, in effect, an external projection upon blacks nationwide of the internal loyalty and discipline that Farrakhan commands in the NoI. Fidelity to the race and its assumed homogeneous collective values and interests overwhelms the pluralism, diversity, and heterogeneity that black Americans in fact clearly, and increasingly, exhibit in political, economic, and social terms in the post–civil rights era. In vigorously projecting himself as the prophetic personification of black Americans' genuine individual and collective racial interests, and as the divinely ordained savior of their fate as a social group in the United States, Farrakhan makes extraordinary claims that few other national black leaders either could, or would, dare to advance. Therein resides some of the most curious but crucial features of his contemporary popular African-American appeal and political success.

SUMMARY

Farrakhan's religious and racially bounded conservative authoritarianism exists within the broader historical tradition of paranoid politics in America. Farrakhan is richly endowed with the several constituent attributes of political paranoia: his belief in the existence of antiblack conspiracies; strident racial militancy; ready identification and frequent demonization of opponents as political enemies; pronounced faith in the possibility of collective African-American redemption; ambivalent anti-intellectualism; and his distinctive leadership contribution to the NoI since 1978. Together these influences distinguish the minister as an unusually powerful contemporary black exemplar of the paranoid style in American politics. In combination with the distinctive cosmological, religious, and ideological positions to which the NoI's leader adheres, Farrakhan's unique black brand of American political paranoia accords him a wholly exceptional leadership status within contemporary U.S. politics in general, and national African-American politics in particular.

Farrakhan represents a reactionary and paranoid political figure whose public rhetoric is deeply imbued by the clearest and most unyielding expressions of hatred, ridicule, and loathing. Admittedly, no list of hate groups has ever been officially compiled by the federal government. Although it maintained a committee in its national legislature dedicated to the monitoring of "un-American activities," the term "hate group" itself has no legal definition, meaning, or judicial standing in the United States. While the FBI maintains a list of active domestic terrorist groups in America, the NoI has not merited inclusion thereon. (Unlike many white supremacist groups and citizen militias, the NoI has not, thus far, engaged in acts of direct physical violence against its many sworn enemies.) Nonetheless, Farrakhan's public discourse is pervaded by expressions of the deepest racial animus and clearest contempt. Although not alone in so doing, the NoI's leader deeply compromises and taints the tone of public life in America by the unceasing venom, vitriol, and viciousness with which he attacks those who he deems to be enemies; and, thereby, at minimum, Farrakhan contributes to an environment that is conducive to further assaults upon them, both verbal and otherwise.[97]

That Farrakhan represents a distinctive, vociferous, and disturbingly dangerous voice among African-American political and religious leaders—and one that many Americans of all races would prefer to be strongly muted or to fall completely silent—is, by now, no doubt clear. Two distinct though related issues that are central to the political evolution of the Farrakhan phenomenon, however, thus far remain unresolved: first, the full extent of the popularity of Farrakhan's particular black brand of political paranoia among African-Americans, and second, its causes and consequences for national black political leadership and American politics more broadly. It is the former that we examine in chapter five.

NOTES TO CHAPTER 4

1. Farrakhan speech at Harlem's Apollo Theatre, New York City, 7 May 1995. Quoted in Malcolm Gladwell, "Farrakhan Seeks End of Rift."

2. Quoted in Martin Walker, "America's Great Divide Widens," *The Guardian*, 2 September 1995, p. 25.

3. M. B. Smith, "Foreword" to J. P. Kirscht and R. C. Dilleehay, *Dimensions of Authoritarianism: A Review of Research and Theory* (Lexington, Ky.: University of Kentucky Press, 1967), p. vi.

4. For a summation of the results, see Cas Mudde, "The War of Words Defining the Extreme Right Party Family," *West European Politics* 19, no. 2 (1996): 225–48.

5. Among the most notable studies are: Hans-Georg Betz, *Radical Right-Wing Populism in Western Europe* (Basingstoke: Macmillan, 1994); Luciano Cheles, Ronnie Ferguson, and Michael Vaughan, eds., *Neo-Fascism in Europe* (New York: Longman, 1991); and Hainsworth, *The Extreme Right in Europe and the USA*.

6. Lipset and Raab, *The Politics of Unreason*, p. 508. See also: Richard Orr Curry, *Conspiracy: The Fear of Subversion in American History* (New York: Holt, Rinehart, and Winston, 1972); David Brion Davis, ed., *The Fear of Conspiracy: Images of Un-American Subversion from the Revolution to the Present Day* (Ithaca, N.Y.: Cornell University Press, 1971); George Johnson, *Architects of Fear: Conspiracy Theories and Paranoia in American Politics* (Los Angeles: J. P. Tarcher, 1983); and Sargent, *Extremism in America*.

7. In this context, see the examples discussed in Zillah Eisenstein, *Hatreds: Racialized and Sexualized* (London: Routledge, 1996); and the excellent review essay by Garry Wills, "The Militias," *The New York Review of Books*, 10 August 1995, pp. 50–55.

8. On the Waco controversy, see Stuart A. Wright, *Armageddon at Waco: Critical Perspectives on the Branch Davidian Conflict* (Chicago: University of Chicago Press, 1995).

9. See: Michael Barone, *Our Country: The Shaping of America from Roosevelt to Reagan* (New York: Free Press, 1990); and Huntington, *American Politics*.

10. On these, see respectively: Barbara Hinkson Craig and David M. O'Brien, *Abortion and American Politics* (Chatham, N.J.: Chatham House, 1993); and Robert J. Spitzer, *The Politics of Gun Control* (Chatham, N.J.: Chatham House, 1995).

11. See Norman Ornstein and Amy Schenkenberg, "The 1995 Congress: The First Hundred Days and Beyond," *Political Science Quarterly* 110, no. 2 (1995).

12. See note 3 .

13. See note 3. None of the studies refer to the incidence of right-wing authoritarian appeals among black Americans in general, much less Farrakhan and the NoI in particular.

14. It is significant, for example, that even in a recent undergraduate textbook on the role and influence of racial minorities in American politics, no reference at all is made to Louis Farrakhan, whereas David Duke and other expressions of antiblack animus receive attention. See Paula D. McClain and Joseph Stewart Jr., *"Can We All Get Along?" Racial and Ethnic Minorities in American Politics* (Boulder, Colo.: Westview Press, 1995).

15. See the collection of primary sources compiled by Sargent, *Extremism in America*.

16. Allen, *The Concise Oxford Dictionary of Current English*, p. 863.

17. Among the most impressive works in an extensive scholarly literature on McCarthy and McCarthyism, see: John G. Adams, *Without Precedent: the Story of the Death of McCarthyism* (New York: Norton, 1983); Edwin R. Bayley, *Joe McCarthy and the Press* (Madison: University of Wisconsin Press, 1981); Richard M. Fried, *Men Against McCarthy* (New York: Columbia University Press, 1976) and *Nightmare in Red: the McCarthy Era in Perspective* (New York: Oxford University Press, 1991); Robert Griffith, *The Politics of Fear: Joseph McCarthy and the Senate* (Rochelle Park, N.J.: Hayden Book Company, 1970); Allen Joseph Matusow, ed., *Joseph R. McCarthy* (Hemel Hempstead: Prentice-Hall, 1970); Richard Rovere, *Senator Joe McCarthy* (New York: Harper and Row, 1973); and Thomas C. Reeves, *The Life and Times of Joe McCarthy: a Biography* (London: Blond and Briggs, 1982).

18. See Richard Hofstadter, *The Paranoid Style*, pp. 3–40.

19. Hofstadter, "The Paranoid Style," p. 29.

20. Sargent, *Extremism in America*, p. 2.

21. A relatively recent example from the white radical right is the white supremacist organization established by David Duke, the National Association for the Advancement of White People. The group's title was a deliberate variant of that of the preeminent civil rights organization for black Americans, the NAACP. See Rose, *The Emergence of David Duke*.

22. Hofstadter, "The Paranoid Style," p. 35.

23. On the general political context and role of the intellectual in American political history, see Richard Hofstadter, *Anti-intellectualism in American Life* (New York: Knopf, 1963).

24. Hofstadter, "The Paranoid Style," p. 39.

25. See, for example: Lynda Wright, "Farrakhan's Mission: Fighting the Drug War—His Way," *Newsweek*, 19 March 1990, p. 25; and Howard Fineman

and Vern E. Smith, "An Angry 'Charmer'," *Newsweek*, 30 October 1995, pp. 42–46.

26. Farrakhan speech in New Orleans at the African American Summit 1989, 23 April 1989, cited in Edsall and Edsall, *Chain Reaction*, p. 238.

27. Farrakhan, *Independent Black Leadership in America*, p. 51. Also, see Farrakhan's interview with John F. Davis, "Farrakhan Speaks," *Village Voice* 29 (22 May 1984) pp. 15–18, 20.

28. See also Farrakhan's address, "Countering the Plan of Genocide Against the Black Male in America," delivered at Bethel A.M.E. Church, San Francisco, 13 September 1995 (audiotape).

29. Louis Farrakhan, "I Am an Alarm Clock," *Black Scholar*, January/ February 1979.

30. Of course, ample documentary evidence exists to support the argument that many black American organizations and individuals have indeed been targeted by the FBI—especially under J. Edgar Hoover—for surveillance, infiltration, and destabilization. In this particular instance, it is not the fact of historic FBI intrigue that is notable but the vast scope and unrelenting character of the Bureau's efforts that distinguishes—and substantially diminishes—Farrakhan's case.

31. See Lynda Wright, "Farrakhan's Mission."

32. Farrakhan, *Independent Black Leadership in America*, p. 32. See also the Farrakhan address, "Farrakhan: The Marked Man for Death!," delivered at Mount Zion Baptist Church, Miami, Florida, 2 October 1995. That Farrakhan has admitted to personally contributing to the atmosphere in which Malcolm was murdered makes one wonder whether the minister holds even himself to be part of the anti-Farrakhan conspiracy.

33. Farrakhan speech, Mosque Maryam, Chicago, 17 January 1995. Quoted in Edward Walsh, "Farrakhan Says U.S. Concocted Plot Charge," *The Washington Post*, 18 January 1995, p. A3.

34. Transcript, Farrakhan's interview with Mike Wallace, "60 Minutes" 14 April 1996 (New York: CBS News, 1996).

35. Farrakhan interview with Mills, "Predicting Disaster." When asked whether he possessed hard evidence to support his assertion about crack dissemination, Farrakhan argued simply that, "Statistics on drug usage will bear me out."

36. See Mark Fitzgerald, "Farrakhan Denounces Critical Stories," *Editor and Publisher*, 8 April 1995, p. 11. The findings of the original four-part series by Gaines and Jackson, "Profit and Promises," were reaffirmed in the two-part investigation by Lorraine Adams, "Nation of Islam."

37. Quoted in Lynne Duke, "At the Core of the Nation of Islam: Confrontation," *The Washington Post*, 21 March 1994, p. A1.

38. Quoted in Thomas, "The Man Who Haunts Jesse Jackson," p. 6.

39. See Farrakhan's article on Jesse Jackson in *Essence*, February 1984.

40. According to Farrakhan, a giant spacecraft called the Mother Wheel floats approximately forty miles above the Earth, in anticipation of the day of divine judgment, when it will release its load of bombs upon whites, while blacks who have embraced the Nation of Islam will be lifted to their full and appropriate majesty (the fate of other blacks is presumably the same as that of whites, though this is not entirely clear from Farrakhan's speeches and writings). Farrakhan stated in 1985 that he had been seized by a vision in which he was taken on board a smaller spaceship, which transported him through a beam of light to the Mother Wheel and where, once docked, Elijah Muhammad spoke to him at length. See Gaines and Jackson, "Profit and Promises."

41. See Gareth G. Cook, "Race: Feeding the Fire," *U.S. News and World Report*, 7 February 1994, p. 12.

42. Cited in Jonathan Kaufman, *Broken Alliance: The Turbulent Times Between Blacks and Jews in America* (New York: Scribner, 1988), pp. 219–20.

43. Quoted in David Kurapka, "Hate Story: Farrakhan's Still at It," *The New Republic* 198, 30 May 1988, pp. 19–21, at 20.

44. The comments are from a Farrakhan speech in Fresno, California, 19 March 1994. Quoted in "Conspired against, Farrakhan says," *Christian Century*, 6 April 1994, p. 347.

45. Quoted in "Farrakhan Sees a Plot Against Him," *The New York Times*, 21 February 1994, p. A11.

46. Cited in Michael Kramer, "Loud and Clear: Farrakhan's anti-Semitism," *New York Magazine*, 18, no. 41 (21 October 1985). Other examples (and discussions) of Farrakhan's anti-Semitic diatribes and warnings of retribution are contained in David Evanier, *The Anti-Semitism of Black Demagogues and Extremists* (New York: Anti-Defamation League, 1992); Lori Linzer, *The Nation of Islam: the Relentless Record of Hate* (New York: Anti-Defamation League, 1995); and Kenneth Stern, *Farrakhan and Jews in the 1990s* (New York: Institute of Human Relations, 1994).

47. Cube has included explicit praise of both Farrakhan and the Nation of Islam in his lyrics and the liner notes of some of his albums, in between his descriptions of black American women as "bitches" and "hos." His fellow rapper, Ice-T, also thanks Khalid Muhammad, Farrakhan's even more vulgarly loquacious lieutenant, in the notes to his 1993 album, "Home Invasion."

48. Farrakhan has also issued rhetorical questions as to why no black American equivalent of the attention devoted to the Jewish holocaust by Spielberg's film, "Schindler's List," exists. The question is typically posed as yielding only one adequate answer: Jewish domination of the film industry that invariably ignores African-American problems. It is less common to hear Farrakhan advocating that the newly emergent group of prominent black filmmakers, such as Spike Lee, John Singleton, and Mario Van Peebles, address their attention to the historic sufferings of African-Americans rather than projecting unsympathetic and negative images of violent and abusive black American males to cinema audiences around the world.

49. See, for example, the discussions in: Kenneth S. Stern, *Farrakhan and Jews in the 1990s*; Paul Shore, "Farrakhan and the Filling of the Mythic Gap," *The Humanist*, July-August 1994, pp. 4–6; Frank Rich, "Bad for the Jews," *The New York Times*, 3 March 1994, p. A17; and Julius Lester, "Blacks, Jews, and Farrakhan," *Dissent* 41, no. 3 (Summer 1994).

50. See: Milton D. Morris and Gary E. Rubin, "The Turbulent Friendship: Black-Jewish Relations in the 1990s," in "Interminority Affairs in the U.S.: Pluralism at the Crossroads," ed., Peter Rose, *The Annals of the American Academy of Political and Social Science* 530 (November 1993); and Edwin Black, "Farrakhan and the Jews," *Midstream* 32 (August-September 1986), pp. 3–6.

51. Cited in Thomas, "The Man Who Haunts Jesse Jackson," p. 6.

52. See Penelope McMillan and Cathleen Decker, "Israel Is a 'Wicked Hypocrisy'," *Los Angeles Times*, 15 September 1983, p. 1, 3.

53. Cited in Christopher Thomas, "The Man Who Haunts Jesse Jackson," p. 6.

54. Cited in "The conscience of Louis Farrakhan," *Dallas Times Herald*, 8 December 1985; and King, "The Farrakhan Phenomenon," p. 20.

55. *The (London) Times*, 26 March 1985, p. 5.

56. Transcript of news conference at the National Press Club in Washington, D.C., 14 March 1996. Also cited in "Media Eye on Farrakhan," *The Final Call* 15, no. 11 (3 April 1996), p. 21.

57. See Adam Gelb, "Farrakhan Calls U.S. Constitution Racist," *Atlanta Journal and Atlanta Constitution*, 13 September 1987, p. E24. The Million Man March was also almost completely bereft of American flags—certainly the largest demonstration in Washington, D.C., in American history to witness so few Stars and Stripes among the crowd.

58. Cited in Erwin Suall, "Look who's in Farrakhan's Corner," *ADL Bulletin* 42, no. 10 (December 1985).

59. Quoted in *Newsweek*, 4 March 1985, p. 25.

60. It was also interesting to observe the presence of white American supporters of Lyndon LaRouche at the Million Man March in Washington, D.C., in October 1995. They had evidently identified a Farrakhan audience as one whose members would potentially be receptive to their own eccentric brand of paranoid and quasi-fascistic politics.

61. See: King, "The Farrakhan Phenomenon"; and Reed, "All for One."

62. Baldwin, for example, makes note of this in *The Fire Next Time*, p. 112.

63. The dictum was first enunciated by Goldwater at the 1964 Republican National Convention, in response to some supporters of Nelson Rockefeller who had sought to portray the Arizona Senator as an unacceptable extremist. A central part of the explanation for Goldwater's winning the electoral college votes of five Deep South states in the 1964 presidential election was his vote against the year's landmark civil rights legislation for southern blacks.

64. Quoted in Bone, "Prophet of Hate." Even some of Farrakhan's most prominent public supporters have disavowed the parts of the NoI leader's belief system that are clearly anti-Semitic. See, for example, "The Andrew Billen interview: Spike Lee," *The Observer*, 14 January 1996, pp. 11–12.

65. Quoted in Munnion, "Farrakhan Tells Whites to Atone for Apartheid."

66. See Nicoll, Ruaridh, "Black Pride on the March Again," *The Observer*, 1 October 1995, p. 23.

67. Farrakhan, *Independent Black Leadership in America*, p. 46.

68. On the links between black American political organizations and white corporate largesse, see Viveca Novak, "Conservatives and Corporations Plug Into Black Power," *Business and Society Review* 71 (Fall 1989): 32–39.

69. Quoted in Gaber, "Lamb of God or Demagogue?," p. 108.

70. It may be, alternatively, that Jackson's inclusion of derogatory references to Jews in his 1995 release, "HIStory" (subsequently withdrawn and reissued without the offending lyrics), outweighed his androgynous sexuality and crossover popular appeal in Farrakhan's evaluation of the singer's racial authenticity.

71. Quoted in Lynda Wright, "Farrakhan's Mission," p. 22.

72. See: Peter Pearl and Edward Walsh, "Muslims Accuse U.S. of Creating Farrakhan Plot," *The Washington Post*, 14 January 1995, p. A1; and Tom Morganthau, "Back in the Line of Fire."

73. On the FBI and black activists, see Nelson Blackstock, *Cointelpro: The FBI's Secret War on Political Freedom*, 3rd ed. (New York: Pathfinder Press, 1995).

74. Most of Farrakhan's public speeches and interviews since 1984 do not include any references to white Americans as "devils." The extent to which such an omission merely represents a strategic political ploy rather than a reflection of a genuinely changed view of whites, though, remains unclear. Given the nature of Farrakhan's theological beliefs, outlined in chapter 2, it seems unlikely that his conception of whites as devils has altered, not least since this alteration would entail a violation of the divine doctrines of Fard and Elijah Muhammad about the essential nature of whites in America. Moreover, in an interview with the BBC's *Panorama* current affairs program ("An American Apartheid?," broadcast in November 1995), Farrakhan stated defiantly that he didn't originally define whites as devils, but God did.

75. Wright, "Farrakhan's Mission," p. 22.

76. Quoted in Gaines and Jackson, "Profit and Promises," p. 10.

77. On the racially driven transformation of American politics, see Edward G. Carmines and James A. Stimson, *Issue Evolution: Race and the Transformation of American Politics* (Princeton, N.J.: Princeton University Press, 1989).

78. On the apparent reluctance of whites to support African-American candidacies, see: Barker and Walters, *Jesse Jackson's 1984 Presidential Campaign*; Colton, *The Jesse Jackson Phenomenon*; and Abdul Alkalimat and Doug Gills, *Harold Washington and the Crisis of Black Power in Chicago* (Chicago: Twenty-First Century Books, 1989).

79. Quoted in Christopher Thomas, "Idol Who Strikes Terror Into Whites," *The (London) Times*, 26 March 1985, p. 5.

80. The term is that of Lincoln, in *The Black Muslims*, p. 269.

81. Cited in J. L. Hochschild, "Blacks and the Ambiguities of Success," in *Prejudice, Politics and the American Dilemma*, eds., Sniderman, Tetlock, and Carmines, pp. 148–72, at 159.

82. Quoted in Gaber, "Lamb of God or Demagogue?," p. 124.

83. Farrakhan, "Farrakhan on Jesse Jackson."

84. Farrakhan, "Farrakhan on Jesse Jackson." Even if governmental involvement in the assassinations of Martin and Malcolm is accepted, no allegations of government complicity in Elijah's death—which occurred of natural causes—have been made by any persons other than NoI members.

85. For an account of this interpretation as applied to Jackson, see Reed, *The Jesse Jackson Phenomenon*. Reed's assessments of Farrakhan in his popular writings also support this argument further.

86. Farrakhan, *Independent Black Leadership*, p. 41.

87. For an account of their reconciliation, see Sullivan, "Call to Harm."

88. Farrakhan, New Orleans speech, quoted in Edsall and Edsall, *Chain Reaction*, p. 238.

89. The reluctance of the Nation of Islam under Farrakhan to condemn present-day slave practices is itself a significant indication of the ambivalence that surrounds the organization's pronouncements upon the issue. See: Paul Liben, "Farrakhan Turns Blind Eye to African Slave Trade," *Human Events* 51, no. 20 (26 May 1995); and Minoo Southgate, "Slavery Ignored," *National Review*, 23 October 1995, pp. 26–27.

90. Harold D. Brackman, *Ministry of Lies: The Truth Behind the Nation of Islam's "The Secret History between Blacks and Jews"* (New York: Four Walls Eight Windows, 1994).

91. Robert Hughes, *Culture of Complaint: The Fraying of America* (London: Harvill, 1994), p. 122.

92. See, in particular: Hofstadter, *The Paranoid Style*; and Lipset and Raab, *The Politics of Unreason*.

93. Quoted from Jim Drinkard, "Farrakhan Denied Permission to Take $1 Billion Libyan Donation," Associated Press Report, 4 September 1996.

94. This ought, in the context of Farrakhan's popularity during the 1990s, to be a source of some political comfort to his critics, at least to the extent that Farrakhan is unable—and perhaps unwilling—to perpetuate his influence through grooming a successor.

95. Quoted in Hacker, *Two Nations*, p. 206.

96. Farrakhan, *Independent Black Leadership in America*, p. 39.

97. In this context, Arthur Magida provides one example of a Jewish man who, having requested to an apparently gracious Farrakhan on an airplane flight in 1994 that the minister "tone down" his rhetoric about Jews, was followed on landing by one of Farrakhan's guards through the airport, who repeatedly muttered, "You fucking Jew bastard. We're gonna get you. Motherfucker. Motherfucker. Fucking Jew bastard." See Magida, *Prophet of Rage*, p. xxiii.

5

The Popularity of Paranoia

> *. . . there can be no substantial or disruptive political action by the Nation of Islam other than akin to the campus gadfly—a nuisance, mildly frightening, but actually not as deadly as the Tse-tse fly. Yet a frightened public or civic authorities, incensed by a sensationalist press, may well be led in such a way to precipitate the fulfilment of alarmist prophecies.*
>
> E. U. Essien-Udom, 1962[1]

> *Anyone who can pull an audience of 10,000 without the benefit of an electric guitar is worthy of some attention.*
>
> Richard E. Cohen, 1985[2]

Louis Farrakhan is considerably more than a one-chord paranoiac wonder, but the harmonic strains of his public discourse are far outweighed by its more deeply discordant tones. Nonetheless, it is precisely through his almost unerring ability to achieve and exploit political controversy that Farrakhan has managed to secure his intermittently disturbing fifteen-minute bouts of national American infamy over the past decade—an ability that has relied centrally upon the eagerly receptive and rapt attentions of the press and television media alike. For while no paranoid political figure in the United States, either previously or subsequently, has exercised a political influence even remotely comparable to that of Senator Joe McCarthy during the early 1950s, Farrakhan, like the Wisconsin Senator before him, has clearly benefited to a substantial degree from the extensive coverage that has been accorded him by the modern American mass media.

The media's role has been crucial to Farrakhan's evolving political career, representing a necessary (if insufficient) condition of his national ascendancy. The central foundation upon which the minister's emergence as a national political phenomenon of consequence has rested has been the increasingly common perception, among both black and white American political elites, that Farrakhan has forged a significant mass base of support among African-Americans at large. Particularly for white Americans, that disconcerting view—that Farrakhan's popular black foundations extend far beyond the narrow ranks of the Nation of Islam (NoI)—has been one whose popular acceptance has been powerfully abetted, if not actively promoted, by the national (and international) media. For many professional journalists and editors, the inviting "story" of racial controversy that Farrakhan regularly stokes has invariably been as difficult to resist replaying in its various dramatic guises as its paranoid protagonist has been a consistently compelling political figure to cover. John Lewis's forceful assessment of the civil rights movement—that, without the accompanying national and international media coverage, it would have constituted "a bird without wings"—is equally applicable to the Farrakhan phenomenon in the post–civil rights era.

The full extent of popular black American support of Farrakhan has hence been strongly challenged by many politicians, media commentators, and academics. Critics of Farrakhan have dismissed the Black Muslim minister as, variously, an ephemeral social force, a marginal political figure, and an essentially hollow and vapid "media creation" whose national public profile is entirely disproportionate to his actual mass black appeal. For still others, however, the jarring combination of Farrakhan's eccentric theological beliefs, extremist political views, and apparent popular black support has instead accorded the NoI leader an especially unusual and dangerous niche in contemporary American politics, one that print and television journalists alike face a responsibility not only to address, but also to challenge strongly and convincingly.

In fact, according to the limited indicators thus far available, Farrakhan does indeed enjoy a broad, supportive political constituency among black Americans. Admittedly, the depth and resilience of that popular appeal remains somewhat unclear and uncertain. Farrakhan elicits very strong disapproval from sections of the national black American community, and it remains the case that the overwhelming majority of African-Americans simply do not share the Black Muslim's beliefs in their entirety. Nonetheless, the minister does receive very positive evaluations from black Americans across a range of important indices. Moreover, Farrakhan's notable political longevity and broad black support in the face of intense, widespread, and persistent personal criticism clearly indicate that the NoI's leader enjoys a level of popular political backing from many African-Americans that is at once significant and surprisingly resilient. However uncomfortable, difficult, and worrying it may be for many Americans to accept the notion of Farrakhan's reactionary and paranoid form of politics securing substantial mass black support, the fact of its occurrence can be neither easily nor convincingly denied.

POPULARITY, CONTROVERSY, AND INFLUENCE: TELLING IT LIKE IT IS?

Students of American politics seeking definitive answers to the questions that are frequently posed about the influence of an individual political institution or actor in the United States invariably encounter powerful conceptual obstacles and methodological difficulties. In providing responses to enquiries about how effective an individual president is, for example, evaluations of the extent of a chief executive's political success must first establish the precise criteria by which to define, and the methods by which to measure accurately, the somewhat inchoate notion of "presidential success." Even if appropriate indices of influence can be clearly defined, their ranking in terms of priorities is itself an often disputatious and contentious intellectual matter. The grounds for meaningful comparison, and the quantification of appropriate indicators of influence, only rarely admit of broad-based and lasting critical agreement.

If the influence of an individual politician is frequently difficult to assess accurately, the project of evaluating such influence is exacerbated even further in the case of nonelected political figures, whose leadership status and claims of public support are not subjected to political accountability through the democratic test of free, fair, and regularly prescribed elections. Although an assuredly imperfect and decidedly partial method of assessing influence, elections are widely accepted in liberal democratic regimes as the most reliable and appropriate opportunities for citizens to express their political will and articulate their preferred policy options by choosing between different candidates or political parties for public office. At a minimum, elections provide some basic indicators of mass approval, and thereby confer upon elected officials a popular legitimacy, however limited and imprecise, that is denied many nonelected activists.

It might be argued, therefore, that attempting to reach accurate, informed, and comprehensive conclusions about the extent and nature of Farrakhan's contemporary political influence in American politics is plagued by intractable, and perhaps even insurmountable, intellectual and methodological hurdles. Not the least of these is the fact that, as a nonelected African-American activist whose organization's precise membership remains unknown, the indices by which to assess the minister's political influence are few in number and weak in character. Reliable, hard, and fast conclusions about Farrakhan and the Black Muslim movement seem to be especially elusive. To move beyond merely impressionistic and tendentious assessments, evaluations of Farrakhan's political impact must, of necessity, draw upon empirical findings from outside the province of American elections and voting behavior studies.

Naturally, the extent to which such an enterprise is useful may quite reasonably be doubted. Contemporary American political scientists, in particular, tend to view with a skepticism verging almost on scorn scholarly inquiries that lack sufficiently abundant, rigorous, and supportive quantitative evidence for their arguments. Nonetheless, few political scientists deny that Jesse Jackson, for example, has represented a key national black American political leader since at least 1984, though until 1990 he had not been elected to any public office and his claims to national African-American leadership rested on limited, unconventional, and contentious grounds. The logic of denying the existence of political significance or influence to an individual on the basis of his not standing for elected office—and therefore being beyond the bounds of standard methods of verifiable quantitative investigation—is both intellectually perverse and extremely stifling to scholarly inquiry, not least in the context of such influential nonelected black American figures such as Martin Luther King Jr., Thurgood Marshall, and Clarence Mitchell.

If elections cannot furnish us with information about Farrakhan's mass black American appeal, some of the available indications of the minister's political ascendancy can nonetheless be located in the sheer quantity of media attention that his various activities have increasingly received over the 1990s. The popular attention and media coverage devoted to Farrakhan during the previous decade had been intermittent, generally being occasioned by Jackson's two presidential nomination campaigns and the accompanying national political furors over alleged anti-Semitism. The 1990s, however, have witnessed a more consistent and stable level of mainstream media coverage of Farrakhan and the NoI, one that has also broadened in scope and acquired a more temperate tone.[3] Primary attention was still devoted to Farrakhan's extremist credentials, paranoid politics, and anti-Semitic pronouncements.[4] In addition, though, more extensive and balanced coverage was accorded the NoI's interventions in inner cities to reduce drug consumption and gang violence[5]; the organization's varied business concerns and plans[6]; the lingering controversy over the circumstances of Malcolm X's assassination and Farrakhan's role therein[7]; and a newfound willingness on Farrakhan's part to grant newspaper interviews and make personal appearances on national network and cable television programs. Speculation that Farrakhan had moderated was a new twist and an unexpected addition to the traditional catalog of post–1984 media spins on the NoI's leader, and contributed to a discernible tempering of the critical tone in which he was conventionally treated in many journalistic accounts.[8] Consonant with this changing political environment, Farrakhan was even accorded the 1995 "Newsmaker of the Year" award by the National Newspaper Publishers Association in Washington, D.C., before being subsequently anointed by *Time* magazine, in 1996, with the accolade of being one of America's "25 most influential individuals."[9]

The new media attention notwithstanding, however, four distinct developments provided important indicators of Farrakhan's increasing political influence and social impact among African-Americans at large during the 1990s. First, Vice-President Al Gore, the U.S. Congress, and the U.S. Commission on Civil Rights independently criticized (and Jewish groups ran full-page newspaper advertisements denouncing) Farrakhan and the NoI, during 1992–96. Most significant, as chapter two noted, the U.S. House of Representatives and Senate approved resolutions explicitly condemning the Kean College remarks of Farrakhan's chief aide and spokesperson, Khalid Abdul Muhammad, as "hate-mongering" and "vicious," by margins of 364:34 (29 voting "present") and 97:0, respectively, in February 1994. Furthermore, in 1995–96, the House convened hearings on the NoI's involvement in obtaining security contracts for inner-city housing projects and on Farrakhan's ongoing relationship with several foreign despots and "rogue regimes."[10]

The 1994 initiative by the federal legislature was especially remarkable. The denunciation of Khalid's speech constituted a rare—

and, according to Rep. Don Edwards (D-CA), then chairman of the House Judiciary Committee's Subcommittee on Civil Rights, wholly unprecedented—instance of the U.S. Congress officially condemning a political speech by an American citizen. An unusual occurrence in any circumstances, such governmental censure would seem especially peculiar if directed against a member of an organization of marginal social consequence or political importance. Moreover, the congressional action also contrasted powerfully with two expressions of antiblack sentiment in America that notably escaped the national legislature's unequivocal censure, one historic and the other more recent.

In terms of the former, the isolation and condemnation of the NoI's spokesperson contrasted sharply with the essentially benign treatment accorded the Ku Klux Klan (and other racist vigilante groups) by Congress in the 1920s and 1930s, when the white supremacist group was enjoying substantial membership and exercising considerable political influence, particularly within southern state Democratic parties.[11] Unlike the KKK, the NoI had committed no documented acts of violence, vigilantism, or terrorism, nor were members of its security arm, the Fruit of Islam, permitted by their own organization to carry offensive weapons of any type. That an organization such as the NoI should merit adverse congressional attention was thus wholly exceptional, even within the peculiar generic family of extremist American cults and militias.

Historic disjunctures, however, were not the only contrast in congressional attentiveness to the incidence of expressions of bigotry and racial animus. Contemporaneous to Khalid's viciously defamatory speech, the Democratic Senator for South Carolina, Ernest "Fritz" Hollings, made a series of deeply offensive remarks about a delegation of black Africans attending a conference in Geneva. Not a politician noted on Capitol Hill for being especially overburdened by either intellect or sensitivity, Hollings referred to the Africans as potentates and cannibals, "in search of a good meal." Although then-CBC chairman Mfume attempted to attach an amendment condemning Hollings's comments to the motion censuring Muhammad, the House of Representatives refused to accept it, while the Senate typically eschewed censuring one of its own.

Although neither the scope of Hollings's remarks nor the form of their expression approximated the comprehensive range and vituperatively virulent nature of Muhammad's speech, the apparent double standard for condemnation of transparently bigoted comments was obvious. That the national legislature of the United States should engage in censure of a member of the NoI was not so much an indication of a newfound sensitivity to prejudice and bigotry on the part of American federal legislators, but more a clear sign of two political developments: first, the increasingly widespread perception and broadly shared consensus in the Congress of the gravity of the threat that Farrakhan's organization represented to social comity and harmonious relations between the races in America; and second, the exclusively beneficial results and political profit to be accrued for almost all congresspersons from attacking Farrakhan and the NoI, a political capital decidedly less marked and far more uncertain for many representatives and senators in the case of repudiating Hollings's offensive remarks.

The decisive and hostile (though inconsistent) response of U.S. federal legislators to the NoI thus offered one indication of Farrakhan's growing political impact. Another, and in many respects more important, set of signals of the minister's rise was provided by the large audiences that Farrakhan's sermons and rallies attracted and by public opinion surveys of support for the Black Muslim minister among African-Americans at large. Both indices powerfully suggested that Farrakhan's popular appeal among black Americans was substantially increasing. Although the material significance of both the rallies and the poll data is open to challenge, it is unusual that a member of a relatively small, unorthodox, and isolated minority religious sect should attract such huge numbers of attenders to his rallies and win widespread approval in opinion surveys of African-Americans at large, and that, partly as a result, Farrakhan should be intermittently accorded the star turn before the world's press corps. Farrakhan's claims of popular legitimation had evidently secured strong sources of popular sustenance and support.

The Million Man March may have easily been his greatest political achievement in mass black mobilization, but Farrakhan's public lecture tours since 1984 have frequently drawn substantial African-American audiences, often of between fifteen and twenty thousand people and rarely fewer than five thousand. His 1985 tour of fourteen American cities, for example, pulled in impressive black American crowds of six thousand in Detroit, Michigan; seven thousand in Atlanta, Georgia; five thousand in Houston, Texas; and seven thousand in Philadelphia, Pennsylvania, all of whom paid $2–3 for the privilege of temporary admittance to Farrakhan's traveling court of reaction and paranoia.[12] Although Reed, in 1991,[13] somewhat caustically and casually dismissed mass African-American attendance at such rallies as a temporarily fashionable act of black radical chic, but one of minimal substantive consequence among African-Americans—akin to attending concerts of the then trendy rap star M. C. Hammer—the consistently large audiences that Farrakhan commands over a remarkably prolonged period of time belies such a complacent interpretation. If Reed's analogy held firm, Farrakhan would have (like Hammer) exited the political pop charts of African-America by the mid-1990s. Instead, the minister's paranoid and reactionary mantra has attracted many more black American buyers and perhaps adherents. (Lincoln, for example, argues that the NoI's newspaper, *The Final Call*, claims the largest regular circulation of any specifically African-American periodical in the United States, at around 600,000 per week.[14])

Farrakhan's exceptional ability to inspire such incredible numbers of ordinary black American citizens to attend his lectures and sermons is indeed striking. The substantial size of the audiences that Farrakhan draws is truly impressive, no matter what comparative standards are invoked. Few, if any, other national black or nonblack American political leaders could aspire to Farrakhan's heights. The minister's rally at New York City's Madison Square Garden in October 1985, for example, drew in excess of twenty thousand African-Americans to the stadium, with another five thousand watching on closed-circuit televisions in a neighboring building, despite (or, more accurately, partly because of) widespread efforts by local black and nonblack public figures to discourage African-Americans from attending the event. In 1992, while 53,000 fans turned out for the opening game of the baseball World Series in Atlanta's Fulton County Stadium, over 60,000 black Americans attended a Farrakhan rally in the Georgia Dome just one mile away—at an entrance fee of $15 per head.[15] And in 1994, approximately 25,000 African-Americans filled the Jacob Javits Convention Center in New York City to listen to Farrakhan's lengthy address. Such startling figures are quite impossible to dismiss as being merely ephemeral social products of passing, faddish, or marginal political significance.

This is especially so given the character of the African-American audiences that the NoI's leader attracts to his rallies. The social composition of those attending Farrakhan's public sermons and lectures is generally far from being homogeneously deprived and disadvantaged in socioeconomic terms. While the majority of attenders are indeed working class and underprivileged black Americans, Farrakhan's meetings also consistently attract large numbers of middle income and relatively affluent African-Americans. One observer, who attended more than 200 such meetings over a twelve-year period, related that Farrakhan's audiences comprised an extremely heterogeneous range of African-Americans, from single black American females to professional football players, accountants, pop singers, physicians, and the unemployed.[16] Moreover, the overwhelming majority of these African-Americans are, of course, not NoI members, either prior or subsequent to attending the Farrakhan rallies.

The impressionistic evidence that such events regularly provide has been supplemented and largely supported by public survey data on Farrakhan. The limited but increasing public opinion poll evidence that exists about the Black Muslim minister has tended to indicate a broad level of support for Farrakhan among black Americans at large, although the exact strength and depth of its foundations remain open to question. An October 1985 poll of African-Americans (commissioned by the Simon Wiesenthal Center), for example, found that Farrakhan had rapidly emerged as the third best-known national black political spokesman, after Jesse Jackson and Andrew Young. It is significant that two-fifths of those African-Americans surveyed who had heard of Farrakhan at the time also wanted to see his political influence increase.[17]

Of course, such an impressive level of name recognition may plausibly have been simply a direct, isolated, and unrepresentative response to the furor over Farrakhan that erupted during the previous year's presidential election campaign. Moreover, name recognition does not necessarily imply public approval. Nonetheless, almost a decade later, according to the University of Chicago's 1993–94 Black Politics Study, in response to the question, "Do you think Farrakhan is a good leader or a dangerous force in the black community?," two-thirds of those African-Americans who answered (67 percent) deemed him a good leader, while a relatively modest 28 percent viewed the minister as dangerous (4 percent said both). On a separate scale of 0 to 100 (from cold to warm), Farrakhan scored 59, a "moderately warm" response. Almost one-third of those African-Americans surveyed, however, failed to answer either question. Michael Dawson, one of the study's coauthors, suspected that Farrakhan's approval rating would have been even higher had more black Americans actually responded.[18]

Such indicators of Farrakhan's mass appeal are also supported by several other surveys that suggest that the minister's role and analyses of black Americans' contemporary plight resonate strongly with many African-Americans nationwide. A Gallup poll in April 1991, for example, revealed that 34 percent of black American respondents believed that African-Americans would benefit if Farrakhan assumed a larger leadership role in their affairs. This figure compared to 72 percent for Jesse Jackson, 42 percent for Colin Powell, and 29 percent for Doug Wilder. By comparison, only 8 percent of white American respondents felt that a larger leadership role for Farrakhan would benefit black Americans, compared to 54 percent for Powell, 46 percent for Jackson, and 18 percent for Wilder.[19] A 1994 poll for *Time* also revealed that 70 percent of African-Americans felt that Farrakhan "says things the country should hear"; 67 percent saw him as an "effective leader"; 62 percent held him to be "good for the black community"; and, perhaps most important, 63 percent believed he "speaks the truth." Only 34 percent of blacks saw him as a bigot and a racist.[20] (These figures compare ironically with an August 1993 Gallup poll that found only 1 percent of African-American respondents citing Farrakhan when asked to name "black leaders."[21])

The reasons for the significant discrepancy in survey evidence are unclear and encompass several plausible possibilities: an understandable reluctance among black American respondents to reveal political support for Farrakhan in public; genuine popular indifference to, or disapproval of, Farrakhan and the NoI; ignorance about the NoI's leader; and attitudinal reactions among African-Americans who may have been conditioned in the post–civil rights era to respond to inquiries about leadership among blacks in terms of conventional, elected officials rather than protest or extrasystemic political actors.

Juan Williams argues that the figures suggest that Farrakhan is not actually viewed by the mass of African-Americans as a leader but that, through repeated exposure by the mass media, he is nonetheless granted authority as an opinion maker.[22] If the core of Williams's argument, however, is that African-Americans do not subscribe wholly, and will not follow unthinkingly, an activist such as Farrakhan, then precisely the same point could be made in regard to virtually any other black American politician, from Jesse Jackson to Baltimore Mayor Kurt Schmoke. Williams's view does not negate the notion that Farrakhan's political support is indeed significant; the generally favorable responses that the Black Muslim receives when his name is mentioned to African-Americans and the sizeable proportions of respondents who publicly endorse an enhanced leadership role for him indicate that both his name recognition and substantive approval among black Americans at large are extensive. Leaders require supporters, however selective and qualified their endorsements, more than sycophants and blind followers in order to propagate their views, acquire national legitimacy and, ultimately, effect meaningful social and political change. And the combination of survey evidence and mass attendance at Farrakhan events clearly suggests that the popular constituency among African-Americans to which the minister successfully appeals for mass black support is far more substantial than negligible in scope.

In addition to his substantial mass African-American approval, the third development indicative of the Black Muslim's increased impact was the growing attention that Farrakhan received from, and his generally improved and increasingly conciliatory relations with, other national black American political and civic elites. The most important political development in this respect was his rapprochement in the early–mid-1990s with the CBC under Mfume and the NAACP under Chavis (discussed in chapter two). Through his resulting partial inclusion in the elite cadre of national African-American political leadership, Farrakhan achieved a notable political triumph that had eluded many black nationalist political activists and organizations in the United States previously. That his inclusion was largely conferred upon him by other elite African-American political actors (some of whom, such as Chavis, occupied leadership positions through bureaucratic patronage politics rather than direct popular election) was of less political importance to Farrakhan's burgeoning leadership role than was his mere presence at national black political leadership forums. The enthusiastic responses of both other panel members and the audience at the 1993 CBC legislative weekend, for example, provided strong confirmation of the important role (as well as fundamental legitimation of the increasing political influence) that the NoI's leader had achieved by 1993. That Farrakhan should have merited such inclusion was testimony to his appeal to a broad social constituency among American blacks.

Fourth, and most incontrovertible, Farrakhan's 1995 Million Man March on Washington, D.C., demonstrated to the entire American nation an exceptional ability on the NoI leader's part to mobilize collective action by African-Americans on an unprecedented and dramatic scale. Although estimates of the true size of the march varied greatly, the remarkable political achievement of the occasion could hardly be disputed.[23] No other contemporary black American political leader could have even contemplated the organization and successful execution of such an impressively well-attended national political event. Indeed, the most emphatic statement of the changing internal balance of the national African-American leadership cadre could partially be inferred from two starkly contrasting demonstrations of 1995. In the spring of that year, Jesse Jackson had barely been able to muster 300 marchers to walk to Martin Luther King's grave in Atlanta, Georgia, to protest against possible federal reversal of affirmative action policies under the Republican-controlled 104th Congress and the Rehnquist Supreme Court. But by October 1995, the man whose public pronouncements Jackson had eventually repudiated a decade previously headed a gathering of over 400,000 African-American men in the nation's capital, striking numbers that were powerfully suggestive of an extensive political reach and a broad social impact wholly exceptional among current national black American political leaders.

Opinion surveys taken both prior and subsequent to the march also provided further confirmation of Farrakhan's popular, if by no means universal, political appeal among black Americans. A *Washington Post-ABC News* poll prior to the march, for example, revealed that over half of all black Americans knew of the march and an overwhelming majority (84 percent) approved of the initiative. Many respondents nonetheless drew a distinction between the public goals of the march, which were overwhelmingly supported, and the character of its principal organizers: both Farrakhan and Chavis had at least as many black detractors as supporters in the poll.[24]

Polls taken subsequently, however, at the time of the march and thereafter, revealed an alternative set of popular black views of Farrakhan. Although, as table 5.1 shows, a mere 5 percent of marchers participated in order specifically to express support for Farrakhan, fully 87 percent of the marchers expressed a favorable opinion of the NoI's leader, while a slightly larger proportion (88 percent) also endorsed his organization. These figures exceeded approval of Jesse Jackson by 15 percent and Bill Clinton by over 30 percent. Most African-Americans

---

TABLE 5.1   The Million Man March*

Single most important reason for participation?

Support for black family	29
Support for black men showing more responsibility for families and communities	25
Support black unity	25
Support black economic strength	7
Support for Farrakhan	5

Favorable or unfavorable impression of:

Nation of Islam	88	Clinton	54
Farrakhan	87	Jewish people	41
Chavis	77	White people	31
Jackson	73	Criminal justice system	15

As a result of the march, will Farrakhan have more influence among black leaders in the African-American community?

	MMM Participants	Blacks Nationally
Yes	80	34
No	14	27

Will Farrakhan have more influence among political leaders in Washington?

	MMM Participants	Blacks Nationally
Yes	55	34
No	14	41

Age		Education		Marital Status	
18–30	33	Less than HS	5	Married	42
30–44	42	HS graduate	22	Single	46
45–60	20	Some college/college grad.	59	Divorced	10
61+	4	Post–graduate	14	Widowed	1

Religion

Protestant	52	Muslim	6	None	14
Catholic	7	Nation of Islam	5		

*Figures are percentages of total number of respondents
Source: *The Washington Post*, 17 October 1995, p. A23.
N=1047, sampling error of +/- 3 percent.

---

also expected Farrakhan to achieve a more influential role among national black leaders as a result of the successful mass mobilization.

Moreover, one of the most important features of the poll in this respect concerns the demographic bases of Farrakhan's support and approval. For in terms of both age and education, in particular, the pool of African-American respondents professing their approval of Farrakhan and the NoI was notably mature, educated, and middle income in character. That Farrakhan should elicit such markedly high approval ratings from a middle-income group of black American males is especially significant. Dismissing the mass black American constituency to which Farrakhan appeals as essentially comprising only the most impoverished, underprivileged, and unrepresentative segment of African-Americans is hence impossible. Although this segment is undoubtedly the mainstay of the NoI's mass base, the minister's signal political achievement is that, as the table clearly shows, his reach actually encompasses very diverse and disparate sections of the national black American community.

Perhaps even more telling than the *Post*'s survey were the results of two opinion surveys for the magazines *Time* and *Newsweek*.[25] The former revealed that the ratio of positive to negative evaluations of Farrakhan by black Americans had hardly altered between February 1994 (at the height of the national furor over Khalid Muhammad's Kean College speech) and October 1995. Almost half of black respondents (48 percent) held that Farrakhan was not a bigot and a racist, while well over half believed him to speak the truth (59 percent). Half of all black respondents also viewed him as a good role model for black youth (59 percent) and as a positive force in the black community (50 percent).

Farrakhan's support admittedly remained far from universal: 36 percent of black respondents held Farrakhan to be a bigot and a racist, and 30 percent did not view him as a good role model for black youth. The *Newsweek* survey also recorded that, while 41 percent of black Americans harbored a favorable opinion of Farrakhan, exactly the same percentage had an unfavorable view of him. Even in the hour of his greatest political triumph, then, the Black Muslim minister found himself unable to command anywhere near universal African-American support.

Such persistently skeptical and hostile responses to Farrakhan from many black Americans serve as the clearest repudiations of naively critical assessments that portray the minister as having won overwhelming and uncritical endorsement and support from American blacks, or as somehow having become the titular "leader" of African-Americans. That the leader of the NoI elicits negative reactions and unfavorable evaluations from many African-Americans is clear and beyond refutation. Given both the esoteric content of his religious and ideological beliefs and the concerted public attacks to which he has so long been subject from black and nonblack American elites, however, this is neither especially surprising nor of momentous political (or analytic) significance. Indeed, it would be far more notable—and immeasurably more worrying for white Americans—if Farrakhan elicited either exclusively, universally, or overwhelmingly positive and favorable responses from black Americans in general.

Far more significant than the fact of negative reactions persisting among blacks toward the NoI's leader, however, is the remarkable proportion of African-Americans who do respond positively to Farrakhan. A sizeable proportion of black Americans consistently view Farrakhan favorably and warmly, seeing him as a positive force within black communities.[26] Moreover, it seems reasonable to assume that a significant percentage of those respondents who either do not answer such surveys or, if they do, answer "not sure" to questions about Farrakhan, also harbor positive dispositions toward the minister. In sum, although the evidence by which to evaluate the question of Farrakhan's popularity and political influence is incomplete, and by no means provides a definitive answer, the achievement by Farrakhan of a substantial political and social impact among African-Americans in the 1990s is extremely difficult—indeed, impossible—to reject. Farrakhan's wary treatment by nonblack politicians and political lobbies, the several indices of his mass black approval, the vacillating responses of black political and civic elites, and the manifest success of the Million Man March together testify to the minister's achievement of an exceptional leadership position among African-Americans at large.

THE FARRAKHAN PHENOMENON: A MEDIA CREATION?

Although the indicators of his increasing mass appeal among black Americans are multiple and undeniably persuasive, the precise extent and nature of Farrakhan's political influence have nonetheless been strongly contested by political commentators in both the American Academy and the mass media. For several critics, Farrakhan's recent national rise essentially provides yet another unfortunate example of the pervasive, if generally unintentional and often adverse, influence of the modern mass communications industry in recent American politics.[27] The necessary political fuel for the Farrakhan phenomenon, in this interpretation, is largely provided by an American press and televisual corps whose principal fascination about national politics in the contemporary United States is dominated by the compelling political dramas of sleaze and sensationalism (whether racial, sexual, or financial), and which appears almost congenitally predisposed to reducing complex and difficult political issues into simplistic and inaccurate narratives. In place of both abstract entities, such as political parties, and substantive issue-oriented national policy debates, a candidate-centered, personality-driven politics and an artificially constructed adversarialism instead increasingly inform the American public's limited consumption of political news.

Certainly, few political scientists dispute the extensive political influence that the fourth estate now exerts in liberal democratic regimes in general and the United States in particular.[28] Far from being a neutral observer of political events, the media, in particular television, has become a central player in political matters in contemporary America, particularly in national and statewide election campaigns.[29] Through its decisions either to run or ignore particular stories and, indeed, through the very decision that a particular event actually merits designation as a story worthy of dissemination to the public, the media participates powerfully in determining the national political agenda. Media journalists both select and screen the political information that American citizens receive. Moreover, not only does that selection process determine what counts as news, but the spin that a story receives from the media also shapes its general, diffuse reception by the mass American public. Television and print editors and reporters thus consistently act as professional gatekeepers to political information, determining what citizens know and the manner in which what they deem relevant information is imparted to the public—a process that powerfully shapes, even if it can neither fully nor consistently determine with precision, what the responses of news watchers are likely to be.

That Farrakhan's politics should have been profoundly affected by the mass media is hardly a shocking or unreasonable proposition, then. Indeed, the American media can be argued to have performed a doubly critical role in shaping Farrakhan's political ascendancy. First, the media have been of cardinal importance in terms of the sheer volume of print and televisual coverage devoted to the NoI's leader since 1984, both of which have increased almost exponentially in scope. Second, the evolving political salience to, and the varied reception of Farrakhan among, the American public has been greatly influenced by

the invariably negative character—whether excessively or insuffi-
ciently so, according to particular subjective tastes—of much of that
media coverage. Farrakhan's national public visibility among both
black and nonblack Americans has thus been crucially raised—and
his political career thereby vitally advanced—by generous, if intermittent, media attention. In both assisting in the initial creation of the Farrakhan phenomenon as a national force, and in subsequently reviving
and sustaining its political momentum, the U.S. media has incontrovertibly played its part in contributing to the minister's national political ascent.

To deny that this is the case would certainly be ludicrous. The
precise extent to which the media has either created or driven the Farrakhan phenomenon, however, remains unclear. Farrakhan's gradual
but inexorable political rise to a position of national influence and
leadership among African-Americans over the past twelve years has
been viewed almost universally as being vitally assisted by the disproportionately large amount—and occasionally histrionic and near-hys-
terical style—of coverage devoted to the Black Muslim leader by
television and, in particular, print reporters. Farrakhan has, by this
interpretation, invoked Marshall McLuhan's most famous dictum to
devastating demagogic effect. If the medium is the message, the message that the combination of the cathode ray and the nationally syndicated column has assisted Farrakhan to propagate across America has
been one of paranoia, fear, and mutual racial animosity combined.
Moreover, in focusing mainly upon the concrete and charismatic individual behind that unedifying message, the media has in effect not
only disseminated his pernicious views but has also elevated—even
transformed—the political legitimacy and social status of the messenger.

Dennis King, for example, views Farrakhan as "very much a
media creature":

> As with many such figures a theatre of illusion is created com-
> prising rhetorical violence, cheering crowds, TV cameras and
> hysterical newspaper editorials. In short, it becomes easy to
> ascribe to Farrakhan an importance much greater than he actu-
> ally possesses.[30]

In arguing further (and persuasively) that the direct threat to American Jews that Farrakhan poses has been vastly overdrawn, King notes

the total absence of physical violence committed by the NoI upon its many enemies. In contrast to many white supremacist American groups, for whom the violence of their racist rhetoric has frequently been matched by the brutality of their actions, no physical attacks on Jews or synagogues or incidents of cemetery desecration have ever been directly traced to the NoI, under either Farrakhan or his predecessors.[31]

King also argues less compellingly that the support that Farrakhan receives from educated and middle-income black Americans is fundamentally "a passive form of support, the product of media hype more than of any organizational skill on Farrakhan's part." In this, Juan Williams, too, concurs that it is the attention that Farrakhan actively and assiduously pursues, and regularly and readily receives, from the American mass media that serves as the necessary fuel for his public notoriety and his national African-American political leadership pretensions.[32]

The central theme of such arguments tends to converge upon a shared notion that Farrakhan has essentially been propelled into a position of national public prominence in America by a media-driven politics of racial sensationalism. In creating a political climate in which demands either for Farrakhan's vigorous denunciation or for solidaristic rallies to his support are easily generated, the media inevitably stokes (and even causes) the controversies and "scandals" surrounding Farrakhan and, thereby, animates the visceral bases of his popular black American appeal. Such are the depths to which contemporary black-white relations have plunged that, as Manning Marable argued, many black Americans "instinctively" recognize that any African-American public figure who so unerringly evokes harsh contempt and unrelenting condemnation from white religious and political leaders in the United States must "necessarily" have something meaningful for them in his program.[33] Black Americans are prompted to rally to Farrakhan mainly because he is quite correctly perceived to be the object of persistently disparaging, abusive, and derogatory public attacks, especially by members of other, nonblack social groups—attacks that, when they occur, are assiduously and expansively featured in national newspaper opinion pages and evening news bulletins.[34] Thus, in encouraging public responses and in relaying nationwide reactions to Farrakhan, the news media thereby contributes to his emergent status as an embattled and courageous black political martyr, boldly seeking to advance African-Americans' collective well-being (whether wisely or misguidedly is essentially beside the point here; the laudatory effort is all that is relevant), but being denounced and defamed by nonblacks in that admirable process.

Such arguments are frequently linked to vehement rejections of the various theses that advance Farrakhan's growing status as an influential national political actor among African-Americans. These rejections tend to adopt one of two interpretive strategies: either to deny or refute the notion that Farrakhan performs a role of some consequence in black American politics at present, and hence to infer that media attention accorded the NoI's leader is entirely unmerited, malapportioned, and inflammatory; or, alternatively, to acknowledge the significant social and political impact achieved by Farrakhan among many African-Americans at the mass level, but to identify this principally as the product of undue and excessive media attention. Thus, in constituting some type of militant, totemic racial figure of paranoid extremism, mass black American support for the NoI's leader is viewed by such critics as being either limited, weak, and fundamentally transient or, alternatively, an artificial consequence of media hyperbole. The inherent contradiction in the two arguments is no doubt sufficiently manifest, but each nonetheless possesses a particular, distinctive, and coherent internal logic. Let us therefore deal with them each in turn.

The first interpretive course tends to reduce Farrakhan's influence to a matter of essentially transient popular symbolism, what can perhaps be defined most appropriately as the "media event" school. According to this reductive line of argument, Farrakhan represents a particularly virulent and compelling example of the increasingly disturbing conflation between sensationalist politics and entertainment that the modern mass media and the phenomenon of "video politics" has wrought in the United States and elsewhere.[35] Farrakhan, in this view, essentially forms part of a continuum of popular cultural references that advance a dual message of collective black American uplift and increasing interracial animosity in the United States. Thus, the NoI's leader occupies an ignominious place in the media's broad spectrum of ugly but compelling social and political ogres, "somewhere between Ice-T and the Ayatollah Khomeini," as Joe Klein memorably put it.[36] Attendance at Farrakhan rallies and lectures represents little more for African-Americans than an essentially vicarious experience of a temporarily fashionable racial fad, of (at best) primarily cathartic value in contributing to those blacks attending a brief and necessarily ephemeral moment of racial pride and uplift—miniature-scale, localized versions of the Million Man March, in essence.[37] Farrakhan's public discourse is merely a marginally more elaborate and pseudosophisticated version of the sounds of gunshots aimed by black Americans at a white victim that introduce a new gangsta rap album.[38] The consuming hatred and the implicit threat of violence that pervade Farrakhan's speeches together contribute to a compulsively marketable national package, fastidiously tailor-made for the mass American public's contemporary consumptive tastes. Shocking and outrageous, to be sure, at times even scandalous, but of neither fundamental, serious, nor lasting material consequence for white America.

The alternative interpretation is at once less hasty and more uncertain that Farrakhan's influence among black Americans at large is either overestimated or can legitimately be viewed as analogous to the consumption of the various visceral racial messages and symbols of interracial dissensus that are invariably disseminated by the modern mass entertainment industry in America.[39] Unlike the media event school, adherents to the "media irresponsibility" interpretation broadly accept that Farrakhan has achieved an influential and serious national political role among African-Americans. Still, they attribute this largely to the very coverage of the NoI's leader in which they and their colleagues themselves frequently engage. The national attention and ready journalistic access that the media typically grant Farrakhan (however intermittently) ensures that his poisonous and pernicious racial message achieves a uniquely privileged political outlet. The minister hence receives a wide and—given the inflammatory nature of the news—unusually attentive American audience; one, moreover, that would otherwise not exist or, at a minimum, would be considerably narrower in scope.

A representative example of this interpretive school is the nationally syndicated black American journalist Carl Rowan, who best encapsulated its outlook when Farrakhan first won widespread media attention and criticism in 1984:

> I cannot silence Farrakhan. I cannot stop the media from exploiting him. I can, I hope, make some of my media colleagues understand the damage they do in chasing down black demagogues and making them national figures.[40]

Rowan subsequently speculated further:

> Media mirror on my wall, who's the dumbest of 'em all? Those
> of us . . . who are making Mr. Farrakhan one of the best-known,
> most-listened-to black persons on earth, even though he offers
> nothing more than religious bilge and racial hatred and is
> preying on the frustrations, the rage, of millions of black
> Americans.[41]

Twelve years on, and Rowan grew ever more frustrated and exas-
perated that, in the face of the national media's continued and seemingly unremitting, deer-in-the-headlight-like fixation upon Farrakhan, "those blacks to whom America's leaders and power-brokers
ought to be listening can rarely get a fair hearing."[42]

Another, equally disenchanted, subscriber to the "media irresponsibility" thesis, political scientist Martin Kilson, also holds that
the American print and televisual media have accorded grossly "disproportionate attention to leaders of the black disenchanted," such as
Farrakhan and Sharpton. "Pseudo-event politics," that is, media-
hyped politics, attempts to equate what Kilson sees as a minority and
marginal strand of ethnocentric black American nationalism with the
more mature, pragmatic, and important electoral "mainplot" of African-American politics.[43] In paying attention to Farrakhan at all, the
U.S. media effectively serve the deeply deleterious political function
of legitimizing his otherwise extremely limited and contentious
national leadership claims as equivalent, though by definition different (and, for Kilson and many others, wholly deficient) to those of
established black American elected and appointive officials.

Although these two interpretations are analytically distinct, the
basic logic that informs their core arguments is nonetheless shared,
simple, and clear. Since the media bear a disproportionate burden of
the unenviably heavy responsibility for Farrakhan's rise, they also
possess the power—and should rapidly grasp the political opportunity—to precipitate his decline: either by ignoring or reducing substantially their excessive coverage of his public speeches and the
NoI's activities (Rowan and King's preferred solution), or by making
absolutely clear the complete unacceptability of Farrakhan's ram-
pantly paranoid bigotry in American public life (the course preferred
by Cohen, Williams, and Klein). As with McCarthy in the 1940s, the
coverage of Farrakhan's activities and paranoid allegations by the
print and television media renders those newsworthy in a manner in

which they would otherwise utterly fail to be. Thus, for Farrakhan, the unmerited and invariably hostile coverage directed toward his speeches and sermons serves strongly to amplify rather than to diminish the extent of his popular African-American support and, hence, to exaggerate rather than reduce the more general political threat that he is perceived to represent. National notoriety, ipso facto, equals news; and notoriety is conferred upon Farrakhan through and by the media, whose unceasingly formidable appetite for the sensational is fed, but rarely satiated, by the minister's more inflammatory public claims, statements, and threats.

Such arguments are, however, neither internally coherent nor especially intellectually convincing. Let us concede, for the moment, that the Farrakhan phenomenon is predominantly, or even exclusively, a media-driven entity. The proposed solution to the minister's national rise—withdrawing or decreasing the level of media attention—seems wholly insufficient to accomplish its instrumental goal of a diminution in Farrakhan's political and social influence. Notwithstanding its ascribed origins, the current popularity of Farrakhan among black Americans is such that simply ignoring his role in current African-American politics would do little, if anything, to modify or dilute his popular black appeal.

In much the same way that Jackson successfully achieved a preeminent leadership status by 1984 as a result of his spectacularly unsuccessful campaign for the Democratic party presidential nomination, which media inattention thereafter did not diminish, so, for Farrakhan, his social impact has reached levels—and his organization achieved a sufficiently widespread mass black admiration and respect—that transcend any coverage the mainstream press and television may now accord him. If the media are either wholly or primarily culpable for releasing the black American demagogic genie from the bottle of racial hatred, it is unclear how the lax and complacent professional culprits can either easily or completely return the bigoted escapee to his original isolated, unfamiliar, and appropriate political home. Containment of those contaminated by such unapologetic racial animus requires far more than a willing suspension of disbelief and pretenses that Farrakhan is an inconsequential national African-American figure.

It is at the very least unclear, though, that the notion that the media created the Farrakhan phenomenon should be accepted at all. Indeed, in searching for plausible explanations for Farrakhan's political rise, the notion that "the media did it" is one that is inherently and deeply flawed in two key respects. First, in sharp contrast to Jackson, the NoI's leader has generally explicitly avoided mainstream media outlets until relatively recently in his leadership career. Of the 110 television channels and 50 radio stations across America (listed in *The Final Call*) that Farrakhan could be heard or seen on in May 1996, for example, no more than a handful could even optimistically be described as "mainstream."[44] Indeed, Farrakhan maintained a complete vow of silence in relation to white media outlets until well into the 1980s, a practice which in part accounts for the striking paucity of both popular and scholarly articles on him prior to 1984, and the relative dearth of them even between 1985 and 1990.[45] Second, when Farrakhan has subsequently appeared on network television or granted lengthy interviews to particularly well-respected newspapers during the 1990s, the content of his core message has barely altered, even though the style of his delivery has softened noticeably from his typically intemperate stump tirades.[46]

Thus, in attributing *Larry King Live, The New York Times,* or *Washington Post* op-ed pieces with providing the complicitous fuel for erroneous claims of Farrakhan's political leadership status among black Americans, media critics seem guilty of an interpretive faculty that is unduly conditioned by the Beltway mentality. One might greet with a reasonably healthy degree of skepticism, after all, the notion that sixty thousand black Americans paid $15 each in Atlanta in 1992 to listen to the NoI's leader because they had been fooled by such editorials— or by appearances on *Donahue*—into thinking that Farrakhan had more to say than he actually did. African-Americans attend because they want to hear Farrakhan's message undiluted, unabridged, and unadorned by commentaries, even if they may neither agree with nor endorse that message in its entirety.

Moreover, to compare Farrakhan's rallies to concerts by popular musicians wholly neglects the explicitly political content—and hence the unusual political significance—of the former. When an accomplished and militant black American agitator, whose speeches consistently feature vicious attacks upon a variety of specified enemies (both in and outside the United States) and whose rhetoric is deliberately infused by incendiary references to violence and death, can pack to overflowing stadia that many popular entertainers can never hope to fill, far more fundamental political questions are involved than that of mere media attention, particularly given the clear longevity of

Farrakhan's mass African-American appeal and the fact that white media are more often absent than present at NoI rallies. The persistence of large black American audiences attending such lectures and rallies over a twelve-year period since Farrakhan's effective national media debut in 1984 is powerfully suggestive of a political appeal among African-Americans at large that stretches far beyond that of mere novelty and cathartic psychological value, or some transient, collective racial fashionability.

If the media event school of interpretation is unconvincing, the irresponsibility variant of the media creation argument, as applied to Farrakhan (and others before him), also seems very weak. For its proponents, such as Kilson and Rowan, the essence of their argument is that coverage devoted to the Black Muslim leader is grossly malapportioned to his original political influence among African-Americans, prior to such undue media attention. They must then, however, confront the vexing issue of defining what would constitute a proportionate level of coverage of Farrakhan. In fact, it is not so much the quantity of coverage that is the real cause of their disapprobation, but the substantive content of the subject's message and the fact of its positive reception among many African-Americans. Farrakhan's face on the cover of *Time* magazine in February 1994 would in itself have been unremarkable, and impossible, were it not for the combination of the reactionary and paranoid content of his discourse and its evident popular appeal among black Americans at large. If Farrakhan's influence is indeed exaggerated, then denunciations would seem wholly out of place; the logic in vigorously denouncing an entirely irrelevant, fatuous, or marginal political force (Lyndon La Rouche, say) is not readily apparent. If, however, Farrakhan's influence is instead conceded to be tangible, ignoring the Black Muslim leader (as Rowan recommended) would appear to be neglecting a pressing responsibility—even a civic imperative—to challenge his pernicious message and to combat his harmful political aspirations. Direct and full engagement is otherwise subsumed by wholesale avoidance, when a combative, candid dialogue and an analysis of the real sources of Farrakhan's mass appeal seems of cardinal importance.

The line between being "merely" a media creation and constituting "more than" a media creation is admittedly as thin in modern American public life as the gulf between the television news headlines and the range of important political events that actually occur in the world is wide. Indeed, in the context of an American politics wherein the two major parties' national conventions were literally made for TV in 1996, separating the media out from "real" politics at times seems an almost futile project. The actual causes of Farrakhan's increasing influence, however, are more appropriately identified elsewhere than in either the American mass media's structural and political biases or its sensationalist predispositions. The blight of many predominantly black-populated urban centers across the United States; the persistence of racial prejudice and discrimination; the increasing social and economic problems affecting many black American communities; the perceived inability of national black political elites—and apparent unwillingness of many whites—effectively to ameliorate and rectify such serious problems together form a critical set of underlying conditions that are especially ripe for Farrakhan to exploit. (The next chapter examines these bases of the Farrakhan phenomenon in detail.)

That mass media attention has substantially assisted the dissemination of Farrakhan's activities and views among both black and nonblack Americans is, of course, undeniable. Farrakhan himself regularly addresses parts of his sermons specifically to the assembled press corps and, in the aftermath of his 1996 World Friendship Tour, ironically thanked CNN for increasing his international stature by its extensive coverage of the Million Man March.[47] The extent to which this has been the central, rather than an admittedly important, contributory factor in the minister's growing role and influence is much less certain. Arguments that the media are responsible for, rather than simply culpable in, Farrakhan's rise are too tenuous, counterfactual, and tendentious to be convincing.

Indeed, the view that sensationalist media attention to, and portrayals of, Farrakhan have been responsible for his political rise also rests uneasily with two distinct (though related) issues of intellectual consistency and reporting double standards. Both concern the full repudiation of bigoted sentiments, no matter what the locus thereof may be. Williams, for example, has argued that black American leaders and elites cannot simply ignore Farrakhan's incandescent rage. Richard Cohen has also held that the media and public attention devoted to Farrakhan and his aides' anti-Semitism is insufficient, and contrasts this with an imaginary white bigot who made equally defamatory remarks about black Americans on a regular basis.[48] Both are surely correct, and it is certainly surprising that even some academic commentators treat Farrakhan's anti-Semitism as a matter merely of "unfortunate" rhetoric.[49] For other critics, though, such as Adolph Reed (as far from being a defender of the NoI leader as any), the opprobrium that is legitimately and deservedly heaped upon black American bigots such as Farrakhan, Leonard Jeffries, and Public Enemy is considerably less than that addressed to the many white Americans who engage in similarly offensive and defamatory expressions of racial prejudice and sexism, from David Duke through right-wing radio "shock jocks" to the rock group Guns'n'Roses.[50]

Condemnation of Farrakhan's more rabidly prejudiced comments is a necessary part of any strategy aimed at effectively confronting his political challenge. But it is also an insufficient one, and one that must be accompanied by a full and frank assessment of the broader and very real conditions to which Farrakhan forcefully speaks, however falsely. Consistency demands an equally forceful repudiation of the Dukes and Helmses and Hollingses, however coded or allegedly jocular a veil the various appeals to baser sentiments of antiblack bigotry in their messages frequently assume. Nonetheless, the prevalence of persistent and grievous historic injustice and discrimination by some white Americans against their black compatriots fails to render African-Americans wholly free from the legitimate accusation of racism. The fact of white prejudice does not exculpate Farrakhan from the fullest and clearest repudiation for the bigotry that he evinces and the manifest injury to racial comity that he causes. Journalists and academics alike face this responsibility, for the bifurcation in racial attitudes and responses to Farrakhan is one that pervades not only popular perceptions but also divides intellectual elites—a powerful testimony to the substantial disjuncture in perceptions about race that characterize current attitudes among black and white Americans in general.

None of the preceding discussion is intended to suggest that Farrakhan has achieved his current status unassisted by the media, nor that the Black Muslim has not zealously sought to exploit the media as often as possible for his own political purposes. It is clear that Farrakhan has seized with increasing eagerness every opportunity available to utilize media outlets in order to disseminate his message as widely as possible. Jackson's 1984 campaign, for example, was interpreted by the NoI's leader as a mechanism that Allah grasped in order to make Farrakhan known to greater numbers of black and white Americans alike.

Farrakhan has also deliberately created media opportunities designed to achieve maximum nationwide publicity for his paranoid views, particularly through his international links, in which Libya looms especially prominent. The minister's attendance at the Second Mathaba in Tripoli in 1986, despite threats of possible arrest and federal prosecution subsequent to his return to the United States, was deliberately intended to provoke the maximum amount of outrage by white American politicians and to ensure that his message was heard in the highest echelons of the federal government.[51] A decade later, Farrakhan's return to Libya to receive that year's "Gadhafi International Human Rights Prize" (surely the ultimate definition of a tragicomic oxymoron) once more yielded outraged coverage in the United States.[52]

Farrakhan's meeting Nelson Mandela in January 1996 was similarly designed to achieve maximum media attention and to compound the increasingly widespread American perceptions of his new political influence that he had elicited in the United States since the Million Man March. Farrakhan's audiences with an unedifying gallery of tyrants and terrorist sponsors in Libya, Sudan, Nigeria, Iran, and Iraq and his public comments on the ultimately doomed fate of the United States were private affairs, of course. But they were also aimed, simultaneously, at provoking the strongest and most hostile of white reactions across America which, he hoped, would once more consolidate his putative martyr status on behalf of African-Americans and the oppressed. The World Friendship Tour epitomized Farrakhan's strategy of winning incredulous headlines and outraged editorials, and thereby political martyrdom, at home by declaring verbal war on America from abroad. As he put it, addressing the U.S. government upon his return from the trip, "I know you want to kill me, but I just raised the price . . . Whatever you do to me over here, they're going to do to you over there."[53] Such provocative proclamations are invariably designed to maximize the amount of public attention and fury that Farrakhan receives from press and television alike; and they frequently succeed in so doing. Witness, for example, the grossly exaggerated assessments of Farrakhan's having graduated from being a "national nuisance" to "a national security threat."[54]

Moreover, media coverage of Farrakhan is used by the leader of the NoI to support his own claims about the deliberate misrepresentation of his views by fearful and furious white elites. The factors that encourage structural bias in American television coverage generally (time constraints, revenue demands from advertisers, fairness doctrine requirements) preclude a full discussion of Farrakhan's public statements in general, and theological beliefs in particular, on network news or elsewhere. Farrakhan is thus able to invoke claims that his real message is deliberately being distorted by a hostile white/Jewish media in order to undermine both his existing and his potential political support among black Americans.[55] Of course, the accusation of distortion ironically is itself a strategy designed to attract additional African-American supporters. Although it is necessarily speculative, it seems reasonable to assume that at least some of the black Americans who attend Farrakhan's rallies and lectures do so from a genuine desire to discover for themselves whether or not the image of the NoI's leader that they have received from media coverage in fact comports with what he represents in person. The charge of media bias is therefore one that functions not only to shield Farrakhan from criticism but also to assist mass black attendance of his public events.

Just as few analysts today, however, would attribute Malcolm X's political influence among American blacks during the 1960s (and subsequently) mainly to the controversy sparked by the Mike Wallace "hate that hate produced" documentary, so Farrakhan's more recent rise rests heavily upon foundations that are far more extensive, deep, and enduring than simple media coverage alone. The intermittent and generally hostile attention of the mainstream print and televisual media has represented an integral and necessary, but far from a sufficient, condition of the NoI leader's political ascendancy and current influence among African-Americans at large. Although the mass media have strongly assisted the faltering propulsion of the Farrakhan roadshow, and continue to cover its more well-attended, important, and exotic stopovers, they certainly did not invent the unseemly spectacle.

THE NEW AND OLD POLITICS OF PARANOIA

The important, but nonetheless limited, extent of the mass media's role in Farrakhan's rise can most appropriately be examined by contrasting the Black Muslim leader with a more familiar American exemplar of traditional paranoid politics from the paranoid white far-right: David Duke. The former KKK leader represents probably the most well-known hate figure on the white radical right in the modern United States. Like Farrakhan, Duke's past associations and activities were extremely dubious and controversial and have rendered him, at times, the brief focus of intense national political attention in America. Unlike Farrakhan, however, Duke sought deliberately and explicitly to moderate his extremist public persona by rejecting elements of his previous behavior as merely the product of youthful indiscretions or harmless mischief. In addition, the process of achieving a mass influence depended for Duke upon the successful cultivation of a conventional and widely acceptable political image via the mass media, and through television in particular. For thousands of white Louisiana voters, by 1990, Duke had done precisely that. In appearance, delivery, and style, Duke's demeanor was virtually inseparable from that of the majority of nattily besuited, softly spoken, and carefully coiffured candidates for federal or state elective office in America.[56]

In contrast to Farrakhan, the Louisianan's rise to statewide, and subsequently national, political attention was accompanied by electoral campaigns for specific elective offices. Prior to his successful bid for a seat in the Louisiana state House of Representatives in 1989, Duke was known only to those active on the fringes of the American far-right. Not until his 1990 campaign for the U.S. Senate and, in particular, his 1991 campaign for gubernatorial office in Louisiana, did Duke reach a national—and international—audience. Moreover, after his abortive bid for the Republican presidential nomination in 1992, Duke's coverage in the mass media dropped precipitously, recovering only slightly with his second abortive Senate bid in 1996. The appropriation of many of his themes by Republicans with less controversial personal histories and associations was one factor in this. Duke's appeal, however, had always been based on a relatively narrow and ephemeral set of state-specific conditions. The centrality of media attention was therefore especially important to his prospects for popular attention, name recognition, and ultimately, elective success.

Farrakhan, by comparison, occupies an entirely different national political milieu. First, he personally has never run, and harbors no apparent ambitions to run, for elective political office in the United States, at any level. In contrast, the electoral process was fundamental to Duke's rise and fall. Duke was in part defeated because of the response of those white Louisianans (and the state's business community, in particular) who recognized the many dangers that the achievement of political office by Duke could potentially pose to their material socioeconomic interests. The symbolism of a former Grand Wizard of the KKK occupying the governor's mansion in Baton Rouge was conjoined to the substantial powers that the gubernatorial office possessed in concentrating both black and white voters' minds in the state. Whatever threat Farrakhan poses, by contrast, derives from factors that are entirely unassociated either with his seeking state power or with the prospect of his attempting to achieve elective public office.

Second, Farrakhan heads a national organization of long-standing (if changeable) repute among black Americans. The Nation of Islam may be a relatively minor player in America's racial politics, but it is not an ephemeral entity in African-American social and political life. With or without the attention of print journalists and television pundits, the organization's laudable and brave efforts to police central city areas, reduce drug consumption, and mediate in gang disputes among African-Americans would doubtless continue apace. The media critique of Farrakhan is thus somewhat misplaced. If he and the NoI have been "discovered" by the media, that discovery has been far more for white American audiences than for black ones. Duke, by comparison, was not only found but was also assiduously amplified to white and black Americans alike, both within and beyond the state of Louisiana, by the media's attention from 1989 to 1992.

Third, the substantive content of media coverage of Duke and Farrakhan emphasizes quite distinctive features in each case. In Duke's, press attention invariably stressed the Louisianan's Klan background and white supremacist associations. A prominent subtheme, however, was the common political agenda and policy preferences that Duke shared with the modern Republican party. Commentators drew attention to the difficulty that Duke posed for then president Bush, whose eventually reluctant approval of the 1991 Civil Rights bill (after he had vetoed the previous year's proposal) was attributed largely to the negative public effects of the Duke candidacy for the GOP nationally. As Duke went down to a decisive defeat against Edwin Edwards in 1991 (one in which he nonetheless captured a majority of the white vote in Louisiana, as he had done previously, in 1990), Kirk Fordice won the neighboring gubernatorial race in Mississippi (and repeated his electoral success in 1995) on a markedly similar platform: addressing welfare beneficiaries, crime, affirmative action, and the status of the United States as an avowedly "Christian nation." Although the racial code words were barely different in the two Deep South state races, Fordice received the Republican National

Committee's assistance while Duke received the mild opprobrium of
its chairman and of the then president.

In Farrakhan's case, by contrast, the emphasis of much popular
coverage is the express distance between the NoI's leader and other
national black American politicians and civil rights figures. By stressing the respectable political credentials of the latter, in order to frame
Farrakhan as a markedly unsavory and exceptional extremist figure,
the terms of debate are, ironically, drawn so starkly and simplistically
that the ultimate strategic advantage frequently accrues more to Farrakhan than to established African-American political leaders. The conceptual prism by which black American leadership is viewed by
African-Americans at large is one in which white assessments frequently function as influential mediating agents. The content of the
bulk of white media coverage of the NoI is clear, however. Farrakhan,
in diametric contrast to Kilson's view, is not typically equated with
established African-American leaders—the threat that he poses them
is an important, though not always explicit, theme in the coverage of
his activities, just as the fact of Farrakhan's winning support is treated
as surprising, not understandable, in most popular accounts.[57] Duke,
by comparison, was rarely interpreted in terms of posing anything
approximating a threat to national white American politicians, whom
he sought to imitate as much as to condemn.

Critics such as Esolen, who view both Duke and Farrakhan as
more or less equivalent opportunistic fame seekers and extremists-
turned-moderates whose appeals to the media conditioned their
changing political creeds, therefore miss the paranoid mark somewhat. Dapperly besuited, bejewelled, and bow-tied though he may
be, Farrakhan has done nothing to approach either a blow-dried
image or a moderated, inclusive message. Although Farrakhan's oratorical abilities and rhetorical style attract some media attention,
many established black leaders also exhibit an impressive and varied
range of public-speaking credentials. The fact that a politician such as
Bill Gray, John Lewis, or Mike Espy is able to adopt a presentational
style that is well-suited to the televisual medium does not preclude
their still possessing a formidable array of oratorical skills in alternative contexts. Espy, for example, was as comfortable displaying a
markedly "southern" style of speech in his reelection activities "at
home" as in moderating his stentorian Mississippian tones on the
Hill.[58] That Farrakhan can alternately rant and rave as a prophet of
rage at his NoI rallies only to soothe subsequently on national televi-

sion as a lucid voice of reason and calm says much about his shrewd intelligence and presentational skills, but very little about an allegedly moderated belief system.

Farrakhan has provided as few reasons for the American public to accept that his traditional views on racial Armageddon, whites, and Jews have sincerely altered as Duke has done for that public to believe that he has genuinely recanted his long-held prejudices about, and barely latent antagonism toward, African-Americans. Both have acquired a natty sartorial sense while neither has shed the nasty opinions of old. Perhaps, since the subtleties and nuances of the peculiarly flawed architecture of their respective belief systems has never attracted either substantial or enduring attention from most Americans, that may not actually matter very much. Hacker's view, for example, that "Farrakhan and Duke are more ideological symbols than expositors of intellectual positions" has some evident merit.[59] The importance of symbolism in American political life, however, is frequently substantial.[60] The Republicans' platform for the 1994 congressional mid-term elections, the "Contract with America," for instance, was a largely symbolic document; but its electoral and policy consequences were marked. Farrakhan's public discourse may similarly contain relatively little that poses as either intellectually distinguished, impeccably rational, or even minimally respectable, but the importance of what he says is substantial nonetheless, if only because many African-Americans listen assiduously to, and frequently agree with, much of the reactionary and paranoid case that he advances.

To exaggerate unduly either Farrakhan's mass appeal to black Americans or the political threat that he represents to whites would be a grave and foolish error. Contrary to many fanciful popular beliefs, the minister has achieved neither universal nor uncritical endorsement from African-Americans. Nor is Farrakhan poised to mount some swift takeover even of Black America, much less the United States. Despite his gruesome links with Gadhafi and other tyrants, Farrakhan poses no clear and present danger to American society. Reed is absolutely right to remind Americans that, unlike David Duke, the NoI's leader has never once held public office in the United States; has never had the slightest input to public policy outcomes at state or local, much less national, levels; and has never enjoyed access to state power or to positions of institutional authority within policy-making bodies.[61] It is as laughable as it is incredible to imagine Farrakhan leading some Black Muslim (presumably non-alcoholic) beer-hall putsch or heading a successful fascistic coup d'état in America.

Still, lack of imagination is a deficiency that rarely justifies wholesale neglect of the substantive threats that even small-time demagogues and fanatics may ultimately represent.[62] The complacently indulgent refrains of the Weimar Republic of 1930 are hardly resonant in the minuscule political threat that Farrakhan personally or the NoI corporately poses to the American nation in the late 1990s. Notwithstanding the extensive media coverage that he frequently receives, however, Farrakhan possesses the resources, ambition, and leadership skills to assume an increasingly important political role among African-Americans. Although a preeminent leadership role among black Americans—a primus inter pares niche in the realms of African-American statesmanship—will doubtless elude him in his remaining years, Farrakhan still retains the disturbing potential to deepen America's yawning racial divide to a profound and perhaps even precipitous point. That prospect, moreover, should be sufficient cause to occasion at least informed and attentive public concern, if not pronounced alarm.

SUMMARY

Farrakhan has emerged in the 1990s as a political leader of substantial popular appeal among African-Americans at large. Although popularity is, of course, only one resource for a political leader seeking influence in the United States, it nonetheless represents an extremely important and valuable commodity, and one that many American public figures find exceedingly difficult to both achieve and sustain. Few politicians in America, from presidents to school board members, are eager to forfeit the considerable political capital that widespread and lasting popular support affords. Moreover, for other envious and fearful political actors, the fact of Farrakhan's popularity partly conditions their own strategic and tactical political behavior. To the extent that other political actors must take his popularity into account in calculating their own electoral interests, determining their voting behavior, and shaping their general political approaches, Farrakhan's political influence may be indirect within the ranks of national African-American leadership. Nonetheless, it remains of manifest political significance.

Like all demagogues through the ages, Farrakhan relies strongly upon the spoken word through which to exert political influence and to forge a popular base. Although the mass media in America have clearly assisted his political rise, however, Farrakhan represents much more than merely an ephemeral or a marginal media creation. The minister's mass appeal among African-Americans has been far more helped than hindered by the recurrent attention of mainstream television and print media, even in its more critical and adverse forms. Nonetheless, Farrakhan's longevity is also powerfully suggestive of a broad political appeal that far transcends the intermittent bouts of national attention accorded by the American news media to his more extreme public pronouncements and quixotic political initiatives.

While the fact of Farrakhan's significant—though limited—mass black American appeal is demonstrable, however, the reasons for the popularity of such an unorthodox, extreme, and polarizing minority religious and political figure have yet to be fully analyzed. By virtue of his theological convictions, reactionary political beliefs, and paranoid political claims, Farrakhan occupies a peculiar and distinctive contemporary niche in national black American politics. That the leader of the NoI should have achieved the social impact and mass appeal among African-Americans that he has over recent years obviously demands explanation. It is to the proximate causes of the minister's political ascendancy and the multiple foundations of the Farrakhan phenomenon that we hence turn next.

NOTES TO CHAPTER 5

1. Essien-Udom, *Black Nationalism*, p. 339.

2. Richard E. Cohen, "Farrakhan and Anti-Semitism," *Torrington (CT) Register-Criterion*, 28 July 1985, p. 15.

3. Mention of Farrakhan in the indexes of newspapers such as *The New York Times* and *The Washington Post* from 1990–1996, for example, was almost twice that of 1984–89.

4. See, for example: Richard E. Cohen, "Farrakhan Too," *The Washington Post*, 16 May 1995, p. A17; Chris Bull, "Farrakhan Under Fire," *The Advocate*, 8 March 1994, p. 25; Thomas W. Hazlett, "The Wrath of Farrakhan," *Reason*, 26 (May 1994), p. 66; and Sullivan, "Call to Harm."

5. See, for example: Lyons, "Muslim Guard Service Grows"; Nathan McCall, "D.C. Council Votes to Praise Farrakhan's Anti-Drug Work," *The Washington Post*, 25 October 1989, p. A1; Sylvester Monroe, "Doing the Right Thing: Muslims Have Become a Welcome Force in Black Neighborhoods," *Time*, 135, 16 April 1990, p. 22; William K. Stevens, "The Muslims Keep the

Lid on Drugs in Capital: The Dealers Simply Move to Another Area," *The New York Times*, 26 September 1988, p. 8; and Wright, "Farrakhan's Mission."

6. Sanson, "Farrakhan Means Business"; and Stodghill, "Farrakhan's Three-Year Plan."

7. See: Farber, "In the Name of the Father"; Purnick, "An Unlikely Matchmaker"; and Terry, "Shabazz Case."

8. See, for example, Turque, Smith, and McCormick, "Playing a Different Tune," p. 30.

9. The association represents approximately 200 black-owned newspapers across the United States and awarded Farrakhan the honor (on 14 March 1996) for his "vision" in putting together the previous year's Million Man March.

10. See the transcript, "Attempts by Rogue Regimes to Influence U.S. Policy," Hearing before the Subcommittee on International Operations and Human Rights, Committee on International Relations, U.S. House of Representatives, 19 March 1996.

11. Perhaps the most notorious instance of congressional insouciance regarding the Klan at this time concerned the 1937 confirmation of former KKK member and then Alabama Senator Hugo Black, as an Associate Justice of the United States Supreme Court. See William E. Leuchtenberg, "A Klansman Joins the Court: The Appointment of Hugo L. Black," in Leonard Dinnerstein and Kenneth T. Jackson, eds., *American Vistas: 1877 to the Present*, 5th ed. (New York: Oxford University Press, 1987), pp. 187–215.

12. Christopher Thomas, "Idol Who Strikes Terror into Whites," *The (London) Times*, 1985, p. 5.

13. See Reed, "All for One."

14. Lincoln, *The Black Muslims*, p. 272.

15. The figure is from Lincoln, *The Black Muslims*, p. 270. Other sources claim that the total number at the Atlanta rally was closer to 40,000. See, for example, Lynne Duke, "Farrakhan Defends Clinton, Asks Critics to 'Get to Know Me Better'," *The Washington Post*, 5 May 1993, p. A22. Whichever figure is the more accurate, the numbers are clearly substantial.

16. McFadden-Preston, "The Rhetoric of Minister Louis Farrakhan," p. 160.

17. *A National Survey of American Blacks* (New York: Simon Wiesenthal Center, December 1985).

18. Dawson made the remarks to (and the figures are also cited by) Juan Williams, "The Farrakhan Paralysis: How the Demagogues of the Disenfranchised Are Silencing Black Leaders," *The Washington Post*, 13 February 1994, p. C2.

19. See "The New Politics of Race," *Newsweek*, 6 May 1991, p. 23.

20. See Henry, "Pride and Prejudice," p. 22.

21. In addition, see Michael Kagay, "Poll Finds Most Blacks Reject Farrakhan's Ideas as Theirs," *The New York Times*, 5 March 1994, p. 8.

22. Williams, "The Farrakhan Paralysis."

23. The most ridiculously inflated estimate of the march's crowd that has been publicly advanced thus far has come from the filmmaker Spike Lee.

Though he didn't personally attend the gathering (instead watching it on television as a result of a medical operation), Lee confidently told a British audience to discount suggestions that only 500,000 African-Americans had attended, stating for the record that, "Two million black men assembled in the nation's capital . . ." See "Why Do the White Thing?," *The Guardian*, 18 November 1995, p. 32.

24. See the poll surveys in *The Washington Post*, 9–10 October 1995, Sec. A.

25. See, respectively: Monroe, "The Mirage of Farrakhan"; and Fineman and Smith, "An Angry 'Charmer'," pp. 42–46.

26. A comprehensive poll by CBS news, for example, revealed that 30 percent of blacks believed that Farrakhan and the NoI "represent the views of most black people in America," while 22 percent of blacks "generally agree" with Farrakhan's positions. Although this may be treated as a relatively small proportion, a further 40 percent of respondents were "not familiar enough" with Farrakhan's views to state an opinion. See "60 Minutes Poll: Louis Farrakhan and Public Opinion, March 27–28, 1996" (New York: CBS News, 1996).

27. See, in particular: Klein, "The threat of tribalism"; King, "The Farrakhan Phenomenon"; and Reed, "All for One."

28. See the excellent volume by Doris Graber, ed., *Mass Media and American Politics* (Washington, D.C.: Congressional Quarterly Press, 1993).

29. See: Butler and Ranney, *Electioneering*; Paul Herrnson, *Congressional Elections* (Washington, D.C.: Congressional Quarterly Press, 1995); Larry Sabato, *Feeding Frenzy: How Attack Journalism Has Transformed American Politics* (New York: The Free Press, 1993); and, on the media's effect on the changing role of national party conventions, Byron E. Shafer, *Bifurcated Politics* (Cambridge, Mass.: Harvard University Press, 1988).

30. King, "The Farrakhan Phenomenon," p. 17.

31. Though King's argument is compelling, it largely neglects the potential indirect consequences of the violent rhetoric of Farrakhan and many of his followers. According to one Anti-Defamation League report, for example, the incidence of anti-Semitic conflagrations on college campuses increased from 54 in 1988 to 114 in 1992–93. This latter figure, an increase of thirteen from 1991, coincided with an 8 percent drop in the number of anti-Semitic incidents reported nationwide during 1992–93. The ADL attributed the increased incidence of campus harassment of Jews in part to the messages of Farrakhan and other black speakers popular with many African-American students.

The issue of violence that surrounds Farrakhan's rhetoric is one that other scholars have also isolated for particular attention. Gaber, for example, in cautioning against devoting attention to the socioeconomic grievances among Farrakhan's supporters, argues that "when violence is finally committed by people full of hate, it hardly matters that they have other, genuine, grievances. What matters is that the innocent get hurt for no good reason." See Gaber, "Lamb of God or Demagogue?," p. 167. Insofar as Farrakhan himself has conceded, in the context of Malcolm X's assassination, that he contributed to the atmosphere in which Malcolm's murder occurred, so it seems

plausible to argue that a persistently violent rhetoric directed toward a particular social group by members of another is indeed likely to contribute toward
the incidence of at least some antagonistic and potentially violent confronta-
tions. There is no evidence, however, that innocents (the NoI may not accept
the term's usage, of course) have been directly harmed by Farrakhan's followers.

32. Williams, "The Farrakhan Paralysis."

33. Marable, "In the Business of Prophet Making."

34. See Reed, "All for One."

35. For expositions of this position, see: Giovanni Sartori, *Comparative
Constitutional Engineering: An Inquiry into Structures, Incentives and Outcomes*
(London: Macmillan, 1994); and his article, "Video-Power," *Government and
Opposition* 24, no. 1 (Winter 1989): 39–53.

36. Klein, "The Threat of Tribalism," p. 15.

37. Dennis King, Manning Marable, and Adolph Reed all subscribe to
this basic view of Farrakhan's rallies. The commentaries by, among others,
Richard Cohen, Julius Lester, and Andrew Sullivan are altogether less sanguine in this regard.

38. Ice Cube, *Lethal Injection* (Fourth and Broadway, 1994).

39. On the subject of the representation of African-Americans in popu-
lar culture and by the mass media, see: Richard M. Merelman, *Representing
Black Culture: Racial Conflict and Cultural Politics in the United States* (New
York: Routledge, 1995); Dent, ed., *Black Popular Culture*; and Van Deburg, *New
Day in Babylon*.

40. Carl Rowan, *The Washington Post*, 6 August 1984, op-ed.

41. Carl Rowan, "Antidote to Louis Farrakhan: Ignore Him," *The New
York Times*, 25 September 1985, p. 22.

42. Carl Rowan, "Farrakhan's Poisonous Journey," *The Buffalo News*, 28
February 1996, p. 3B.

43. Martin Kilson and Clement Cottingham, "Thinking About Race
Relations: How Far Are We Still From Integration?," *Dissent*, Fall 1991, pp.
520–30, at 525.

44. Figures calculated by the author from *The Final Call*, 15, no. 17 (21
May 1996), p. 11.

45. For a breakdown of the latter, see Gaber, "Lamb of God or Demagogue?"

46. For examples of the latter, see Farrakhan's appearances on: *The Phil
Donahue Show*, 13 and 15 March 1990; *The Arsenio Hall Show*, 25 February 1994;
and *Larry King Live*, 16 October 1995.

47. See Byron White, Jerry Thomas, and Shirley Salemy, "Farrakhan
Defends World Tour: Nation of Islam Leader Welcomes Showdown," *Chicago
Tribune*, 26 February 1996, p. 1.

48. Richard E. Cohen, "At Nuremberg-on-Potomac," p. 7.

49. Washington, "Jesse Jackson," p. 93.

50. Reed, "All for One."

51. See McFadden-Preston's account of Farrakhan's "triumphant
return" address, in "The Rhetoric of Minister Louis Farrakhan," chapter five.

52. Farrakhan was the guest of honor at celebrations in September 1996 to commemorate the twenty-seventh anniversary of the coup that overthrew Libya's monarchy and installed Gadhafi as leader. In accordance with the decade-long American sanctions on most financial transactions between the United States and Libya, Farrakhan was banned by the U.S. Treasury Department from accepting the $250,000 prize that accompanied the award.

53. Quoted in White, Thomas, and Salemy, "Farrakhan Defends World Tour."

54. Peter King, "'PC' Handling of Farrakhan Is Wrong," *Newsday* (Nassau Edition), 8 March 1996, p. A47.

55. An editorial in *The Final Call*, for example, claimed in relation to Farrakhan's World Friendship Tour that the "national mainstream media fuelled a frenzy when they misportrayed the purpose of the tour," while then giving scant coverage to Farrakhan's explanatory press conferences and speeches upon his return home. See "Media Consistent on Farrakhan Coverage," *The Final Call*, 21 May 1996, p. 16.

56. See the collection of essays in Rose, *The Emergence of David Duke*. A more polemical discussion is contained in Clarence Lusane, *African Americans at the Crossroads*, pp. 87–92.

57. See, for example, Fred Barnes, "Farrakhan Frenzy: What's a Black Politician to Do?," *New Republic*, (28 October 1985), pp. 13–15.

58. See, for example, the account of Espy's electioneering style in Rob Gurwitt, "A Quest for a Breakthrough," *Congressional Quarterly Weekly Report*, 25 October 1986, pp. 2645–46.

59. Hacker, *Two Nations*, p. 150.

60. Murray Edelman, *The Symbolic Uses of Politics* (Urbana: University of Illinois Press, 1964).

61. Reed, "Behind the Farrakhan Show," p. 16.

62. It was partly for this reason that the Clinton Administration's refusal to allow Farrakhan to accept the financial assistance offered by Gadhafi to the NoI elicited such widespread approval in both the United States and Europe in September 1996.

6

Explaining Farrakhan

Black people exist on the edge of outrage against white people.
Farrakhan provides an outlet. He gives whitey hell.

Reverend Wyatt Walker[1]

This is a man whose political identity is constituted by antago-
nism to the self-image of America.

Henry Louis Gates[2]

Popular interpretations of the Farrakhan phenomenon frequently
present a racial hatred borne of the most widespread disillusion and
deep black despair as the exclusive foundation of the minister's charismatic version of paranoid American politics; all else is embellishment and detail. E. J. Dionne, for example, encapsulates the views of
many critics of the Nation of Islam (NoI) leader when he attributes
the source of Farrakhan's popularity among African-Americans to "a
loss of faith" by the black community in white U.S. society.[3] William
Schneider, too, viewed Farrakhan's political ascent as essentially a
reflection of increasing black–white antipathies, as signaling "a new
direction in black politics and a new division between the races."[4] A
leading international newspaper even identified a distinctive "Farrakhan style of leadership," entailing that African-American politicians
behave "outrageously" and shout "that your critics are racists until
they shut up."[5] For such commentators, Farrakhan's rise is fundamentally a matter of unfavorable black responses to white Americans. It
reflects, in large part, what Adolph Reed identified as the central fascination that many whites invariably find in the Farrakhan phenomenon and in the vexed issue of race more generally: what do black
Americans think about whites?[6]

Such interpretations, focusing upon a diffuse African-American despondency and disillusion, are superficially compelling in their appeal, and they comport with many popular conceptions of current black–white disjunctures in beliefs, values, and attitudes. These views, however, obscure the pronounced complexity of the causes of Farrakhan's growing appeal and social impact among African-Americans. Moreover, in their monodimensional aspect, they also evince a somewhat paternalistic and inaccurate interpretation of black Americans' views of the most propitious prospective forces for their own social and economic advancement in the post–civil rights era (i.e., whites) and the most effective method of African-American leadership (i.e., a single heroic figure capable of somehow transforming their collective fortunes).

Of course, Farrakhan is a manifestly charismatic black American political leader. An accomplished and often compelling orator, the minister seems able mellifluously to tap deeply and powerfully into mass black hopes and fears, almost at will. In full flow, Farrakhan frequently appears able to steal the sunrise past the proverbial rooster. Farrakhan's popular appeal among African-Americans, however, relies upon a multiplicity of factors, most of which are far more complex in character than simple notions of a Weberian type of charismatic authority are able either to capture or convey. In Farrakhan's case, the individual leader and the collective social group to which he addresses his activism are frequently—and falsely—conflated. As Harold Cruse argued three decades previously, this problem of confusing the individual black leader with the broader African-American political movement (and of his personality with the wider societal forces and fissures upon which his support is based) is a familiar one over the course of black American history:

Individual leaders can project ideologies of many kinds and color them with the hues of their own personal aspirations which very often obscure the very fundamental issues which are of crucial interest to the people for whom the leaders speak. Then historians come along and completely forget or overlook what the basic issues were for the people in the mass, and center their attention on the personal characteristics of the leaders.[7]

The caution expressed by Cruse is especially apposite to analyses of Farrakhan, wherein disproportionate attention to his extreme rhetoric and paranoid tendencies can overshadow the extent to which a significant number of his public views clearly accord with many mass black American beliefs, attitudes, and values. (Moreover, of course, if the mere possession of charismatic authority was the principal basis of Farrakhan's political rise, many other African-American politicians who also display great personal qualities of charisma, such as Julian Bond and Ron Dellums, ought logically also to have established more influential national political roles over recent years.) Farrakhan's leadership role relies heavily upon several foundations that far transcend his prodigious charismatic appeals.

The sources of Farrakhan's political ascendancy are at once multiple, distinctive, and interconnected. Farrakhan has achieved an influential political role in the 1990s partly through a combination of innovative political leadership of the NoI and sensitive political judgment of the opportunities and constraints facing an African-American "protest" leader in the post–civil rights era. While Farrakhan has certainly exploited the manifest crises of many black Americans in the post–civil rights era to great personal advantage, however, it is not only a loss of confidence in the possibility of achieving an integrated America (and of black and white citizens' support for that ideal) that is central to his popular appeal among African-Americans. It is also, crucially, the confusion and negative attitudes that black Americans harbor toward members of their own communities; the increasingly distant prospect of the socioeconomic regeneration of many central cities at a time of pronounced fiscal constraint; the sometimes remarkable dissonance between the policy preferences of African-Americans at large and their putative national political leaders, along several issue dimensions; the material actions and achievements of the NoI among black city communities; and Farrakhan's running for black leadership by running against black leaders that are together fundamental to the minister's contemporary political role, popular appeal, and national influence. In sum, divisions among black Americans, as much as between blacks and whites, are critical in accounting for Farrakhan's contemporary black appeal.

THE TWO CRISES OF BLACK AMERICA

Like his white right-wing paranoid predecessor, Senator Joseph McCarthy, Farrakhan's recent ascendancy in national American politics has depended upon two analytically distinct but closely related factors: first, the existence of a manifest sense of crisis and the presence of seemingly intractable social, economic, and political problems affecting American citizens in general, or a particular, discrete group thereof; second, the plausibility of the aspirant leader's claims as to both the origins of the crisis and the most effective means of its possible resolution. The more acute the nature of the crisis, the more plausible and legitimate (even rational) a status otherwise unconventional analyses and simplistic political solutions are apt, respectively, to assume for many of those either affected by or concerned with the cataclysmic situation at hand. Although, like McCarthy previously, Farrakhan certainly does considerably more to aggravate than ameliorate the dual crises, his persistent activism serves, simultaneously, to elevate his personal public recognition to national and international dimensions—a critical feature of the demagogue's political project.

For Joe McCarthy, the crisis-level problems confronting Americans in the immediate postwar era were notoriously cast in terms of the apparently relentless advance of atheistic international communism and the cardinal threat that this was held to pose to America's vital political, economic, and security interests. The preferred solution that the senator consistently and confidently advanced—vigorous diplomatic and military defense of those interests abroad by the United States and unrelenting domestic vigilance against the many alleged subversive enemies and radical malcontents at home—was at once straightforward, clear, and (lest it be forgotten) widely appealing.[8]

That appeal achieved a pronounced political salience and won significant popular support among Americans not least as a result of its immediacy. The clear emergence of the United States as the world's foremost—indeed, hegemonic—superpower after 1945 was very rapidly accompanied by broad and acute fears of foreign military aggression, domestic political subversion, and the prospect of an incipient, third, catastrophic global war. McCarthy's activities were therefore undertaken in the context of a wholly new, complex, and disturbing national and international environment. Although, from the perspective of the post–Cold War era (and with the benefit of the impeccable clarity of analytic vision that hindsight invariably affords), the structure of superpower relations from 1947 to 1989 was in fact relatively clear and stable, its initial emergence in the late 1940s was then characterized by profound confusion and deep dissensus; an uncertainty paralleled currently by the continuing search for an appropriate paradigm by which U.S. foreign policy should be conducted in the 1990s.[9]

McCarthy's paranoid claims—and his mercifully brief political ascendancy, from 1950–1954—were therefore advanced during a period of profound American unease over the prospective shape of international relations.

By comparison, in the post–civil rights era, the political, economic, and social development of black Americans has provided an especially fertile environment in which Farrakhan's demagogic and paranoid appeals have been able to achieve a national political salience and mass popularity. For many blacks, material social and economic conditions lend their desperate circumstances a critical status. In turn, Farrakhan's analyses are widely accorded elements of persuasiveness, however repugnant or ludicrous these appear to most black and white Americans. To many African-Americans, Farrakhan's prescriptions for improving black socioeconomic welfare assume a political importance that extends far beyond their cathartic and uplifting psychological value. The NoI's leader does not promise salvation in an afterlife, but constantly stresses instead the achievability of human dignity and a decent material and spiritual life on Earth. The current appeal of that promise is an extremely sad, but very powerful, indictment of many black Americans' parlous social and economic position in the most prosperous nation-state on the planet at the close of the twentieth century.

Moreover, compared to McCarthy's paranoid assertions, Farrakhan's unremitting claims of a conspiracy against black Americans are forged upon a basis prima facie more plausible to many African-Americans, given two hundred years of slavery, de jure and de facto segregation, racial discrimination, and prejudice. Whereas the Cold War was, even at the height of McCarthyism, a relatively new international political phenomenon,[10] and fear of foreign threats fundamentally a psychological condition, the plight of disadvantaged African-Americans is one of the more enduringly undistinguished—and the brute fact of black political, economic, and social inequality one of the most depressingly constant—and objective features of American historical development since the republic's founding in the eighteenth century. What is perhaps most surprising, in this context, is not so much that an unprepossessing national figure such as Farrakhan has arisen in the dramatic fashion that he has over recent years, but more that it has taken so long for this actually to have occurred.

Indeed, the very longevity of broadly based black American inequality—the enduring and disproportionate disadvantage faced by

African-Americans—serves as an important focus for starkly dissonant interpretations of Farrakhan's reactionary and paranoid praxis. Conspiracy theorists typically invoke their claims of malevolent and secret plots in order to account for a set of events or developments for which no otherwise obvious or immediate explanation seems plausible, that is, to explain a situation which is, in most respects, inexplicable. In the nineteenth and early twentieth centuries, for example, mass immigration into the United States (particularly from southern Europe) was viewed by nativist American groups as grievously undermining the purported unity of the young nation through irreparably disturbing its relative ethnic homogeneity. The only reasonable explanation for the influx of such "aliens" had, for many established Americans, to reside in the sinister conspiratorial activities of elite governmental authorities.

In the twentieth century, the steady spread of international communism, to which the United States appeared passive and irresolute in effectively opposing, was similarly attributed by McCarthy and others largely to internal forces of subversion. In the 1950s and 1960s, the decisive intervention of the federal government in advancing desegregation of public facilities in the South was viewed by many white southerners as being inherently rooted in antisouthern conspiracies and elitist northeastern seaboard designs deliberately hatched to destroy traditional ways of life in Dixie. The presence of communists and Jews in the civil rights movement appeared to lend some credence to many southerners' suspicions (along with the tacit, and sometimes outspoken, agreement of FBI head J. Edgar Hoover). Subsequently, in the 1970s and 1980s, attempts by the federal and state courts to achieve racially integrated schools through busing; to provide welfare benefits to indigents; to outlaw prayer in public schools while permitting sex education, legalized abortion, and "obscene" art and literature have all suggested to discrete groups of Americans the existence of a destructive conspiracy of unrepresentative and effete elites in Washington, D.C. The historical lineage and extensive scope of conspiratorial claims is therefore pronounced in American public life.

The invocation of such assertions of conspiracy is largely associated with (though not exclusively confined to) periods of rapid political, social, and economic change. As Lipset and Raab rightly observe, extremist movements have historically been movements of disaffection that typically occur during periods of incipient, but potentially broad-ranging, change in traditional modes of life and established customs. Such movements invariably address social groups that have either already been, or are about to be, deprived of something they perceive to be important or, alternatively, that experience rising aspirations that lead them to feel that they have always been deprived of something that they now strongly desire. Such a widespread sentiment of deprivation is typically accompanied by a profound sense of political dislocation, with the groups concerned casting increasingly unfavorable, suspicious, and wary eyes upon an established polity (and, especially, an existing party structure) that no longer seems able to serve their needs or wants.[11]

At such transitional moments, traditional patterns, structures, and established ways of life are threatened by being forced—by hostile outside entities—to undergo dramatic and rapid transformations. Where this "threat" seems especially potent, and the scope of change particularly great, the popular plausibility of conspiracy theories—and the accompanying mass appeal of their most articulate, vigorous, and skillful proponents—has been considerable. For many Americans at the time, for example, the international advance of communism in Europe (Eastern and Western), Asia, Africa, Latin America, and the Caribbean during the 1950s did indeed appear to be peculiar, dangerous, and virtually inexplicable. For many white southerners then, and over subsequent decades, the external federal government "interference" in regional practices that had been established for well over sixty years did seem not only shocking, but also without legitimate precedent or adequate explanation; the region seemed to many to be subject to special and intensely adverse treatment. Only the existence of malign forces conspiring to advance deleterious sectional goals appeared to be a sufficiently persuasive explanation to account for the rapid changes that were occurring to traditional forms of racially segregated existence in Dixie.

In its many distinct guises, the disconcerting process of change has therefore rendered many millions of Americans particularly susceptible to the proponents of conspiratorial analyses at different points in American history. In the case of African-Americans, however, the brute historic fact of persistent and disproportionate political, social, and economic inequality is so self-evident—and its causes so lengthily and well-enumerated—that no pressing imperative to invoke conspiracies seems to be incumbent upon analysts of the racial minority's plight. There are few, if any, mysteries about the state and the multiple sources of black deprivation. The manifest character of black American history provides a dramatic and powerful indication of the perversity of claims of the existence of an insidious, widespread, and sinister antiblack conspiracy on the part of Jews, whites, or the federal government. Conspiracies are normally invoked to explain the existence of a phenomenon that seems otherwise inexplicable, but compelling explanations for black American disadvantage do not require such invocations of conspiracy theories to be sufficiently persuasive.

For many African-Americans however,—and in particular for those blacks whose political socialization has been shaped in and by the politics of the post–civil rights era, with the experience of de jure segregation a relatively distant memory—the persistence of grievous and disproportionate maladies among black communities nationwide renders such claims of an antiblack conspiracy more palatable and plausible. This is so, in particular, because the prescriptive content of Farrakhan's analysis rests upon such stark and persistent indices of many African-Americans' continued material social and economic dislocation since 1964–65. Both the critical and popular recitation of figures detailing black socioeconomic deprivation in the post–civil rights era have admittedly become so frequent in recent years as to render the notion of disproportionate problems affecting African-Americans familiar to all. But the sheer scale and scope of the social and economic devastation that afflicts many predominantly black urban communities nonetheless require particular emphasis and are worth detailed elaboration so as to be absolutely clear about their dramatic and critical qualities.

Even the most cursory glance through studies of contemporary black American socioeconomic conditions makes for deeply distressing reading. Both absolute and relative indicators of social and economic well-being register demonstrably poor advances for millions of blacks in the post–civil rights era. In 1990, for example, African-Americans were collectively:

> . . . over twice as likely as whites to be jobless. The median black family income is 56% of a white family's. Nearly a third of all blacks, as against 10 percent of whites, live below what is officially reckoned to be the poverty level. A new-born black baby is twice as likely as a white baby to die before its first birthday. The 31 million or so blacks are 12 percent of America's population but supply nearly half its prison population. A black man is

six times as likely as a white man to be murdered; homicide is the leading cause of death of young black men.[12]

For some social scientists, such as William Julius Wilson, these statistics, while in the main accurate, nonetheless obscure a crucial point: that the problems conventionally associated with issues of race are in fact problems more accurately and comprehensively linked to issues of social class.[13] Such analysts are prone to adopt more optimistic diagnoses for the future of America's blacks (and for U.S. race relations in general) than are others for whom the scar of race is emphatically the central and dominant explanatory variable in the marked disjunctures in black/white life chances. According to this class-centered view, the relentlessly broad scope and seemingly intractable character of the socioeconomic problems facing many African-Americans is at least partially alleviated by the growing economic security and increasing prosperity of the substantial black middle class, even though, for those many blacks excluded from its burgeoning ranks, the statistics remain a lengthy litany of acute and broadly based pain.[14]

Thus, for example, the 1990 American census found that of approximately 30 million black American citizens, over 9 million lived in households with a total annual income of $35,000 or more, the conventional definition of a middle-income status in contemporary America. Clear and substantial black progress has also occurred along several other important socioeconomic dimensions. In educational terms, for example, in 1965, there were five times as many high school dropouts among black Americans as there were college graduates. By 1995, among blacks aged 25–44, the figures were even. In 1970, only 15.3 percent of black Americans had any college education or better; twenty-five years later, fully 48.3 percent did (compared to 59.8 percent of whites). Moreover, in many suburban residential areas across America, such as Carson, California, and Queens, New York, the median black household income is equal to, or in excess of, that of whites. A generation on from the civil rights era, material progress is indeed a reality, not an illusion, for millions of black Americans.

Nonetheless, while such figures (and the analyses of scholars such as Wilson) provide some significant grounds for optimism about many black Americans' life prospects, the differences between the races on many important indices of collective social and economic welfare remain nothing less than startling in the 1990s. Overall, for example, the average black household income is currently a mere 63 percent of that of white Americans. In 1993, almost one-third of all African-American families (31 percent, or 2.5 million) were officially designated as poor, compared to just under one-tenth (9 percent, or 5.4 million) of white families. No temporal progress was in evidence here. African-American families were more than three times as likely as white families to be poor in 1993, a ratio that was actually somewhat larger than that obtained in 1969 (28 percent compared to 8 percent). Fully 33 percent of black Americans were poor in 1993, an overall increase of 1 percent from 1969, while the poverty rate for blacks was more than twice that for whites (at 12 percent), in both 1993 and 1969.[15] Thus, almost a quarter-century of post–civil rights era development has witnessed no enduring progress for black Americans, collectively, in comparison with whites.

Furthermore, black Americans are also twice as likely as whites to be unemployed, three times more likely to be recipients of welfare, and four times more likely to be serving time in prison than are whites. In both 1993 and 1980, the civilian unemployment rate for African-Americans was more than twice that for their white compatriots (14 compared to 6 percent). The unemployment rate for black Americans grew from 14 percent in 1980 to a high of 20 percent in 1983, before dropping to 11 percent in 1989, and then rising again to 14 percent in 1993.[16] Black American teenage males are also six times more likely to be murdered than their white counterparts currently, and homicide is the leading cause of death among black males aged 15–24. Although representing only 6 percent of the national population, black American men constitute a massive 47 percent of the total U.S. prison population. A study by the National Center on Institutions and Alternatives discovered that, on an average day in 1991, fully 42 percent of the black male population of Washington, D.C., aged 18–35, was either incarcerated, on probation or parole, awaiting trial, or being sought by authorities on an arrest warrant.[17] In 1995, one in three black men in America was in some form of penal care. Clearly, this terrain is depressingly barren, but it also provides demonstrably fertile and propitious ground for Farrakhan's many appeals to resonate among African-Americans.

Moreover, even the notable expansion of the black American middle class over recent decades—a development that might be thought partially to retard the nascent appeal of the NoI's leader—offers significant opportunities for Farrakhan to secure substantial political support for, if not actual recruits to, his separatist organization. Deprivation in the black community, after all, assumes both absolute and relative forms. As Lipset and Raab argued during the 1970s, the very improvement of the material circumstances of some African-Americans can actually serve to aggravate the sense of deprivation harbored by many others, providing additional reasons for alienation, beyond the absolute deprivation experienced by many vis-a-vis the white American community.[18] Such a crisis of rising expectations has, historically, been among the most influential catalysts for revolutionary and protest movements, from the French Revolution of 1789 to the anti-Vietnam war demonstrations of the 1960s. The unique status of black Americans as the only social group in the United States to be depressed by American society, rather than by their countries of origin, plausibly adds a further sense of collective bitterness to their mood and accentuates demands for immediate and effective remedies: for reparations as well as progress.

The claims of an antiblack conspiracy that Farrakhan regularly advances are thus neither outlandish nor preposterous to the hard-pressed inhabitants of metropolitan areas of America, urban landscapes that resemble not so much the central cities of the most prosperous nation in the world but more battle zones of an undeveloped country teetering in the bloody throes of an ongoing civil war. Such inhospitable areas are more than merely "no-go" zones for whites who happen to value their lives. They also represent Hobbesian territories that are fundamentally off bounds and wholly unknown to the majority of black Americans. In appalling conditions barely fit for human habitation, in which life is assuredly nasty, brutish, and short, the conspiratorial claim that only inhuman forces can have allowed these areas to deteriorate to such a barbaric state of nature is not prima facie implausible. Thus although, for example, many black Americans would vigorously disagree with paranoid claims that the "war on drugs" of the Reagan and Bush administrations actually constituted a deliberately coercive and genocidal government effort directed at further dislocating black Americans in U.S. inner cities, few would deny that it was almost totally ineffective in stemming the spread of hard drugs and drug-related crime.[19]

For the NoI's principal target group of inner-city blacks, in particular, the ravaged urban environment therefore represents a much more visible confirmation of the plausibility of claims of a conspiracy's existence than did McCarthy's communists to many Americans previously. In comparative terms, the loss of China and the communist threat to Korea were far more abstract and much less substantial blows than the devastatingly tangible losses of work, family, or life, the deep symbolic significance of the former notwithstanding. Farrakhan and the NoI target such deprived city areas, rather than prosperous black American suburbs, for the most obvious and simple of strategic reasons: the prospects for a sympathetic hearing are especially great in the former. Farrakhan's central message certainly encompasses middle-income "Buppies," but it is directed primarily toward reaping a harvest of new adherents and supporters from the many seeds of acute despair that are scattered throughout inner-city black communities across America.

The disproportionate dimensions of black disadvantage also render conspiracy theories especially plausible for many African-Americans. While the threat of Soviet and Chinese expansionism in the postwar years did not discriminate between Americans by race or ethnicity, the socioeconomic plight of African-Americans has always been, and remains, especially acute compared to that of other social groups in the United States. Farrakhan consistently challenges Americans of all races to look directly at the persistently skewed racial distribution of social and economic deprivation in the United States ". . . and tell me if there's not a plot. Twenty-five percent of our black youth in prison, black males destroyed in the cities . . . the black man crushed."[20] As many black politicians often argue, were such dramatic proportions of white America to be afflicted by similar social and economic problems, a full-scale national emergency would likely be declared and prompt ameliorative action undertaken as a matter of course.

In addition to the basic socioeconomic conditions being ripe for notions of a conspiracy's existence to take hold, more black Americans (in relative, and perhaps also absolute, terms) have directly encountered adverse experiences with the putative agents of Farrakhan's claimed conspiracies—Jews, whites, the federal government, and accommodationist blacks—in the postwar years than had Americans in general personally encountered communists in the 1940s and 1950s. Admit the possibility of the conspiracy, and the existence and identification of those forces that target its victims become both necessary and desirable. In this respect, the dismissal of Farrakhan's supporters and sympathizers as somehow naive (or worse), by virtue of his conspiratorial claims, reveals a surprising and significant degree of ahistoricism. Many more Americans adhered to McCarthyite tenets about the extent and multiple forms of domestic communist subversion on the basis of more meager and tendentious information and limited personal experience. It is worth recalling, after all, that Farrakhan, unlike McCarthy, occupies no position of institutional influence that requires that U.S. presidents must consider his reactions when contemplating their future policy options and public pronouncements.

If the potential for African-Americans encountering the alleged agents of antiblack conspiracies is, in principle at least, greater than that of discovering communists was during the 1950s, it is also clear that Farrakhan's anti-Semitism taps into a sizeable reservoir of latent prejudice among some African-Americans toward Jews.[21] Anti-Semitism admittedly has never acquired a mass political following among black Americans, and the vast majority of black Americans have probably not directly encountered Jewish Americans at all.[22] Shared experience of discrimination and prejudice has, historically, constituted the basis for a consonance of political goals and a remarkably resilient relationship between the two groups. Moreover, the incidence of such prejudices has been viewed by some social scientists as being merely the particular expression of a more diffuse antiwhite sentiment among African-Americans, rather than reflecting a specific anti-Semitic bias and antagonism.[23]

Some blacks, however, clearly do harbor prejudices toward Jews regardless of the presence or absence of their personal contact with members of the latter social group. Moreover, these prejudices extend beyond the narrow perceptions of economic exploitation that resulted from historic patterns of black migration during the first half of the twentieth century, which saw disadvantaged African-Americans move into urban areas in which Jews ran businesses and owned dwellings (prejudices that rest uneasily with the social groups, such as Koreans, currently owning businesses in central cities). The breakdown of the black–Jewish alliance of the civil rights era has fissiparous roots that extend deeply, and black American stereotyping of Jews (as more loyal to Israel than America, and as aggressive and therefore irritating, for example) is not restricted to economic issues, no matter how central to anti-Jewish prejudices such issues remain.[24]

In some respects, the crude anti-Semitism that Farrakhan exploits and promotes resembles not so much interracial hatred as more ethnic rivalry. The principal locus of conflicts between blacks and Jews have been the cities of New York and Chicago, historic migrant magnets whose conurbations comprise significant proportions of both populations. The competition over economic resources and political power that is endemic between American ethnic and social groups in general also informs black–Jewish rivalries in particular. In this sense, the extent and importance of anti-Semitic attitudes among black Americans is perhaps exaggerated and overstated.

Nonetheless, the gratuitous opprobrium regularly heaped upon Jews by Farrakhan and his NoI acolytes is exceptional. No other American ethnic group in the modern era faces the type of recurrent public vilification and intense hostility from a national political figure that Jews regularly confront from Farrakhan and his followers. The NoI's leader may, very plausibly, forfeit more potential African-American support than he attracts through his anti-Semitic appeals. Many of the working class and poor black Americans to whom his message appeals would no doubt be equally supportive and appreciative of Farrakhan without the virulent tirades against Jews. More affluent and educated African-American elites would also, almost certainly, be far more willing to accord Farrakhan greater legitimacy and respect in the absence of such pernicious and repugnant comments. The critical attention and national visibility that attends the more controversial public pronouncements that Farrakhan makes, however, are central to both his public profile and political ascendancy. In affording him notoriety as an allegedly independent and outspoken leader, anti-Semitism is inextricably bound to Farrakhan's rise, even if it does not constitute either a necessary, dominant, or sufficient part of his mass black American appeal.

The litany of socioeconomic woes that plague black Americans is, therefore, evidently critical to the popularity of the NoI leader. To attribute Farrakhan's political ascendancy to the existence of persistent social and economic problems among many black American communities, however, is an interpretation that is too simplistic and ahistorical to be intellectually convincing. By comparison, for example, the 1920s and 1930s, periods of deep economic dislocation among African-Americans, witnessed relative moderation among black political and civic elites. Garvey's pan-Africanist movement was eclipsed and undermined by the integrationist NAACP by the early 1920s and failed to revive during the acutely harsh economic conditions of the post–1929 Depression. Noble Drew Ali's Moorish Science movement

was never more than a tiny cult. Even the original NoI's period of substantial growth in membership occurred during the late 1950s and
early 1960s, years of sustained (though, for African-Americans, un-
evenly distributed) economic growth. Economic deprivation is therefore very much a necessary and important, but by no means a
sufficient, condition of the contemporary success of the Farrakhan
phenomenon.

For it is not only the existence of deeply adverse socioeconomic
conditions among many black American communities that informs
Farrakhan's rise. The responses of elite American actors—both white
and black—have also critically shaped Farrakhan's fluctuating political fortunes. In particular, the reactions of African-American political,
economic, and social elites to the Black Muslim have powerfully conditioned his emergent role and influence. As C. Eric Lincoln argued, it
is Farrakhan's:

> . . . inexplicable attractiveness to the responsible element of the
> black community that constitutes the major source of threat and
> irritation that the Muslim leader seems to pose.[25]

In fact, however, Farrakhan's resonance with middle-class black
Americans is by no means inexplicable. Central to Farrakhan's popular appeal is an unusual ability, derived principally from the more
ambiguous elements of the ideological message that he propounds,
effectively to exploit both elite and mass intrablack cleavages. Farrakhan falls squarely within the category of "preservatist" right-wing
American movements, which typically require some type of symbio-
sis or ongoing commonality of interests between members of the
upper and the lower economic stratas in order to achieve significant
and lasting political influence. Such movements:

> . . . are guarding different kinds of self-interest together. The
> common grounds they find are some symbolic and effective
> aspects of the changing times: a disappearing way of life, a van-
> ishing power, a diminishing group prestige, a heart-sinking
> change of social scenery, a lost sense of comfort and belonging-
> ness. This is status deterioration which is seen in political terms
> as a general social deterioration.[26]

Farrakhan has sought deliberately, consistently, and carefully to
safeguard together quite distinct types of particular, discrete black

American interests within the same collective, universal, and organic racial message. In doing so, his political appeal has essentially cut across intrablack cleavages of social class, gender, age, religion, and region to forge a broad base of pro forma African-American support. The NoI's free-market economic principles, for example, coincide substantially with the dominant economic agenda of the black American petit bourgeoisie. However objectionable many middle income African-Americans find his bizarre theological claims, militantly unrepentant anti-Semitism, and traditionalist cultural prescriptions, Farrakhan's avowed brand of economic individualism resonates among black American elites. Even Coretta Scott King—whose personal history is so intimately linked to the philosophy of racial integration and the achievement of a multiracial democracy—argued that Farrakhan's self-help philosophy is "something we can all agree on."[27] The frustrations and anger that middle-class black Americans feel as members of a racial minority still subject to prejudice and discrimination and their conventional American aspirations to a secure, prosperous, and affluent lifestyle intersect in Farrakhan's distinctive combination of cathartic racial militancy, black nationalism, and economic conservatism.[28]

Conversely, for many poorer and disadvantaged black Americans, the combined appeal of the NoI's noneconomic message and the organization's direct action interventions to reduce drug consumption and combat intrablack crime in disintegrating urban centers far outweighs the more negative features of Farrakhan's antigovernment, laissez-faire agenda. Noneconomic demands to rid inner-city communities of dope addicts, beggars, and gangsters win support from those many black Americans who have to confront that decaying and dangerous urban environment on a routine basis. Thus, when otherwise sharply astute critics (such as Richard Cohen) casually compare defenders of Farrakhan to those of Benito Mussolini, for reserving their full disapprobation and unequivocal censure on account of the good works that the authoritarians have achieved, they miss a vitally important distinction: the NoI's efforts to improve black city communities assume an entirely different qualitative—and an immeasurably more pressing—human importance than simply "making the trains run on time." For many black Americans, the NoI is bravely engaged in nothing less than a struggle of life and death.

Moreover, popular African-American demands are frequently matched, however imperfectly, by the NoI's organized actions. The Nation of Islam Security Agency, a licensed corporation and business unit of the organization, secured contracts to patrol apartment complexes in crime-ridden areas of Washington, D.C., Chicago, Baltimore, and Los Angeles, where its presence has been widely accredited with achieving a tangible difference in the quality of life of these areas' inhabitants. The Black Muslims commenced patrols of Mayfair Mansions and Paradise Manor (two housing projects in Washington) in 1988, and won notable praise from both tenants and police officers for their dedicated efforts. According to the former, the NoI's guards were not only more committed than were regular police officers to the pressing goals of crime reduction and community regeneration, but they also commanded more popular respect among African-Americans at large, not least from some of the initially skeptical black elderly residents in the projects.[29] The licenses that NoI-affiliated groups secured from local government authorities testified both to the deeply inhospitable nature of the central city environs and the almost total lack of competing sources of effective security for their beleaguered residents.

The response of the late black American novelist, James Baldwin, to Elijah Muhammad's NoI in the early 1960s is indicative of the type of emotions aroused by the actions of Farrakhan's organization (and its offshoots) during the 1990s. Baldwin, as both an avowed and courageous opponent of racial separatism and an outspoken, cosmopolitan homosexual, was by no means a sympathetic observer of Elijah's NoI. Nonetheless, though he wrote about Elijah, Baldwin expressed laudatory sentiments that are equally applicable to Farrakhan's organization currently, for many blacks:

> [He] has been able to do what generations of welfare workers and committees and resolutions and reports and housing projects and playgrounds have failed to do: to heal and redeem drunkards and junkies, to convert people who have come out of prison and to keep them out, to make men chaste and women virtuous, and to invest both the male and the female with a pride and serenity that hang about them like an unfailing light. He has done all these things, which our Christian church has spectacularly failed to do. How has Elijah managed it?[30]

Substitute Farrakhan's name for that of Elijah, and it should become apparent that, despite the many contradictions and controversies that surround the NoI's activities, it is extremely difficult—if not entirely impossible—for many blacks unequivocally to reject the minister. There are some elements of Farrakhan's public message and his organization's activism that are accepted, admired, and approved of by most African-Americans. Therein resides one of the most important features of Farrakhan's mass black appeal.

Unhindered by the demands of public office, in which his many avowed convictions and prescriptions would require support through roll-call votes, legislative results, and effective implementation, Farrakhan's protest-centered posture permits the vigorous articulation of policy positions, economic self-help programs, and proactive social initiatives that—shorn of their eccentric theological accompaniments—few African-Americans would dismiss in toto. The combination of public prescriptions that are shared by many blacks and tangible social and economic accomplishments in central cities that are admired by still more represents an especially powerful resource for Farrakhan consistently to extol and to capitalize upon for substantial personal political advantage.

INTER- AND INTRA-RACIAL DIVISIONS

Interracial Dissensus

Farrakhan has zealously exploited the fact of pronounced interracial tension in America, the existence of which undeniably remains one of the nation's most prominent and persistent societal features. The NoI's leader has been assisted in this undistinguished task by the continued existence in the post–civil rights era of pronounced socioeconomic disparities between white and black America. The massive growth of the African-American middle class since the mid-1960s has not caused two fundamentally separate and estranged black and white American societies to converge to any meaningful extent.

Dionne was thus quite correct to argue that mass black disillusionment with white America has had a fundamental and extensive role to play in enlarging Farrakhan's effective political and social constituency among African-Americans over recent years. This process, however, has occurred in three quite distinct ways that, when isolated into their component parts, go considerably beyond a simple loss of faith among African-Americans in whites' idealism, benevolence, and support for black aspirations in the United States, and instead imply a far more deep racial chasm, a chasm that Farrakhan at once exploits and exacerbates still further.

The first dimension—which forms the implicit but dominant theme of Dionne's argument—is that black and white Americans harbor strongly divergent and discrepant opinions upon both the extent of, and the explanations for, current African-American socioeconomic deprivation (both relative and absolute). Opinion surveys clearly and consistently demonstrate that black Americans powerfully disagree with white Americans on a range of important questions: on whether the post–civil rights era economic situation has improved for blacks; on whether more opportunities for racial minorities exist in the 1990s; on whether interracial competition for employment now occurs on a fair and equitable basis; and on whether the extent of white racism and prejudice toward blacks in America has diminished.[31]

In addition, and most important, clear and persistent racial disjunctures exist in relation to the appropriate role of government in general—and the U.S. federal government in particular—in promoting black American welfare. The majority of African-Americans continue to believe that the American state has a moral obligation to provide entitlement programs and other forms of public benefits to black (and also nonblack) U.S. citizens. Compared to white Americans, most blacks are particularly supportive of the notions that jobs should be guaranteed by the federal government and that the government should ensure a decent standard of living for all of its citizens. According to the most comprehensive database available—the 1988 Black Election Study—African-Americans decisively support greater spending by the government than do whites in all policy areas, bar defense, the environment, and space/scientific research (see table 6.1).

Black Americans' enduringly robust support for an active and interventionist federal government has represented one of the most consistently important and manifest differences between the races in the post–civil rights era. Moreover, it substantially (though not completely) explains the striking racial differences in electoral support for the two main American political parties since 1968.[32] The vast bulk of black Americans continue in the 1990s to favor the type of purposive government intervention, redistributive economic policies, and comprehensive social welfare programs that have historically been associated with the post–New Deal Democratic party. White Americans, who in the main do not endorse such interventionist policies, tend instead to support the GOP in national elections, particularly—though not, as the 1994 mid-terms revealed, exclusively—in the quadrennial presidential elections. The Democratic party has thus emerged in the post–

TABLE 6.1. Differences between White and Black Public Opinion

Issues	Whites	Blacks	+/-
Support increased spending on government services	33	63	30
Support decreased defense spending	31	47	16
Support government health insurance	39	49	10
Believe government should provide jobs and a good standard of living	21	57	36
Support increased federal spending on:			
Social security	53	82	29
Food stamps	16	49	30
Fighting AIDS	71	83	12
Protecting the environment	64	58	-6
Financial aid to college students	39	72	33
Assistance to the unemployed	24	65	41
Child care	53	78	25
Public schools	61	83	22
Care for the elderly	73	90	17
Homeless	61	90	29
War on drugs	74	82	8
Support decreased federal spending on:			
Aid to Nicaraguan Contras	50	51	1
Star Wars	40	53	13
Space and scientific research	31	25	-6
Political identifications:			
Consider self a liberal	27	41	14
Consider self a Democrat	40	83	43
Like something about the Democratic party	51	63	12
Dislike something about the Democratic party	48	20	-28
Like something about the Republican party	52	22	-30
Dislike something about the Republican party	47	50	3

Sources: Adapted by the author from: 1988 American National Black Election Panel Study; and Michael Dawson, *Behind the Mule: Race and Class in African American Politics* (Princeton, N.J.: Princeton University Press, 1994), p. 183.

civil rights era as the party of racial liberalism, whereas the Republican party has taken up the banner of racial conservatism with increasing alacrity and enthusiasm.

While the GOP's racial conservatism may be driven largely by a (theoretically, at least) "race-neutral" economics and by opposition to an activist federal government among whites, not by the crudely overt racism of the old Dixiecrat, the role of race still remains a crucial one for Republicans. Considerations of race have become so deeply embedded in the strategy and tactics of modern U.S. politics, in competing conceptions of the appropriate role and responsibility of the federal government, and even in American voters' very conceptions of moral and partisan identity, that few national elections now occur without some reference to latent racial tensions and ongoing conflicts. As Stanley Greenberg's influential research into the "Reagan Democrats" of the 1980s found, white Democratic defectors expressed a "profound distaste for blacks, a sentiment that pervades everything they think about government and politics." African-Americans constituted "the explanation for their (white defectors') vulnerability and for almost everything that has gone wrong in their lives; not being black is what constitutes being middle class; not living with blacks is what makes a neighborhood a decent place to live."[33] The combination of an antigovernment appeal and either explicit or implicit racial signals in Republican campaigns (busing, "law and order," the "welfare queen," minority quotas, Willie Horton) has hence proven to be a reliable midwife to the regular delivery of powerful electoral bases for GOP candidates—federal, state, and local—since 1968. A clear result has been that racial disjunctures in partisan identification, affiliation, and electoral support have emerged in the past thirty years as more profound and persistent than ever.[34]

Although Farrakhan's economic beliefs enthusiastically embrace laissez-faire principles more congenial to Republicans than liberal Democrats (rather than government-oriented programs), the disjuncture in racial attitudes to black American welfare nonetheless provides an attractive opportunity for him to exploit for political gain among black Americans. The core themes that Farrakhan relentlessly develops and advances in his public discourse—that white America is largely responsible for black problems and that whites collectively desire to be rid of African-Americans entirely—are themes that the differences in racial attitudes outlined above seem, to many African-Americans, to confirm. A government ostensibly of all Americans appears to some blacks to be implacably unwilling to address the needs and desires of a long-oppressed racial minority, whose historic deprivation is thereby effectively sanctioned, perpetuated, and worsened. Although the reasons for white Americans' opposition to new government programs to benefit blacks are far more complex than simple racial prejudice alone—and while white opposition to such programs is far from being either universal or immutable in character[35]—the very existence of white opposition is a sufficiently galvanizing force for Farrakhan's attempts to win mass political support through stoking up black American animosity and thereby exacerbating interracial tensions still further.

Dissensus over economics therefore strongly informs continued discrepancies in racial life chances and powerfully buttresses Farrakhan's frequent assertions of the incompatibility of the races in America: in this view, even peaceful coexistence between black and white Americans represents a chimera. While interracial differences in opinions, however, are principally focused upon distributive and redistributive policy concerns, the clear disjunctures in attitudes between the races also extend far beyond narrowly economic issues. Especially in regard to some of the most notable foci of societal conflicts involving race in recent years, such as the Rodney King beating in 1992 and the O. J. Simpson trial of 1994–95, black and white Americans differed dramatically in their assessments of the relative and absolute guilt and innocence of the involved parties.

Consider, for example, the reaction to the King beating and the subsequent Los Angeles riots of April 1992. Although an overwhelming majority of both black and white Americans believed that the four white police officers found not guilty of beating King should have been found guilty, the broader inferences that they drew from the affair diverged dramatically. For example, while 78 percent of black Americans agreed that the King verdict demonstrated that blacks simply cannot achieve justice in America, only 25 percent of whites (admittedly, a significant figure in itself) concurred with that view. Only 1 percent of African-Americans, compared with fully 47 percent of whites, held that the police in most U.S. cities treat blacks as fairly as whites, while a mere 8 percent of blacks (against a substantial 46 percent of whites) believed that black Americans and other minorities received equal treatment in the American criminal justice system as a whole.[36] The vast gulf between the races in their dissonant perceptions of the same evidence, events, and politicosocial institutions is such that Farrakhan's repetitive central message—that America's racial chasm is now beyond the reach of any bridge—is one that resonates with increasing popular force.

Farrakhan's popularity among many black American college students, as well as inner-city blacks, also reflects this pronounced gulf and the marked extent to which even middle-income black Americans in the post–civil rights era still hold race to be a formidable obstacle to their individual advancement and to the enjoyment of full citizenship in the United States. Simplistic characterizations of Farrakhan as the "gangsta of choice on college campuses, a trendy demagogue"[37] entirely fail to address the complex intraracial cleavages and the particularly salient issues upon which the Black Muslim's appeal among educated (as well as uneducated) black Americans is founded. The centrality of race that Farrakhan invokes constantly in his analyses of America's plight is a factor that middle-class black Americans, aspiring to upward social and geographic mobility, also perceive to be absolutely fundamental—and far more often constraining than beneficial—to their own individual and collective futures. Disjunctures between black and white conceptions along a range of important questions are thus a crucial feature of the interracial conflict that Farrakhan invariably highlights.

The second dimension in which Farrakhan's appeals win popular black American support, however, is based more clearly and comprehensively on a shared black antipathy toward white Americans and/or the governmental and political institutions that are perceived to be dominated or controlled by them. Several of the paranoiac themes that Farrakhan emphasizes in his public discourse are themes that evidently resonate with popular black American attitudes. In particular, the pronounced mistrust of government in general, and the federal government in particular, shared by both Farrakhan and white supremacists—albeit for different reasons and from discordant motives—is one that many blacks at the mass level also demonstrably harbor. A poll in the *New York Times* in 1990, for example, revealed that 77 percent of black Americans (compared with 34 percent of whites) think it either "true, or most likely true" that the government singles out African-American politicians for investigations in order to discredit them. Fully 60 percent of black Americans (compared with only 16 percent of whites) believed that the government intentionally makes drugs easily available in poor black neighborhoods to harm African-Americans. In addition, a remarkable 29 percent of African-Americans (but just 5 percent of whites) thought that it was true, or possibly true, that the AIDS virus was created deliberately to decimate the black population and to advance its genocide.[38]

What is most striking about these figures is not simply the substantial proportion of black Americans who adhere to these notions—although, obviously, this is itself impressive—but also the clear and marked differences that exist between the races on the above questions. The figures indicate very strongly that not only does a significant pool of potential black support for Farrakhan exist when he addresses issues such as FBI harassment of black American politicians and the dissemination of hard drugs and the HIV virus in black neighborhoods, but also that the minister's linking these themes to prevailing conceptions of a diffuse white American hostility or increasing indifference toward African-Americans compounds their popular appeal among many blacks. No matter how ludicrous, preposterous, and repugnant the propositions are to many white and black Americans alike, Farrakhan unapologetically articulates sentiments about drugs and AIDS that are shared by substantial numbers of blacks.

Farrakhan's demonization of whites and the federal government as enemies of black Americans is not, therefore, as much a high-risk strategy as it is one that is certain to accord favorably with many popular black attitudes. If white Americans and a white/Jewish-run federal government truly are capable of deliberately disseminating lethally addictive drugs and deadly sex-related viruses among blacks in order to hasten African-American genocide—as many blacks currently believe is the case—it is hardly surprising that Farrakhan's strident calls for racial separation (whether cultural or physical) in the United States win him significant popular black support. It would be immeasurably more surprising, in fact, if his vocal pleas actually fell upon deaf ears, in this context. Separate racial development represents not just a matter of empowering black Americans politically, economically, and socially, by this interpretation. It is also a fundamental prerequisite for the very survival of the African-American race in the United States. Farrakhan's militant demeanor and uncompromising demands are thus entirely appropriate to—and even required by—the broader context of deteriorating U.S. race relations for many African-Americans.

The third facet of popular black American disillusionment with whites concerns the widespread perception among African-Americans of a deep and growing white political backlash against the landmark black political and social gains secured, after protracted and costly struggle, during the 1960s. The roots of the Farrakhan phenomenon thus extend beyond simple white indifference about, or neutrality toward, African-Americans or black welfare in the 1990s. Rather, several recent developments in national American politics instead point clearly toward an increasing and dangerous level of white hostility to blacks, with white Americans actively and aggressively seeking to reverse established public policies that were originally designed to assist black Americans in particular.

The most significant historical development in this respect was the election and reelection of Ronald Reagan to the United States presidency in 1980 and 1984, respectively. The civil rights gains of the 1960s and 1970s appeared to come a screeching halt with the election of one of their most vocal and consistent conservative opponents. As a presidential candidate more broadly and deeply despised by black Americans than any since George Wallace, and as a president whose political aspirations were more distant from those of African-Americans than any occupant of the White House since Herbert Hoover, Reagan undoubtedly—though inadvertently—antagonized, galvanized, and politicized blacks nationwide. In many respects, in fact, Reagan was the perfect national white foil for expanding Farrakhan's popular black political base. For many African-Americans, the president vividly personified the racial insensitivity, indifference, and ignorance of white America and, moreover, fathered the socioeconomic conditions that gave rise to the antiblack backlash of the "angry white male" during the 1990s.[39] Although his unabashed conservatism was viewed by Farrakhan as being ultimately beneficial to the cause of racial separatism (Reaganite attacks upon public welfare programs were seen by the minister as evidence that the president had been dispatched by God to set blacks free), the very values that led African-Americans ardently to oppose Reagan and to support Farrakhan ironically saw the latter deliver the president's own brand of conservative individualism back to them once more, albeit this time in a racially militant and paranoid black separatist guise.

That hostile national political environment—the sense of a white America that no longer needs, but does not know precisely what to do with, African-Americans—has in several respects been exacerbated even further since Reagan's departure from Washington in 1989. After two decades as mainstream public policy items, for example, both the United States Supreme Court and Republican elected officials in federal, state, and local office have struck down affirmative action policies and minority set-aside programs that had been specifically designed to assist black Americans' opportunities for education, employment, and private enterprise. Having upheld the practice of concentrating racial minorities into particular congressional districts in order to increase black representation in representative assemblies in 1986 (a process dubbed "affirmative gerrymandering" by its critics), the Supreme Court moved in four critical decisions during the 1990s to reverse that policy, condemning it as a form of "political apartheid" repugnant to both a color-blind U.S. Constitution and civilized American sensibilities. Having won control of both houses of Congress in 1994, the GOP majority even managed to abolish the relatively meager support services and limited funding of minority congressional caucuses (such as the Black and Hispanic Caucuses) on the first day of the 104th Congress.[40] And, in 1995–96, a wave of arson attacks on over thirty black churches—what the SCLC's Joseph Lowery termed "the soul of the black community"[41]—across the American South vividly recalled the most brutal terrorist attacks of white supremacist groups during the 1960s.

In sum, a deepening racial tumult seemed to have engulfed American race relations. At a popular level, opinion polls also revealed the growing mutual animus that animated racial attitudes to national public policy debates. By 1995, only 12 percent of black Americans and a mere 23 percent of whites held race relations to be either "excellent or good." Of white Americans, 54 percent professed to a belief that "we have gone too far in pushing equal rights in this country," while a decisive 73 percent opposed giving "special consideration" to black Americans in opportunities for college places, jobs, and employment promotions. Of African-Americans, 70 percent (compared with only 25 percent of whites) held it to be "very important" that legislative districts remained drawn to increase black representation in assemblies.[42] Two-thirds of white Americans believed that "it is their own fault that blacks cannot get ahead," with only one-third attributing lack of black progress to the persistence of racial discrimination, figures that represented a complete reversal of the proportions that had obtained thirty years previously.

For some observers, locating the origins of this third dimension of interracial dissonance in collective white anger, fear, and resentment was a profoundly misplaced and misleading exercise. White Americans' attitudes toward black Americans was, in this context, not so much one of overt hostility or pronounced disinterest, but rather of fundamentally benign indifference. Some of the more strident of these critics, such as Jared Taylor, author of *Paved with Good Intentions: The Failure of Race Relations in America*, locate the core of contemporary tension between the races in America instead at a problem of black

Americans viscerally hating whites. Taylor identifies an all-consuming black American racial hatred, an antipathy expressed in the ferocious and violent rhetoric of rap music; manifest in the incidence of black American criminal acts against white citizens (such as the appalling rape of a white woman jogger in New York's Central Park in 1990, the beating of Reginald Denny in Los Angeles in 1992, and the indiscriminate mass murder of white passengers committed by Colin Ferguson on a suburban Long Island commuter train in December 1993[43]); discernible in widespread white perceptions of an underlying mood of sullen, smoldering rage among African-Americans in general; and articulated with varying degrees of eloquence and bile by figures such as Farrakhan, Fulani, Sharpton, Savage, and the notorious Sister Souljah.

The harsh tone of Taylor's conservative treatise and the condemnatory critical responses to it both testified to the stark interracial dissensus in which American public life has become so thoroughly mired during the 1990s.[44] Although, in looking to the future, whites remained more optimistic that the pattern of contemporary race relations could improve than did blacks (according to Taylor), the fact of enduring and extensive interracial animus remained brutally clear, whatever its principal motivating locus.[45] So, while Andrew Hacker is undoubtedly correct that effective political measures intended to redress relations between the races require from white Americans either "support, neutrality or indifference,"[46] it remains the case that, over recent years, issues of race have become far too salient to elicit indifference, too controversial to allow neutrality, and too divisive to produce decisive white support. With such a febrile social canvas as his striking backdrop, it should hardly be surprising that Farrakhan's inflammatory picture of an incipient American racial nightmare should both catch and retain the attention of so many African-Americans.

Intraracial Dissensus

The existence of pronounced interracial cleavages is a familiar enough theme in American politics, even if the three dimensions of interracial dissensus and disaffection outlined above are only infrequently delineated with particular clarity or precision. The disaggregation of the distinct components of the factors animating black–white tensions provides clear and substantial evidential support to

the arguments of Dionne and other critics that the basis of Farrakhan's mass black political appeal resides in his unremitting exploitation of (and impressive contribution to) a diffuse but palpable sense
of growing racial antagonism in contemporary America.

Conflict and antipathy between the races nonetheless forms only
one of the core foundations for Farrakhan's rise, albeit a very important one. The external focus upon white Americans that is commonplace in critical commentaries on Farrakhan substantially obscures the
internal African-American dynamics that also powerfully inform the
Black Muslim leader's politics. For not only is interracial antipathy a
critically important theme in the Farrakhan phenomenon, but intraracial differences and heterogeneous black attitudes are also influential
in expanding the NoI minister's popular appeal among African-Americans. Farrakhan's persistent (and largely successful) provocation of
extensive dissensus within, as well as between, the races is a central
and often-neglected component of his political ascendancy and of the
continuing political controversy that has conditioned his gradual but
steady path to national notoriety.

In this respect, the central intellectual problem posed by the general phenomenon of political authoritarianism and first identified by
Adorno et al.—its being a function principally of either personality or
ideology—is especially relevant to explanations of Farrakhan's ascendancy. In particular, the existence among many black Americans of
markedly negative self-images provides a rich and propitious basis
for Farrakhan's demagogic, reactionary, and paranoid appeals to
secure popular African-American support. Paul Sniderman and Thomas Piazza, for example, record how, on a series of explicitly negative
stereotypes of African-Americans, black respondents actually concurred with every one of the characterizations even more than
whites.[47] As table 6.2 shows, the median level of black American
agreement on the five selected negative racial stereotypes of blacks
exceeds that of white Americans by over 10 percent.

Such findings are striking and powerful, and they go a long way
toward accounting for Farrakhan's recent popular appeal among many
black Americans. Farrakhan's core political message of individual
responsibility, personal discipline, and collective black racial pride is
likely to find a responsive and receptive African-American audience
far beyond the comparatively few members of the NoI: among black
Americans both disillusioned at the increasing disintegration of black
communities and disgruntled at existing African-American politicians

TABLE 6.2.   Acceptance of Negative Stereotypes of
African-Americans by White and Black Americans

	Percent in Agreement		
Stereotype	Whites	Blacks	Difference
Blacks are more aggressive or violent	52	59	7
Blacks are boastful	45	57	12
Blacks are complaining	41	51	10
Blacks are lazy	34	39	5
Blacks are irresponsible	21	40	19
Median	38.6	49.2	10.6

Source: Adapted from Paul M. Sniderman and Thomas Piazza, *The Scar of Race*
(Cambridge, Mass.: Harvard University Press, 1993), p. 45, and the 1991 National
Race Survey. N=1744 whites, 182 blacks.

Note: Acceptance is defined by assigning a value of 6 or higher on a scale of 0 to
10.

and other established civic leaders. Reed speculated in 1991 that Farrakhan's political aspirations were staked upon a terrain somewhere
between actual mass membership of the NoI and a more limited form
of pro forma black support.[48] According to these figures that ground is
exceedingly responsive to the discordant seeds of bitterness that Farrakhan sows.

It was, of course, precisely that fertile terrain that Farrakhan exploited through the Million Man March and its central theme of black
male atonement, at once an opportunity for individual atonement
and collective African-American redemption and an explicit admission of both individual sins and collective guilt. The inward-looking
parochialism manifest in the march—the exclusive focus on intrablack affairs and the often errant practice but great potential of black
American males—was without precedent for such a mass gathering
in Washington, D.C. Never before had so many American citizens
gathered together in the nation's capital to engage in an explicitly cele-
bratory occasion that was so deeply suffused by self-recrimination,
regret, and remorse. Whatever its subsequent material effects, the
march represented an unequivocal, public mass black confession, a
national expiation that spoke directly to the negative self-evaluations
of—as well as the adverse external stereotypes widely held about—
African-American men.

In addressing those self-evaluations, some of the march's success (and of Farrakhan's visceral appeal to black men generally) relied on the gender differences within African-American communities that have fueled widespread popular perceptions of the black male as being increasingly emasculated. Farrakhan publicly seeks, and purports in his prescriptions to offer, the restoration of male authority—an authority that the growing employment and educational achievements of African-American women are easily portrayed as undermining. In socioeconomic terms, for example, by March 1993, the civilian U.S. labor force was populated more by black women than men; African-American women's educational attainment levels exceeded those of African-American men; and a higher proportion of black women than men were employed in managerial and professional jobs, as well as service occupations, by 1994.[49] The latter disjuncture, especially, represented not only a matter of black females constituting a decisive majority of the total number of African-Americans occupying such positions, but also of the diminishing opportunities for black men to obtain traditional blue collar and public sector employment that had occurred since 1980.[50]

Although the discrepancies between male and female black income, educational achievements, and employment prospects are not as pronounced as among other American racial and ethnic groups, the substantial differences that clearly do exist are nonetheless important in conditioning Farrakhan's appeals to black men. For all his protestations about the heavy burdens of black American women, Farrakhan's message (like that of his mentor, Elijah) is concentrated primarily upon the regeneration of male responsibility, the revival of male authority, and the reinstitution of an essentially patriarchal and paternalist sexual order. The compelling image of the African-American male as not only endangered but as also emasculated is a constant refrain in Farrakhan's pronouncements. When conjoined to the statistics of the likelihood of black men being homicide victims or convicted criminals, and of U.S. Census Bureau conclusions that "less than 3 out of 4 Black women will eventually marry,"[51] for example, it is also an image that becomes especially resonant—and understandably so—with many popular black sentiments.[52]

The resonance of such an appeal and the figures contained in table 6.2 clearly undermine the argument that it is either exclusively or primarily a loss of black Americans' faith in white support or benevolence that explains the rising popularity over recent years of black nationalist sentiment in general among African-Americans, or Farrakhan's variant thereof, in particular. Central though perceptions of white Americans' indifference and hostility to black interests and aspirations undoubtedly remain to popular African-American support for the NoI's leader, it is also the complex nature of contemporary intrablack attitudes and elite–mass relations within the black community that is critical to the increasingly advanced political effectiveness of Farrakhan's reactionary and paranoid appeals.

Farrakhan's political strategy is to confirm rather than deny the accuracy of these adverse self-perceptions among black Americans. As the minister succinctly observed in his Million Man March speech, "I point out the evils of black people like no other leader alive."[53] His explicit public message is that many African-Americans are indeed irresponsible, lazy, dependent, and so forth. Issued by any white American politician (and most black ones, too), such negative remarks would naturally invite wholesale censure. Farrakhan, however, qualifies his aggressive and repudiative rhetoric by invoking two (admittedly unsubtle) qualifications: first, that the institution of slavery is held responsible for leaving blacks in America in such a profound state of collective emotional and psychological disarray; second, that that abject state is one that is open to challenge and change, providing that black Americans heed Farrakhan's message and "fly to Islam." The reeducation of black Americans is thus premised upon their purported existing mental, social, and psychological inadequacies and the fundamental mutability of those deficient characteristics.

Of course, Farrakhan's exploitation of negative black American self-images also comprises an explicit attempt vigorously to challenge and change them for the better. Such challenges are common enough among more conventional political, religious, and civic figures in black American communities, dating back to the earliest days of the republic. What distinguishes Farrakhan's appeals from those of other African-American leaders, however, is his intensity, his theologically derived analysis, and the notable public alacrity and marked insouciance with which he persistently charts black Americans' purported defects and deficiencies. Established black American leaders do not stress the alleged consuming emotive and psychological poverty of the mass of African-Americans with either the frequency, emphasis, or eloquence that Farrakhan does as a matter of course. Other African-American leaders do not share the minister's religious beliefs in the divinely ordained crippling of American blacks' individual and collective wills. However much its derivation is ultimately premised upon love and respect, Farrakhan's public message is one of apparent revulsion for many of his black compatriots and one that is delivered, it should be added, almost with relish.

Indeed, it is ironic that, for a national black leader who invariably places such pronounced importance upon racial exclusivity, essentialism, organicism, and unity—to the extent of excluding nonblacks and African-American women from his lectures and rallies—Farrakhan harbors so few public inhibitions about discussing black deficiencies in the presence of nonblacks. Since his controversial national media debut in 1984, Farrakhan's willingness to engage in public declarations about the many maladies of African-Americans and to offer elaborate explanations of black American malfeasance in a variety of nationwide forums has increased exponentially. By 1990, even the Phil Donahue show—with a mostly white studio and nonstudio audience alike—was graced by the Black Muslim leader's presence.[54] In front of a predominantly white audience, Farrakhan proceeded to articulate in detail, and without circumspection or reticence, his firm belief in black Americans' welfare mentality and the infantile mental state of African-Americans at Emancipation. For many other black American public and private elites, such public candor is far less appealing and wholly self-defeating in seeking to challenge and alter preexisting racial stereotypes of African-Americans as incompetent, amoral, violent, and bestial savages. It is inconceivable that a white American politician could engage in similar rhetorical gambits without provoking an intense national controversy and inviting justifiable public censure.[55] Furthermore, were any other established black American politician to do so, the grave charges of race betrayal and Uncle Tomism would no doubt be forthcoming.

For Farrakhan, however, such marked discrepancies in approach are themselves effectively demanded by the strategic and tactical political deficiencies of the existing national black political leadership cohort in America. As the minister noted (with a characteristically ambiguous mixture of pride and regret) during his keynote speech at the Million Man March, of all contemporary black American political figures, only he assiduously draws attention to the evils that many African-Americans commit. In order to encourage African-Americans to achieve moral rectitude, Farrakhan must apparently first highlight black failings. In conferring a nobility upon the black dispossessed,

Farrakhan must, of necessity, address the more base aspects of African-American actions and attitudes.

Moreover, not only do negative self-images evidently exist among African-Americans and demand to be squarely confronted and challenged, but the inadequate and inaccurate representation of black American interests by black elite organizations and elected politicians is also an important contributory factor abetting Farrakhan's national political ascent. Thus, in addition to the notable political capital that the NoI's leader gains from challenging negative self-conceptions at the mass level, Farrakhan's popular appeals are also in part based upon his persistent exploitation of the disjunctures between elite black attitudes and popular African-American beliefs. In particular, Farrakhan's authoritarian and traditionalist prescriptions mirror the existence of majorities among African-Americans favoring conservative policy preferences, particularly on so-called "social issues," that is, those issues that encompass conflicts over cultural and moral values. Farrakhan's strong endorsement of traditionalist and morally repressive stances and his adamant rejection of negative conceptions of liberty (in essence, the notion of "freedom as license" and the absence of constraints upon autonomous individual action) clearly strike a resounding chord with African-Americans at a mass level.

Although most pronounced among southern blacks, this traditionalism also encompasses nonsouthern blacks. In fact, by some indicators, social conservatism is actually significantly more pronounced among black than white Americans, and has been so for many years. In 1980, for example, 50 percent of black Americans replied "harmful" or "unsure" when asked about the benefits of social welfare programs, while 52 percent said "no" to legalized abortion for women, even if married.[56] Fewer African-Americans than whites approve of married women working (70 versus 76 percent) or like the idea of female politicians (65 versus 75 percent). More black Americans than whites, however, favor prayer in public school (82 percent of blacks versus 68 percent of whites). More black Americans than whites also disapprove of abortions on demand (41 versus 28), though blacks and whites are evenly divided against abortion restrictions on the victims of rape and incest (47 versus 46 percent). A survey of 750 African-Americans by the Joint Center for Political and Economic Studies, in June 1992, found one-third of respondents agreeing that abortion should be legal under any circumstances and an additional 47 percent favoring its legality under some circumstances. A poll of black activists for the magazine *Emerge* at the 1992 Democratic Convention also found that 50 percent agreed that abortion should always be legal, with only 4 percent believing it should never be legal. Nonetheless, even among these activists, 38 percent agreed with the statement that "abortion is genocide"[57]—precisely the view of the NoI's leader.

Stereotypical conceptions of black Americans as overwhelmingly liberal in values and beliefs, while generally accurate when confined exclusively to economic questions, tend to neglect the strong cultural conservatism of many African-Americans, a conservatism that comports well with the avowed preference of Farrakhan for well-ordered and traditionalistic social relations among black Americans.[58] As with empirical indicators of Farrakhan's popularity among black Americans, opinion poll evidence is by no means conclusive or foolproof and should not be taken as such. Increased support for Farrakhan, however, is certainly consistent with the well-documented trend away from blacks describing their ideology as "liberal" and with critical arguments that "Black support for conservatism is likely to accelerate, as gaping cracks and fault lines appear in black liberalism."[59] At a minimum, the figures in table 6.2 suggest strongly that the deeply conservative cultural convictions of the NoI's leader are also attractive to a significant proportion of African-Americans at large.

Moreover, these traditionalist political positions are only infrequently reflected in, for example, the roll-call voting of CBC members and the public statements of other organized black interest lobbies, who consistently adopt more liberal and socially progressive positions on issues such as federal government funding for abortion clinics or public school prayer than do black Americans at large. Indeed, the disjunctures between the opinions of the mass of African-Americans and black elites are pronounced, especially on issues of a noneconomic nature. A poll by the American Enterprise Institute—contrasting a black "leadership" sample with a "national" black sample—found that 83 percent of the national sample approved of prayer in public schools, compared with only 40 percent of the leadership sample; 53 percent of the national sample approved of the death penalty, compared with only 33 percent of the leadership; and 53 percent of the national sample opposed busing for school integration, compared with 68 percent of the leadership who favored the policy.[60] Many of these differences clearly reflect divergent concerns between elite and mass blacks. On the death penalty, for example, as the conservative black economist Glenn Loury has observed, for black political and civic leaders, the issue of criminal justice is primarily one of police brutality and coercion; for many ordinary blacks, however, intraracial violence has caused them to view the death penalty as a means of improving the fragile security of their inner-city neighborhoods.

Thus, for many black Americans, the NoI's religious doctrines and Farrakhan's eclectic theological claims are most appropriately regarded as representing merely the embellishment of more fundamental traditionalist and populist political tenets: respect for the institution of the family; clear demarcation of strictly defined, traditional gender roles; condemnation of nontraditional sexual practices; and disapproval of stimulants of all kinds. Explanations of Farrakhan's ascendant leadership status among African-Americans must, to be accurate, take appropriate account of more than just interracial differences. The Black Muslim's mass black appeals are vitally founded not only upon the profound differences in political values and attitudes that exist between black and white Americans, but also upon the partial failure of black political elites faithfully and consistently to represent the policy preferences of African-Americans at a mass level.

Both intra- and inter-racial cleavages therefore inform Farrakhan's popular appeal among African-Americans. As Carol Swain argues, for effective political representation on these types of social issues, blacks currently need to look beyond both the Democratic party and their established national political representatives, whether African-American or nonblack.[61] For many blacks, they evidently find an approximation of or a functional substitute for such representation in Farrakhan. By virtue of his nonelected status, that representation is necessarily imperfect in ensuring the achievement of an effective contribution to national public policy processes and their ultimate policy outputs. Nonetheless, Farrakhan's appeals partly rest upon the clear conviction that conventional political methods have failed, and will remain inadequate, to redress fully black American grievances and demands. Changes in the social behavior and attitudes of both individuals and groups can assuredly be effected by methods other than the passing of laws and resolutions by governmental institutions. Indeed, the NoI's political strategy is precisely to prove the accuracy of that contention through its proactive private initiatives and interventions in urban centers across the United States. If Farrakhan and the NoI stand squarely and uncompromisingly outside established institutions, and are hence denied an influence upon their internal deliberations and decisions, this serves more as an indication of their strength than their weakness, an unmistakably clear sign of their incorruptibility and dogged resistance to the established system of oppression.

Thus, it is partly upon the indices of traditionalist and illiberal attitudes outlined above that Farrakhan carefully cultivates a broader supportive mass African-American constituency, far beyond the NoI's narrow membership base, much as Malcolm X has become a popular black American icon more by virtue of the secular, nonreligious values he is widely perceived to symbolize than either his religious convictions or his material political, economic, and social achievements.[62] Malcolm's charismatic personal leadership qualities—stridency, courage, fearless desire to challenge, eloquence, and political commitment—constituted a substantial part of his popular mass black appeal, both during his lifetime and subsequently. His status as an "authentic" black man, unbowed, unbought, and unbeaten by the very formidable pressures of being an African-American in the United States in the middle years of the twentieth century, was central to his mass black American popularity, both then and over subsequent decades.

Like Malcolm X, Farrakhan's exceptionally charismatic and stylistic qualities—not least his ability to "tell it like it is"—powerfully assist the winning of many African-American adherents and sympathizers in the 1990s. Like Malcolm, too, Farrakhan's proselytizing politics is also premised upon a bifurcated black public appeal of racial love and hate. As Reverend Walker rightly observed, Farrakhan eagerly serves as an outlet for African-Americans' angst, anger, and antipathy, for black rage against the failure of America to include blacks as substantively equal members of its polity: Farrakhan gives whitey hell. That dubious but recurrent donation is a central, unedifying, and wholly inextricable part of his popular appeal among African-Americans. Nonetheless, like Malcolm previously, black Americans do not escape Farrakhan's fulsome censure and venomous fury either.

Unlike Malcolm, however, Farrakhan's consuming racial wrath and his righteous rebuke of his fellow black Americans occasionally approach a form of almost megalomaniacal loathing and contempt, in both its content and tone. Addressing the (white) editorial board of the markedly conservative Liberty Lobby's house journal, *The Spotlight*, for example, Farrakhan explained:

> Not one of you would mind, maybe, my living next door to you, because I'm a man of a degree of intelligence, of moral character.

I'm not a wild, partying fellow. I'm not a noisemaker. I keep my
home very clean and my lawn very nice . . . With some of us
who have learned how to act at home and abroad, you might
not have problems . . . Drive through the ghettos, and see our
people. See how we live. Tell me that you want your son or
daughter to marry one of these. No, you won't.[63]

As such comments amply demonstrate, Farrakhan makes
deeply derogatory pronouncements about the African-American community that other black political leaders either do not believe or will
not state publicly, for a multiplicity of understandable reasons. The
gratuitous and deep opprobrium that Farrakhan frequently directs at
both black and white races in the United States—their distinct motiva-
tions and effects notwithstanding—assumes a crucial constituent of
his popular black American appeal. So, too, does the generally
adverse and hostile attention that Farrakhan directs at elite black
American actors in general, and the established national African-
American leadership cadre, in particular.

SPATIAL LEADERSHIP: RUNNING FOR BLACK LEADERSHIP, RUNNING AGAINST BLACK LEADERS

Although Farrakhan has never publicly articulated a desire to win
elective office in America, the NoI's leader has effectively exercised a
distinctive version of what the British political scientist Michael Foley
terms "spatial leadership."[64] Drawing upon the seminal research of
the distinguished American scholars, Richard Fenno and Morris Fiorina, on incumbent behavior in the United States Congress, Foley
refined further the notion of running *for* public office by running
against the institution to which one actually aspires to join or become
a part of.[65] The attack upon the particular institution is, ironically, an
especially advantageous method of achieving membership therein. In
particular, when the institution is one that is collectively perceived as
unpopular or ineffective, the individual-level strategy of presenting
oneself as an outsider, untainted by the institution's faults and (potentially, at least) able to clean it up and rectify its many defects, is politically very attractive.

Farrakhan, by analogy, seeks neither to join a representative as-
sembly nor a branch of government in the United States, nor directly as
a candidate to challenge incumbent African-American elected officials
(or others); but the Black Muslim leader assiduously runs for national

African-American leadership by running against the cohort of established black American leaders. This is not to imply a deliberate or concerted political campaign by Farrakhan but simply to observe that, both implicitly and explicitly, the NoI's leader persistently focuses popular black (and nonblack) American attentions upon the particular crisis of national African-American political leadership, as well as that of many black American communities more broadly. In so doing, Farrakhan deliberately seeks to draw a clear, powerful, and unmistakable contrast between what is being done by the NoI under his inspirational leadership to resolve the problems of blighted African-American communities, in comparison with the more limited and largely ineffective efforts of elected black officials and black interest lobbies. Thereby Farrakhan also highlights, and seeks to enhance, his relative leadership credentials compared to the latter, established national black American political leadership cadre.

Farrakhan shrewdly aspires not to government but instead to orchestrating the diffuse forces of African-American protest against the status quo, to shaping those sonorous and disparate voices of black disaffection into a commanding crescendo of righteous and invincible anger whose militant chorus sings exclusively from his personal hymn sheet of malice and hatred. Farrakhan persistently presents himself as an outsider to established black American leadership (a status that the public demands for, and accompanying expressions of, his repudiation serve consistently to assist) who, by virtue of that external locus, can inject the necessary vitality, innovation, and integrity to bring about its more general revival. As an avowed spiritual redeemer, from outside the conventional political realm and hence untainted by its corrupting demands and cooptive tendencies, Farrakhan and the NoI can purify black American civic and political leadership and thereby regenerate black communities nationwide.

As Reed argued, Farrakhan shares with Ronald Reagan the same essential style of self-promotion, as the redemptive vanguard of an antipolitical politics, a politics largely bereft of substantive commitments and programmatic specifics and instead heavily reliant upon a rich catalog of comforting homilies to the fundamental goodness of the ordinary citizen, along with caustic criticisms of the sellouts and betrayals of that citizen by corrupt, venal, and even degenerate national political elites. Similar to the inchoate antiestablishment appeals that informed both H. Ross Perot's 1992 independent presidential candidacy and the substantial popular support for a potential Colin Powell bid for the Oval Office in 1996, Farrakhan's leadership aspirations are founded upon an explicit leadership status as being expressly outside the established political arena.[66] Farrakhan's legitimacy is partially founded upon this expressly external locus, as apparently representing a genuinely formidable challenge to the political establishment and the governmental status quo.

Thus, Farrakhan's distinctive, paranoid brand of spatial leadership invokes his pronounced ideological, religious, and stylistic distance from mainstream black American politicians precisely in order to gain entry into the ranks of national African-American leadership. Farrakhan argues, for example, that the "current crop of leaders, black and white, have been ineffective in purging black communities of drugs, crime, and other social ills." In archetypal American populist mode, the minister excoriates African-American politicians who "used the people to get what they want, then forget to serve the people." After Mayor Barry's infamous drug bust in Washington, D.C., in 1990, Farrakhan promised that Black Muslim politicians—a notion that would have been entirely oxymoronic in Elijah Muhammad's days as the NoI's leader—would provide "upright alternatives." Alternative black American leaders' analyses—should they depart from Farrakhan's—are, by definition, incorrect and misleading, lacking both the divine derivation accorded the NoI leader's interpretations and the minister's full and unbowed political independence. In acidly attacking existing black politicians, Farrakhan aspires to secure increasing national recognition as an authoritative and independent black leadership figure.

In his more vituperative mode, Farrakhan's populist critique of established black political leadership becomes dramatically more extreme, acerbic, and vehement in its explicit denunciations:

> Black leaders have become whores, and we sell ourselves to whomever pays the bills and so we don't have too many independent Black leaders who have their hands in their own people's hands exclusively. They have one hand or finger in the Black community's hands and nine fingers and their feet under the table of some white person.[67]

By implication, of course, Farrakhan's ten dextrous digits are firmly and irrevocably entwined in those of African-Americans nationwide. Or, as his NoI lieutenant Khalid Muhammad summarized the dilemma facing authentic black leaders such as Farrakhan and himself (typically, in even more luridly offensive and vulgar fashion than his own superior):

> When white folks can't defeat you, they'll always find some Negro, some boot-licking, butt-licking, bamboozled, half-baked, half-fried, sissified, punkified, pasteurized, homogenized nigger that they can trot out in front of you.[68]

Unconstrained by representing a particular, discrete constituency of black Americans to which he is politically accountable by formally prescribed mechanisms, such as free and fair elections, Farrakhan instead projects himself (and is zealously promoted by erstwhile supporters such as Khalid) as the representative of all, the ultimate and exemplary repository of collective black interests. As the prophetic and enlightened savior of the entire black race, Farrakhan modestly desires simply to be a "good shepherd" for a race of people who have had "thieves and robbers in front of them as leaders."[69] To this noble end, by 1988, even Jesse Jackson was described by Farrakhan as possessing a "slave mentality,"[70] whereas, eight years later, those African-Americans who publicly raised concerns that Farrakhan was opportunistically exploiting his post–Million Man March fame as a vehicle for pursuing his own religious and political agenda overseas were roundly ridiculed by the humble minister as being blinded by the fear of whites, as constituting black critics who slavishly "live in the ghetto, stay in the ghetto, and . . . only go where the master says it is safe."[71]

The overarching purpose of such virulent attacks upon the established cadre of black American political leaders is clear. Denigration and ridicule of his African-American political peers is designed by Farrakhan to secure mass black support as an outspokenly independent force for meaningful social change and, by virtue of that popular support, to obtain the respect, envy, and fear of other black leaders. The link between the bleak and deteriorating conditions of many black American communities in the post–civil rights era and the apparent failure of established black leaders to halt and reverse that devastating decline is one that is designed to bolster powerfully Farrakhan's personal claims to legitimate national leadership status among African-Americans. As Marable argued, "Black people don't listen to Farrakhan because of his anti-Semitism. They listen to him because the traditional civil rights establishment and most black elected officials have failed miserably in providing any effective leadership or vision."[72] It is in the de facto co-optation of black leadership by establishment forces, which Farrakhan explicitly identifies, that the minister simultaneously locates much of the responsibility for African-American communities' continued socioeconomic problems and also isolates one of his most vulnerable elite targets for unrelentingly populist attack.[73]

Farrakhan uses his various aggressive appeals, denunciations, and claims of popular black American support to demand a "seat at the table" of the national African-American leadership cadre, in a manner analogous to Jesse Jackson's attempts to gain respect and recognition from Democratic party elites during the party's primaries and conventions in 1984 and 1988. Although neither of the African-American preachers had won election to public office (the most conventional, if limited, indication of public support in liberal democratic regimes), both used their claims of widespread popular support to achieve effective recognition from recalcitrant, unenamored, and skeptical political elites: Jackson, in the form of party delegate selection rules changes, particular platform planks, and prime-time convention speeches; Farrakhan, in the form of public tributes, media attention, and inclusion in black American umbrella organizations and special national black events.

Moreover, despite the fact that their presence and activism in African-American communities could be assessed in terms of decades, both Jackson and Farrakhan's distinctive exercise of spatial leadership enabled them, at different times, successfully to develop and project public images as new entrants into national black political life. For Jackson, the presentational task was rendered possible by the mass media's focus upon the novelty and significance of the first "serious" campaign for the Democratic party's presidential nomination to be mounted by an African-American. For Farrakhan, the media's assistance principally assumed the form of disseminating his reactionary and paranoid message (and the accomplished demagogic style in which it was invariably delivered) to as wide a national American audience as possible. The more years that have passed in the post–civil rights era, the greater the contrast (if not the conflict) has become between protest agitators and increasingly well-established and experienced elected black political leaders. In achieving formal political equality and expanding the ranks of black American elected officials operating "inside" the American political system, the old protest credentials of extrasystemic African-American actors were ironically accorded a peculiar novelty and an intrinsic value that facilitated the presentation of Jackson and Farrakhan as new outsiders.

That status, as essentially outside the increasingly dominant domain of black American politics has also, necessarily, encompassed a locus beyond the conventional realms of mainstream U.S. party politics. Farrakhan's political appeal is based to a substantial extent upon—and seeks consistently to exploit—the continued strategic dilemma facing black American elected officials in particular and African-American voters in general in the U.S. two-party system. Farrakhan vigorously promotes himself as an unceasingly independent voice for black America and for black political autonomy, whether in the form of an independent black American political party or presidential candidate in national American elections—a strategy that has often been advanced by African-Americans but, thus far, never realized.[74]

That this should be the case is unsurprising. The institutional logic imposed by the plurality American electoral system upon its party system is fundamentally coalitional in character. Independence is either impossible or self-defeating.[75] Continued participation in and loyalty to the Democratic party, however, has won insufficient concessions in the form of material public policy outputs and redistribution of resources to improve the quality of life of millions of African-Americans. For Ronald Walters, black Americans occupy a position of "dependent-leverage."[76] As a minority group operating in a political system replete with other minorities, blacks must necessarily compete within the same distributional framework as all other American social groups. Securing distributive benefits depends centrally, as for those other groups, on the political and economic capital that African-Americans can muster, either to exchange favors, demand concessions, or bargain effectively in policy-making institutions. Black Americans' status as a numerical rather than a racial minority of the U.S. population is shared by all other social groups. The manifest urgency of black American demands, however, is a factor that is of at best marginal consequence to most other groups in either American election campaigns or the institutional distributive bargaining nexus that ultimately determines public policy outcomes. The policy benefits eventually accorded black Americans are therefore limited in volume and scope and remain woefully inadequate to change the plight of depressed black communities materially and decisively for the better.

The resulting mass–elite disjuncture in attitudes toward the Democratic party among African-Americans is hence especially pronounced and deeply problematic. As Marable and other African-American critics have argued, most contemporary black American political leaders are mentally, emotionally, and ideologically committed to the Democratic party, even if many of their African-American constituents increasingly are not.[77] For Farrakhan, such a tenacious attachment represents yet another particular political expression of the more generally compliant, unchallenging, and self-defeating slave mentality the long-lasting presence of which among black Americans the minister constantly bemoans and seeks to challenge. In this sense, Farrakhan's consistent message to African-Americans to achieve collective autonomy and complete independence represents as much a desperate cry of black American political frustration as it does one of either political defiance or hope.

Indeed, with regard to Farrakhan's exploitation of black American disaffection from the established political system in general, the reactions of Jesse Jackson's delegates to Farrakhan at the Democratic party's national convention at San Francisco in 1984 were also revealing. As table 6.3 demonstrates, whereas only 5 percent of Walter Mondale and 3 percent of Gary Hart's delegates were at all favorable to Farrakhan (presumably comprising mostly their respective black American delegates), fully 65 percent of Jackson delegates had a positive impression of the NoI's leader, and more than a quarter had a "very favorable" view.

Robert Newby's conclusion, that the gap "marks the vast ideological differences that separated the Jackson candidacy from that of the more mainstream candidates" is, however, unpersuasive.[78] That affinity for Farrakhan among Jackson delegates was partly a function of the minister's deep disdain for "the system" is certainly plausible. The ideological content of this view, though, is at best marginal. Rather, it is the unusual mixture of ideological dimensions—a reactionary set of cultural values combined with an unremitting commitment to black separatism—that is central to Farrakhan's public message, and the resulting ambiguity (one that nonetheless comprises no obvious internal contradictions), couched in the most strident black nationalist rhetoric, that is fundamental to his cross-cutting appeal among African-Americans at large.

TABLE 6.3. Delegate Views of Minister Louis Farrakhan by Candidate, Preference (%)

	Candidate Preference		
Views on Farrakhan	Mondale	Hart	Jackson
Very favorable	0	0	27
Somewhat favorable	5	3	38
Somewhat unfavorable	16	22	14
Very unfavorable	56	58	8
Not aware of him	23	17	13
Total %	100	100	100
*of responses	(N=1699)	(N=1111)	(N=305)

Source: Los Angeles Times Delegate Survey. Cited in Lucius J. Barker and Ronald W. Walters, *Jesse Jackson's 1984 Presidential Campaign* (Chicago: University of Illinois, 1989), p. 171.

That appeal is itself built, fragilely, upon a telling paradox. For though Farrakhan persistently preaches a public gospel of intraracial unity and self-love among black Americans, the minister's national leadership aspirations and popular support have depended critically upon his identifying and magnifying the available forces of disharmony, disunity, and disaggregation among African-Americans. Professing to be seeking black harmony, Farrakhan attacks African-Americans who do not subscribe to his views, who dare to criticize his beliefs and methods, and who depart from his divine script of racial salvation. The minister may be no modern Machiavelli, but Farrakhan's politics of intraracial love and reconciliation is premised fundamentally upon one of the oldest but most effective political tactics of divide and conquer, reflecting a deliberate and consistent strategy of provoking racial polarization and division nationwide, not just between black Americans and whites, but also, crucially, among African-Americans themselves. By making scrupulous support for Farrakhan a de facto litmus test of unswerving fidelity to the race and of black authenticity, the NoI leader effectively guarantees that dissension, division, and fragmentation all prosper within black ranks.

For other black American politicians, however, the Farrakhan phenomenon is an especially difficult one to deal with and to counter successfully. In 1985, for example, Mayor Tom Bradley of Los Angeles—an exemplar of the type of effective biracial coalition-builder that

Farrakhan regularly lambastes as treacherously selling black Americans out—was asked by local Jewish leaders to denounce the minister prior to the NoI's leader delivering an address in the city. Bradley refused, on the basis of an informal agreement that he had concluded with Farrakhan, in which the latter vowed to keep his upcoming speech entirely free of anti-Semitic remarks. Predictably enough, the agreement meant nothing. Farrakhan insouciantly proceeded, as he had in other major cities that year, to articulate explicitly anti-Jewish sentiments in the speech, and Bradley duly denounced the NoI's leader.[79]

The Bradley experience was not, however, an isolated or exceptional instance.[80] For established black American politicians more broadly, reaching an effective accommodation with Farrakhan represents a delicate enterprise fraught with many potential political costs and few substantive rewards. For the leader of the NoI, by contrast, the exercise of spatial leadership is one that entails very few political penalties of consequence and offers many welcome benefits. Most important, the fact that established African-American leaders feel it necessary to forge tentative and amorphous agreements—whether formal or informal—with Farrakhan serves to bolster his burgeoning political credentials and claims of leadership respect, while Farrakhan's ability nonchalantly to flout such agreements serves only to embellish his claims of political independence and autonomy.

The immense political difficulty that black leaders confront in dealing effectively with the NoI's leader is therefore one that is also central to Farrakhan's rise. As table 6.4 shows, the divisions within the then 38-member Congressional Black Caucus on the vote to condemn Khalid's Kean College diatribe closely reflect such strategic and tactical calculations. CBC members' votes did not reflect differential black voting age populations in their districts; if the votes for the resolution are compared with those who voted either against, present, and did not vote or make a position known, the difference is less than five percentage points. Nor did the intra-CBC dissension reflect differences in seniority in the House, the median term length being five terms for those voting for, four for those voting against. For most CBC members, the vote was evidently more a matter of personal philosophy and tactical convictions regarding Farrakhan and the NoI. As such, the marked dissensus within the CBC spoke powerfully to the difficult political dilemmas that Farrakhan and his followers have continued to pose his erstwhile black leadership allies.

TABLE 6.4.   CBC Votes on Khalid Resolution*

CBC Member	State/ District	Black VAP	Term	Vote	CBC Member	State/ District	Black VAP	Term	Vote
Dixon	CA 32	40	9th	Y	Dellums	CA 9	29	13th	N
Tucker	CA 37	34	2nd	Y	Waters	CA 35	44	3rd	N
Franks	CT 5	5	3rd	Y	McKinney	GA 11	60	2nd	N
Brown	FLA 3	50	2nd	Y	Rush	ILL 1	68	2nd	N
Meek	FLA 17	54	2nd	Y	Fields	LA 4	63	2nd	N
Bishop	GA 2	52	2nd	Y	Thompson	MS 2	58	2nd	N
Lewis	GA 5	57	5th	Y	Clay	MO 1	48	14th	N
Reynolds	ILL 2	66	2nd	Y	Payne	NJ 10	57	4th	N
Collins	ILL 7	60	12th	Y	Towns	NY 10	60	7th	N
Jefferson	LA 2	56	3rd	Y	Watt	NC 12	53	2nd	N
Wynn	MD 4	56	2nd	Y	Washington	TX 18	49	3rd	N
Conyers	MI 14	65	16th	Y					
Wheat	MO 5	21	7th	Y	Mfume	MD 7	68	5th	P
Owens	NY 11	72	7th	Y	Collins	MI 15	68	3rd	P
Rangel	NY 15	47	13th	Y	Clayton	NC 1	53	2nd	P
Stokes	OH 11	55	14th	Y	Ford	TN 9	54	11th	P
Blackwell	PA 2	58	2nd	Y					
Clyburn	SC 6	58	2nd	Y	Hilliard	ALA 7	64	2nd	?
Johnson	TX 30	47	2nd	Y	Hastings	FLA 23	46	2nd	?
Scott	VA 3	61	2nd	Y	Flake	NY 6	54	5th	?
					Median				
					Votes For	—	50.6	5th	—
					Votes Against	—	55.3	4th	—

*H. Res. 343. Adoption of the resolution to express the sense of the House condemning the "hate-mongering" and "vicious" speech given by Khalid Abdul Muhammad at Kean College in Union, N.J., on 29 November 1993, and condemn all anti-Semitic, anti-Catholic, and racist forms of expression. Adopted 361–34: R 169–2; D 192–31 (ND 126–22, SD 66–9); I 0–1, Feb. 23, 1994.

P= voted "present," ? = did not vote or otherwise make position known.

Source: Adapted by the author from *Congressional Quarterly Weekly Report* 52, no. 8 (26 February 1994), pp. 506–7.

Farrakhan's running for black American leadership has thus been crucially founded upon a persistent praxis of running against— and running down—established African-American political leaders. The effective exercise of spatial leadership by Farrakhan has depended upon his successful exploitation of intrablack cleavages at both elite and mass levels, and his retention of a novel political identity and dis-tinctive outsider locus among current national black American politi-cal actors. It is however, ironic that in partially compromising that

novelty through his increasing participation in national politics, Farrakhan has made his political influence subject to its own (albeit limited) internal constraints.

INFLUENCE IN ISOLATION

As chapter five argued, while they have contributed to perpetuating
the national prominence and to sustaining the name recognition of
the NoI's leader, the American mass media did not create the Farrakhan phenomenon. It has been the Black Muslim minister's ability to
secure increasing popular black support without resorting to conventional methods of media manipulation—by steadily amassing direct
links with poorer black urban communities and engaging in a long-
running campaign to increase his elite and mass African-American
prestige—that has distinguished Farrakhan's steady rise to national
attention. Media coverage can of course assist an individual's campaign by amplifying his activism and disseminating his message. To
the extent that television viewers and newspaper readers are more
than passive receptors, however, the grounds for a positive predispo-
sition must typically be in place already for any media-filtered message to achieve significant mass resonance. Rather than create
Farrakhan, media coverage has served at best to animate preexisting
attitudes among African-Americans that were already favorable to
selective features of both the Black Muslim messenger and to parts of
the multifaceted message that he propounds.

In Farrakhan's instance, the positive reception of his message
has substantially been a function of the poverty of conditions—material, spiritual, and psychological—of many members of his putative
African-American audience. Farrakhan's popular black influence,
however, also depends in large part upon his continued political isolation and clear distance from the cadre of established national black
American political leadership. Reflecting widespread elite concern
about the minister's sharp and disrespectful criticisms of his fellow
African-Americans, Charles Rangel argued after the Million Man
March that Farrakhan would not intermittently "go off on the deep
end" in attacking parts of the black community if the minister was
actually seeking a genuine political leadership role.[81] Such a view,
while eminently rational, naively fails to acknowledge the centrality
of such spatial attacks to Farrakhan's overall political project. It is in
his vividly standing apart from conventional American political

procedures and processes—such as running for public office or lobby-
ing legislative assemblies—that Farrakhan bases a substantial part of
his mass black appeal, and upon which his political legitimacy largely
depends. The NoI's leader rests many of his claims and aspirations to
national political leadership of African-Americans upon his protest
credentials and upon his manifest unwillingness to engage in the
horse-trading, deal-making, and log-rolling that are the very essence
of many (indeed, most) American politicians' electoral and institutional lives.

Therefore, Farrakhan's flirtation with elected politicians and his
tentative overtures to other black organizations since 1984 have,
paradoxically, partially compromised what had, until that point,
represented an entirely novel political niche among national African-
American leaders. The most delicate and demanding of political
balancing acts is required of Farrakhan, between making only anti-
Semitic and paranoid appeals that accord him no leadership credentials at all (thereby reducing him to an absurd, Sharptonesque cartoon
figure of local notoriety but minimal national political and social consequence) and becoming an accepted and familiar part of the national
black leadership cadre by tempering his extremist and hateful discourse (thereby appearing to be no more of a distinctive voice for African-Americans than conventional black politicians). Much as the
increasingly enthusiastic and effective participation over the last two
decades of evangelical Christian preachers, such as Jerry Falwell and
Pat Robertson, in Republican party politics frequently endangered the
base of their popular support among the fundamentalist Christian
right, so Farrakhan's political role is fraught with potential dangers
for the Black Muslim's organizational and popular African-American
bases. The less distinctive and exceptional the message that he propounds (and the less vitriolic, offensive, and provocative the manner
in which he publicly does so), the more Farrakhan forfeits his monop-
oly upon the niche market of paranoid black American politics.

It is also here that one of the paradoxes of Farrakhan's role and
influence—and also of the reactions to him by other black and nonblack actors—assumes an especially pronounced political importance.
Since his popular black appeal is based extensively—though not
exclusively—on his protest credentials, the most logical course for
those seeking to reduce that appeal is not, as Rowan and others
argue, to censor Farrakhan by denying him the oxygen of national
publicity. Rather, the most propitious course is actually to accord him

the opportunity—even the responsibility—for implementing effective political, economic, and social change. By properly incorporating him within the national African-American leadership cadre, the strategy offers the opportunity of casting the Black Muslim as merely another conventional American politician. The credibility of his position then rests crucially upon the effective delivery of his many promises, a delivery inevitably complicated and frustrated by the realities of America's plural society and the complex cross-pressures that it exerts upon the governing institutions of the American polity.

Not only does the strategy involve substantial risk for established black American leaders, however—as Bradley found in 1985, as Mfume discovered in prematurely announcing the CBC–NoI Sacred Covenant in 1993, and as many blacks disappointingly found with the World Friendship Tour of 1996—but it also presumes that Farrakhan would actually be willing to compromise his oft-touted independent political credentials by agreeing to participate. Neither eventuality is likely. Having achieved an influential national leadership role through an explicitly unconventional protest route, by stressing and demonstrating the possibilities of private economic initiative, and by vigorously fanning the flames of nationwide political controversy, Farrakhan's desire to risk sacrificing his independence and popularity through being incorporated fully into the ranks of conventional black American political leaders is unlikely to be great.

As Gates compellingly observed, Farrakhan's political identity has been forged upon an uncompromising and unremitting antagonism to the self-image of America. So much of what Farrakhan does is expressly aimed at embellishing and flaunting that antagonistic image for all that it is worth: abusing established public American figures and institutions; attacking the United States as corrupt, degenerate, and doomed; and attaching himself to anti-American despots in Iran, Iraq, and Libya who most Americans understandably loathe and despise. In this respect, Farrakhan is no doubt sincere when he denies desiring entry into any American mainstream; but not so much because that mainstream is tainted and corrupt, more because such entry would inevitably deprive him of the irresponsible leadership role to which he has become so delightfully accustomed and that he has made his peculiar own. For the NoI's leader, giving comfort and solace to the enemy by conciliating with the existing system of oppression would be an utterly unforgivable betrayal of all that he has stood so resolutely for over the past forty years. Farrakhan's express role has consistently been—and remains—that of an unrecalcitrant and unapologetic black gadfly, not a constructive consensus-seeker. The marginal influence accorded any individual politician by public office in the United States has never proven remotely attractive to the NoI's leader. The final resting place in modern American history that Farrakhan evidently craves is less that of a repentant healer of the polity's deep societal wounds, and more that of a misunderstood martyr, unjustly crucified upon the cross of its chasmic racial divide.

SUMMARY

Farrakhan's growing appeal among African-Americans over recent years has its roots in the inter- and intra-racial fissures that remain deeply (if not intractably) embedded in American society in the 1990s. Widespread disillusionment with, and pronounced antipathy toward, white Americans explains much of the popular black appeal of the NoI's leader and accounts for the limited harm that Farrakhan's esoteric theological and conspiratorial claims inflict upon his mass impact. Farrakhan's biblical analogies of America as Babylon are largely tangential and superfluous to his broad appeal, but the belief that American society is fundamentally racist remains widely held by African-Americans. Events such as the King beating in 1992, the Fuhrman revelations in the Simpson trial of 1995, and the spate of black church attacks in 1995–96 confirmed for many black Americans their underlying skeptical beliefs about white Americans, the federal government, and the political and criminal justice systems—all familiar targets of Farrakhan's righteous fury and contempt.

Farrakhan undoubtedly has emerged as an uncompromising and aggressively articulate expression of the intense anger and deep frustration felt by the millions of black Americans desperate to halt and reverse the declining conditions of their individual lives and collective communities. Farrakhan represents a vicariously soothing funnel into which black resentments, fears, and bitterness toward white America can be poured, there to be cathartically replenished. Nonetheless, antiwhite sentiment represents a necessary, but by no means a sufficient, condition of the recent success of the Farrakhan phenomenon. Farrakhan's popular black appeal also rests crucially upon factors specific to African-Americans alone: the existence of strongly negative self-images and stereotypes; the high incidence among blacks of conservative and traditionalist social attitudes, values, and beliefs; the partial and imperfect reflection of those conservative con-victions by established African-American political leaders in representative governmental institutions; and the material actions and accomplishments of the NoI in many deprived urban black communities across the United States. In running for black leadership by running against and running down black leaders, Farrakhan attacks not only white, but also black, Americans. This combination of attacks accords the minister the exceptional role and the unique leadership niche that he occupies in American politics.

The slight prospect of Farrakhan's full and enduring incorporation into mainstream national black leadership also provides an acute strategic political dilemma for both black and nonblack American politicians in terms of their relations with the NoI's leader and his organization. At once too extreme to be readily and wholly accepted into the national black leadership mainstream and too popular among black Americans to be either ignored entirely or marginalized successfully, the threat that the emergent Farrakhan phenomenon poses to the established national African-American political leadership cohort in the United States is simultaneously substantial and difficult to counter effectively and enduringly. It is this threat, and the Farrakhan phenomenon's broader social and political significance in contemporary America, that we address in the concluding chapter.

NOTES TO CHAPTER 6

1. Quoted in Thomas, "Black Radical Taunts U.S. Jews," p. 7.
2. Gates, "The Charmer," p. 131.
3. E. J. Dionne Jr., *Why Americans Hate Politics* (New York: Simon and Schuster, 1991), pp. 336–37.
4. William Schneider, "The Black Vote and a Powell Candidacy," *National Journal* 27, no. 44 (28 October 1995), p. 2690.
5. See "Black Politics (2): Incivility," *The Economist*, 15 June 1996, p. 55. The article was in relation to Mayor Marion Barry's criticisms of the efforts of the control board, appointed by the 104th Congress, to balance the Washington D.C. budget.
6. Reed, "All for One."
7. Harold Cruse, *The Crisis of the Negro Intellectual* (New York: Quill, 1984), p. 157.
8. See Rovere, *Senator Joe McCarthy* (New York: Harper and Row, 1973).

9. Michael Cox, *U.S. Foreign Policy After the Cold War: Superpower without a Mission?* (Chatham, N.J.: RIAA, 1995).

10. See William Chafe, *The Unfinished Journey: America Since World War Two*, 2nd ed. (New York: Oxford University Press, 1991).

11. Lipset and Raab, *The Politics of Unreason*, p. 428.

12. "American Survey," *The Economist*, 3 March 1990.

13. See: Wilson, *The Declining Significance of Race* and *The Truly Disadvantaged*; and James Jennings, ed., *Race, Politics, and Economic Development* (New York: Verso, 1992).

14. See also: *The State of Black America 1994* (New York: National Urban League, 1994); and Hacker, *Two Nations*.

15. Claudette E. Bennett, *The Black Population in the United States: March 1994 and 1993*, U.S. Bureau of the Census, Current Population Reports, P20–480 (Washington, D.C.: U.S. Government Printing Office, 1995), p. 24.

16. Bennett, *The Black Population in the United States*, pp. 17–19.

17. See Stanfield, "Black Frustration," p. 1166.

18. Lipset and Raab, *The Politics of Unreason*, p. 509.

19. Clarence Lusane and Dennis Desmond, *Pipe Dream Blues: Racism and the War on Drugs* (Boston, Mass.: South End Press, 1991).

20. Quoted in Wright, "Fighting the Drug War."

21. See Seymour Martin Lipset, "Blacks and Jews: How Much Bias?," *Public Opinion*, July-August 1987.

22. See Morris and Rubin, "The Turbulent Friendship"; and Marable, "In the Business of Prophet Making."

23. See, for example, Sheila S. Walker, "The Black-Jewish Paradox: Ambivalence of U.S. Race Feeling," *Patterns of Prejudice*, 7, no. 3 (1973): 19–24.

24. See Kaufman, *Broken Alliance*; and the essay by Taylor Branch, "The Uncivil War: Blacks and Jews," *Esquire*, May 1989.

25. Lincoln, *The Black Muslims*, p. 271.

26. Lipset and Raab, *The Politics of Unreason*, p. 429.

27. Quoted in Barnes, "Farrakhan Frenzy."

28. See Reed, "All for One."

29. See: Nancee Lyons, "Muslim Guard Service Grows," *Emerge*, February 1993, p. 9; and Tate, *From Protest to Politics*, p. 161.

30. Baldwin, *The Fire Next Time*, p. 72.

31. See the opinion polls in: "The New Politics of Race," *Newsweek*, 6 May 1991, pp. 22–31; and Ron Faucheux, "Affirmative Reaction," *Campaigns and Elections*, April 1995, pp. 5, 45–46.

32. See Carmines and Stimson, *Issue Evolution*.

33. Stanley B. Greenberg, *Report on Democratic Defection* (Washington, D.C.: The Analysis Group) 15 April 1985, pp. 13–18.

34. It is especially noteworthy, in this regard, that analyses of American election results increasingly contain breakdowns of party identification and voting behavior categorized according to race. Black and white patterns are treated as almost entirely separate analytic foci. See, for example, Paul R. Abramson, John H. Aldrich, and David W. Rohde, *Change and Continuity in the 1992 Elections* (Washington, D.C.: Congressional Quarterly Press, 1995).

35. Sniderman and Piazza, *The Scar of Race*.

36. See the poll evidence in *The Washington Post National Weekly Edition*, 11–17 May 1992, p. 10.

37. Klein, "The threat of tribalism, p. 28."

38. The poll was based on telephone interviews with 1047 New Yorkers (484 whites and 408 blacks; persons with no opinions were excluded from the analysis). See *The New York Times*, 29 October 1990, Sec. A.

39. Reagan's launching of his 1980 presidential campaign at Neshoba County Fair, Philadelphia, near the site of the brutal murder of three civil rights workers in 1964, was a barely concealed nod in the direction of racial conservatives. With his espousal of the merits of states' rights, the traditional southern white defense for segregation during the 1950s and 1960s, the choice of venue was powerfully symbolic to both white and black Americans, in and outside the South.

40. Robert Singh, "The Rise and Fall of Legislative Service Organisations in the United States Congress," *Journal of Legislative Studies* 2, no. 2 (Summer 1996): 79–102.

41. Quoted in "Black Politics: No Sanctuary," *The Economist*, 15 June 1996, p. 55.

42. Faucheux, "Affirmative Reaction," p. 45.

43. Ferguson's actions won praise from Farrakhan's former national spokesperson, Khalid Muhammad, who claimed in a speech at Howard University that he "loved" Ferguson. According to Muhammad, "God spoke to Ferguson and said, 'Catch the train, Colin, catch the train.'" See Wendy Melillo and Hamil R. Harris, "Dissent Raised as Ex-Farrakhan Aide Returns to Howard," *The Washington Post*, 20 April 1994, p. B1.

44. One critic, for example, described the Taylor tome as "classic racism in a new form, a Protocols of the Elders of Africa written for a White suburban audience." See Mark Naison, "Jared Taylor's America: Black Man's Heaven, White Man's Hell," *Reconstruction* 2, no. 3 (1994): 64–66, at 66.

45. According to a *Time/CNN* poll in October 1995, 65 percent of whites believed that race relations in America would eventually improve, compared with only 44 percent of black Americans. While 56 percent of African-Americans did not think that discrimination against them would ever diminish, only 27 percent of whites agreed. See Richard Lacayo, "A Critical Mass," *Time*, 30 October 1995, pp. 34–35.

46. Hacker, *Two Nations*, p. 200.

47. See the discussion of "Negative Characterizations of Blacks," in Sniderman and Piazza, *The Scar of Race*, pp. 38–46.

48. Reed, "All for One."

49. In 1994, 73.8 percent of African-American women had at least a high school graduate education, compared with 71.7 percent of black men. Thirteen percent of black women and 12.8 percent of black men held a bachelor's degree or more. See Bennett, *The Black Population in the United States*, p. 10. Just over 7 million African-American women, compared to approximately 6.9 million men, were in the civilian labor force (p. 1).

50. In terms of the total number of African-Americans employed, black women made up 63.8 percent of all professional, 55.0 percent of all managerial, and 62.6 percent of all technical positions, compared with just 27.6 percent of blue collar ones, in 1990. See Hacker, *Two Nations*, p. 115.

51. See Arthur J. Norton and Louisa F. Miller, *Marriage, Divorce and Remarriage in the 1990s* (Washington, D.C.: U.S. Government Printing Office, 1992), Bureau of the Census, Current Population Reports, Series P23, No. 180, p. 4.

52. The lack of employment opportunities for African-American males in metropolitan centers is documented and discussed at length by Wilson in *The Truly Disadvantaged*.

53. Quoted in Don Terry, "In the End, Farrakhan Has His Day in the Sun," *The New York Times*, 17 October 1995, p. A19.

54. See "Minister Farrakhan Speaks," *The Phil Donahue Show*, 13 and 15 March 1990.

55. Indeed, the continued sensitivity of racial issues was made especially clear by the intense conflict that surrounded the publication in 1994 of the controversial book on race and intelligence, *The Bell Curve*.

56. Gallup poll cited by Martin Kilson, "Problems of Black Politics: Some Progress, Many Difficulties," *Dissent*, Fall 1989, p. 527.

57. Julianne Malveaux, "Black America's Abortion Ambivalence," *Emerge*, February 1993, pp. 33–34.

58. A detailed discussion of current African-American social and economic beliefs is contained in Lawrence Sigelman and Susan Welch, *Black Americans' View of Racial Inequality* (Cambridge, Mass.: Cambridge University Press, 1991).

59. Adam Meyerson, "Manna 2 Society: The Growing Conservatism of Black America," *Policy Review* 68 (1994), p. 5.

60. American Enterprise Institute poll, quoted in Kilson, "Problems of Black Politics," p. 527.

61. Carol M. Swain, *Black Faces, Black Interests: The Representation of African Americans in Congress* (Cambridge, Mass.: Harvard University Press, 1993), p. 11.

62. See the collection of essays in Joe Wood, ed., *Malcolm X: In Our Own Image* (New York: Anchor Books, 1994).

63. Quoted in Reed, "All for One."

64. The three most influential academic works in this respect are: David Mayhew, *Congress: The Electoral Connection* (New Haven: Yale University Press, 1974); Richard Fenno, *Home Style: House Members in Their Districts* (Boston: Little, Brown and Company, 1978); and Morris Fiorina, *Congress: Keystone of the Washington Establishment*, 2nd ed. (New Haven: Yale University Press, 1989).

65. Michael Foley, *The Rise of the British Presidency* (Manchester: Manchester University Press, 1993).

66. Reed, "All for One."

67. Farrakhan, *Independent Black Leadership in America*, p. 39.

68. Quoted in Williams, "Hiding from This Rage."

69. Excerpt from a Farrakhan speech at Cobal Hall, Detroit, Michigan, 8 February 1985. Cited in Gaber, "Lamb of God or Demagogue?," p. 111.

70. See "Farrakhan: Jackson has 'slave mentality'," *The Boston Globe*, 15 August 1988, p. 10.

71. Quoted in White, Thomas, and Salemy, "Farrakhan Defends World Tour."

72. Quoted in Nicoll, "Black Pride on the March Again."

73. See, for example, his addresses: "Disappointment in Leadership," delivered at Muhammad Temple No. 27, Los Angeles, California, 27 May 1987; and "The Need for Leadership: When Did It Begin?," delivered at Chicago, Illinois, 21 June 1987.

74. See: Walters, *Black Presidential Politics*; and Walters "Strategy for 1976: A Black Political Party," *Black Scholar* 7, no. 2 (1975): 8–19; and Chuck Stone, "Black Politics: Third Force, Third Party or Third-Class Influence?," *Black Scholar* 1, no. 2 (1969): 8–13.

75. Among a voluminous literature on American political parties, perhaps the most elegant and comprehensive analysis is provided in Leon E. Epstein, *Political Parties in the American Mold* (Madison: University of Wisconsin Press, 1986).

76. Walters, *Black Presidential Politics*. Aside from the profound inelegance of the term, the content of Walters's argument is not particularly persuasive. The dichotomy of independence and dependence is a largely artificial conceptual device, which hinges upon a notion of political independence that is asserted but never fully or adequately defined. Precisely what constitutes independence in a system that is inextricably fused by institutional structures that compel associative and coalitional forms of political behavior by individuals and collective groups alike, is difficult to establish.

77. Manning Marable, "Race, Identity, and Political Culture," p. 300.

78. Robert G. Newby, "The 'Naive' and the 'Unwashed': The Challenge of the Jackson Campaign at the Democratic Convention," in Barker and Walters, *Jesse Jackson's 1984 Presidential Campaign*, pp. 160–177, at 170.

79. See the account of Raphael J. Sonenshein, "Biracial Coalition Politics in Los Angeles," in Rufus P. Browning, Dale Rogers Marshall, and David H. Tabb, *Racial Politics in American Cities* (New York: Longman, 1990), pp. 33–48, at 45.

80. For a D.C. comparison, see Brian Kelly and Harry Jaffee, "The Farrakhan Fiasco," *Regardies*, (January 1990), pp. 47–55.

81. See Michael A. Fletcher and Dan Balz, "Farrakhan Seeks Wider Role: Some Black Leaders Are Conciliatory, Others Cautious," *The Washington Post*, 18 October 1995, p. A12.

7

Toward an American Apartheid: Farrakhan and Black Leadership in the 1990s

You are going to have to live with me. To some, I'm a nightmare.
But to others, I'm a dream come true.

Louis Farrakhan, 1995[1]

Should Americans be concerned by the recent rise of Louis Farrakhan? Should they endeavor to counter him and the Nation of Islam (NoI) and, if so, how? Such questions have informed the plentiful public and private discussions of the minister and his organization that have occurred both before and since the Million Man March. Most American critics, however, have responded with notably sanguine and subdued assessments of the scale and seriousness of the threat that Farrakhan represents to American racial comity. Their clear and concerted repudiation of his views notwithstanding, the fissiparous dangers that the Farrakhan phenomenon poses to the national fabric of American social relations have been conventionally interpreted as being so slight as to be barely worth either prolonged or animated consideration; as straining that otherwise robust fabric, perhaps, but not as causing anything remotely resembling its unraveling or eventual decomposition.

Such phlegmatic sagacity is founded upon a confidence about the American polity's fundamental resilience, and its effective resistance to forces of fragmentation, that is historically well-rooted. After all, as the Oxford political scientist, Desmond King, has rightly observed, "The United States has a remarkable capacity, demonstrated by its history, to absorb and transcend social and political problems."[2] Few political extremists have ever managed to constitute more than passing and minor irritants to the American body politic; few societal conflicts have been so enduring as to be unamenable to resolution; and still fewer social problems have animated a pervasive sense of their complete intractability. Such historic precedents must surely augur well for the many critics and opponents of Farrakhan today, and should also instill among seekers of racial comity in the United States a reasonably well-grounded optimism and informed confidence: that the burden of proof for those who discern in the "American Dilemma" a problem that defies full or enduring resolution resides more firmly and heavily upon their pessimistic side of skepticism and doubt.

At a minimum, however, the Farrakhan phenomenon represents a clear, rich, and timely warning to Americans of undeniable political importance. The oft-touted African-American rationale for dealing with the NoI's leader—of ignoring the fireman's background in the scorching face of a rapidly burning national home—in itself implicitly concedes that Farrakhan's political beliefs, paranoid appeals, and popular black impact are at once exceptional, contentious, and deeply disturbing to many American citizens. That Farrakhan attracts such extensive and antipathetic public and media attention currently—and frequently evokes the most extreme and vituperative of critical reactions—by virtue of his distinctive role, uncompromising message, and aggressive approach in contemporary American politics is transparent enough to even the most inattentive of observers. That many elements of Farrakhan's paranoid and reactionary message should resonate so strongly among African-Americans is powerfully indicative of the grievously strained and mutually suspicious relations of America's races in the 1990s. And that thousands of African-Americans should even contemplate seeking an appropriate solution to their desperate plight in Farrakhan (much less actually finding one) is a stunning and tragically eloquent indictment of the parlous social and economic environment that many black citizens continue to endure in the United States.

For Farrakhan to have become a genuine player within the national African-American leadership cadre is hence, without doubt, a legitimate cause for widespread concern among Americans of all races. The NoI leader's seemingly unerring facility to be accorded such extensive (albeit intermittent) media attention and to cause such recurrent bouts of nationwide public anxiety, anger, and distress is testimony both to his shrewdly demagogic political skills and tactics and to the unusual constellation of social and political forces propelling his outspoken message across America. The rivers of ink that have been spilled on discussing, denouncing, and defending Farrakhan—a charismatic and intelligent man whose delusions of personal grandeur and visions of all-encompassing conspiracies entertain few apparent bounds or doubts—represent a peculiar homage to a curious American public figure whose many eccentricities and contradictions have more helped than hindered his steady national political ascendancy. Farrakhan's prophetic convictions may rightly be ridiculed and his eclectic doctrinal beliefs roundly repudiated, but no thoughtful American can any longer dismiss the deeply resonant and disharmonic chords that the minister has clearly struck among black Americans at large.

Nonetheless, the distinctive features of the Farrakhan phenomenon also reveal a more fundamental and important fact about current national black American leadership in the United States more broadly, namely, its advanced incorporation within mainstream American politics. Although frequently overlooked, national black American political leadership in the 1990s reveals the pluralistic features that have traditionally been common to conventional American politics more generally: fragmentation, differentiation, competition, dissensus, and the overarching need to forge majority coalitions in order to achieve desired public policy goals. The modernization of national black leadership, in so far as this entails its exhibiting characteristics more familiar than exceptional in American politics more broadly, has reached an unprecedentedly mature mark and a seemingly entrenched level. Farrakhan, then, represents paradoxically both a confirmation and an indirect product of the very success, rather than the failure, of the aspirations of civil rights era activists to black political empowerment.

In this respect, although it is undeniably politically significant that national black American political, religious, and civic leaders have thus far failed collectively to condemn Farrakhan, it remains of markedly less political importance than their near-universal and persistent refusal to embrace him—a dogged and determined refusal that even the Million Man March failed fundamentally to alter. While that commendable and consistent reluctance remains intact, as it surely must, Farrakhan and the NoI pose no consequential threat to white Americans. They remain a nagging irritation and a grievous offense to many, a gnawing annoyance and an ugly political curiosity to most, certainly. Neither Farrakhan nor his unconventional organization, however, ought to preoccupy white American and Jewish attentions unduly. Farrakhan's impact on public policy in America has been minimal. Despite the march and the new political legitimacy that it undoubtedly conferred upon Farrakhan, his NoI has not won legions of new African-American recruits; its leader has not obtained elite black agreement with his reactionary public philosophy and its avowedly separatist racial goals; nor has Farrakhan's extremely unorthodox Islamic creed secured anything remotely approximating mass adherents among black Americans at large. The palpable scar that the Farrakhan phenomenon has left upon the American body politic is a relatively minor one, and an unfortunate political abrasion the ultimate indelibility of which remains in doubt. Not only are the many obstacles to his further advance strong, but Farrakhan is also, fundamentally, the symptom, not the cause, of the twin current crises of black American communities and national African-American political leadership.

Rather, it is the multifarious grounds of the Farrakhan phenomenon that demonstrably represent the more entrenched, formidable, and dangerous threats to the racial and ethnic fabric of American social life as the end of the twentieth century approaches. And it is to the several pillars upon which the shaky yet resilient edifice of Farrakhan's politics of organized hate is constructed that Americans must closely and assiduously attend, if that repellent and reprehensible form of politics is to be convincingly challenged and ultimately overcome: the continuing, disproportionate social and economic maladies of black Americans; the perpetuation of prejudice, discrimination, and negative stereotypes of blacks among both white and African-Americans; and, not least, the national dialogue about race in America that occurs substantially in private and in isolation, all of which assist the advance of an impending epoch in which black and white Americans know each other as fellow citizens only in the most shallow and superficial of fashions, vicariously and involuntarily, from the books they read, the films they watch, the music to which they listen, and the multicultural courses for which they are required to register—not from personal contact and uncoerced experience.

For the increasingly pervasive culture of group separation in the United States that Farrakhan enthusiastically celebrates and promotes is also one that is increasingly sustained by civics texts and sanctified in American universities. It is also, moreover, a culture that can serve as the midwife to a taciturn child of racial ignorance, the catalyst of an American public discourse about race in which the principal actors—

in city centers, college campuses, and civic groups alike—are frequently accustomed to talking at and across, rather than to, each other. And it is upon the lack of meaningful, candid, and, above all, empathetic dialogue about race that Farrakhan's poisonous and pernicious appeals to mutual racial fear, ignorance, and hostility partially rest.

Neither white nor black Americans bear the exclusive responsibility for the growth of an American public life whose distinguishing feature is the degree to which contemporary race relations are animated by deep mutual suspicion and a starkly intense animosity. Until both African-American and nonblack politicians, however, achieve a substantial material improvement in the everyday lives of most black citizens in the United States, the several grounds of the Farrakhan phenomenon will stay abundantly fertile for the destructive seeds of civic discord that the minister so widely and eagerly scatters. No matter how sincere and deeply held are the convictions of those public figures and politicians that subscribe to a genuinely multicultural public philosophy, that contemporary mantra has instead, in its present form, given rise to a series of effectively monocultural American enclaves. Although, in sharp contrast to the old South African regime, the process has neither express legal sanction nor an explicit public rationale, the United States is assuredly moving toward a twenty-first century society in which black and white Americans lead wholly separate lives, inhabit markedly dissimilar worlds (both physically and culturally), and regard each other with increasing dismay, suspicion, and hostility as aliens and strangers in the same land: a veritable American apartheid.

THE TALISMAN OF THE PAST

In heralding, and in large part hastening, the impending arrival of that ignoble and parlous adversarial state, Farrakhan's abiding apostolic role has been one that has rightly been accorded increasingly fulsome critical attention in America. For Farrakhan has undoubtedly emerged as the most charismatic, shrewd, and successful leader that the NoI has enjoyed in its entire institutional existence thus far. In pioneering the resurgence of the revived and fundamentalist NoI, Farrakhan has represented an especially innovative and determinedly bold leader, not least in his carefully guiding the organization's gradual (though still only partial and faltering) entry into the national American political arena.

Nonetheless, for all his impressively effective strategic and tactical innovations, and his unprecedentedly unremitting self-promotion, Farrakhan's leadership also evinces important continuities with Elijah's NoI. In particular, Farrakhan's invocations of an apparently prosperous future of racial separatism for black Americans are based in large part upon a clear summoning of, and an abiding return to, the past. In style, rhetoric, message, and even personal appearance, Farrakhan explicitly recalls and revives the legacy of Malcolm X during his NoI period. In analysis, Farrakhan's explanations for contemporary black American socioeconomic ills powerfully echo those of the Black Muslims in the pre–civil rights era (and, before them, those of Booker T. Washington and Marcus Garvey). In prescriptions, Farrakhan seeks to reformulate the black nationalist and separatist agenda of the early-middle years of the twentieth century for the fin de siècle. And in his outsider, spatial leadership stratagem, Farrakhan evokes the "prepolitical," protest era of mass black American agitation (albeit with a venom toward other black leaders with which the internal clashes of the desegregation movement brook no comparison). The Million Man March on Washington represented Farrakhan's most audacious attempt to revive and, in the process, successfully to surpass the triumphant direct action mobilization efforts of the civil rights movement during the 1960s—an innovative political initiative in the context of the 1990s, but one that purposefully recalled earlier periods of mass black action and one, moreover, whose principal function of drawing a vivid contrast with other contemporary black leaders would have no doubt made Elijah Muhammad particularly proud.

In sum, Farrakhan represents a reactionary American figure par excellence, not only in his profoundly conservative (indeed, unabashedly repressive) worldview, but also in the sense that he adheres to a core conviction that "the past was better than the present and that society should be turned completely around."[3] Separation of the races, internal black unity based upon a presumed—almost metaphysical—commonality of African-American interests, and the vigorous reinstitution of conservative, traditionalist cultural values together represent the only possible paths to a full and virtuous reinvigoration of black Americans (whether in the United States itself or abroad in a new African homeland, under Farrakhan's benevolent dictatorship). Farrakhan's authoritarian prescriptions and paranoid prophecies are thus truly constitutive of a peculiar, "back to the future" conception of collective African-American welfare and black empowerment. A mythical, idealized past (albeit in a somewhat different guise), however, is one that many thousands of white Americans are also apt to find especially comforting and congenial in the disconcerting midst of profound socioeconomic change and pervasive uncertainty about the future. Few Americans reject the largely inchoate, but instinctively appealing, incantations of "family values" and homilies to "community," whatever their race or religion. Indeed, one of the few features that links together Farrakhan, Newt Gingrich, and Hillary Rodham Clinton is the often trite platitudes and disturbingly vacuous paeans to family and community that so frequently punctuate their various speeches and publications.

The minister's reactionary strategy, however, is also one that is designed to serve Farrakhan's personal political objectives. In both evoking and invoking the past, Farrakhan necessarily, and clearly, draws the attention of African Americans at large (as well as that of nonblacks) to the present configuration and limited influence of the national black political leadership cohort. Notwithstanding his barely concealed public aspirations to join—indeed, to assume the supreme or preeminent leadership position within—its elite ranks, Farrakhan's express presence outside the conventional constellation of elective national black political leaders has served a dual function for the NoI leader: as a fundamental bulwark of his individual political authority, and as a transparent indication of the inadequate structure, Pyrrhic achievements, and deeply entrenched internal fissures of the existing leadership cadre of African-Americans. As the symbolic black American talisman of the past, Farrakhan thus forges a potent popular political appeal for the present, in the face of which his established national black leadership colleagues are apt to muster only a tremulous, uncertain, and vacillating response.

The political irony in this respect is indeed a very powerful one. For in the aftermath of the brutal assassinations of Malcolm X and Martin Luther King Jr. in the 1960s, national black American politicians invariably sought to stress the pressing political imperative of developing collective leadership mechanisms. Reliance upon a single, heroic, concrete leadership figure as some form of exceptional and especially enlightened savior for black Americans collectively was subject to a near-universal rejection, in favor of a more abstract and diffuse set of discrete, electorally accountable career politicians. As then CBC chairman Parren Mitchell (D-MD) put it in 1977, African Americans could no longer afford the tragically expensive "luxury" of a single black leader—titular or otherwise—in the post–civil rights era.[4]

The persistence, however, of pronounced socioeconomic inequalities and the deep malaise of many black communities during a period in which African-American politics has become regularized along the lines of dominant American politics have increasingly seemed to attest only to the practical inadequacy of that very notion. The dramatic emergence of Jesse Jackson in the 1980s, and later Farrakhan in the 1990s, has in part answered a desire among many black Americans—and also among whites seeking to simplify increasingly complex and pluralistic collective black leadership structures—to vest their hopes and aspirations instead in a single, readily identifiable black leadership figure, an incontrovertible "race fighter" capable of dealing directly and effectively with white power-brokers. The old paternalistic white question of "what do your people want?" is assuredly more easily posed when addressed to an individual black leader. Indeed, one of the more curious ironies of Farrakhan's rise, in this regard, is that it lends that very staid and patronizing question renewed salience and vigor for many whites, by obscuring not only the pronounced pluralism of modern black political structures but also the marked heterogeneity of black Americans' policy priorities and preferences at the mass level.

However acute that irony appears, though, it is one that is most definitely not lost upon the leader of the NoI. In fact, it has powerfully informed Farrakhan's strategic political calculus for well over a decade now, in making unmistakably clear the vivid and substantial contrast between himself and other national black political leaders. Like the overwhelming majority of their nonblack counterparts, African-American leaders currently emphasize electoral mobilization at the expense, though not the complete exclusion, of protest or extrasystemic political tactics. Those tactics that a generation earlier had been at the very heart of the landmark movement for black freedom (sit-ins, boycotts, teach-ins, selective buying campaigns, strikes, civil disobedience, and popular demonstrations of all kinds) have subsequently become minimized by, and have steadily emerged as marginal to, the increasingly dominant behavioral framework of current national black political life in the United States.

Farrakhan therefore seeks to cast himself in a distinctive contemporary political light by establishing a symbolic political link to the historic legacies of major African-American activists of the past, such as King, Malcolm, Paul Robeson, Fannie Lou Hamer, and A. Philip Randolph, all of whom were decidedly influential and respected figures in national black politics, yet none of whom were elected public officials nor drew their considerable political authority expressly from the electoral arena. Farrakhan would no doubt agree with the forceful assessment of Manning Marable, that current black American politicians have forgotten the past's lessons and tactics, and instead invest too heavily in a systemic political process that was never really designed either to articulate black grievances effectively or to address their demands fully.[5] But it is, nonetheless, to this apparent crisis of national African-American leadership that Farrakhan opportunistically addresses many of his public lectures and bases much of his own popular political appeal.

Of course, it is at minimum mildly surprising that precisely at the time that black political representation is at its height in federal, state, and local government, national black political leadership is widely held (far beyond Farrakhan) to be in such an acute state of crisis. Although the periodic issuance of such critical charges has been a relatively familiar feature of academic and journalistic discourse about national black politics in the United States for the last two decades now, the current crop of scathingly negative assessments possess a strong and compelling resonance in historical terms, in large measure precisely because of the successful incorporation of black Americans into mainstream political processes. The argument that national-level African-American politics has moved "from protest to politics" is now sufficiently well-established as to be unremarkable, and almost staid, in character. Indeed, U.S. political scientists have extensively documented the marked degree to which many contemporary black politicians resemble white political entrepreneurs in their organizational bases, campaign styles, and institutional behavior.

The rich resonance of interpretations of a black American leadership crisis is not, however, entirely perverse as the twenty-first century approaches, at least when the socioeconomic fortunes of African-Americans collectively are considered. For most social groups in the United States, the achievement of government office and representation in legislative assemblies has, after all, either resulted in or coincided with significant improvements in their social and economic conditions. Black Americans historically not only suffered far more grievously from slavery, legally sanctioned and heinously enforced segregation, and informal discrimination and prejudice than did other

Americans, but the difficult and immensely costly struggle to secure their basic civil and political rights has also occupied many painful decades. African-Americans have only been included in American politics and society as full citizens for a marked minority of the nation's history. The relative lack of progress for black Americans collectively—and the deterioration in day-to-day living conditions that many have experienced in both relative and absolute terms—therefore assumes a particularly pronounced, profound, and puzzling problem when juxtaposed with their growing political empowerment in the post–civil rights era.

Thus, the formal inclusion of black Americans as full citizens in the U.S. political system since 1965 has been accompanied not by universal material improvements, but instead by the continued exclusion of millions of African-Americans from the type of economic prosperity, security, and social well-being that is taken virtually for granted by most American citizens. At the same time, and especially since the early 1990s, black elective office-holding has attained proportions almost commensurate with the percentage of African-Americans in the U.S. population as a whole. The traditional explanation offered by many social scientists for the overrepresentation of African-Americans in the section of U.S. society conventionally classified as poor, namely, their underrepresentation in democratic governmental institutions, therefore no longer appears so persuasive. Moreover, with federal, state, and local public policies that are geared specifically to assist black Americans having been on the statute books for almost three decades now (such as affirmative action and minority set-aside programs), and with the arrival in America since 1965 of other racial and ethnic groups who have also faced deep prejudice (but nonetheless achieved remarkably impressive levels of economic affluence and educational attainment), the persistence of grievous and disproportionate African-American deprivation represents an entirely exceptional state that demands explanation. And, as we have seen earlier in this book, the NoI's leader has many strikingly distinctive, extremely elaborate, and logically related explanations for black Americans' contemporary fortunes readily at hand.

As Farrakhan is well aware, the contemporary crisis of national African-American leadership has thus emerged not from a period of sullen and rapid retreat, but rather from a process of substantial political advancement, that is, the near-complete achievement of "fair" minority representation in government offices and legislative assemblies.

The passage of the 1965 Voting Rights Act, its subsequent amendment in 1970, 1975, and 1982, combined with the Supreme Court's *Thornburgh v. Gingles* (1986) decision, together served powerfully to expand the number of black American politicians elected to representative assemblies at both state and federal levels. That expansion nonetheless advanced the focus of black aspirations to the delivery of material, distributive benefits and to the enactment of effective policy changes to improve directly the lives of most African-Americans nationwide. These substantive benefits, thus far, for many African-American communities have been either few, inadequate, or nonexistent. For inner-city black Americans, especially, the social and economic problems have been exacerbated by the diminishing populations of central city areas and, in consequence, the steeply declining congressional representation and contracting tax bases of the (increasingly black) governing city regimes.[6] And it is this fundamental and acute dilemma that lies at the very heart of the current leadership problems facing African-Americans occupying positions in urban government offices and representing metropolitan districts in Congress: the jarring juxtaposition of increasing political empowerment and persistent material deprivation.

That acute dilemma is also seriously compounded by the relative lack of feasible electoral, party, and policy options that are available to mainstream national black American politicians in the U.S. political system. Collective black electoral independence is as much a political chimera for African-Americans as it is for all other social groups in the United States. The logic of the single-member plurality American electoral system strongly encourages competition between political parties to assume a two-party character. Third parties and third candidates at the presidential level invariably fare notoriously badly in such a majoritarian system (much as they do in the U.K.'s parliamentary, but plurality, system). Only those parties and candidates with a well-defined issue appeal and a geographically concentrated base of substantial electoral support enjoy the prospect of some success in national American elections. Black Americans, dispersed across the nation and in no state representing anything near a majority of the voting age population, simply cannot afford the false luxury of separate, third-party efforts, of "refusing to compromise" with the remainder of the U.S. electorate. Although it certainly cannot guarantee their effective delivery, only a politics of cross-racial coalition-building offers the genuine prospect of African-Americans securing substantial concessions in the form of policy outputs by the state; a politics of electoral separatism is ultimately self-defeating, for black Americans as much as—indeed, crucially, more than—for any other social group.

In this regard, although regularly promoted by some black politicians and commentators as a viable method of advancing black Americans' policy priorities and preferences to material effect, the electoral prospects for a third black political party in the United States are not at all impressive. An independent black political party or independent African-American presidential candidate would be unable to call upon a sufficiently concentrated demographic base of electoral support to secure either legislative seats in Congress or electoral college votes; would be highly unlikely to win the unanimous political endorsement of black elected officials; would probably not manage to attract anything resembling a unanimous black popular vote; and would inevitably be subject to the compelling charge of black votes being "wasted" in the particular cause. (This is notwithstanding the likely prospect of an antiblack reaction or backlash among nonblack voters nationwide.) The inherent logic of such a black party or individual candidacy would ultimately replicate on a national scale that of the third-party black candidate, Charles Evers, in the Senate contest in Mississippi in 1978: in splitting the most anticonservative political forces and thereby allowing the more conservative, Republican candidate (then Thad Cochran) to emerge electorally victorious.[7] Political independence in U.S. elections represents a fundamentally doomed and delusory design for genuine black progress.

In electoral and party terms, then, the vast majority of black elected officials in America are, and will in all probability remain, firmly but uncomfortably wedded to the Democratic party, the home of racial liberalism since 1964. Even with the Democrats as the majority party in Congress, however, the policy concessions that African-American officeholders have been able to achieve for blacks nationwide have been relatively modest (though certainly not insignificant). As a numerical minority of a minority legislative party—as occurred in the 104th Congress after the dramatic Republican sweep in the 1994 congressional mid-term elections—such policy concessions would invariably be more meager still. The strategic political options available to black elected officials and voters seeking a greater attentiveness by national policy makers in the United States to the grievous conditions and disproportionate problems facing many African-American communities are thus exceedingly few, weak, and unattractive.[8]

It is partly for this reason that Farrakhan has increasingly been able to pose such ample and acute strategic and tactical difficulties for established national black political and civic leaders during the 1990s. For nonelected black activists such as Farrakhan, the plentiful seeds of frustration, resentment, and anger that years of benign neglect have sown among many African-Americans offer a potentially rich, though exceedingly bitter, political crop for strident racial militancy and reactionary extremism to reap. The issuance of viscerally extreme indictments and nonnegotiable demands; the outspoken conspiratorial claims of deliberate, malign neglect by whites, government, and Jews alike; and the aggressively populist proselytizing in favor of simplistic political solutions to persistently grave and complex socioeconomic problems—the false fanaticist panaceas that Farrakhan offers of racial separation, cultural disengagement, and economic and social retrenchment—together attract much media attention and win the NoI leader significant popular support and sympathy among African-Americans. They consistently avoid, however, the most fundamental and pressing issues of how a deprived minority in the United States, whose policy preferences on matters concerning the role of government in ensuring the citizenry's collective economic welfare are simply not shared by the vast majority of Americans, can best utilize its limited economic muscle, social resources, and political capital in order to secure substantive and enduring advances for its members. The rotten political harvest that Farrakhan has personally gathered in from a politics of organized racial hatred fundamentally lacks any semblance of either a coherent public program or a plausible bargaining strategy by which to realize material gains for the putative objects of his nationwide activism.

Lest that damning failure occasion an indulgent complacency among observers of Farrakhan's peculiar national progress, however, it is worth emphasizing that the dilemma of achieving effective political influence for a racial minority is not one that is solely confined to black elected officials and other African-American elites. For, as 1992's L.A. riots so vividly and devastatingly demonstrated to the entire nation, the tinderbox of latent racial tension and animosity in America that has been so inexorably crafted over three turbulent centuries of conflict still requires only a few potent sparks to ignite. The resulting explosions may have left the destructive economic and social debris scattered primarily among the already-strained urban communities of the African-American underprivileged themselves; but the social and political wounds remain visibly and deeply etched upon the American body politic more broadly. The apprehensions of white Americans prior to the Simpson verdict and the Million Man March, for example, were sufficiently palpable as virtually to clear the downtown areas of L.A. and D.C., respectively, in two days in October 1995.

While African-Americans cannot see clear and substantial benefits in the form of material policy outputs from their elected cadre of officials, the hollow and false blandishments of unelected extremist figures promising a better future by returning to a mythical past of collective order and group autonomy will therefore doubtless remain tenaciously attractive. The starkly brutal racial animus that informs such prescriptions will also continue to render white reservations and suspicions of their African-American compatriots ever more broad, deep, and fearful. And it is in these respects that Farrakhan, an undistinguished but exceptionally dedicated architect of black pride and white fear alike, stands as the clearest contemporary counterpoint to and confirmation of the "Americanization" of the national black leadership elite that has occurred since 1965.

THE AMERICANIZATION OF BLACK LEADERSHIP: THE DIMENSIONS OF INCORPORATION

The move of black American politics into the national mainstream has often been taken for granted by critics of U.S. politics, yet has rarely been appropriately or fully disaggregated. In discussing this notion, it is important to stress immediately that black and white politics have not yet reached a state of full parity. Most notable, whereas black Americans across the United States remain conspicuously willing to vote for white candidates in American elections, whites generally display a pronounced reluctance to endorse black candidates for elective office, at federal and state levels in particular. Much of this bifurcation in the incidence of cross-racial voting is of course explicable in terms of traditional liberal-conservative ideological divisions rather than race per se. Ideology, however, explains only part of the elective racial dichotomy. With black candidates in statewide (and federal) contests, as Sonenshein argues, "even when race is not an overt campaign issue, it is deeply embedded in the election."⁹ The transformation that has been wrought so dramatically in American racial politics since 1965 has clearly not yet encompassed the achievement of a truly race-neutral U.S. polity.

Black American politics, however, has itself become American-ized over these years: that is, it has come to evince the same character-istics and core traits of mainstream American politics more generally. In this respect, the Farrakhan phenomenon serves as a very useful window upon the five central features of national black political lead-ership in the 1990s: fragmentation, differentiation, dissensus, competi-tion, and incorporation. The responses of national black political elites to Farrakhan—and their commendably protracted resistance to his spatial leadership appeals—has both reflected and rested upon the advanced incorporation of African-American leadership into conven-tional political structures and dominant modes of U.S. political behav-ior more generally. For the NoI's leader, that incorporation serves as both an enticing opportunity and a significant constraint. The former, in that it affords Farrakhan a novel niche as an unelected, outsider, protest-style activist, able to appeal to African-Americans on the basis of forging a collective solidarity and unity in the face of great racial adversity. The latter, in that Farrakhan's prophetic project necessarily founders upon the pluralistic dimensions of the African-American community and its national black leadership cadre. Although he can claim his damaging and pernicious place therein and continue to court its many well-respected and responsible members, the preemi-nent and commanding position to which Farrakhan aspires among national black leaders is also one to which he remains denied.

The fragmentation of black leadership has accompanied the exponential growth in the number of black elected officials since 1965 and has occurred along both vertical and horizontal dimensions. Divi-sions now exist not only between different African-American groups at the federal and state levels but also within them. To the traditional civil rights organizations such as the NAACP, SCLC, and NUL have been added new and substantially expanded umbrella and peak groups such as the Leadership Conference on Civil Rights; national black organizations representing elected African-American officials (such as the CBC, National Conference of Mayors); organized interest lobbies for minority enterprises and corporations (such as the Black Business Council); research institutes specializing in African-Ameri-can political, economic, and social affairs (such as the Washington,

D.C.–based Joint Center for Political and Economic Studies); and accomplished individual black political entrepreneurs (such as Jackson, Wilder, Mfume, and Schmoke).

Such leadership heterogeneity was also apparent at the 1995 CBC legislative weekend, the annual national gathering of black American political and social elites. The event was not only the largest ever for the caucus in terms of numbers, but also its most diverse in terms of attendees. The CBC itself encompassed an unprecedentedly large and diverse membership in terms of region, gender, partisanship, seniority, generation, and urban-rural cleavages. The previous year, Mfume, chairman during the 103rd Congress, had been moved publicly to state that the organization could no longer operate on the principle of unanimity—a belated recognition of a long-established reality.

Leadership fragmentation also reflects a growing process of differentiation among black Americans. This intrablack differentiation process has occurred along both economic and territorial cleavages, with a growing African-American middle class increasingly located outside the central city in suburban or near-suburban residential areas. As chapter six argued, Farrakhan has sought to exploit this development, to the extent that the economic foundations of the NoI's public program (such as it is) coincide with the economic agenda of the growing African-American petit bourgeoisie. However bizarre, distasteful, and objectionable his theological convictions, anti-Semitism, and the noneconomic dimensions of the NoI's program, Farrakhan's ringing endorsement of private and individualistic principles of economic behavior resonates powerfully among black American elites.

Farrakhan's exploitation of such cross-pressures within the black community is also linked to the development of national black political leadership dissensus. These problems of dissensus have centered primarily upon the pressing questions of both political objectives and strategies. In relation to the former, confidence in both the possibility and the desirability of achieving an integrated U.S. society has been waning dramatically among black Americans at large since the late 1980s. Skepticism over the Democratic party's commitment to black American priorities has become widespread at a mass level among African-Americans, as well as among many national black political elites. Moreover, according to the Black Politics Study, support for an independent black American political party and other forms of self-segregation and black nationalism had reached an all-time high among African Americans by the early 1990s. Fully half of all black Americans surveyed supported the idea of an independent black political party.

Against this background, established black political and civic leaders have confronted powerful strategic incentives to adopt accommodationist tactics toward those African-American activists (including, most notably, Farrakhan and the NoI) who consistently eschew the politics of moderation, conciliation, and interracial coalition-building in favor of militancy, nonnegotiable demands, and separatist racial extremism. The marked political dissensus surrounding Farrakhan provides telling and important indicators of his current role and influence. At its simplest, for other national black political actors, Farrakhan is simultaneously too influential to ignore completely and too controversial to embrace fully. The responses of many national black political and social elites to the NoI and its leader, consequently, appear to some observers as an astonishingly unimpressive and ineffective melange of inconsistency, equivocation, and uncertainty. The termination of the CBC–NoI Sacred Covenant, the intra- and extra-CBC divisions on rebuking Khalid Muhammad's viciously anti-Semitic and homophobic Kean College diatribe, and the appearance of leading and well-respected national African-American politicians on public platforms with Farrakhan all reveal the very acute difficulties facing established national black civil and political leaders in seeking an effective and enduring rapprochement with the Black Muslim leader.

Such dissensus has, moreover, reflected and reinforced the existence of growing competition among national black political elites in the United States. Although present to a limited extent for many decades previously, intrablack competitive pressures have increasingly assumed three especially dominant forms in the 1990s: electoral, financial, and policy. Each arena of competition testifies to an African-American political leadership cadre that manifests characteristics that powerfully resemble those of nonblack elite politics. Each, moreover, affords Farrakhan further political opportunities to embellish his self-proclaimed status as the most indefatigable, articulate, and dedicated defender of authentic mass black American interests.

Electoral competition among black Americans now occurs both within and between the two major political parties. Reform of the Voting Rights Act has caused unprecedented numbers of black American candidates to win election to federal and state legislatures. Increasing numbers of black congressional incumbents have confronted general and primary election challenges and several were defeated in both the 1992 and 1994 election cycles. Moreover, black partisan identification has also begun to shift perceptibly. While black Americans still identify overwhelmingly with the Democratic party, unanimous black support has begun to crumble. White gubernatorial candidates in Illinois and Ohio in 1994, for example, captured over 30 percent of the African-American vote. Increasing numbers of black Republicans have also contested and won congressional and state legislative elections, the two most notable being Gary Franks (R-CT), the first black Republican elected to the House since the New Deal, and J. C. Watts (R-OKL). Both admittedly represented majority-white districts, but their careers demonstrate—at a minimum—the increasing willingness of aspirant black American politicians to identify and align with the Republican party. Indeed, of sixty-two African-American candidates for Congress in 1994, fully twenty-four were Republicans. Even the candidacy of Alan Keyes for the Republican party's 1996 presidential nomination, though doomed from the very outset, represented an important symbolic breakthrough in black American penetration of the GOP's elite political circles, while Colin Powell's joining the party has provided the Republican party with its most nationally prominent and well-respected black member this century, in what may well come to be seen by future American historians as a landmark political event. The sixty-year lock of the Democrats upon black politicians' career aspirations and mass African-American electoral loyalties remains decidedly strong, but it is no longer free from serious, shrewd, and increasing challenge.

The financial dimension of intrablack competition has centered on the need of individuals and organizations to attract sufficient funds to achieve and maintain economic viability—a requirement compounded by the relative lack of available resources among black American communities. For established organizations such as the NAACP, for example, the need to acquire new members in order to operate effectively is fundamental. In the NAACP's case, this need served as an extremely powerful incentive to Ben Chavis to adopt a more aggressive black nationalist stance in 1993–94. Indeed, the acute financial crisis of the nation's leading historic civil rights organization over 1993–96 served as a stark and powerful reminder of the changing dynamics—political, generational, social, and ideological—of national black American politics in the 1990s.[10]

Policy competition has also developed between rival black American organizations to develop appropriate policy proposals and programs, capable of successful legislative passage and effective implementation, to address black Americans' social and economic concerns. Even within black progressive ranks, skeptical voices have been raised over established liberal public policy and juridical totems, such as racial quotas in education and employment and affirmative gerrymandering. In addition, though, the growth of a significant cadre of both conservative (Sowell, Loury, Williams) and revisionist liberal African-American intellectuals (Steele, Carter, Wilson), skeptical of existing public programs such as affirmative action and minority business set-asides, has strongly increased the competitive character of policy entrepreneurship among national black elites. Although the extent and material mass significance of the intrablack elite dissensus has been widely called into question, the very fact of its existing and provoking a vigorous response—if not quite a dialogue—between the distinct contemporary and historic intellectual tendencies in African-American critical thought is a development of cardinal political importance. [11]

The four preceding emergent features of current national black political leadership, however, also indicate the fifth and, incontestably, the most important dimension of contemporary national black American politics in the United States: incorporation. As the Million Man March demonstrated so vividly, the responses of many African-American elites to the NoI leader have assuredly lacked either clear direction or notable conviction. Those reactions have certainly alternated, at times oscillating rapidly, between accommodationist impulses and exclusionary political strategies. In the process, though, these very responses have served to indicate the marked extent to which national black American political leadership in the United States has been powerfully regularized and incorporated into, and now exhibits the same fundamental features as, American politics more generally: fragmentation, differentiation, dissensus, competition along several dimensions, and the overriding strategic imperative to compromise, conciliate, and cooperate in order to overcome institutional divisions and societal conflict in order to achieve desired policy and political goals.

Whether it is given the essentially neutral appellation of "entering the mainstream" or instead is pejoratively termed "co-optation," the extent and importance of this incorporative development is of critical political significance—and is sometimes lost amidst the often vehement demands made by nonblack observers for Farrakhan to be denounced in the clearest terms possible by his African-American compatriots. For some critics of Farrakhan, the most perplexing and infuriating aspect of the NoI leader's recent public prominence has been the ignominious failure of many national black politicians to condemn him. The 1984 controversy over the particular case of Jesse Jackson has been broadened subsequently to include a vast range of black American politicians across the United States, for whom the crucial litmus test of winning or maintaining political and other forms of support—particularly, but by no means exclusively, from whites and American Jews—has been their complete repudiation of Farrakhan and his methods, beliefs, and style. As Morris and Rubin have observed, many Jewish Americans, especially, fear that in failing to admonish Farrakhan for his anti-Semitic comments, those pernicious beliefs will receive an indirect public sanction from black leaders, and thereby gain greater popularity and legitimacy among African-Americans at large, than would otherwise be the case. That fear is one that many white and black Americans also share and one, moreover, that elite and mass African American support for Farrakhan-orchestrated initiatives such as the Million Man March does nothing at all to dispel.

In the context of black political incorporation, however, the continued and pronounced reluctance of many African-American politicians to associate with Farrakhan, despite the electoral and reputational profit that such action would in many instances evidently yield, is much more important than their failure to condemn him unequivocally and unanimously. The process of black political incorporation in the United States, which commenced with the passage of the civil and voting rights legislation of 1964 and 1965, respectively, has reaped thousands of electoral rewards for African-Americans. The subsequent three decades have been distinguished by a gradual evolution of black American participation in conventional methods of seeking, achieving, and maintaining political power. The victories in 1989 of Dinkins in the New York City mayoral campaign and Wilder in the gubernatorial election in Virginia represented the most nationally noteworthy manifestations of increasing black electoral success, but across the entire U.S. black candidates for elective office had made substantial strides forward by the beginning of the 1990s.

Yet, in their immediate aftermath, the incidence of popular and scholarly discussions of the putative death of black American politics was also notable. For many of those most closely involved in the struggle to secure black civil and political rights, and subsequently to achieve public office and effect policy change, the notion of the demise of a distinctive black politics was as inaccurate as it was wholly irrelevant to achieving meaningful black empowerment. Rather, by the 1990s, many of the core political goals of the civil rights struggle had, after long and costly struggle, been realized. Not only were the ranks of black voters and elected officials substantially swelled after 1965, but proposals once widely viewed as naively ambitious—if not wildly eccentric—became mainstream public policy items: affirmative action programs, Aid to Families with Dependent Children, food stamps, racial redistricting, and minority set-asides. To the extent that a movement succeeds in achieving its objectives, then, its death is to be expected and desired; its life would otherwise testify to a continued exclusion and an incomplete achievement.

It is, nonetheless, true that the very success of the civil rights movement during the 1960s rendered it something of a victim of its own remarkable achievements. Similarly, the expansion of the cadre of black public officeholders in America over the last two decades has rendered national black American politicians peculiarly vulnerable to preincorporative era protest appeals. Precisely by virtue of its success, then, the process of political modernization has left open a significant vacuum for protest appeals to garner popular African-American support. And, since 1984, that vacuum has been increasingly filled—assiduously, vigorously, and extremely effectively—by the shrewd, enthusiastic, and indefatigable leader of the NoI.

As an outsider figure, one untainted by Washington politics and its richly negative public connotations in contemporary America, Farrakhan has aggressively exploited his wholly distinctive black leadership niche to disconcerting national effect. Although only one of the explanations for its success, it was the nonelected, outsider character of Farrakhan's leadership status that proved absolutely vital in mobilizing black Americans to come to the nation's capital in October 1995. Unlike other elected and nonelected black leaders, however, Farrakhan has forged a popular African-American base through exploiting the profoundly negative features associated with, and the substantial divisions within, the black community in the United States. Farrakhan's recent popularity is parasitic not only upon the disproportionate persistence of grievous economic and social maladies among many black communities and the ongoing failure—if not the inability—of their political representatives (both black and white) in federal, state, and local governments to secure their amelioration. It is also heavily reliant upon the deeply negative evaluations of African-Americans harbored by many black and white Americans alike.

That Farrakhan is increasingly treated by national black American political elites as a legitimate and important voice on behalf of a sizeable constituency is therefore a profoundly eloquent testimony both to the transformation of the NoI under his leadership and to the current Americanization of established black political and civic leadership elites in general. As Martin Kilson has persuasively argued, the increasing diversification of black Americans' attitudes, voting patterns, candidates, and policy concerns Americanizes the black political profile in a fashion imitative of the Americanization of Jewish Americans that occurred during the 1970s. For Kilson, this process provides an opportunity for black and white Americans to link their political fortunes in combination, and for what he terms a "transethnic imperative" increasingly to inform black life in general, and its politics in particular. The goal of that imperative is to interlink the leadership of black and white sociopolitical institutions in common cause. Thus, much as during earlier periods in American history, white ethnics such as the Irish penetrating WASP-dominated positions from the 1890s to the 1930s, or Jews penetrating WASP and Irish-dominated milieus from the 1930s onward, so politics remains the most appropriate and immediately available sphere for transethnic penetration by black Americans.[12]

In this context, rather than viewing Farrakhan as further evidence of the continuing racial organicism and essentialism widely attributed to black American politics (as Adolph Reed argues), it is hence more accurate instead to view the minister's relations with national black political and religious elites as testimony to the deracialization and class analyses favored by Kilson, Wilson, and others. Although the racial dimension of Farrakhan's appeal has of course been critical to his national ascendancy, it is the intraracial differentiation of African-Americans in the 1990s—and its associated representation, partial representation, and misrepresentation by national black elites—that informs the political boundaries in which the Farrakhan phenomenon has occurred. No one political actor can fill the mythic role of a national black spokesperson, as if African-Americans actually agree upon all political and social issues, and Farrakhan does not fully bridge—much less reconcile—the many important differences between, and divisions among, African-Americans; but his composite mass appeal is sufficiently diffuse to accord him an exceptional national leadership niche that no other black politician has managed (and relatively few have even sought) to achieve. In this respect, however, Farrakhan's political rise and influence indicate not so much a return to the politics of protest by African-Americans than the clear ascendancy—incomplete but overwhelming—of conventional politics among black Americans in the 1990s.

THE END OF PROTEST AND THE FARRAKHAN PHENOMENON

The mass black popularity of Farrakhan during the 1990s is partially the product, but is also wholly symptomatic, of the deeply entrenched racial divisions and fissures in the United States that have been painfully hewn over many turbulent decades. It is also indicative of the profound tactical and strategic political dilemmas confronting many national black politicians in the post–civil rights era. The long-awaited achievement of formal civil and political equality for black Americans has not realized subsequently the type of marked improvement in African-American social and economic welfare that most Americans— black and nonblack alike—hoped to witness as possible, and that many envisioned as probable. The bright prospect of collective material advancement once harbored by black leaders has gradually dissipated into a deep skepticism among African-Americans at both elite and mass levels about both the possibility and the probability of genuine improvement for literally millions of African-Americans.

The gradual but inexorable evolution of national black American politics from protest to politics is therefore one that has left many black Americans at large confused, puzzled, and angry about their continued exclusion from the social and geographical mobility, and the accompanying economic security, affluence, and prosperity, that so many Americans of all races continue to enjoy, almost as a matter of course or birthright. Even during an age of relative economic decline and increased interdependence for the United States as a whole, the disproportionate locus of African-Americans among the poor, the jobless, the malnourished, the disease-ridden, the victims of homicide, and the jailed is one that continues starkly to differentiate black from white America. In consequence, progress—that notion that remains so central to U.S. political culture, popular belief, and arguably to American national identity itself—continues to stand as a partial, uncertain, and distant prospect for many African-Americans as the twentieth century draws to its close.

That apparent distance provides much of the fuel for Farrakhan's venomous vehicle of black American paranoid and reactionary politics. Farrakhan's success is ultimately the story of a shrewd black opportunist who has zealously capitalized upon America's continuing failure to deal with its serious and abiding racial problems; in this sense, at least, the minister cannot be seen as an unfortunate aberration in American history. As the aggressive and articulate apostle of an impending American apartheid, Farrakhan addresses, amplifies, and aggravates the existing racial division of America. Not just whites and Jews, but Koreans, Palestinian Arabs, and homosexuals have all merited inclusion in Farrakhan's far-reaching compass of bigotry, contempt, and scapegoating. The racial and ethnic tensions contaminating America that his political opportunism exploits with such vulgarly ostentatious relish, however, existed long before the minister was even conceived and, equally, loom as a deeply divisive and precipitously polarizing prospect long after Farrakhan's pernicious political opportunism finally fades away. And that most unedifying prospect is immeasurably more disconcerting and in need of candid and concerted challenge than the crude political posturing, jet-setting antics, and verbally offensive pyrotechnics of Farrakhan currently.

In this respect, constantly isolating Farrakhan for denunciation is a reaction that, no matter how understandable, legitimate, and defensible, serves mainly to elevate the stature of the messenger at the expense of the broader forces upon which the message relies for its mass resonance. The reactionary and paranoid appeals of the NoI's leader depend for their contemporary popularity among African-Americans principally upon the continued economic and social devastation of many black communities across the United States and upon Farrakhan's very effective exploitation of crosscutting political, economic, and social cleavages among blacks nationwide. The underlying social and economic causes of fear, distrust, and resentment will also, in the absence of their effective amelioration, continue to form a potentially powerful popular basis for Farrakhan's demagoguery among African-Americans. Although Farrakhan has undeniably profited greatly from these conditions, however, it would be entirely wrong to view him as a somehow aberrant, unique, or exceptional phenomenon. As Richard Hofstadter cautioned over a quarter-century ago, the paranoid style in American politics is, unfortunately, peculiarly apt to recur in different guises over time. There are other Farrakhans, it seems certain, who will assuredly assume the same ignominious national mantle of organized hatred by capitalizing on the deprivation, disadvantage, and despair of millions of black Americans, should they continue apace.

If the tragic and woeful conditions that have given rise to the minister's political successes merit attention, conceding that there are many causes of Farrakhan's approval and support nonetheless cannot exempt the leader of the NoI from legitimate and extensive criticism. For Farrakhan represents the most starkly brutal and unequivocal repudiation of the commendable liberal principles of diversity, tolerance, and pluralism of all modern national African-American public figures in the United States. Preaching racial reconciliation, Farrakhan practices a politics of polarization and division; proselytizing for racial comity, he advances mutual racial animus; proclaiming his boundless humanitarian love, he readily capitalizes upon the basest sentiments of ignorance, fear, and hatred. Farrakhan's antipolitics is one of negation, condemnation, and malice: a vociferous, unequivocal and comprehensive rejection of the traditional American doctrine, "e pluribus unum." No tentative olive branches offered to Jewish and white Americans can obscure the opprobrious venom that has been so eagerly heaped by Farrakhan, for almost all of his adult life, upon those many nemeses against whom he and his God take offense. No amount of good works that his organization accomplishes in inner cities can disguise premeditated racist demagoguery behind a saintly mask of beneficent justice. No amount of peremptory preaching for racial harmony can hide a public praxis forged disgracefully upon hatred and hypocrisy. Were the tone in which America's race relations discussed in national public life less shrill and adversarial, no doubt many more national figures of all racial, ethnic, and religious shades would concede publicly that Farrakhan writes checks of racial comity that draw upon a long-bankrupt account of the deepest intolerance and insensitivity.

Furthermore, Farrakhan has had opportunities in abundance, in America and elsewhere, to disavow his ubiquitous expressions of racial malice and division. If those plentiful expressions have always been wholly unnecessary to instill racial pride, self-dignity, and individual responsibility among African-Americans—as they most clearly have been and so remain—the minister could perhaps still achieve a position of note by clearly and sincerely repudiating them. Why, then, does Farrakhan compromise a potentially positive historic legacy by engaging in vitriolic expressions of the grossest animosity and bigotry? Why must Farrakhan continually devalue the laudable project of revitalizing downtrodden communities and despairing African-American individuals by invoking an entirely extraneous litany of the most ignoble, base, and repellent prejudice?

The resolution of those vexing questions can only reside in the unfortunate but unmistakable fact—one that the briefest investigation of Farrakhan's voluminous speeches and writings confirms beyond reasonable doubt—that such deep animus is at once integral to the Bilalian faith, inextricable from the NoI's worldview, and completely inseparable from Farrakhan's personal political project. Carefully coded distinctions between despising whites and hating the mind-set of white supremacy are no more persuasive now than were southern white segregationists' claims in the 1950s that they never had a race problem until outside activists came down to Dixie to stir up trouble among their otherwise placid and pliant blacks. The rhetorical subtleties that put a woman's base rather than place in the home, similarly, do not render the NoI's patriarchal belief system any less sexist, rigid, and demeaning to women. It is upon this undistinguished legacy of prejudice, paranoia, and reaction that Farrakhan forfeits a broader public admiration, endorsement, and multiracial support. For black Americans, especially, Farrakhan represents less the light at the end of the tunnel of oppression than the blinding headlamps of the oncoming train.

The appropriate response to the leader of the NoI is therefore one that entails recognizing the Farrakhan phenomenon for what it essentially is: a virulently bigoted, paranoid, and authoritarian expression of mass disillusion not only with white America, but also with African-Americans as well. Defenders of Louis Farrakhan labor under the most heavy burden of legitimizing the prejudice and reaction with which his public discourse is so replete; whereas his many critics, adversaries, and denunciators must correspondingly attend to more than the particular political figure in their condemnatory remarks if they are to witness the full atrophy of the Farrakhan phenomenon. For however repulsive and ridiculous much of the content of Farrakhan's sermonizing and paranoid pontificating most certainly is, some of the minister's views clearly jibe with the attitudes and beliefs of thousands, perhaps even millions, of African-Americans. Bereft of acknowledging the desperate plight of many blacks and the collapsing infrastructure of many black communities, impulsive insults and contemptibly dismissive, self-righteous, and disparaging rebukes are unlikely to dissuade African-Americans at large of the merits of Farrakhan's dubious case. They can instead serve to exacerbate the visceral bases of Farrakhan's appeal by seeming to confirm the very allegations and accusations that he levels at the putative enemies of black America, rendering the NoI's leader more a modern-day black martyr to prejudiced attacks than a political monster who promotes bigoted inter- and intra-racial animus. If Farrakhan is genuinely viewed by thousands of African-Americans as a messianic figure and the Million Man March is similarly seen sincerely as a miraculous and millennial event, those views partially derive from the frequently condemnatory, derisive, and unduly defamatory reactions of whites.

Ultimately, the Farrakhan phenomenon represents both an expression and a function of the abiding American dilemma of race. Its political fate thus far reveals the pronounced extent to which black and white Americans in the United States continue to retain sharply divided conceptions of what it means actually to be an American citizen in the 1990s. Despite the substantial political, economic, and social advances made by black Americans over recent decades, the many sharp fissures in American society and politics centered around race remain deeply entrenched and especially controversial at the close of the twentieth century. Though it occupies no place in either the creedal values or the great promise of American democracy, racial and ethnic bigotry represents an ugly but unmistakably influential and prominent part of America's political history. It remains the province of responsible citizens, critics, and politicians alike to render both those original values and the immense, but imperfectly realized, promise of American democracy a reality if the avowed status of the United States as a truly liberal, pluralist, and inclusive political regime is finally to be achieved. To that admirable end, it is not only the particular paranoid perorations of a Farrakhan and the siren calls of a barren racial separatism that should be implacably resisted and strongly challenged (although they most certainly should). It is also to the root causes of those deep fissures based upon race that the fullest political attention and the most extensive, enlightened, and empathetic public candor must be devoted if the Farrakhan phenomenon—and its related current expressions and future successors—is ever likely to fade.

NOTES TO CHAPTER 7

1. Quoted in Fletcher and Balz, "Farrakhan Seeks Wider Role," p. A1.

2. King, *Separate and Unequal*, p. viii.

3. Sargent, *Extremism in America*, p. 3.

4. Quoted in Alan Ehrenhalt, "Black Caucus: A Wary Carter Ally," *Congressional Quarterly Weekly Report*, 21 May 1977, p. 969.

5. Marable, "Race, Identity and Political Culture," p. 297.

6. See Demetrios Caraley, "Washington Abandons the Cities," *Political Science Quarterly* 107, no. 1 (1992): 1–30.

7. See Lamis, *The Two-Party South*, pp. 45–61.

8. The issue bases of the firm locus of African-Americans within the Democratic fold is also well-documented in Byron Shafer and William Claggett, *The Two Majorities* (Baltimore, Md: Johns Hopkins, 1994).

9. Raphael J. Sonenshein, "Can Black Candidates Win Statewide Elections?," *Political Science Quarterly* 105, no. 2 (1990): 219–40, at 241.

10. For some of the acute ethical and political problems that the need for funds generates, see Novak, "Conservatives and Corporations Plug Into Black Power."

11. The most prominent exponent of the view that affirmative gerrymandering in a single-member, plurality electoral system is inadequate in realizing political equality for black Americans is Lani Guinier. See the collection of her essays, *The Tyranny of the Majority*. Shelby Steele's views are best encapsulated in *The Content of Our Character* (New York: St. Martin's Press, 1990).

12. Kilson, "Problems of Black Politics," p. 528.

Bibliography

Abilla, Walter D., *The Black Muslims in America: an introduction to the theory of commitment* (Kampala: East African Literature Bureau, 1977).

Abramson, Paul R., John H. Aldrich, and David W. Rohde, *Change and Continuity in the 1988 Elections* (Washington, D.C.: Congressional Quarterly Press, 1990).

——, *Change and Continuity in the 1992 Elections* (Washington, D.C.: Congressional Quarterly Press, 1995).

Adams, John G., *Without Precedent: the Story of the Death of McCarthyism* (New York: Norton, 1983).

Adams, Lorraine, "Nation of Islam: A Dream Past Due," *The Washington Post*, 1 September 1996, pp. A1, A28–29; 2 September 1996, pp. A1, A8.

Ali, Amir M., *Islam or Farrakhanism?* (Chicago: Institute of Islamic Information and Education, 1991).

Alkalimat, Abdul and Doug Gills, *Harold Washington and the Crisis of Black Power in Chicago* (Chicago: Twenty-First Century Books, 1989).

Allen, R. E., ed., *The Concise Oxford Dictionary of Current English*, 8th ed. (Oxford: Clarendon Press, 1990).

Altman, Dennis, *AIDS and the New Puritanism* (London: Pluto Press, 1986).

Badger, Anthony, *The New Deal: the Depression Years, 1933–1940* (New York: Hill and Wang, 1989).

Bakst, Jerome H., ed., "Louis Farrakhan: An Update," *Anti-Defamation League Facts* 30, Spring 1985 (New York: Anti-Defamation League, 1985).

Baldwin, James, *The Fire Next Time* (New York: Dell, 1963).

Barboza, Steven, *American Jihad: Islam after Malcolm X* (New York: Doubleday, 1994).

Barker, Lucius J., and Ronald W. Walters, eds. *Jesse Jackson's 1984 Presidential Campaign: Challenge and Change in American Politics* (Chicago: University of Illinois Press, 1989).

Barnes, Fred, "Farrakhan Frenzy: What's a Black Politician to Do?" *New Republic*, 28 October 1985: 13–15.

Barone, Michael, *Our Country: The Shaping of America from Roosevelt to Reagan* (New York: The Free Press, 1990).

Bayley, Edwin R., *Joe McCarthy and the Press* (Madison: University of Wisconsin Press, 1981).

Bell, Derrick, *And We Are Not Saved: The Elusive Quest for Racial Justice* (New York: Basic Books, 1979).

Bennett, Claudette E., *The Black Population in the United States: March 1994 and 1993*, U.S. Bureau of the Census, Current Population Reports, P20–480 (Washington, D.C.: U.S. Government Printing Office, 1995).

Benz, Ernst, "Der Schwarze Islam," *Zeitschrift fur Religion und Geistesgeschichte* 19 (2) 1967: 97–113.

Berger, Morroe, "The Black Muslims," *Horizon* 6 (1) 1964: 49–65.

Betz, Hans-Georg, *Radical Right-Wing Populism in Western Europe* (Basingstoke: Macmillan, 1994).

Beynon, Erdman D., "The Voodoo Cult Among Negro Migrants in Detroit," *American Journal of Sociology* 43 (July 1937–May 1938): 894–907.

Bibb, Leon Douglas, "A Note on the Black Muslims: They Preach Black to be the Ideal," *Negro History Bulletin* 28 (6) 1965: 132–33.

Black, Earl and Merle Black, *Politics and Society in the South* (Cambridge, Mass.: Harvard University Press, 1987).

———, *The Vital South: How Presidents Are Elected* (Cambridge, Mass.: Harvard University Press, 1992).

Black, Edwin, "Farrakhan and the Jews," *Midstream* 32 (August-September 1986): 3–6.

Blackstock, Nelson, *Cointelpro: The FBI's Secret War on Political Freedom*, 3rd ed. (New York: Pathfinder Press, 1995).

Blake, J. Herman, "Black Nationalism," in *Annals of the American Academy of Political and Social Science* 382 (1969): 15–25.

Bolce, Louis, Gerald D. De Maio, and Douglas Muzzio, "Blacks and the Republican Party: The 20 Percent Solution," *Political Science Quarterly* 107 (1) 1992: 63–79.

———, "The 1992 Republican 'Tent': No Blacks Walked In," *Political Science Quarterly* 108 (2) 1993: 255–70.

Bone, James, "Prophet of Hate," *The London Times (Magazine)*, 3 February 1996: 26–30.

Bontemps, Arna, and Jack Conroy, *They Seek a City* (Garden City, N.Y.: Doubleday, 1945).

———, *Anyplace But Here* (New York: Hill and Wang, 1966).

Bositis, David, *The Congressional Black Caucus in the 103rd Congress* (Washington, D.C.: Joint Center for Political and Economic Studies, 1994).

Brackman, Harold D., *Ministry of Lies: The Truth Behind the Nation of Islam's "The Secret Relationship between Blacks and Jews"* (New York: Four Walls Eight Windows, 1994).

Branch, Taylor, *Parting the Waters: America in the King Years, 1954–1963* (New York: Simon and Schuster, 1988).

———, "The Uncivil War: Blacks and Jews," *Esquire*, May 1989.

Breger, Marshall J., "Discriminating in Favor of Farrakhan," *The Wall Street Journal*, 24 July 1995: A12.

Breitman, George, ed., *Malcolm X Speaks: Selected Speeches and Statements* (New York: Grove Press, 1965).

———, ed., *The Last Year of Malcolm X* (New York: Pathfinder Press, 1967).

———, ed., *By Any Means Necessary: Speeches, Interviews and a Letter by Malcolm X* (New York: Pathfinder Press, 1970).

———, ed., *Leon Trotsky on Black Nationalism and Self-Determination* (New York: Pathfinder Press, 1978).

Breitman, George, Herman Porter, and Baxter Smith, *The Assassination of Malcolm X* (New York; Pathfinder Press, 1976).

Broder, David, "Farrakhan reminder that U.S. still has its own racial problems," *The Atlanta Journal*, 18 September 1985: A15.

Brodie, Ian, "Muslim Racism Sparks Uproar," *The London Times*, 4 February 1994: 12.

Browning, Rufus P., Dale Rogers Marshall, and David H. Tabb, *Racial Politics in American Cities* (New York: Longman, 1990).

Bruce, Steve, *The Rise and Fall of the New Christian Right, 1978–1988* (Oxford: Clarendon Press, 1988).

Bryce, James, *The American Commonwealth* (New York: Macmillan, 1888).

Bull, Chris, "Farrakhan Under Fire," *The Advocate*, 8 March 1994, p. 25.

Butler, David and Austin Ranney, eds., *Electioneering: A Comparative Study of Continuity and Change* (Oxford: Clarendon Press, 1992).

Caldwell, Wallace E., "Black Muslims Behind Bars," *Religious Studies* 34 (4) 1966: 185–204.

———, "A Survey of Attitudes Towards Black Muslims in Prison," *Journal of Human Relations* 16 (2) 1968: 220–38.

Caraley, Demetrios, "Washington Abandons the Cities," *Political Science Quarterly*, 107 (1) 1992: 1–30.

Carmines, Edward G. and James A. Stimson, *Issue Evolution: Race and the Transformation of American Politics* (Princeton, N.J.: Princeton University Press, 1989).

Carter, Stephen L., *The Confirmation Mess: Cleaning Up the Federal Appointments Process* (New York: Basic Books, 1994).

Chafe, William, *The Unfinished Journey: America Since World War Two*, 2nd ed. (New York: Oxford University Press, 1991).

Cheles, Luciano, Ronnie Ferguson, and Michael Vaughan, eds., *Neo-Fascism in Europe* (New York: Longman, 1991).

Chong, Dennis, *Collective Action and the Civil Rights Movement* (Chicago: University of Chicago Press, 1991).

Clay, William L., *Just Permanent Interests: Black Americans in Congress, 1870–1991* (New York: Amsitad Press, 1992).

Cohen, Richard E., "Farrakhan and Anti-Semitism," *Torrington (CT) Register-Criterion*, 28 July 1985, p. 15.

———, "Hatred Covenant," *The Washington Post*, 15 October 1993, p. 25.

———, "At Nuremberg-on-Potomac, A Chanting of Jews, Jews," *International Herald Tribune*, 3 March 1994, p. 7.

———, "Farrakhan Too," *The Washington Post*, 16 May 1995, p. A17.

———, "Marching behind Farrakhan," *The Washington Post*, 19 September 1995, p. A18.

Colton, Elizabeth O., *The Jackson Phenomenon: The Man, the Power, the Message* (New York: Doubleday, 1989).

Cone, James H., *Martin and Malcolm and America* (London: HarperCollins, 1991).

Cook, Gareth G., "Race: Feeding the Fire," *U.S. News and World Report*, 7 February 1994, p. 12.

Cox, Michael, *U.S. Foreign Policy After the Cold War: Superpower Without a Mission?* (Chatham, N.J.: RIAA, 1995).

Craig, Barbara Hinkson, and David M. O'Brien, *Abortion and American Politics* (Chatham, N.J.: Chatham House, 1993).

Crick, Michael, *Militant* (London: Faber and Faber, 1984).

Cronon, Edmund David, *Black Moses: The Story of Marcus Garvey and the Universal Negro Improvement Association* (Madison: University of Wisconsin Press, 1962).

Cruse, Harold, *The Crisis of the Negro Intellectual* (New York: Quill, 1984).

———, *Plural But Equal: A Critical Study of Blacks and Minorities in America's Plural Society* (New York: Quill, 1987).

Curry, George, "Farrakhan, Jesse, and Jews," *Emerge*, 5, July-August 1994, p. 28

———, "Unity in the Community: Can Ben Chavis Pull It Off?" *Emerge*, 5 September 1994, p. 28

Curry, Richard Orr, *Conspiracy: The Fear of Subversion in American History* (New York: Holt, Rinehart, and Winston, 1972).

Cushmeer, Bernard, *This Is the One: Messenger Elijah Muhammad—You Need Not Look for Another* (Phoenix, Ariz.: Truth Publications, 1970).

Davis, David Brion (ed.), *The Fear of Conspiracy: Images of Un-American Subversion from the Revolution to the Present Day* (Ithaca, N.Y.: Cornell University Press, 1971).

Davis, John F., "Farrakhan Speaks," *Village Voice*, 29 22 May 1984: 15–18, 20.

DeCaro, Louis, *On the Side of My People: A Religious Life of Malcolm X* (New York: New York University Press, 1996).

De Tocqueville, Alexis, *Democracy in America* (New York: Vintage Books, 1945).

Dent, Gina, ed., *Black Popular Culture* (Seattle: Bay Press, 1992).

Dionne, E. J., *Why Americans Hate Politics* (New York: Simon and Schuster, 1991).

———, "So Many Could Have Been There," *The Washington Post*, 17 October 1995, p. A17.

Duke, Lynne, "Farrakhan Defends Clinton, Asks Critics to 'Get to Know Me Better'," *The Washington Post*, 5 May 1993, p. A22.

———, "Congressional Black Caucus and Nation of Islam Agree on Alliance," *The Washington Post*, 17 September 1993, p. A3.

———, "At the Core of the Nation of Islam: Confrontation," *The Washington Post*, 21 March 1994, p. A1.

Edelman, Murray, *The Symbolic Uses of Politics* (Urbana: University of Illinois Press, 1964).

Edsall, Thomas Byrne, and Mary D. Edsall, *Chain Reaction: The Impact of Race, Rights, and Taxes on American Politics* (New York: W. W. Norton, 1991).

Ehrenhalt, Alan, "Black Caucus: A Wary Carter Ally," *Congressional Quarterly Weekly Report*, 21 May 1977, p. 969.

Eisenstein, Zillah, *Hatreds: Racialized and Sexualized* (London: Routledge, 1996).

Epstein, Leon E., *Political Parties in the American Mold* (Madison: University of Wisconsin Press, 1986).

Esolen, Gary, "More Than a Pretty Face: David Duke's Use of Television as a Political Tool," in *The Emergence of David Duke and the Politics of Race*, ed. Douglas Rose (Chapel Hill: University of North Carolina Press, 1992), pp. 136–55.

Essien-Udom, E. U., *Black Nationalism: A Search for an Identity in America* (Chicago: University of Chicago Press, 1971).

Eure, Joseph D. and Richard M. Jerome, *Back Where We Belong: Selected Speeches by Minister Louis Farrakhan* (Philadelphia, PA: PC International Press, 1989).

Evanier, David, *The Anti-Semitism of Black Demagogues and Extremists* (New York: Anti-Defamation League, 1992).

Farber, M. A., "In the Name of the Father," *Vanity Fair* 58, June 1995, pp. 52–60.

Farrakhan, Louis, *Seven Speeches by Minister Louis Farrakhan* (New York: Ministry Class, Muhammad's Temple No. 7, 1974).

———, "I Am an Alarm Clock," *Black Scholar*, January-February 1979, pp. 12–14.

———, "Farrakhan on Jesse Jackson: A Warning to Black Leaders, A Warning to Black People," *Essence*, February 1984, pp. 30–34.

———, *The Honorable Louis Farrakhan: a minister for progress; the complete historic interview with Michael Hardy and William Pleasant from The National Alliance* (New York: Practice Press, 1985).

———, *Independent Black Leadership in America: Minister Louis Farrakhan, Dr. Leonara Fulani, Reverend Al Sharpton* (New York: Castillo International, 1990).

———, *A Torchlight for America* (Chicago: FCN Publishing, 1993).

———, "Excerpts of Interview," *The Washington Post*, 1 March 1990, pp. A16–17.

———, "Nation of Islam Offers True Liberation for Muslim Women," *The Final Call*, 24 August 1992, p. 28.

Faucheux, Ron, "Affirmative Reaction," *Campaigns and Elections*, April 1995, pp. 5, 45–46.

Fenno, Richard, *Home Style: House Members in Their Districts* (Boston: Little, Brown and Company, 1978).

Fineman, Howard, and Vern E. Smith, "An Angry 'Charmer'," *Newsweek*, 30 October 1995, pp. 42–46.

Fiorina, Morris, *Congress: Keystone of the Washington Establishment*, 2nd ed. (New Haven: Yale University Press, 1989).

Fitzgerald, Mark, "Farrakhan Denounces Critical Stories," *Editor and Publisher*, 8 April 1995, p. 11.

Fletcher, Martin, "Anti-Semitic Gibes Mar Million Man March," *The London Times*, 16 October 1995, p. 10.

———, "Prophet of Hatred Becomes Voice of Black America," *The London Times*, 18 October 1995, p. 11.

Fletcher, Martin, and Tom Rhodes, "Washington Mass Rally Rekindles Black Pride," *The London Times*, 17 October 1995, p. 11

Fletcher, Michael A. and Dan Balz, "Farrakhan Seeks Wider Role: Some Black Leaders are Conciliatory, Others Cautious," *The Washington Post*, 18 October 1995, pp. A1, A12.

Fletcher, Michael A., and Hamil R. Harris, "Farrakhan Announces Voter Drive," *The Washington Post*, 19 October 1995, p. A3.

Foley, Michael, *American Political Ideas* (Manchester: Manchester University Press, 1991).

———, *The Rise of the British Presidency* (Manchester: Manchester University Press, 1993).

Fried, Richard M., *Men Against McCarthy* (New York: Columbia University Press, 1976).

———, *Nightmare in Red: the McCarthy Era in Perspective* (New York: Oxford University Press, 1991).

Friendly, Michael, *Malcolm X: the Assassination* (New York: Carroll and Graf, 1992).

Gaber, Julia E., "Lamb of God or Demagogue? A Burkean Cluster Analysis of the Selected Speeches of Minister Louis Farrakhan" (unpublished Ph.D. thesis, Bowling Green State University, 1986).

Gaines, William and David Jackson, "Profit and Promises," *Chicago Tribune*, 12 March 1995, sec. 1., pp. 1, 16–17; 13 March sec 1., pp. 1, 10; 14 March, sec. 1, pp. 1, 10; 15 March sec. 1, pp. 1, 10.

Gaiter, Dorothy J., "Civil Unrest," *The Wall Street Journal*, 10 June 1994, p. A1.

Gallen, David, *The Malcolm X Reader* (New York: Carroll and Graf, 1994).

Gardell, Mattias, *Countdown to Armageddon: Louis Farrakhan and the Nation of Islam* (London: Hurst, 1996).

Garrow, David J., *Bearing the Cross: Martin Luther King, Jr. and the Southern Christian Leadership Conference* (London: Jonathan Cape, 1988).

Garvey, Amy-Jacques, *Philosophy and Opinions of Marcus Garvey* (New York: Universal Publishing House, 1923).

Gates Jr., Henry Louis, "A Reporter at Large: The Charmer," *The New Yorker*, 29 April–6 May 1996, pp. 116–31.

Gelb, Adam, "Farrakhan Calls U.S. Constitution Racist," *Atlanta Journal and Atlanta Constitution*, 13 September 1987, p. E24.

Gerth, Hans and C. Wright Mills, *From Max Weber: Essays in Sociology* (London: Routledge, 1991).

Gladwell, Malcolm, "Farrakhan Seeks End of Rift with Shabazz; Apologizes for Hurt but Denies Involvement in Malcolm X Death," *The Washington Post*, 8 May 1995, p. A1.

Goldman, Peter, *The Death and Life of Malcolm X*, 2nd ed. (Urbana: University of Illinois Press, 1979)

Gooding-Williams, Robert, ed., *Reading Rodney King/Reading Urban Uprising* (New York: Routledge, 1993).

Graber, Dorothy, ed., *Mass Media and American Politics* (Washington, D.C.: Congressional Quarterly Press, 1993).

Greenberg, Stanley B., *Report on Democratic Defection* (Washington, D.C.: The Analysis Group, 1985).

Griffith, Robert, *The Politics of Fear: Joseph McCarthy and the Senate* (Rochelle Park, N.J.: Hayden Book Company, 1970).

Guinier, Lani, *The Tyranny of the Majority: Fundamental Fairness in Representative Democracy* (New York: The Free Press, 1994).

Gurwitt, Rob, "A Quest for a Breakthrough," *Congressional Quarterly Weekly Report*, 25 October 1986, pp. 2645–46.

Hacker, Andrew, *Two Nations: Black and White, Separate, Hostile, Unequal* (New York: Ballantine Books, 1992).

Hainsworth, Paul, ed., *The Extreme Right in Europe and the USA* (London: Pinter, 1992).

Hamby, Alonzo L., *Liberalism and Its Challengers: FDR to Reagan* (New York: Oxford University Press, 1985).

Hamilton, Alexander, James Madison and John Jay, *The Federalist Papers*, with introduction by Isaac Kramnick (Harmondsworth, England: Penguin, 1987), No. 10.

Hamilton, Charles V., *The Black Preacher in America* (New York: William Morrow and Co., 1972).

———, *The Black Experience in American Politics* (New York: Putnam, 1973).

Harlan, Louis R., *Booker T. Washington: The Making of a Black Leader, 1865–1901* (New York: Oxford University Press, 1972).

———, *Booker T. Washington: The Wizard of Tuskegee, 1901–1915* (New York: Oxford University Press, 1983).

Harper, Frederick, "The Influence of Malcolm X on Black Militancy," *Journal of Black Studies* 1 (4) 1971: 387–402.

Harris, Hamil R., "March of Black Men Is Planned in District; Farrakhan Seeks a Turnout of 1 Million," *The Washington Post*, 19 July 1995, p. B1.

Hartz, Louis, *The Liberal Tradition in America* (New York: Harcourt, Brace, and World, 1955).

Hazlett, Thomas W., "The Wrath of Farrakhan," *Reason* 26, May 1994, p. 66.

Henry, Charles P., *Culture and African American Politics* (Bloomington: Indiana University Press, 1990).

Henry, William A., "Pride and Prejudice," *Time*, February 26, 1994, pp. 21–27.

Hentoff, Nat, "Black Bigotry and Free Speech," *The Progressive*, May 1994, pp. 20–21.

———, "A Black Response to Black Bigotry," *The Washington Post*, 23 July 1994, p. A21.

Herbert, Bob, "The Hate Game," *The New York Times*, 9 February 1994, p. A18.

Herrnson, Paul, *Congressional Elections* (Washington, D.C.: Congressional Quarterly Press, 1995).

Higginbotham Jr., A. Leon, "Why I Didn't March," *The Washington Post*, 17 October 1995, p. A17.

Hobsbawm, Eric, *The Age of Extremes: The Short Twentieth Century* (London: Abacus Books, 1995).

Hofstadter, Richard, *The American Political Tradition* (New York: Knopf, 1948).

———, *Anti-intellectualism in American Life* (New York: Knopf, 1963).

———, *The Paranoid Style in American Politics* (Chicago: University of Chicago Press, 1979).

Holland, Bernard, "Sending a Message, Louis Farrakhan Plays Mendelssohn," *The New York Times*, 19 April 1993, p. C11.

Hook, Janet, "Mfume Cuts Renewed Ties to Nation of Islam," *Congressional Quarterly Weekly Report*, 5 February 1994, p. 219.

———, "House Denounces Remarks as 'Racist' Speech," *Congressional Quarterly Weekly Report*, 26 February 1994, p. 458.

Hughes, Robert, *Culture of Complaint: The Fraying of America* (London: Harvill, 1994).

Humphries, Cameron, "The Sacred Covenant," *Diversity and Division*, 3 (3) Spring-Summer 1994.

Huntington, Samuel P., *American Politics: The Promise of Disharmony* (Cambridge, Mass.: Belknap/Harvard University Press, 1981).

Jennings, James, ed., *Race, Politics, and Economic Development* (New York: Verso, 1992).

Johnson, George, *Architects of Fear: Conspiracy Theories and Paranoia in American Politics* (Los Angeles: J. P. Tarcher, 1983).

Jones, Charisse, "Farrakhan-Shabazz Meeting Kindles Hopes," *The New York Times*, 6 May 1995, pp. 16, 23.

Joyce, Faye S., "Farrakhan Warns Press on Jackson," *The New York Times*, 10 April 1984, pp. 1, 7.

Kagay, Michael, "Poll Finds Most Blacks Reject Farrakhan's Ideas as Theirs," *The New York Times*, 5 March 1994, p. 8

Kaplan, H. M., "The Black Muslims and the Negro American's Quest for Communion: A Case Study in the Genesis of Negro Protest Movements," *British Journal of Sociology* 20 (2) 1969: 164–76.

Karenga, Maulana, "Jesse Jackson and the Presidential Campaign: The Invitation and the Oppositions of History," *Black Scholar*, 15 (5) September-October 1984.

Karim, Benjamin, *Remembering Malcolm* (New York: Carroll and Graf, 1992).

Kaufman, Jonathan, *Broken Alliance: The Turbulent Times Between Blacks and Jews in America* (New York: Scribner, 1988).

Kelly, Brian, and Harry, Jaffee, "The Farrakhan Fiasco," *Regardies*, 10, January 1990: 47–55.

Kifner, John, "With Farrakhan Speaking a Chorus of GOP Critics Join In," *The New York Times*, 17 October 1995, p. A18.

Kilson, Martin, "Problems of Black Politics: Some Progress, Many Difficulties," *Dissent*, Fall 1989, pp. 526–34

Kilson, Martin, and Clement Cottingham, "Thinking About Race Relations: How Far Are We Still From Integration?" *Dissent*, Fall 1991, pp. 520–30.

King, Dennis, "The Farrakhan Phenomenon: Ideology, Support, Potential," *Patterns of Prejudice* 20 (1) 1986: 11–22.

King, Desmond S., *Separate and Unequal: Black Americans and the U.S. Federal Government* (Oxford: Oxford University Press, 1995).

King, Peter, "'PC' Handling of Farrakhan Is Wrong," *Newsday* (Nassau Edition), 8 March 1996, p. A47.

Kirman, Joseph M., "The Challenge of the Black Muslims," *Social Education* 27 (7) 1963: 365–68.

Kirscht, J. P. and R. C. Dilleehay, *Dimensions of Authoritarianism: A Review of Research and Theory* (Lexington, Ky.: University of Kentucky Press, 1967).

Klein, Joe, "The Threat of Tribalism," *Newsweek* 123, 14 March 1994, p. 28.

Kotlowitz, Alex, "A Bridge Too Far?" *The New York Times Magazine*, 12 June 1994, pp. 41–43.

Kotzin, Michael C., "Louis Farrakhan's anti-Semitism: A look at the record," *The Christian Century* 111 (1994), pp. 224–25.

Kramer, Michael, "Loud and Clear: Farrakhan's anti-Semitism," *New York Magazine* 18 (41) 21 October 1985.

Krauthammer, Charles, "The 'Validation' of Louis Farrakhan," *The Washington Post*, 20 October 1995, p. A19.

Kurapka, David, "Hate Story: Farrakhan's Still at It," *New Republic* 198, 30 May 1988, p. 19–21.

Labash, Matt "Inside the March: Farrakhan Is King," *The (Washington, D.C.) Weekly Standard*, 23 October 1995, p. 26–29.

Lacayo, Richard, "A Critical Mass," *Time*, 30 October 1995, pp. 34–35.

Lamis, Alexander P., *The Two-Party South*, 2nd ed. (New York: Oxford University Press, 1990).

Laue, James H., "A Contemporary Revitalization Movement in American Race Relations: The Black Muslims," *Social Forces* 42 (3) 1964: 315–323.

Lawson, Steven F., *In Pursuit of Power* (New York: Columbia University Press, 1985).

Lee, Martha F., *The Nation of Islam: an American millenarian movement* (Lewiston, N.Y.: E. Mellen Press, 1988)

Lemann, Nicholas, *The Promised Land: The Great Black Migration and How It Changed America* (London: Macmillan, 1991).

Lester, Julius, "Blacks, Jews, and Farrakhan," *Dissent* 41 (3) Summer 1994.

Letwin, Shirley R., *The Anatomy of Thatcherism* (London: Fontana, 1992).

Leuchtenberg, William E., "A Klansman Joins the Court: The Appointment of Hugo L. Black," in Leonard Dinnerstein and Kenneth T. Jackson, eds., *American Vistas: 1877 to the Present*, 5th ed (New York: Oxford University Press, 1987), pp. 187–215.

Liben, Paul, "Farrakhan Turns Blind Eye to African Slave Trade," *Human Events* 51 (20) 1995.

Lincoln, C. Eric, *The Black Church in the African American Experience* (Durham, N.C.: Duke University Press, 1990).

———, *The Black Muslims in America* 3rd ed. (Grand Rapids, Mich.: William B. Eerdmans, 1994).

Linzer, Lori, *The Nation of Islam: The Relentless Record of Hate* (New York: Anti-Defamation League, 1995).

Lipset, Seymour Martin, "Blacks and Jews: How Much Bias?" *Public Opinion* July-August 1987.

Lipset, Seymour Martin and Earl Raab, *The Politics of Unreason: Right-Wing Extremism in America, 1790–1977* (Chicago: University of Chicago Press, 1978).

Loury, Glenn C., "One Man's March," *The New Republic*, 6 November 1995, pp. 18–22.

Lusane, Clarence, "Black Political Power in the 1990s," *The Black Scholar*, January/February 1989, pp. 38–42.

———, *African-American Politics at the Crossroads: The Restructuring of Black Leadership and the 1992 Elections* (Boston: South End Press, 1994).

Lusane, Clarence and Dennis Desmond, *Pipe Dream Blues: Racism and the War on Drugs* (Boston: South End Press, 1991).

Lyons, Nancee, "Muslim Guard Service Grows," *Emerge*, February 1993, p. 9

Magida, Arthur J., *Prophet of Rage: A Life of Louis Farrakhan and his Nation* (New York: HarperCollins, 1996).

Malveaux, Julianne, "Black America's Abortion Ambivalence," *Emerge*, February 1993, pp. 33–34.

Mamiya, Lawrence H., and C. Eric Lincoln, "Minister Louis Farrakhan and the Final Call: Schism in the Muslim Movement," in *The Muslim Community in North America*, eds. Earle Waugh, Baha Abu-Laban, and Regular Querishi (Edmonton: University of Alberta Press, 1983), pp. 234–51.

Maolain, C. O., *The Radical Right: A World Dictionary* (Harlow, U.K.: Longman, 1987).

Marable, Manning, *How Capitalism Underdeveloped Black America: Problems in Race, Political Economy, and Society* (Boston: South End Press, 1983).

———, *Race, Reform and Rebellion: The Second Reconstruction in Black America, 1945–1982* (Jackson, Miss.: University of Mississippi Press, 1984).

———, *Black American Politics: From the Washington Marches to Jesse Jackson* (London: Verso, 1985).

———, "In the Business of Prophet Making," *New Statesman*, 13 December 1985, pp. 23–25.

———, "Race, Identity, and Political Culture," in *Black Popular Culture*, ed. Gina Dent (Seattle: Bay Press, 1992), pp. 292–302.

———, *Beyond Black and White: Transforming African-American Politics* (New York: Verso, 1995).

Marsh, Clifton E., *From Black Muslims to Muslims: The Transition from Separatism to Islam, 1930–1980* (London: Scarecrow Press, 1984).

———, *From Black Muslims to Muslims: the resurrection, transformation, and change of the lost-found Nation of Islam in America, 1930–1995*, 2nd ed. (Lanham, Md.: Scarecrow Press, 1996).

Marshall, C. Alan, *The Life and Times of Louis Farrakhan* (New York: Marshall Publications, 1992).

Martin, Ben L., "From Negro to Black to African American: The Power of Names and Naming," *Political Science Quarterly* 106 (1) 1991: 83–107.

Matusow, Allen Joseph, ed., *Joseph R. McCarthy* (Hemel Hempstead: Prentice-Hall, 1970).

Mayhew, David, *Congress: The Electoral Connection* (New Haven: Yale University Press, 1974).

McAdam, Doug, *Political Process and the Development of Black Insurgency, 1930–1970* (Chicago: University of Chicago Press, 1982).

McCall, Nathan, "D.C. Council Votes to Praise Farrakhan's Anti-Drug Work," *The Washington Post*, 25 October 1989, p. A1.

McClain, Paula D. and Joseph Stewart Jr., *"Can We All Get Along?" Racial and Ethnic Minorities in American Politics* (Boulder, Colo.: Westview Press, 1995).

McFadden-Preston, Claudette, "The Rhetoric of Minister Louis Farrakhan: a pluralistic approach" (unpublished Ph.D. thesis, Ohio State University, 1986)

McMillan, Penelope and Cathleen Decker, "Israel is a 'Wicked Hypocrisy'," *Los Angeles Times*, 15 September 1983, p. 1, 3.

McNall, Scott Grant, "The Sect Movement," *Pacific Sociology Review* 6 (2) 1963: 60–64.

Meier, August, Elliot Rudwick, and Francis L. Broderick, eds., *Black Protest Thought in the Twentieth Century*, 2nd ed. (New York: Macmillan, 1971).

Melillo, Wendy and Hamil R. Harris, "Dissent Raised as Ex-Farrakhan Aide Returns to Howard," *The Washington Post*, 20 April, 1994, p. B1.

Merelman, Richard M., *Representing Black Culture: Racial Conflict and Cultural Politics in the United States* (New York: Routledge, 1995).

Merida, Kevin, "Black Caucus Says It Has No Official Working Ties with Nation of Islam," *The Washington Post*, 3 February 1994, p. A16.

———, "Lawmakers Uneasy Over Farrakhan: Black Officials Split on Summit Invitations," *The Washington Post*, 17 June 1994, p. A3.

Mervin, David, "Malcolm X and the Moderation of Black Militancy," *PAIS Papers*, Department of Politics and International Studies, University of Warwick, Coventry, UK, Working Paper no. 107 (April 1992).

Meyerson, Adam, "Manna 2 Society: The Growing Conservatism of Black America," *Policy Review* (68) 1994: 4–6.

Miller, David, ed., *The Blackwell Encyclopaedia of Political Thought* (Oxford: Blackwell, 1991).

Mills, Barbara Kleban, "Predicting Disaster for a Racist America, Louis Farrakhan Envisions an African Homeland for U.S. Blacks," *People* 34 (11) 17 September 1990.

Monroe, Sylvester, "Doing the Right Thing: Muslims Have Become a Welcome Force in Black Neighborhoods," *Time* 135, 16 April 1990, p. 22.

———, "They Suck the Life from You," *Time*, 28 February 1994, p. 24.

———, "The Risky Association," *Time* 143, 27 June 1994, p. 39.

———, "Khalid Abdul Muhammad: Is the Fiery Speaker Undermining the Nation of Islam?" *Emerge* 5, September 1994, p. 42.

———, "The Mirage of Farrakhan," *Time* 144, 30 October 1995, p. 52.

Monteil, Vincent, "La Religion des Black Muslims," *Esprit* 32 (16) 1964: 601–29.

Morganthau, Tom, "Back in the Line of Fire," *Newsweek*, 23 January 1995, p. 20.

Morris, Aldon D., *The Origins of the Civil Rights Movement: Black Communities Organizing for Change* (New York: The Free Press, 1984).

Morris, Lorenzo, ed., *The Social and Political Implications of the 1984 Jesse Jackson Presidential Campaign* (New York: Praeger, 1990).

Morris, Milton D. and Gary E. Rubin, "The Turbulent Friendship: Black–Jewish Relations in the 1990s," in "Interminority Affairs in the U.S.: Pluralism at the Crossroads," ed., Peter Rose, *The Annals of the American Academy of Political and Social Science* 530 (November 1993).

Morrisson, Toni, ed., *Race-ing Justice, En-Gendering Power: Essays on Anita Hill, Clarence Thomas, and the Construction of Social Reality* (London: Chatto and Windus, 1993).

Mudde, Cas, "The War of Words Defining the Extreme Right Party Family," *West European Politics* 19 (2) 1996: 225–48.

Muhammad, Elijah, "The Demands and Beliefs of the Black Muslims in America," *Islamic Review* 52 (10) 1964, pp. 25–27.

——, *Message to the Black Man in America* (Chicago: Muhammad's Temple No. 2, 1965).

——, *How to Eat to Live* (Chicago: Muhammad's Temple No. 2, 1968).

——, *The Fall of America* (Chicago: Muhammad's Temple of Islam No. 2, 1973).

Muhammad, Jabril, *Farrakhan, the Traveller* (Phoenix, Ariz.: PHNX SN and Co., 1985).

Munnion, Christopher, "Farrakhan Tells Whites to Atone for Apartheid," *The London Daily Telegraph*, 29 January 1996, p. 11.

Murray, Charles, *Losing Ground: American Social Policy, 1950–1980* (New York: Basic Books, 1984).

Muwakkil, Salim, "Leaders Lacking in a Black and White World," in *Inside the L.A. Riots: What Really Happened and Why It Will Happen Again* (New York: Institute for Alternative Journalism, 1992), pp. 106–08.

Myrdal, Gunnar, *An American Dilemma: The Negro Problem and Modern Democracy* vols. 1 and 2 (New York: Harper and Row, 1944, 1964).

Naison, Mark, "Jared Taylor's America: Black Man's Heaven, White Man's Hell," *Reconstruction* 2 (3) 1994, pp. 64–66.

Nicoll, Ruaridh, "Black Pride on the March Again," *The Observer*, 1 October 1995, p. 23.

Norton, Arthur J., and Louisa F. Miller, *Marriage, Divorce and Remarriage in the 1990s* (Washington, D.C.: U.S. Government Printing Office, 1992) Bureau of the Census, Current Population Reports, Series P23, no. 180.

Norton, Philip, "Black Nationalism in America: the Significance of the Black Muslim Movement," *Hull Papers in Politics*, University of Hull, no. 31, 1983.

Novak, Viveca, "Conservatives and Corporations Plug Into Black Power," *Business and Society Review* 71 (Fall 1989): 32–39.

Ornstein, Norman and Amy Schenkenberg, "The 1995 Congress: The First Hundred Days and Beyond," *Political Science Quarterly* 110 (2) 1995.

Ovenden, Keith, *Malcolm X: Socialism and Black Nationalism* (London: Bookmarks, 1992).

Pear, Robert, "Despite Praising Farrakhan in 1983, Thomas Denies anti-Semitism," *The New York Times*, 13 July 1991, pp. 1, 7.

Pearl, Peter and Edward Walsh, "Muslims Accuse U.S. of Creating Farrakhan Plot," *The Washington Post*, 14 January 1995, p. A1.

Perry, Bruce, *Malcolm: The Life of a Man Who Changed Black America* (Barrytown, N.Y.: Station Hill, 1991).

Perry, Huey L. and Wayne Parent, *Blacks and the American Political System* (Gainesville: University Press of Florida, 1995).

Phelps, Timothy M. and Helen Winternitz, *Capitol Games: The Inside Story of Clarence Thomas, Anita Hill, and a Supreme Court Nomination* (New York: HarperPerennial, 1993).

Pierce, Paulette, "The Roots of the Rainbow Coalition," *Black Scholar*, March/April 1988: 2–16.

Pinckney, Darryl, "Slouching Towards Washington," *The New York Review of Books*, 21 December 1995, pp. 73–82.

Preston, Michael B., Lenneal S. Henderson, and Paul Puryear, eds., *The New Black Politics* 2nd ed. (New York: Longman, 1987).

Purnick, Joyce, "An Unlikely Matchmaker," *New York Times*, 8 May 1995, pp. B1, B12.

Queenan, Joe, "America's Most Demented; A Startling Scientific Analysis," *The Washington Post*, 30 May 1993, p. C1.

Rae, Nicol C., *Southern Democrats* (New York: Oxford University Press, 1994).

Reed Jr., Adolph, *The Jesse Jackson Phenomenon: The Crisis of Purpose in Afro-American Politics* (New Haven: Yale University Press, 1986).

———, "The Rise of Louis Farrakhan," *The Nation* 252, January 21, 1991, pp. 51–52, 54–56.

———, "All for One and None for All," *The Nation* 252, January 28, 1991, pp. 86–88, 90–92.

———, "Behind the Farrakhan Show," *The Progressive* 58, April 1994, pp. 16–17.

———, "Black Leadership in Crisis," *The Progressive* 58, October 1994, p. 16

Reeves, Thomas C., *The Life and Times of Joe McCarthy: A Biography* (London: Blond and Briggs, 1982).

Rich, Frank, "Bad for the Jews," *The New York Times*, 3 March 1994, p. A17.

Robinson, Cedric J., *Black Marxism: The Making of the Black Radical Tradition* (London: Zed Press, 1983).

Rose, Douglas, ed., *The Emergence of David Duke and the Politics of Race* (Chapel Hill: University of North Carolina Press, 1992).

Rovere, Richard, *Senator Joe McCarthy* (New York: Harper and Row, 1973).

Rowan, Carl, "Antidote to Farrakhan: Ignore Him," *The New York Times*, 25 September 1985, p. 22.

———, "Farrakhan's Poisonous Journey," *The Buffalo News*, 28 February 1996, p. 3B.

Sabato, Larry, *Feeding Frenzy: How Attack Journalism Has Transformed American Politics* (New York: The Free Press, 1993).

Sanson, Michael, "Farrakhan Means Business," *Restaurant Hospitality*, April 1995, pp. 22–23.

Sargent, Lynne Tower, ed., *Extremism in America* (New York: New York University Press, 1995).

Sartori, Giovanni, "Video-Power," *Government and Opposition* 24 (1) (Winter 1989): 39–53.

———, *Comparative Constitutional Engineering: An Inquiry Into Structures, Incentives, and Outcomes* (London: Macmillan, 1994).

Scheim, David E., *The Mafia Killed President Kennedy* (London: W. H. Allen, 1988).

Schlesinger Jr., Arthur M., *The Disuniting of America: Reflections on a Multicultural Society* (New York: Norton, 1992).

Schneider, William, "The Black Vote and a Powell Candidacy," *National Journal*, 27 (44) 28 October 1995, p. 2690.

Shafer, Byron E., *Bifurcated Politics* (Cambridge, Mass.: Harvard University Press, 1988).

Shafer, Byron and William Claggett, *The Two Majorities* (Baltimore, Md.: Johns Hopkins, 1994).

Shaikh, Farzana, ed., *Islam and Islamic Groups: A World-Wide Reference Guide* (Harlow, U.K.: Longman, 1992).

Shipp, E. R., "Candidacy of Jackson Highlights Split Among Black Muslims," *The New York Times*, 27 February 1984, p. 10.

Shore, Paul, "Farrakhan and the Filling of the Mythic Gap," *The Humanist*, July-August 1994, pp. 4–6.

Sigelman, Lawrence and Susan Welch, *Black Americans' View of Racial Inequality* (Cambridge, Mass.: Cambridge University Press, 1991).

Singh, Robert, "The Congressional Black Caucus in the United States Congress, 1971–1990," *Parliaments, Estates and Representation*, 14 (1) June 1994: 65–91.

———, "The Rise and Fall of Legislative Service Organisations in the United States Congress," *Journal of Legislative Studies* 2 (2) Summer 1996: 79–102.

Smith, Robert, "Black Power and the Transformation From Protest to Politics," *Political Science Quarterly* 96 (3) 1981: 431–43.

Smith, Tom W., "Changing Racial Labels: From 'Colored' to 'Negro' to 'African American'," *Public Opinion Quarterly* 56 (4) Winter 1992: 496–515.

Sniderman, Paul, Philip Tetlock, and Edward G. Carmines, eds., *Prejudice, Politics, and the American Dilemma* (Stanford: Stanford University Press, 1993).

Sniderman, Paul M., and Thomas Piazza, *The Scar of Race* (Cambridge, Mass.: Harvard University Press, 1993).

Sonenshein, Raphael J., "Can Black Candidates Win Statewide Elections?" *Political Science Quarterly* 105 (2) 1990: 219–41.

Southgate, Minoo, "Slavery Ignored," *National Review*, 23 October 1995, pp. 26–27.

Sowell, Thomas, *The Economics and Politics of Race* (New York: Morrow, 1983).

———, *Civil Rights: Rhetoric or Reality?* (New York: Quill, 1984).

Spitzer, Robert J., *The Politics of Gun Control* (Chatham, N.J.: Chatham House, 1995).

Stanfield, Rochelle, "Black Frustration," *National Journal*, 16 May 1992, pp. 1162–66.

Steele, Shelby, *The Content of Our Character* (New York: St. Martin's Press, 1990).

Stern, Kenneth S., *Farrakhan and Jews in the 1990s* (New York: Institute of Human Relations, 1994).

Stevens, William K., "The Muslims Keep the Lid on Drugs in Capital: The Dealers Simply Move to Another Area," *The New York Times*, 26 September 1988, p. 8.

Stodghill, Ron, "Farrakhan's Three-Year Plan," *Business Week,* 13 March 1995, p. 40.

Stone, Chuck, "Black Politics: Third Force, Third Party or Third-Class Influence?," *Black Scholar* 1 (2) 1969: 8–13.

Suall, Erwin, "Look Who's In Farrakhan's Corner," *ADL Bulletin,* 42 (10) December 1985.

Sullivan, Andrew, "Call to Harm: the Hateful Oratory of Minister Farrakhan," *The New Republic* 203, 23 (1990), pp. 13–15.

Swain, Carol M., *Black Faces, Black Interests: the Representation of African Americans in Congress* (Cambridge, Mass.: Harvard University Press, 1993).

Tate, Katherine, *From Protest to Politics: The New Black Voters in American Elections* (Cambridge, Mass.: Harvard University Press, 1993).

Terry, Don, "Shabazz Case: A Gain for Farrakhan," *The New York Times,* 3 May 1995, pp. A15, B8.

———, "In the End, Farrakhan Has His Day in the Sun," *The New York Times,* 17 October 1995, p. A19.

Thomas, Christopher, "The Man Who Haunts Jesse Jackson," *The London Times,* 8 August 1984, p. 6.

———, "Idol Who Strikes Terror into Whites," *The London Times,* 26 March 1985, p. 5.

———, "Black Radical Taunts U.S. Jews with 'God's Oven' Gibe," *The London Times,* 10 October 1985, p. 7.

T'Shaka, Oba, *The Political Legacy of Malcolm X* (Chicago: Third World Press, 1983).

Turque, Bill, Vern E. Smith, and John McCormick, "Playing a Different Tune: Louis Farrakhan Is Trying to Reach Out to the White Mainstream," *Newsweek* 121, 28 June 1993, p. 30.

Tyler, Lawrence L., "The Protestant Ethic Among the Black Muslims," *Phylon,* 27 (1) 1966: 5–14.

Van Deburg, William L., *New Day in Babylon: The Black Power Movement and American Culture, 1965–1975* (Chicago: University of Chicago Press, 1992).

Vincent, Theodore G., *Black Power and the Garvey Movement* (San Francisco: University of California Press, 1972).

Walker, Martin, "America's Great Divide Widens," *The Guardian* 2, September 1995, p. 25.

Walker, Sheila S., "The Black–Jewish Paradox: Ambivalence of U.S. Race Feeling," *Patterns of Prejudice* 7 (3) 1973: 19–24.

Wallace, Mike and Louis Lomax, "The Hate that Hate Produced," Newsbeat, WNTA-TV, 10 July 1959.

Walsh, Edward, "Farrakhan Says U.S. Concocted Plot Charge," *The Washington Post,* 18 January 1995, p. A3.

Walsh, Kenneth T., "The New Drug Vigilantes," *U.S. & World Report,* 9 May 1988, p. 20.

Walters, Ronald W., "Strategy for 1976: A Black Political Party," *Black Scholar* 7 (2) 1975: 8–19.

———, *Black Presidential Politics in America: A Strategic Approach* (New York: State University of New York Press, 1988).

———, "The American Crisis of Credibility and the 1988 Jesse Jackson Campaign," *Black Scholar* 20 (2) March/April 1988: 31–44.

Walton, Hanes, *Invisible Politics: Black Political Behavior* (New York: State University of New York Press, 1985).

Washington, James Melvin, "Jesse Jackson and the Symbolic Politics of Black Christendom," *Annals of the American Academy of Political and Social Science*, 480, July 1985: 89–105.

Watson, Denton L., "Chavis's NAACP: Embracing Farrakhan," *The Washington Post*, 29 June 1994, p. A23.

Weisbord, Robert, *Genocide? Birth Control and the Black American* (Westport: Greenwood Press, 1975).

Weiss, Nancy, *Farewell to the Party of Lincoln: Black Politics in the Age of FDR* (Princeton: Princeton University Press, 1983).

West, Cornel, *Race Matters* (Boston: Beacon Press, 1993).

———, "Learning to Talk of Race," in *Reading Rodney King/Reading Urban Uprising*, ed. Robert Gooding-Williams (New York: Routledge, 1993), pp. 255–60

Whalen, Charles and Barbara Whalen, *The Longest Debate: A Legislative History of the 1964 Civil Rights Act* (New York: New American Library, 1985).

Wheen, Francis, "Voice of Islam," *The Guardian*, 8 November 1995, Sec. 2, p. 7.

White, Byron, Jerry Thomas, and Shirley Salemy, "Farrakhan Defends World Tour," *Chicago Tribune*, 26 February 1996, p. 1.

White, John, *Black Leadership in America: From Booker T. Washington to Jesse Jackson*, 2nd ed. (London: Longman, 1990).

White, R. X., "Minister Ava Muhammad: An Inspiration for Black Women," *The Final Call*, 27 January 1992, p. 17

Wilentz, Sean, "Backward March," *The New Republic*, 6 November 1995, pp. 16–18.

Williams, Juan, *Eyes on the Prize: America's Civil Rights Years, 1954–1965* (New York: Viking-Penguin, 1987)

———, "The Farrakhan Paralysis: How the Demagogues of the Disenfranchised Are Silencing Black Leaders," *The Washington Post*, 13 February 1994, p. C2.

———, "Hiding from this Rage Is Harmful," *International Herald Tribune*, 18 February 1994, p. 7.

———, "President Colin Powell?" *Reconstruction* 2 (3) 1994, pp. 67–78.

Williams, Walter, *The State Against Blacks* (New York: McGraw-Hill, 1982).

Wills, Garry, "The Militias," *The New York Review of Books*, 10 August 1995, pp. 50–55.

Wilson, William Julius, *The Declining Significance of Race* (New York: McGraw-Hill, 1978).

———, *The Truly Disadvantaged: The Inner City, the Underclass, and Public Policy* (Chicago: University of Chicago Press, 1987).

———, "The Underclass: Issues, Perspectives, and Public Policy," in "The Ghetto Underclass: Social Science Perspectives," *Annals of the American Academy of Political and Social Science* 501 (January 1989).

Wines, Michael, "Farrakhan Is Bitterly Denounced by House Black Caucus Member," *The New York Times*, 5 February 1994, pp. 1, 7.

Wright, Lynda, "Farrakhan's Mission: Fighting the Drug War—His Way,"*Newsweek*, 19 March 1990, p. 25.

Wright, Stuart A., *Armageddon at Waco: Critical Perspectives on the Branch Davidian Conflict* (Chicago: University of Chicago Press, 1995).

Wolfenstein, Eugene Victor, *The Victims of Democracy: Malcolm X and the Black Revolution* (London: Free Association Books, 1989).

Wood, Joe, ed., *Malcolm X: In Our Own Image* (New York: Anchor Books, 1994).

X, Malcolm, and Alex Haley, *The Autobiography of Malcolm X* (New York: Penguin Books, 1968).

Index